SERVICE &
THE ART OF HOSPITALITY

CREATING A DINING EXPERIENCE

3rd Edition

Johnson & Wales University

Project Manager	Paul J. McVety, Ed.D.
Assistant Project Manager, Senior Editor	Debra Bettencourt
Associate Project Manager	John Chiaro
Associate Project Manager	Edward Korry
Associate Editor	Eileen DeMagistris
Photographer	Ron Manville
Graphic Designer	Bill Westwood

This book was printed and bound by Imago in China

JOHNSON & WALES
UNIVERSITY

10 9 8 7 6 5 4 3

ISBN 13: 978-09742491-3-1

ISBN 10: 0-9742491-2-2

ISBN 978-0-9742491-3-1

Service Defined *1-9*

1

The Restaurant Environment *18-29*

3

Service *and* The Restaurant Industry *10-17*

2

The Server *30-61*

4

Table of Contents

Styles *and* Sequence of Service 62-69

5

Beer *80-101*

7

The Beverage World 70-79

6

Spirits *and* Liqueurs *102-111*

8

Mixology   *112-141*   **9**

Decoding the Label   *168-195*   **11**

Enology   *142-167*   **10**

CELEBRATING A CENTURY OF INNOVATION

THE LEADING EDGE OF 21ST-CENTURY CULINARY EDUCATION

Our education is different. Lately, just about every college is talking about experiential education. And that's because it works. At Johnson & Wales, we've been perfecting this approach for 100 years.

A pioneering university ahead of its time, Johnson & Wales has been combining industry-focused curricula and strong ties to employers since its founding in 1914. That's what our founders, Gertrude Johnson and Mary Wales, set out to do from the beginning — speaking with employers to discover their needs and with students to uncover their career aspirations.

They created a path for students to achieve their goals and then worked to place them in companies that were a right fit. The combination of professional studies and connecting students to employment opportunities established an institutional DNA that still thrives today.

Our increasing stature in the higher education arena has not gone unrecognized. That's why both *Forbes* and

U.S. News & World Report rank JWU among the best colleges and universities in the United States.* And why the National Society for Experiential Education conferred upon JWU its highest honor: the 2014 William M. Burke Presidential Award for Excellence in Experiential Education.

As a globally-recognized culinary educator, Johnson & Wales is at the leading edge of 21st-century culinary education. Our unique approach blends the craft and art of cooking with science and nutrition, leadership and management skills, global citizenship and work experience, to help graduates pursue their passion for food anywhere around the world.

That's because it's not just food: it's business, and art, and science, and medicine, and more. And that's why at JWU, you'll become more than a great chef. You'll learn to change the way the world eats.

Where will your passion take you?

*Rankings are for the U.S. northeast region.

Dear Student,

The College of Culinary Arts of Johnson & Wales University is committed to your success as a future leader in the food service profession. Our revised culinary arts curriculum is a reflection of our ongoing commitment to continuous improvement. This carefully designed, flexible curriculum provides you with an exciting challenge to learn and to excel in your chosen career.

Johnson & Wales University delivers a multidisciplinary educational experience for driven students who are serious about success and seeking a competitive edge. JWU was the first to offer a Culinary Arts & Foodservice Management bachelor's degree in 1993, the first to offer a Baking & Pastry Arts bachelor's degree in 1997, and the first to offer a bachelor's degree in Culinary Nutrition in 1999. A JWU education integrates rigorous academic and professional skills, related work experiences, leadership opportunities, career services and our unique experiential education model. Students graduate from our university with the knowledge and skills necessary to achieve success in a global economy. Opportunities for practical and cooperative education complement laboratory and related classroom studies and provide valuable on-the-job experiences.

Your formal education in culinary arts is only the beginning of your lifelong study. However, this education is the foundation upon which your future will be built; a foundation established by *Culinary Fundamentals* and *Service and the Art of Hospitality: Creating a Dining Experience.* From these texts you will learn that food and beverage service is a multifaceted field that is constantly growing and changing to respond to the needs and desires of the customer. In studying the fundamentals, you will learn the facts and theories of preparation and presentation. These fundamentals will prepare you to explore, discover and create your own food frontiers.

The faculty and staff of the College of Culinary Arts have dedicated countless hours to these texts. They bring their passion for their craft and years of knowledge and experience to the development of this curriculum. I encourage you to take advantage of this combined wisdom. Within the covers of *Culinary Fundamentals* and *Service and the Art of Hospitality: Creating a Dining Experience* you will discover a truly enjoyable learning experience.

John J. Bowen '77 | *Chancellor*

Acknowledgements

Professionals who truly love educating students have written *Culinary Fundamentals 3rd edition* and *Service and the Art of Hospitality: Creating a Dining Experience 3rd edition.* I am grateful for all the faculty members, administration, students, and friends of the University for their support and participation in this tremendous undertaking.

Paul McVety, Ed.D. | *Dean of Academic Program Development / Project Manager*

EDUCATIONAL TASK FORCE

Paul McVety, Ed.D.
Project Manager

Deb Bettencourt
Assistant Project Manager
Senior Editor

John Chiaro
Associate Project Manager
Director of Artwork

Edward Korry
Associate Project Manager

Eileen DeMagistris
Associate Editor

GRAPHIC DESIGNER

Bill Westwood

JWU DESIGN & EDITORIAL SERVICES

Brian Murphy   Scott Cohoon   Lisa Kaufman

ALUMNI and RESTAURANTS

Gracie's
Chef Joseph Hafner

Persimmon
Chef / Owner Champe Speidel

Siena
Chef / Owner Anthony Tarro

Jacky Ko
Owner Jacky's Galaxy

EDUCATIONAL REVIEWERS

Max Ariza
Jennifer Broderick

Ed Korry
Jim Flader

TJ Provost
Jeremy Houghton

Gershwin Narraidoo
Jennifer Pereira

STUDENT REVIEWERS and ASSISTING with PHOTOS

Schweta Hegde   Natalie Kehbeck   Miranda Micaela   Donald Paredes

FACULTY ASSISTING with PHOTOS

Jennifer Broderick   Ed Korry   Linda Pettine   Robert Weill

A special thank you is extended to Deb Bettencourt, John Chiaro, Edward Korry, Jennifer Pereira, and Eileen DeMagistris for their professional work ethic and assistance. To Don Brizes, Maureen Dumas, Barbara Kamp, David Petrone, Branden Lewis, and Rollie Wesen, thank you for your expertise in authoring new chapters.

PHOTOGRAPHER

Ron Manville

Sangiv Dhar
Chef/Owner Kabob and Curry

Ellen Slattery, Matthew Varga, and Melissa Denmark
Owner, Executive Chef, Pastry Chef
Gracie's

Linda Pettine

Catherine Rabb

Angelina de Jesus

Teixera de Pedra

Jafar Wilson

Jennifer Pereira

T.J. Provost

Acknowledgements

The College of Culinary Arts Culinary Educational Task Force would like to thank the College of Culinary Arts Deans and Faculty members for their ongoing support.

DEANS

Peter Lehmuller, Ed.D.
Dean Providence Campus

Susan Marshall, Ed.D.
Associate Dean Providence Campus

Jorge De La Torre
Dean Denver Campus

Jerry Lanuzza
Dean Charlotte Campus

FACULTY

Allison Acquisto	Robert Brown	Jean-Luc Derron	Mark Harvey
Jeffrey Adel	Tim Brown	Birch DeVault	Peter Henkel
Jeff Alexander	Christoph Bruehwiler	Paul DeVries, Ed.D.	Katrina Herold
Michael Angelo	Wayne Bryan	John Dion	Gilles Hezard
Michael Angnardo	Frances Burnett, Ed.D.	Kim Dolan	Rainer Hienerwadel
Schellie Andrews	Johannes Busch	Ellen Duke	Ciril Hitz
Maxence Ariza	Michael Calenda	Kevin Duffy	Jeremy Houghton
Charles Armstrong	Tim Cameron	Valerie Ellsworth	William Idell
John Aukstolis	Brian Campbell	Robert Epskamp	Steve Johansson
Adrian Barber	Jack Chiaro	Amy Felder	Barbara Kamp
Ed Batten	Thomas Choice	Cynthia Ferron	Peter Kelly
Susan Batten	Luminita Cirstea	Paula Figoni	Linder Kender
Joseph Benedetto	Kristen Cofrades	Jim Flader	Juergen Knorr
Alan Bergman	Jerry Comar	Gian Flores	Mika Kochi
Claudia Berube	Robert Corey	James Fuchs	Kevin Kopsick
Mary Bodensiek	Kevin Crawley	Jennifer Gallagher	Edward Korry
Paul Bolinger	Elaine Cwynar	Marcella Giannasio	Marcia Kramer
Marina Brancely	Jamie B. Daugherty	Dorothy Gilbert	Cece Krelitz
Drue Brandenburg	David Dawson	Stacy Griest	Amy Kweller
Olga Bravo	T.J. Delle Donne	Armin Gronert	Larry La Castra
Robert Brener	Marc DeMarchena	Lauren Haas	Jean-Louis Lagalle
Donald Brizes	Richard DeMaria	Fred Haddad	Susan Lagalle
Jennifer Broderick	Thomas DeRosa	Christina Harvey	Debra Lambert

VENDORS

American Metal Craft, Inc.	Cookshack	F. Dick Corporation	John Boos & Co.
American Roland Foods Corporation	Demarle, Inc. USA	Happy Chef	Lincoln Foodservice Produc
Ateco	Detecto	Hobart Corporation	Matfer Group
Carlisle Food Service Company	Dexter-Russell, Inc.	JB Prince Company	M.F. Foley Fish

Bruce Ozga
Dean North Miami Campus

Emily LaRose

Ronald Lavallee

Dean Lavornia

Alan Lazar

Carrie Hegnauer

Branden Lewis

Robert Lucier

John Maas

Ana Machado

Michael Makuch

Paul Malcolm

Theodore McCall, E.d.D.

Ray McCue

Ashley McGee

Joseph Melanson

Stacy Mirabello

Richard Miscovich

Valeria Molinelli

Kim Montello

Mary Etta Moorachian, Ph.D.

Francis Mullaney

Mitch Murad

Gershwin Narraidoo

James O'Hara

Rene Olmeda

Shelly Owens

Neath Pal

Patti Parkis

Kelly Patkus

Yves Payraudeau

Shane Pearson

Harry Peemoeller

Ronald Pehoski

Robert Pekar

Jennifer Pereira

Linda Pettine

David Petrone

Craig Piermarini

Maureen Pothier

Jonathan Poyourow

T.J. Provost

Catherine Rabb

Joseph Peter Reinhart

David Ricci

Barbara Robinson

Ronda Robotham

Colin Roche, Ph.D.

Joshua Rosenbaum

Robert Ross

Janet Rouslin

Roger Ruch

Adam Sacks

Stephen Scaife

Bernhard Schrag

Louis Serra

Todd Seyfarth

Michael Skufca

Victor Smurro

Mark Soliday

Mitch Stamm

Gill Stansfield

Carrie Stebbins

Rhonda Stewart

Christopher Stone

Karl Stybe

Robin Stybe

Marleen Swanson

Frank Terranova

Fred Tiess

Todd Tonova. Ph.D.

Lynn Tripp

Peter Vaillancourt

Frank Vollkommer

Chris Wagner

Bradley Ware, Ph.D.

Robert Weill

Gary Welling

Rollie Wesen

Kenneth Wollenberg

John Woolley

Emmerich Zach

Robert Zielinski

Russ Zito

Ray Zoller

Monini USA

Morton International Inc.

Ohaus Corporation

Robot Coupe

Saint-Gobain-Norton

Scandicraft

Sid Wainer & Son

Tablecraft Products Company

Taylor Precision Instruments

The Vollrath Company L.L.C.

Town Food Service Equipment Company

Update International

1. Service Defined

Service is a critical ingredient in a restaurant's recipe for success. Guests often have different expectations of service, depending on the type of establishment they visit. Cleanliness, consistency, and friendly, competent service may bring customers back to fast food restaurants, but the expectations of service are much higher for fine dining establishments. In addition to delicious food and elegant décor, guests expect service that enhances the fine dining experience. Service goes far beyond the mechanics or procedures for delivering food and beverage to guests. It reflects an ethos of professionalism, encompasses the highest level of civility, exhibits a passionate respect for the food and beverages served, and is suffused with the spirit of hospitality.

Service is a term that has been overused and oversold by service-oriented industries that advertise the great service they provide but all too often fail to deliver. It is no wonder that today's consumers frequently view the term "service" cynically. Do most consumers recognize great service when they receive it? Yes. Today's consumer is more sophisticated due to an increased exposure to brands, the media attention given them, and the number and level of experiences they have previously enjoyed. The consumer perceives service as more than a perfunctory greeting such as 'thank you' or 'have a nice day'. Although most consumers cannot list all the elements that contribute to great service, they can certainly identify the feeling and sense of caring that is silently transmitted from server to guest.

In addition to delivering a product in a professional way, **service** conveys the feeling to guests that the 'server' is there for them, tuned in to their food and beverage wants and needs. It also transmits the belief that the server will do whatever it takes to ensure that they receive what was 'promised' and will work to create an 'experience' that makes them feel special. Such is the Art of Hospitality.

Quality Service

Although the components of service may seem intangible, poor service can drive away customers, even if the rest of the dining experience is excellent. Conversely, service may bring guests back to an establishment that has otherwise disappointed them.

Servers can only understand how to exceed guests' expectations by first examining what those expectations might be. Servers must have a solid understanding of table manners, civility, and dining etiquette to provide quality service that exceeds guests' expectations. Since all guests have different expectations, the art of hospitality includes the ability to "read the guest."

Table Manners

Table manners change with the times but are an essential component of civility. Most people are offended by behaviors that are perceived as unwelcome or inappropriate, such as individuals chewing food with the mouth wide open. The sight of food being masticated by someone fails terribly in enhancing the dining experience of other guests.

Table manners are inseparable from civility. They exist out of consideration for the feelings and sensibilities of others and a respect for their environment and the food they are consuming. Social manners are also essential skills that must be mastered by individuals selecting the hospitality industry as their profession. It is debatable whether these traits are innate or learned, but with proper training and coaching the majority of people do have the potential to become good hosts.

Since early times, civility and manners have been essential in establishing a community of trust in which people might live and peacefully share a meal together. A mastery of table manners also allows individuals to feel more comfortable in a social setting because they are aware of everyone's expectations. The chart that follows includes a list of **table manners;** behavior that is considered acceptable or unacceptable by most in today's society.

While table manners are important for servers to recognize as part of the dining etiquette, it is important to remember that there are considerable differences in acceptable table manners throughout the world. In today's global village, it is necessary to have knowledge of the table manners of other cultures so as not to be judgmental when eating with or serving individuals of these cultures. Eating with the hands, for example, is acceptable in many societies. In much of the world, eating finger foods using the left hand is seen as unacceptable because the left hand is associated with toilet activities. In this country, we eat with both hands, which may seem revolting to those where the habit of eating with the left hand is taboo. Belching at the table is not only viewed as acceptable in some Asian countries but is considered a sign of appreciation for the food just consumed. In the United States, such an act would be perceived as rude. There are a number of subtle as well as not so subtle differences in the eating styles and table manners of Western and Eastern cultures.

Guest's Table Manners

Appropriate	Inappropriate
Pull out chairs for other guests, in particular for ladies and elders	Sitting down without consideration for others
Put cell phones on vibrate or turned off—never used at the table—in an emergency excuse oneself to take a call	Answering phone calls at the table
Sit straight, with hands on the lap or on the edge of the table. Allow server room to serve and clear	Leaning back in one's seat or slouching on the table
Rest forearms on the table if necessary	Placing arms or elbows on the table
Keep arms within immediate area of the chair so as not to impede service	Stretching arms or elbows in boredom or wildly gesturing while "talking with your hands"
Place and leave the napkin on the lap. Fold and place it to the side when leaving the table	Leaving the napkin on the table while seated
Make eye contact when approached by a server	Failing to address the server and making eye contact
Speak clearly and politely when addressing a server or guest	Mumbling or muttering when responding
Leave the placement of china, flatware, and glassware where it is originally positioned by the server unless in use or if you are left handed	Moving the placement of glassware, china or flatware, especially when finished with the item
Politely ask the person next to you to pass something that is out of reach, such as the salt shaker	Reaching across the table for any reason
Hold stemware by the stem; a base glass by its base	Grabbing a stemmed glass by the bowl or a base glass at the top of the glass
Use the appropriate utensils for each course	Using a knife to put food in the mouth
Use sip sticks, stirrers or straws for stirring or sipping and set aside if not needed on a bread and butter plate	Sticking fingers in a glass or chewing on sip sticks
Hold coffee and tea cups using the handle	Gripping a coffee or tea cup with the whole hand
Sip a beverage	Gulping or slurping a beverage
Offer the person seated next to you bread, butter or a condiment before serving yourself	Serving oneself bread from a bread basket or butter or another condiment without first offering these to others
Wait to eat until all at the table are served	Start eating before everyone has been served
Always taste food before adding seasoning	Add salt and or pepper before tasting the food
Cut or slice foods to an appropriate bite size one mouthful at a time	Placing too much or too large a piece of food on the fork or precutting all food before eating
Scoop food away from you	Scoop food towards you
Let very hot food cool down on its own	Blowing on hot food to cool it off
Remove grape pips, fruit stones, olive pits, fish bones, or gristle using the fork or napkin	Spitting out pips, fruit stones etc., onto a plate
Chew with the mouth closed and only speak when food is not present in the mouth	Chewing with the mouth open or speaking with a mouth full of food
Avoid noisy scraping of the plates or bowls	Noisily scraping china with flatware to get the last bit of soup or sauce
Rest used flatware on edge of plate or underliner while not in use	Placing used flatware on linen
When finished, place the soup spoon on the underliner or the knife and fork in a closed position	Placing dirty/used flatware on the table or cloth/top
Use a napkin to dab the mouth	Wiping the entire face with a napkin or using a sleeve or the back of one's hand to wipe the mouth
Allow servers to crumb the table as part of service	Using the hands to wipe unwanted food particles from the table onto the floor
Politely ask for the check	Getting up before the check is presented
Tooth picks are for use in private	Using a tooth pick for cleaning teeth in a restaurant or in public
When visiting areas with unfamiliar cultures, inquire about customs and standards before dining as a guest or serving as a host	Assume your customs and standards are the only ones of value and others should adhere to them

Since the United States is a melting pot of cultures, it has adopted many types of cuisine and dining habits, which include the consumption of finger foods of all shapes and sizes a the use of chopsticks and flatbreads as utensils for scooping food into the mouth. *See 1.1*

Something as simple as eating bread and butter may be a challenge if one is not aware of the 'rules' governing bread and butter etiquette, which varies from one country to another. In the United States, a small piece of butter should be placed on the bread & butter plate using the bread & butter knife. The knife is then returned on the plate in its original position. A small bite-sized piece of bread should be torn off and then it should be buttered before eating. The whole piece of bread should not be buttered prior to breaking off a piece as the fingers would become greasy and might soil the glassware or other table items. As an added note, the rules may differ if a roll rather than a piece of bread is served. It is perfectly proper to tear a role in half and to use one's knife to place butter inside the center of the roll.

Most rules for proper **table etiquette** are founded on a respect and consideration for other diners and the property of others. A host or hostess who has spent time polishing crystal glasses would feel less than flattered when the glasses are smudged with grease to detract from the general appearance of the table. A greasy finger on an item that is being passed to someone else is also less than appealing. The server at a fine dining restaurant who has spent time polishing and cleaning will also question the value of time spent on "making everything perfect."

In France, there are fewer reservations about how bread should be eaten. The use of bread as a sponge for sauce left on a plate is quite proper, while such a practice would not be seen in the same light in this country. The habit may stem from the common use of a tranche or manchette in the Middle Ages, which was a large piece of old bread that was used as a plate to soak up juices and oils and was eaten mostly by the poor.

1.1 It is common to see a broad range of eating styles within the food service industry.

Quality Service

Servers need to be aware of these service components:

- **Smiling**

- **Eye contact** with the guest

- **Reaching out** hospitably to every guest

- Viewing **every** guest as **special**

- **Inviting** guests to **return**

- **Creating** a warm **environment**

- **Exceeding** guests' **expectations**

1.2 The Continental method of using flatware

1.3 The American or "Zig Zag" method of using flatware

Continental *and* American Styles

There are two basic styles of using flatware when eating: the Continental and the American style (sometimes known as the Zig-Zag style).

The **Continental style** is defined by the diner holding a fork and knife in the left and right hands respectively, cutting a bite-sized piece of food and then placing the food onto the tines of the fork and into the mouth, while still holding onto the knife in the right hand. *See 1.2.*

In contrast, the diner who uses the **American style** typically cuts a bite sized piece of food, then pauses to switch the fork from the left hand to the right, before placing the knife onto the rim of the plate and eating the food from the fork with the left hand on the lap or on the edge of the table. It has been suggested that the origin of this practice might be attributed to the nonexistence of forks in America during colonial times when only knives and spoons were used. Today's society recognizes either method as a demonstration of proper table manners. *See 1.3.*

In Chapter 5, "Styles and Sequence of Service," the menu course sequencing, which is part of dining styles, also demonstrates the influence of other cultures, in particular those of France and Italy. In France, for example, it is traditional that salads are served after the entrée because the vinegar-based dressings would overpower the accompanying wine. The salad is also served at this time to re-stimulate the appetite so that a cheese or dessert course might be enjoyed to complete the meal. In contrast, salads or vegetable courses are served before the entrée in Italy and usually without the accompanying vinaigrette. *See 1.4.*

Gazpacho
Puree of tomato, cucumber, green peppers, onion, garlic and olive oil served chilled with seasoned croutons, chopped tomatoes, cucumber and green pepper
or
Spanish Vegetable Soup
Chorizo, potatoes, turnip and aromatic vegetables simmered in a saffron-infused beef stock
----
Tapas
Chef's choice
or
Mesclun, Figs and Cabrales Salad
Mesclun greens, roasted figs and toasted pine nuts tossed in a honey/lemon dressing and topped with crumbled Cabrales (blue) cheese.

Paella Valenciana
Saffron rice cooked in chicken stock with chicken, chorizo, snails, squid, lobster, clams and fresh pea pods
Pork & Clams Cataplana
Pieces of pork and fresh littleneck clams simmered in dry white wine with garlic, Piri Piri and paprika
Chicken with Almond and Saffron Sauce
Chicken thighs braised in white wine and chicken stock with crushed almonds, garlic, parsley, saffron and fresh lemon juice - garnished with chopped hardboiled egg.
Veal with Sherry
Veal cutlets braised in sherry wine and veal demi glace with shallots, ham, green peppers, tomatoes, mushrooms, & olives

1.4 Salad may be served before or after the entrée depending on the menu and the cultural context.

Dining Etiquette *and* Protocol *for* Ladies *and* Gentlemen

In addition to table manners, there are standards of etiquette and protocol of which both the guest and the server should be aware (especially in a more formal setting).

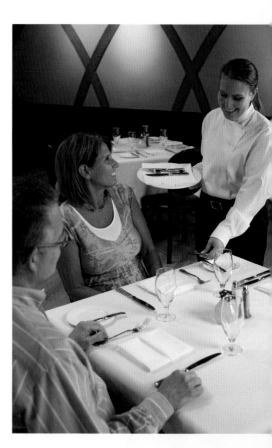

1. Pull out the chairs for ladies and the elderly first.

2. Gentlemen should stand up from their seats when ladies get up from the table.

3. When leaving the table, fold the napkin and place it to the right of the place setting, not on the back of a chair.

4. Serve the guest of honor first, if there is one, and the host last.

5. Serve children, women, and then men (eldest first), in that order.

6. Do not call the server "honey," "dear," "sweetie," "boy," "garçon," or use any other disrespectful term.

7. Do not start eating until everyone has been served, unless another guest's meal has been delayed, and he or she insists that you begin eating (especially if the food is served hot).

8. The plate or bowl does not need to be wiped clean. Garnishes may be left on the plate.

9. When finished with the soup course, place the spoon on the underliner plate.

10. When finished with an appetizer or entrée course, place the fork and knife together on the plate facing 12:00.

11. Use glassware that is placed to the right of the place setting.

12. If you prefer not to be served wine and already have a preset wine glass, politely indicate to the server or host that you prefer not to have any. Do not turn the glass upside down.

13. Use the china or plateware that is set to the left of the place setting and the cup and saucer on the right.

14. If the person to your left has taken your bread & butter plate, ask the server for another.

15. If you are uncertain about how to eat something, watch others at the table and imitate them.

16. If in doubt as to whether something should be eaten with the fingers, use a knife and fork.

17. If eating peas or other similarly difficult foods to maneuver, use the knife to push them onto your fork.

18. Do not eat something from another's plate unless dining with just one other individual with whom you are intimate or familiar.

19. Never rush through a meal. It will make others at the table who are taking their time uncomfortable. Do take cues from the occasion's host regarding the pace of the meal.

20. If coughing, turn away from the table and cough into the napkin to prevent the spread of germs. If the coughing is uncontrollable, politely leave the table and visit the restroom. Clean your hands properly before returning.

Service Protocol *and* Etiquette

Standards of protocol or precedence of service support guest etiquette. Protocols are rules or sets of procedures that are set by establishments and organizations, including governments.

....

SERVER PROTOCOL

The following standards are those that have been adopted as best practices by Johnson & Wales University, based on the premise that a server is there to serve the guest's needs, and that only safety issues should supersede these standards.

1. Always allow guests the right of way when walking through an establishment.

2. Try not to interrupt guests who are engaged in conversation. If the need arises, politely request their attention first.

3. The guest of honor, if there is one, is served first, and the host last.

4. Serve young children, women, and then men. It is also preferable to take age into consideration as an additional sign of respect.

5. Serve all guests at a table at the same time so no one waits for his or her food.

6. Serve and clear beverages from the guest's right side, as long as you are "open" to the guest.

7. Wait until everyone at the table has finished a course before clearing.

8. Clear the bread & butter plate from the left side.

9. Carry flatware on a serviette or a STP (**standard transport plate**).

10. Carry glassware on a beverage tray.

11. Do not reuse flatware for a subsequent course.

12. Do not reach across a guest if you can approach from the other side.

13. Do not touch a guest, and do not allow a guest to touch you.

SERVER ETIQUETTE

Most guests are less concerned with the techniques of service than with the attitude and manner in which they are served. Intrusive service is annoying, regardless of the server's skill level. Considerate service is both efficient and gracious, and it is likely to persuade a guest to return.

General rules:

1. Always address the customer in an appropriate manner. Do not use terms such as "you guys."

2. Carry plates and drinks so that the fingers are well away from the food or rim of a glass. Attention to detail in this area may be critical to your guest's satisfaction, as observant guests may choose not to eat or drink from a plate or glass they consider to be unsanitary or unappealing.

3. Never rush the guest by bringing the courses to the table too quickly.

4. Position the plate of food in front of the guest as the chef intended it to be presented.

5. Place plates onto the cover carefully and quietly.

6. Try to anticipate guests' requests rather than simply responding after the request is made.

7. Serve each guest without asking what was ordered (**food auctioning**).

8. Take the time to clean or **groom the table** before serving a course if needed, particularly after the entrée.

9. Serve each guest in a timely manner to prevent repeated requests for service.

10. Take note of any physical limitations or characteristic preferences, such as left-handedness, and make the necessary adjustments.

11. When clearing, don't ask guests, "Are you done?" Politely ask if you may clear the plates.

As customs and manners have changed over the centuries, the evolution of the restaurant and the role of the food and beverage industry continue to evolve. The expectations of guests have also contributed to the enormous variety of restaurant styles, menus, and service needs. As today's guests are growing more sophisticated about food and beverage options, technology innovation is becoming an important component of service in the restaurant industry.

Serving Children & People with Disabilities

According to the National Restaurant Association (NRA), dining out is still one of America's favorite family activities, and restaurants have served as the foundation of many communities with families dining out on average 3.5 times a week. Clearly, these numbers show that servers must address the needs of children.

The following guidelines apply for serving children up to the age of eight.

• Ask whether a booster seat or high chair is needed.

• Ensure that the seats are clean and that the trays on high chairs are clean and sanitized.

• Remove any sharp objects from the table.

• Remove glassware from the covers of small children. If lidded plastic containers are available for children's beverages, parents generally appreciate their use.

• Talk to the children as you serve them.

• If the establishment offers children's activities such as paper placemats and crayons, bring these to the table.

• If parents approve, help children select an appropriate menu item.

• Serve children as quickly as possible, and serve them first.

• Quietly discuss dessert options with a parent before offering dessert to the children.

• After the guests depart, make sure the area beneath the table is thoroughly swept.

Under the Americans with Disabilities Act (ADA), restaurants are required to provide accommodations for wheelchair users and other disabled guests. Servers should address disabled guests directly, without assuming that they want or need help. With disabled children under eight years of age, servers should take both verbal and non-verbal cues from the parent or guardian when serving the child.

Restaurant Management, Costing *and* Profitability

Today's restaurant industry managers are called upon to provide leadership; manage people, products, and equipment; and perform a variety of tasks in the process while accountable for the bottom line. One would be remiss if the costing and profitability concerns of a restaurant were not discussed and considered as an important piece of the "big picture" in this industry.

ROLE OF MANAGEMENT

Managers are responsible for ensuring guest satisfaction by forecasting, planning, executing, and controlling many restaurant functions that add value for the guest. Guest satisfaction is key for repeat business and continued revenue for the restaurant. There are different levels of management within the restaurant with various responsibilities, but in general terms, the daily goal is a consistently profitable business enterprise through the use of realistic goal setting and problem-solving skills. Management may not be identified by some as the reason for a well-run restaurant but is generally blamed when profitability, productivity, service, and guest satisfaction results are considered poor. For best results, each shift should receive the urgent focus of all managers and staff to result in the consistency guests crave. When done correctly, seamless service delivered by a well trained, prepared staff results in an exceptional dining experience for the guests.

RESTAURANT COSTING AND PROFITABILITY

Operating a restaurant includes monitoring and controlling the planned and unplanned expenses that can occur within the business. The restaurant's Profit and Loss Statement summarizes income, expenses, and inventory illustrating a time period, usually a month's worth of information. This helps managers remain organized and focused on the costs they face while operating the business.

The 2008 recession greatly impacted many businesses, and the restaurant industry suffered many closures of long-established restaurants. Competition has remained fierce in many areas including quality staffing for productivity, value pricing for guests, and top line sales. Managers who watched pennies previously are now even more careful with regard to hiring decisions, menu offerings, and marketing options.

Labor is one of the largest expenses in the industry. The costs associated with hiring, training, and retaining good productive employees can be staggering if not forecasted and planned. Employee productivity can be tracked, mainly through the use of POS (Point of Sale) program technology, permitting managers the information necessary to make good decisions during a shift, as well as to identify current needs and trends. Basic formulas that can assist managers in daily decisions are the calculation of the check average, a labor cost percentage, and the calculation of the percent of revenue from areas of the menu such as beverages.

The check average can be used to illuminate a specific server's abilities to sell the menu and acts as an identifier of productivity, by showing the "per person" average spent at each table.

> **Total Sales ($360)**
> **÷ Total Guests (6)**
> _____
> **= *Check Average ($60 per person)***

The labor cost is generally understood as a percentage of sales and fluctuates as the sales rise or fall in comparison with the number of employees on the clock at any given time. A labor cost percentage can also indicate productivity to a degree but should not be used as the sole determining factor.

> **Payroll ($825)**
> **÷ Total Sales($4500)**
> _____
> **= *Labor Cost Percentage (18.33%)***

The revenue percentage from beverages or food can be used as an indicator of successful marketing campaigns, additional training needs, and areas in need of attention to increase profitability and return on investment results.

> **Beverage Sales ($1320)**
> **÷ Total Sales ($4500)**
> _____
> **= *Percentage of Revenue from Beverage Sales (29.33%)***

Other restaurant costs that seem minor but add up quickly without proper education of the staff are **smallwares**; all beverage products, standard condiments, sauces or syrups, and paper goods. Smallwares also include garnish tongs, measuring cups, shakers, pumps, and pieces of coffee or tea service equipment that can be easily lost or damaged. When considering costs, just the garnish tray behind the bar can become a source of many dollars lost. For example, filling the tray at 9:30PM and then breaking down at 10:30PM to perform pre-closing duties in which someone throws out the product just filled can result in a lack of product available for the next shift in addition to the unnecessary monetary loss of that product from inventory. Whether it is a teaspoon in the trash, coffee spilled or brewed too soon, or napkins dropped in a puddle and rendered unusable, seemly small losses add up to larger issues. Care, concern, and ownership for the value of all products must be discussed, trained, and instilled in the employees by management to meet profitability goals for the restaurant. Through guidance from managers and discussion of business fundamentals, employees will begin to understand the importance and benefits of cost savings and controls, thereby helping them feel like a partner in the process.

2. Service *and* The Restaurant Industry

Great civilizations of the past enjoyed elaborate banquets, and travelers throughout history have relied on wayside stations where they could buy food and drink. The actual restaurant concept where anyone could go to enjoy a complete meal prepared and served by someone else; however, dates back only to 1765. In that year, A. Boulanger, a soup vendor, opened his business in Paris offering only a "restorative" or **"restaurant"** of sheep's feet simmered in white wine. It is from this humble beginning that the tradition of Paris's luxurious restaurants grew.

The "restaurant" idea spread to the United States in 1827 when Giovanni and Pietro Delmonico opened a café in New York City. Three years later, the first American restaurant, "Restaurant Français," opened in an adjacent building.

The Restaurant *and* Banquet Industry Today

According to the National Restaurant Association, the U.S. restaurant industry is a $683.4 billion industry, which currently employs over 13.5 million employees or 10% of the work force at over 990,000 locations. Restaurant industry employment is expected to increase over the next decade to 14.8 million by 2024. It is the largest employer after the federal government. The restaurant industry has outperformed overall U.S. employment growth for the last 13 years. Nearly half of all adults in the United States have worked in the restaurant industry at some point during their lives, and one in three persons obtained their first job in the restaurant industry. One in ten American workers are currently employed in the restaurant industry. Many of those workers, thanks to growth opportunities, are headed for long-term successful careers in the industry. Eight out of ten restaurant owners began in entry-level positions.

As reported by the 2014 annual Gallup Work and Education poll, positive consumer ratings place the restaurant industry as the top business sector in America, with the computer industry coming in second. According to the Bureau of Labor and Statistics, in 2012, there were approximately 2.4 million servers in the food industry and an additional 551,000 bartenders. By 2022, the projection for servers includes an additional 131,800 employed and 65,600 more bartenders will be sought. The over 320,000 current restaurant management positions are projected to increase to 325,000 by 2022. The Bureau of Labor and Statistics noted that those with a combination of a hospitality or food service management degree along with long-term industry experience would have the best employment opportunities.

SERVERS

Servers are most frequently referred to as waiters, waitresses, waitstaff, sales associates, or cast members. The term "waitron" coined in the 1980s reflects a common view that servers take orders robotically and serve without any social skills. The server's job is also most often perceived as a transitory position that requires little skill or attributes. It is not viewed as a "profession" because it has traditionally lacked credentialing or certification. More recent developments in certifications by organizations such as the Federation of Dining Room Professionals have elevated the perception of professional servers to one that is challenging and requires skills. The server's qualities are discussed in greater detail in Chapter 4: "The Server." The position of server is considered entrepreneurial in nature because the server controls the potential tip income. The individual also works at a place of business that assumes the costs and provides all the tools necessary to derive an income. Usually, the greater sale the server generates, the larger the tip income, as tipping is an established American custom. In general, servers earn between 10 % and 15% of their sales. In fine-dining restaurants, the percentage increases closer to 20% on average, and the server's food and beverage sales are significantly higher as well.

There are also other factors that contribute to a server's income: the number of shifts worked, the type of shift (dinner usually being much more lucrative than lunch), the day or night of the week, holidays, seasons, weather conditions, and staffing shortages. Waitstaff in many states are paid a cash wage of $2.89 per hour and their employers are allowed to apply a **"tip credit"** of $6.11 that makes up the difference between this wage and the federal minimum wage of $9.00 per hour, unless the state minimum wage is higher, in which case the state minimum supersedes the

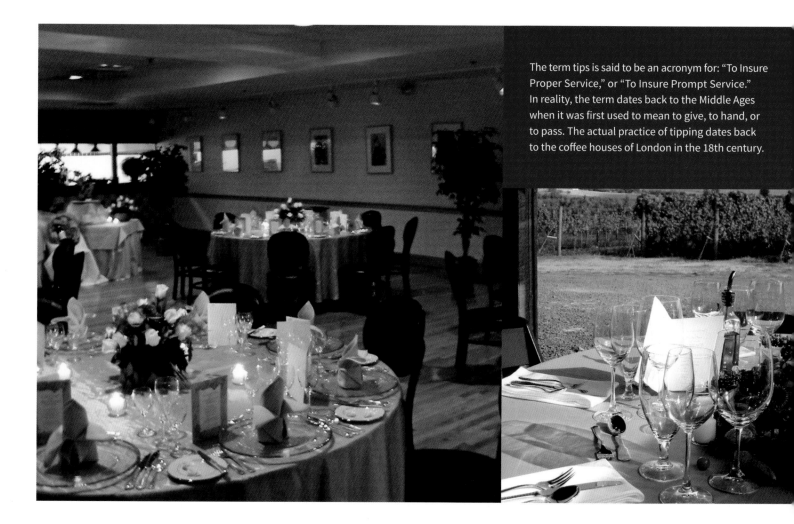

The term tips is said to be an acronym for: "To Insure Proper Service," or "To Insure Prompt Service." In reality, the term dates back to the Middle Ages when it was first used to mean to give, to hand, or to pass. The actual practice of tipping dates back to the coffee houses of London in the 18th century.

federal. According to the 2015 report by the National Conference of State Legislatures, 14 states have legislative plans to increase their state minimum wage over the next few years, and 29 states already have minimum wages above the federal minimum wage. Restaurant owners do not have to directly pay the minimum wage, but they are responsible for declaring employee tips at a minimum rate of 12% of sales on payroll taxes. Owners are held criminally liable if they fail to carry out this law.

While the system of tipping is predicated on the belief that a **tip** is a reward for good service (theoretically the better the service the higher the tip), there are restaurants where employees must 'pool' tips. All tips are placed into a single **'pool'** and are shared equally by waitstaff of the same ranking or level. This system has its critics because it is said to remove the primary incentive for good service. Yet, servers whose main focus is on the tips, typically tend to not be the best servers or employees.

There are also some fine-dining establishments that pay their waitstaff salaries and automatically charge a service charge of 17% to 20% on the bill, including tax. The purpose of this method, which is the European model of how servers are paid, is to provide servers with a steady income, to offer them health and other benefits, and to provide greater parity between the income of the chefs and kitchen personnel and the income of the front of the house staff. It will be interesting to see if more restaurants eventually adopt this same strategy. When servers are paid salaries, their chance of being 'stiffed' is also reduced. This term is applied when a server is not given a sufficient tip. It is up to the restaurant's management to ensure that the waitstaff provides the very best service regardless of the tip potential. When compensation is based on both a salary and benefits, the turnover rate of the front of the house employees is usually reduced, and their jobs are viewed as more professional.

BANQUET SERVERS

There are food and beverage servers and bartenders who work in establishments other than restaurants such as hotels and catering operations. The income of these individuals is usually determined by higher wages that are supplemented by an 18-20% service charge that is automatically imposed on clients. While the social and technical skills of these individuals are similar to those of restaurant servers, and the service they provide is commensurate, staff need not rely on selling skills. The roles of bartenders and their compensation will be examined in greater detail in Chapter 6, "The Beverage World."

BANQUET AND CATERING

Formal protocol and service etiquette originated with the banquets of ancient times. Banquets and catering continue to be an important aspect of the dining service industry. A **banquet** is defined as a meal or event in which food and beverage has been ordered for a predetermined number of people. A formal legal contract between the host of the event and the establishment is signed, and a deposit is made when the event is first booked. Establishments have various policies regarding the amount they require in advance as a deposit. Most properties request 75% to 100% deposit prior to the event.

Banquets range from very elaborate receptions and dinners to the off-premise catering of an informal picnic. Restaurants may sometimes have a banquet room or hall to accommodate these functions or may choose to even close their restaurants to the general public to allow for a catered affair.

Types *of* Restaurants

There are basically 4 types of commercial restaurants that cater to every occasion, budget, and taste. According to the National Restaurant Association, restaurants provide more than 70 billion "meal and snack occasions" and on a typical day, "more than 130 million individuals are food service patrons."

FINE-DINING RESTAURANTS

A **fine-dining restaurant** offers excellent food, fine wines, and highly skilled and attentive service in an upscale environment. The preparation of more complex food and more obscure and exotic ingredients result in high menu prices. Meals are served in several courses at a relaxed pace and usually last between one and a half to two hours. Most job opportunities in fine-dining establishments require both training and work experience. Many fine-dining restaurants are independently owned.

DINNER-HOUSE RESTAURANTS

Dinner-house restaurants provide moderately priced, easily prepared meals. Some dinner-house restaurants have added ethnic dishes to their menus in response to the growing multicultural market. Most serve alcoholic beverages. Dinner-houses are frequently part of a national chain or a franchise but may be independently owned and operated.

CASUAL OR FAMILY RESTAURANTS

Casual or family restaurants offer customers a relaxed atmosphere. These operations feature moderate prices, home-style cooking, and child-friendly menus. Some casual or family restaurants serve alcoholic beverages.

QUICK-SERVICE RESTAURANTS

Quick-service restaurants provide a limited, fairly consistent selection of food at very reasonable prices. The menu is usually **à la carte** with items priced either individually or as combination meals. Customers place their orders and pay at the counter or the drive-thru window. These restaurants form the largest segment of the food-service industry. The chart below demonstrates a correlation between the type of restaurants and guests' expectations, the type of menu, the ambience and layout of the restaurant, the service provided, and the associated cost.

Correlation of the Type of Restaurant to Guests' Expectations, Menus, Service, and Cost

Type of Restaurant	Guests' Expectations	Menu	Ambience Table Layout	Type of Service	Cost
Fine-Dining Examples: Per Se, No 9 Park, Le Bernardin	Highest	À la carte/ semi- à la carte/ prix fixe/ table d'hôte	Designer driven, luxurious. Free standing Linen covers Banquettes	Highly skilled and knowledgeable brigade/team tableside/individualized crafted cocktails and knowledgeable wine service	$$$-$$$$
Dinner-House Examples: Red Lobster, Chili's, TGI Fridays	Moderate +	Semi à la carte	Themed Place mats or table top Booths/ free standing tables	Skilled to moderate skill & knowledge plated/ family style/waiter/ busser/ limited alcohol beverage knowledge and service	$$-$$$
Family/Casual Examples: Cracker Barrel, Friendly's, Johnny Rockets	Moderate	Semi à la carte	Counter/ Booths/ free standing	Moderate skill and Minimal knowledge, very limited to no alcohol beverage service	$-$$
Quick-Service Examples: McDonald's , Burger King	Low to moderate	À la carte and semi à la carte fixed menu	Booths/ free standing	Limited skill and knowledge No alcohol beverage service	$

The Menu

The menu impacts every element of a food service operation, including the type of customer the establishment attracts. Numerous factors need to be considered when planning a menu. Both the target market and operational needs, including profitability, must be evaluated. Identification of the target market, an evaluation of its ability to sustain the establishment, and a knowledge of the income level of the market are necessary. Extensive market research must be conducted to determine the feasibility of an operation.

Other Factors to consider include:

1. **Type** of food
2. **Price** structure
3. **Equipment** analysis
4. **Skill level** of employees
5. **Geography**
6. **Social factors** such as religion or ethnicity
7. **Nutritional** concerns
8. **Age** and **Health** issues

TYPES OF SALES MENUS

The four most common pricing structures for sales menus include à la carte, semi-à la carte, prix fixe, and table d'hôte. An establishment may combine elements of one or more pricing structures. Additionally, the menu may either be a fixed or a cycle menu. Each system affects the organization of the servers' time management, and ability to build the check.

The **à la Carte** Menu

Each course or item is priced individually: appetizers, soups, salads, entrées, and desserts are priced separately. Accompaniments such as vegetables may also be ordered at a cost.

The **Semi-à la Carte** Menu

When items are served together and priced as a combination on a menu, this is known as a **semi-à la carte** menu. Entrées may be priced with the inclusion of a salad or a side dish, while the appetizer, soup, dessert, and beverage are priced separately.

The **Prix Fixe** Menu

The term **prix fixe** is French for "fixed price." The prix fixe menu consists of multiple courses offered at one fixed price regardless of the entrée selected. A supplementary charge may be added for a small selection of items that have costly ingredients.

Pesce

- $26
s fillet finished with
my scallion sauce.

Pesce Spada
Thick center cut domestic
caper, roasted yellow

o° - $25
ttlenecks, baby mussels,
and calamari stewed in a
d vegetable broth.
pped with fried onion rings.

Gamberi
Four jumbo shrimp sau
and fresh thyme le
creamy Parmi

Salmone alla Griglia - $21
Grilled salmon fillet dressed with lemon juice and olive oil.
-ved over a summer salad tossed with a roasted tomato vinaigrette

Contorni (sides)
All sides are available for 2 or 4 persons

- $5/$9
e oil, lemon.

Patatine
Parmesa

a - $5/$9
mesan.

Pisseli e Pr
Tender baby peas sautée

Risotto Bianco - $5/$8
ked Arborio rice folded with Parmigiano-Reggiano cheese and cream

---

LIP SMACKING SUMMER SPECIALS

CHOWK KI TIKKI
Hand rolled potato patties stuffed with green chillies, peas, fresh ginger and mango powder.   (4.99)

SHAKARKANDI KE KOFTE
Sweet potato dumplings stuffed with cheese dumplings and cooked in a butternut squash sauce.   (10.99)

DHANIA COCONUT CHICKEN
White meat of chicken marinated with roasted coriander seeds, curry leaves and fresh coconut. Roasted in a Tandoor. Accompanied by basmati rice and vegetable of the day.   (12.99)

LAMB TIKKA MUGHLAI
Boneless lamb loin morsels. Marinated in a paste of pistachios and papaya. Cooked to perfection in a Tandoor. Accompanied by basmati rice and vegetable of the day.   (14.99)

INTRODUCING OUR SPECIAL FINE MICRO BREWERY BEERS

DOG FISH HEAD INDIA PALE ALE	- 4.00
RADEBERGER, PILSNER, GERMANY	- 4.00
BROOKLYN LAGER, NEW YORK	- 4.00
MAGIC HAT, LUCKY CAT, VERMONT	- 4.00

★ *Chef's Tasting Menu*
Our tasting menu is designed to surprise and ex
palate. We believe this is the best way to dine at
Each course is personally designed for you à la minut
wine pairings are specially selected to enhance every fl
The entire table must experience the tasting together

5 Course 65/95

7 Course 85/125

Take the time to sip, savor and enjoy...

---

other food from anima

In addition to considering the needs of the target market and the operational constraints, an establishment must design a menu that offers variety (ingredients, cooking techniques, textures, taste, and serving temperatures), balance and plate composition, descriptive copy, truth-in-menu, and menu labeling regulations.

The **Table d'Hôte** Menu

A menu in which the price of a multiple-course meal changes according to the entrée selected is known as a **table d'hôte** menu. Steak au poivre at $24.95 might include a soup, salad, and dessert while grilled chicken with the exact same courses sells for $16.95.

Menu Guidelines

To ensure good ethical practices and to accurately represent menu items, it is prudent to adhere to **truth-in-menu guidelines.** It is imperative that servers avoid misrepresenting the products they are trying to sell in an effort to make sales.

The twelve truth-in-menu guidelines for dining establishments and servers that follow, have been created by the National Restaurant Association:

1. **Brand names must be accurately represented**—The advertised product must be the one served; for example, another brand of hot sauce cannot be substituted for Tabasco® sauce.

2. **Dietary and nutritional claims must be exact**—To protect consumers from potential health hazards, health claims and nutritional information must be accurate. Low-sodium and fat-free foods must be correctly prepared to ensure the protection of customers. Nutritional claims must be supported with statistical data.

3. **Description of food preservation methods must be accurate**—Food may be preserved as follows: frozen, chilled, dehydrated, dried such as by sun or smoking, bottled, and canned. Terms used must be accurate. For example, fish cannot be listed as "fresh" on the menu if it has been frozen.

4. **Quantity must be correct**—Whenever a menu item indicates that it contains a certain number of items, that number must be served. Weights given for steaks or other cuts of meat should be identified on the menu as weight prior to cooking.

5. **The origin of ingredients must be truthful**—Blue cheese; for example, must not be substituted for Roquefort cheese.

6. **The quality or grade must be exact**—A steak advertised as "charcoal-grilled" must be grilled over charcoal, not merely grilled.

7. **Cooking techniques must be accurately described**—When a cooking technique is given on a menu; i.e. broiled, the chef must prepare the food using the described technique.

8. **Pictures must be precise**—A photo of apple pie with ice cream must be used to represent "apple pie à la mode."

9. **Food product descriptions must be accurate**—A menu that describes shrimp salad made with jumbo shrimp should not consist of medium-sized shrimp.

10. **Pricing structure must be clearly stated**—The menu must indicate whether the price includes a cover charge, gratuity, or service charge. Any supplement charged for side items with more costly ingredients should be listed.

11. **Menus must indicate if substitutions are made**—Substituting one item for another is a common practice because of delivery problems, availability, or price. Examples of substitutions might include maple-flavored syrup for maple syrup or capon for chicken.

12. **Merchandising terms must be accurate**—Food service establishments may exaggerate in advertising food items as long as they are not misleading customers. Saying, "We are the best in town" or "We serve only the finest beef" is acceptable, but implying that the beef is prime when it is not is misleading.

In addition to the printed menu, which is the primary vehicle for marketing the items an establishment has for sale, selections may be promoted by highlighting items, including clip-ons, using table tents and menu boards, as well as using a website. The Internet has provided innovative and technologically adept restaurateurs with an additional advertising resource. Web site development has become a cost efficient and effective way to disseminate a menu.

RESERVATIONS SYSTEMS

The guest's first contact with an establishment may be through its reservation system. Many destination restaurants and those that are more upscale, commonly accept reservations. Some restaurants use online services, such as **"OpenTable."** Other restaurants only accept reservations on special occasions, such as Mother's Day, and for parties of six or more.

Manual reservation systems rely on the host or hostess to answer the phone to record the details, and if it is management's policy, to record a credit card number as a guarantee. The host or hostess may also have to answer questions, give accurate directions to the restaurant, and provide clear information about parking.

Conversely, OpenTable users can book a table through the website from mobile apps available for many smartphones or via OpenTable partners such as Google, Yelp, and Zagat at any time of day or night that is convenient for them. This translates to no missed bookings for the over 31,000 restaurants currently using the OpenTable reservation system. The system also has marketing capabilities that can be used to foster repeat business.

3. The Restaurant Environment

The environment of an establishment relates to the type of menu and the style of service that are employed. This symbiotic relationship creates a "concept" to which the guest can easily relate. Environment refers to the colors, textures, sounds and smells that create an image and experience for the guest. Fine-dining restaurants have traditionally offered carpeted floors, richly decorated wall and window treatments, full comfortable chairs, and table linens. But today, it is not unusual to find less formality in décor. Fine-dining establishments may have beautifully polished hardwood floors and deliberate design elements that accentuate the volume of noise to make the atmosphere seem more 'alive'.

When replacing the traditional "environment," it is important to remember that certain creative elements might be rather inappropriate. Harsh lighting would be inimical to creating a soft and romantic mood. The playing of heavy metal music in a fine-dining restaurant would be equally discordant. Unpadded hardwood chairs would also fail to provide a relaxing leisurely fine-dining restaurant experience. The exotic spicy aromas of Indian cuisine would be an anomaly in an Italian restaurant.

Restaurant Layout *and* Flow

The layout of the establishment and the dining room in particular, must accommodate the uninterrupted traffic flow of both guests and servers. The location of the restrooms should not interfere with servers' walkways. Tables should not be positioned to slow down the servers' route to and from the kitchen. The guests should not be caused any discomfort by excessive server traffic. *See 3.1.*

3.1 Dining room traffic flow impacts the guest experience

Well laid out dining room.

Poorly laid out dining room.

OPENING AND CLOSING DUTIES

Quality service begins with the availability and proper placement of all the equipment needed to ensure smooth and efficient service. Establishments should have clearly defined duties for each service member to perform prior to the opening or closing of the dining room to the public. Some of these responsibilities may be scheduled daily or by the shift, while others may be required but once a week. These duties are referred to as "side work."

Though side work varies by establishment, it typically includes:
- Setting tables for service.
- Cleaning and refilling salt and pepper shakers.
- Refilling sugar bowls.
- Cleaning and refilling vinegar and oil cruets.
- Folding napkins for service.
- Polishing flatware and glassware.
- Stocking side stations for service.
- Emptying flower vases and storing flowers under refrigeration.
- Vacuuming, sweeping, and washing any tiled floors.
- Emptying the vacuum after use.
- Ensuring that all light bulbs are in proper working condition.
- Recording refrigeration or glass washer temperatures in log books as necessary.
- Cleaning doors, mirrors, and designated surfaces.
- Cleaning the legs or bases of tables.

Dining Room Equipment *and* Serviceware

The tableware and serviceware are as significant as the layout. They must reflect the concept that the establishment is trying to create. Tableware and serviceware refer to all utensils, glassware, china, and service pieces used in the coverage of a meal. Servers must have an extensive understanding of the inter-relationship of dining room equipment and its proper usage as well as knowledge of all the related factors to provide quality service.

3.2 Assigned table numbers contribute to efficient service

THE TABLE

Although there are many styles of tables from which to choose, it is important to consider durability, size, and aesthetics when making purchases. There are free standing, booth, banquette, statler, and round tables of different sizes. A **banquette** table is positioned against a wall and offers continuous seating. A **statler** is a square table that opens into a round. The choice of table surface is largely determined by whether it will be covered with linen. Regardless of choice, servers need to ensure that tables are level, free of wobbling, and are kept in good condition by checking the underside for chewing gum.

A primary concern in selecting tables is size. Both the lay-out of the dining room and the amount of space available for each guest must be considered. The style of menu and service also dictate the type of cover that is used and the amount of space needed for that cover. The **cover** may be as simple as a napkin and a bread-and-butter plate or as elaborate as a show plate, appetizer fork and knife, soup spoon, salad fork and knife, dinner fork and knife, a dessert fork and teaspoon, a bread and butter plate, a water glass, and three wine glasses.

The arrangement of tables in the dining room is also a significant factor when selecting tables. Table placement establishes a sense of uniformity, which is important in creating a positive first impression on the guest. Placement also affects the flow of traffic in the room, which impacts the guest's comfort. Tables should be numbered in a logical manner to allow for point of sales systems, check writing, and quick identification by all service personnel. *See 3.2.*

SEATS AND SEAT NUMBERING

In addition to numbering tables, each seat, and thus each guest, should also have a number, which usually flows clockwise around the table from a **fixed or focal point,** such as the entrance of the restaurant. Using this system, the seat closest to the entrance at each freestanding table is numbered position 1. *See 3.3.*

At a booth or banquette table, the numbering begins at the position where a server stands to take an order. *See 3.4 and 3.5.*

Using this system helps to improve communication among staff members to provide better service. For instance, a busy server can easily ask another server to check on the coffee at Table 5 and to make sure that positions 3 and 4 have fresh hot water for their tea.

The type of seat is also important and must fit the concept of the establishment. A comfortable chair lends itself to a more leisurely paced dining experience and should be selected for fine-dining restaurants rather than quick-service operations.

3.3 Numbering the seats of a freestanding table

3.4 Numbering the seats of a booth table

3.5 Numbering the seats of a banquette table

TABLE SETTINGS

The table setting or cover is determined by the type of menu: à la carte, both traditional and modern or basic, and the banquet/prix fixe.

À la carte

There are two possibilities for presetting the cover for à la carte dining: the traditional and the modern. In a true à la carte set-up, the establishment does not know what or how many courses a guest will select; therefore, the pre-set cover does not include silverware or flatware. If the establishment offers a complimentary **amuse-bouche,** a small, bite-sized sampler, then a cocktail fork might be provided.

The traditional setup includes little but the show plate, napkin, a bread-and-butter plate, and knife. The modern or basic place setting is dictated by aesthetics and the assumption that the guest will order at least an entrée. A less barren place setting might include a show plate, napkin, dinner knife, dinner fork, bread-and-butter plate, butter knife, and water glass. *See 3.6.*

Prix fixe

A prix fixe menu includes a variety of courses such as a soup/appetizer, salad course, and entrée; therefore, the flatware for those courses is included in the pre-set. A wine glass may also be set as a suggestive marketing tool or as a wine pairing offering that is included in the prix fixe. *See 3.7.*

Banquet or pre-set

A **pre-set menu** is one that has been determined ahead of time. The table setting depends on what is being served and includes the utensils and glassware necessary for each course. A bread-and-butter plate, butter knife, salad fork, dinner fork, dinner knife, spoon, coffee cup, wine glass, water glass, dessert spoon, dessert fork, napkin, and show plate may be included. *See 3.8.*

THE SERVICE TRAY

A large oval food tray known as a **service tray** is used to allow servers to carry several dishes to the table at one time. Food trays are usually lined with cork or rubber to prevent slippage. If food trays are not lined, a service napkin is used to prevent slippage. *See 3.9.*

In some casual or family restaurants, plates are arranged on the tray by an expeditor using the guest's seat number from the kitchen slip and following a consistent pattern. This allows a food runner to deliver to the guest's table without auctioning off the food.

TRAY STANDS/JACKS

Tray stands or jacks are collapsible frames on which to rest trays. The frames may be plastic, wood, or metal. Some include a low-level shelf that may be used as a small side stand. When not in use, stands should be collapsed and placed out of busy traffic lanes to prevent accidents. Some establishments designate permanent locations in the dining room for tray stands, while others require that service staff carry the stands with them as they transport food trays in and out of the dining room. *See 3.9.*

3.6 À la Carte "Classic" Place Setting

À la Carte "Modern" Place Setting

3.7 Prix Fixe Place Setting

3.8 Banquet Place Setting

3.9 The service tray and tray stand can increase service efficiency.

THE BEVERAGE TRAY

The **beverage tray** is a round (12" to 14" in diameter) hand-held, skid-free tray on which to carry beverages. Beverage trays should be clean and dry. *See 3.10.*

THE HAND TRAY

The **hand tray** is a small tray used to carry a single small item such as a drink, a napkin or the check.

GLASSWARE

Glassware available for food service operations includes common glass, fully tempered, and crystal. Restaurateurs are faced with selecting glassware that comes in a variety of types, patterns, costs, and qualities. Operators are responsible for purchasing the glassware that best suits the particular needs of the establishment. The glass size must also be appropriate to the serving so that a proper pour may be accommodated.

Another important consideration is whether to purchase a glass with a rim that is beaded. The glass will chip less if beaded, although most high end market consumers prefer to drink beverages, especially wine, in an unbeaded rimmed glass.

Caution should also be taken when selecting patterns because patterns are frequently discontinued, and it becomes difficult or expensive to replace glassware. Glassware is available in a variety of sizes and shapes. Standard sizes and shapes are shown in *3.11 Standard shapes and sizes of restaurant glassware.*

Fully tempered or toughened glassware

Commercial operations commonly use fully tempered or toughened glassware for both practical and safety reasons. This glassware is stronger than other types and will shatter into small fragments rather than dangerous shards. It is also more scratch, chemical, and shock resistant.

Lead crystal glassware, which is also called 24% lead crystal, is known for its brilliance and clarity, but it is expensive. It is best suited for fine-dining establishments.

3.10 The beverage tray is a formal implement for carrying drinks.

3.11 Standard shapes and sizes of restaurant glassware.

 White Bordeaux

Irish Coffee

Brandy Snifter

Martini

Red Burgundy

 Goblet

Hurricane

Margarita

 Tasting Glass

 Water/Soda

 Highball

Sour

Champagne Tulip

 Pilsner

Zombie

 Rocks

Carafe

 Footed Pilsner

 Old Fashioned

Cordial

Handling glassware

Glassware must be handled with care at all times.

The following guidelines should be used:

- Glassware should be free of cracks or chips.
- Glassware should be stored upside down in an appropriate glass rack. The height of a glass rack should exceed the length of a glass and should allow ample room so that the bases of the glasses do not touch.
- Glassware stored on a shelf must be placed upside down on air mats.
- When handling glassware, always hold the glass by the stem or base. *See 3.12.*
- If polishing a clean glass, use a lint free cloth, and do not exert pressure when the bulb of the glass is being turned in one direction and the stem or base being held is turned in another. *See 3.13.*
- Clean all glassware so that it is immaculate. (Polishing methods will be detailed later under server skills.)
- Use a beverage tray when carrying glasses in the dining room. *See 3.14.* When carrying clean, stemmed glassware by hand, invert the glasses and place their bases between the fingers. Depending on dexterity, hand size, and experience a server may carry as many as 10 to 16 glasses at once.

CORKSCREWS

Although the Romans used cork as stoppers, it was not until 1681 that the first known written reference to the use of a corkscrew was made by an Englishman. Today, there are a variety of cork-screw models that range in sophistication, from the first patented design of the Henshall, to the Leverpull of the 1980s. The key to selecting a good corkscrew is to look for one that has a worm that is not too thick and has edges that are sharp enough to cut into the cork, rather than tear it. The most common corkscrew in the food service industry is known as the **"waiter's friend."** *See 3.15.* This corkscrew usually has a knife blade to cut the capsule of the wine bottle, and its edge should be kept sharpened. This corkscrew should have 5 turns to the screw, and the server should ensure that the worm is not bent, in order to maximize its effectiveness. In the past 10 years, the "waiter's friend" has been adapted with a double hinge or two step lever that makes it even easier for the server to open the bottle of wine. Another modification of the original is the substitution of a foil cutter for the small knife blade.

3.12

Correct Glass Handling

Incorrect Glass Handling

3.13 Use clean, lint-free linen to polish glassware.

3.14 Use a beverage tray to carry glassware in the dining room.

3.15 The Waiter's Friend

POTTERY

The term *pottery* applies to clay products made of unrefined clays. As a generic name, pottery includes all fired clayware. More specifically, the term pottery describes low-fired porous clayware, which is generally colored. Ceramic products acquire strength through the application of heat. Along with the heat, the chemical composition of the materials used determines the strength, porosity, and vitrification of the fired product.

There are many types of tableware available to the restaurateur. The final choice is usually determined by how appropriate the tablewares are to the concept and the cost of the products.

Some of the different types of tableware available are:

Earthenware Earthenware is a porous ceramic product that is fired at comparatively low temperatures to produce an opaque body that is not as strong as stoneware or china. The product may be glazed or unglazed.

Stoneware Stoneware is a nonporous ceramic product made of unprocessed clays, or clay and flux additives, which are fired at elevated temperatures. It is quite durable but lacks the translucence and whiteness of china. It is resistant to chipping. Stoneware is available in a variety of colors that are produced by the iron or other impurities in the clay.

Ironstoneware Ironstoneware is the historic term for durable English stoneware. The composition and properties of this product are similar to those of porcelain, although the body of ironstoneware lacks translucency and is off-white in color.

Cookingware Cookingware is the broad term applied to earthenware, stoneware, porcelain, and china designed for cooking, baking, or for serving. It has a smooth, glazed surface and is strong and resistant to thermal shock.

Fine China Fine china refers to a thin, translucent, vitrified product that is generally fired twice at relatively high temperatures: first, to mature the purest of flint, clay, and flux materials; and secondly, to develop the high gloss of the beautiful glaze. It is the highest quality tableware made for the domestic or retail trade.

Porcelain Porcelain is a term that is frequently used for china in Europe. European porcelain, like china, is fired twice. In the United States, porcelain may be fired in a one or two fire process. Porcelain has a hard, nonabsorbent, strong body that is white and translucent. European porcelain is made primarily for the retail market, but manufacturers such as Lennox and Rosenthal make commercial grade porcelain that is purchased by upscale hotels and fine-dining establishments.

Bone China Bone china is a specific type of china that was primarily manufactured in England. The body of this china contains a high proportion of bone ash that produces a greater translucency, whiteness, and strength. Like fine china, it is made primarily for the retail trade.

Restaurant China Restaurant china is a uniquely American blend of china and porcelain, which is designed and engineered specifically for commercial operations. Its body was developed in the United States to give it greater impact, strength, and durability as well as an extremely low absorption, which is required of china that is used in public establishments. *See 3.16.* Decorations are applied between the body and the glaze to protect the decoration on the china during commercial use. Most of this tableware is subject to a high temperature during its first firing and a lower temperature during the second. However, some restaurant china is fired in a one-fire operation during which the body and glaze mature at the same time. Like fine china, America restaurant china is vitrified.

3.16 Each china pattern will be available in a range of plate sizes and shapes.

Coffee Cup

Coffee Mug

Fruit/Nappé

Creamer

Casserole Dish

Appetizer/Salad Plate 9 1/2"

Pasta Plate

Saucer

Bouillon Cup with handles

Monkey Dish

Sugar Caddy

Sauce Boat

Dessert Plate 8"

Soup Plate/Bowl

Demitasse

Sugar Bowl/Cover

Coffee Pot

Salt and Pepper Shakers

Dinner 12"

B&B Plate 6 1/2"

Oval Plate

The following guidelines should be observed when **Handling China:**

- Check all china for **cleanliness** prior to service. *See 3.17.*

- Store all china by **category**.

- Store china **soup** and **coffee cups** in their appropriate **racks**.

- Handle china plates by the **rim**. *See 3.18.*

- Avoid **overstacking** china cups.

- Do **not** stack cups with **handles**.

- Use **underliners** for china cups and bowls.

- **Bleach** all coffee cups every two weeks or according to the establishment's policies.

- Do not use china that has **chips** or clearly visible **cracks**. The cracks may be harboring harmful bacteria. *(The manager should make the decision on how to dispose of damaged china.)*

3.17 Polish clean china with linen napkins and hot water.

3.18 Handle hot plates by the rim with a captain's towel.

The server's hand should never touch the guest's food

DOLLIES

Dollies are carts of different shapes and sizes with casters, which are used for storing and transporting glassware. By placing racks onto dollies, the glassware is stored at a minimum of 6 inches above the floor. Plate dollies include standard adaptable partitions that provide enabling the safe and snug placement of stacks of about 50 specific sized plates in each compartment. Glassware dollies (about 21 inches square) hold racks of glasses that should be stacked no higher than one's ability to see over them for safety reasons. They should always be kept clean and sanitized.

FLATWARE–CUTLERY

The term flatware refers to all dining utensils such as forks, spoons, and knives. *See 3.19.* The origin of the word cutlery is from the Old French word for knife, coutel. The term 'silver' is also frequently used because flatware was made from silver until the mid 19th century when a less expensive process using stainless steel was created.

The selection of flatware should be determined by the concept of the establishment. The more elaborate the establishment, the more specialized and varied the pieces of flatware should be. The composition of flatware varies in grade qualities of stainless steel to silver. Many flatware styles are also available.

Some restaurants place the forks with the tines facing down, although most place them facing up. The tradition of placing forks on the table with the tines down stems back to the 16th century when forks were first introduced in the West. The fork would have the family crest engraved on the back of the handle, which the owners would display on the table. When forks became more readily accessible due to mass production, an engraver's mark replaced the crest. By placing the forks with the tines facing up, the potential for damage to table linens is also reduced.

3.19 Flatware

Knives Knives come in different shapes and may have serrated or flat edges. Standard industry knives include: dinner knives, with or without serrated edges; steak knives; fish knives for filleting fish more easily; appetizer knives that are often used for salad and desserts courses; and bread and butter knives, which are usually shorter than appetizer knives and may be rounded at the top.

Forks Forks are produced in different sizes and shapes for specific functions. Standard and readily available sizes include: the dinner fork that is used for the entrée; the appetizer fork, which may also be used as a salad or dessert fork; a fish fork that is equal in size to the dinner fork but has a flattened tine to prevent the fish from falling off the fork; and a cocktail fork for foods such as oysters on the half shell.

Spoons Spoons include: teaspoons that are used for hot beverages such as coffee, tea, and hot chocolate and for sorbets and soft desserts; demi-tasse spoons for espresso service; soup spoons, which are also referred to as **potage spoons,** for thick or cream based soups; bouillon spoons, which are shaped so that the diner can sip from the side of the spoon *(see 3.20);* a sauce spoon that has a slight notch to prevent excess sauce from dripping off onto the diner; and other specialty spoons such as long handled ice tea spoons.

Service Set

The **service set** refers to a service spoon and fork that are used to **pince or pincer:** a technique of picking up foods such as rolls, and placing them on a plate. *See 3.21.*

HOLLOWARE

Holloware is a term that originally described service pieces that were hollow. Today, this term includes: chafing dishes, coffee urns, samovars, coffee pitchers, tea pots, creamers, water pitchers, sauce boats, goose necks, sugar bowls or basins, tureens, silver salt and pepper shakers, butter dishes, compotes, silver bowls, oval platters, round platters, rectangular serving trays, plate covers, cloches, torte stands, tiered pastry stands, cake server holders, wine stands, wine buckets and coolers, champagne buckets, candlesticks, and candelabras. *See 3.22.*

Holloware may be of different quality levels, from grades of stainless steel to sterling silver. Their purpose is to enhance the presentation of a meal, which can only occur if the correctly sized piece of holloware is used and if it is properly maintained and cleaned.

3.20 A potage spoon is used for thick soups while a bouillon spoon is used for thin soups.

3.21 "Pince Bread Service" utilizes a service set.

3.22 Assorted hollowware or service pieces

Soup Tureen with Lid

Champagne Bucket

Wine Bucket

Cake Server Holder

**Teapot (8 oz.)
Coffee Pot (32 oz.)**

Soup Ladle

Plate Cover (stackable)

Cloche (plate cover)

Square Basin

Sauce Boat

**Pastry Display Stand
(three tier)**

Wine Stand

Sauce Ladle

Water Pitcher

Table Crumber/Scraper

3.23 The guéridon or service cart

THE GUÉRIDON

The **guéridon** is a service cart or trolley. It is a portable work station that is used for all tableside preparations including portioning, cooking, finishing, and plating. The guéridon is generally 18 inches wide by 30 inches long so that it is narrow enough to be placed between rows of tables. *See 3.23.*

The guéridon generally has three shelves: the top shelf is used for the preparation and plating of the dishes; the middle shelf to store underliners, napkins, condiments, and service sets; and the lower shelf for storing the carving board and carving sets.

All the shelves on the guéridon should be covered with linen. The linen on each shelf of the guéridon should be neatly folded so that it does not drape or hang over the sides of the shelf.

THE RÉCHAUD

The **réchaud** is a portable stove designed to cook, flambée, or keep food warm. It is usually made of stainless steel, copper, brass, or silver plate. The base is cylindrical of varying heights with a detachable grate. The pan rests on the grate. *See 3.24.* The heat sources used are propane gas, alcohol, or solid fuel. It is used in the dining room for the tableside preparation of food items. Some *réchauds* are built into the *guéridon*, while others must be placed on the top of the *guéridon*. Most *réchauds* have been replaced by portable butane gas stoves.

3.24 The copper réchaud and blazer pan are well suited to tableside cookery.

BLAZER PANS

Blazer pans may be oval, rectangular, or round. The oval blazer-type pan should be made of copper or stainless steel. Copper, a more efficient conductor of heat, provides an even spread of heat throughout the pan relatively quickly. Copper has a greater aesthetic value and is thus preferred. The shape of the pan is generally designed to suit particular items, although its use is not restricted to those items. For example, Crêpes Suzettes pans are copper plated shallow pans, normally ranging from 9 to 16 inches in diameter. They are primarily used for tableside dessert items, particularly Crêpes Suzettes.

CHAUFFE-PLATS

These heat retaining panels may be stacked in a small battery at a convenient service point inside the dining room and brought to the guéridon when required. Chauffe-plats are used for keeping foods warm when tableside plating is performed, or when a direct flame is not needed.

CENTERPIECES

Centerpieces are decorative attention-getters that many establishments use to enhance their table presentations. They may be small and discreet, such as a bud vase with a single flower or large and flamboyant, such as an ice sculpture on a buffet table. The choice and style of centerpieces depends on the establishment's concept and overall mood. Of the five types of centerpieces—floral and foliage, edible, sculpted, ceramic, and lighting—floral and foliage pieces are the most common.

Floral and Foliage

Floral and foliage centerpieces may be made from fresh flowers and greenery, dried flowers, or silk or synthetic flowers and foliage.

When choosing a floral centerpiece, several factors affect the final selection:

- **Expense**—Fresh arrangements are expensive and need to be frequently replaced. Good-quality dried and artificial arrangements are initially expensive but can last almost indefinitely with good care and storage.
- **Proportion**—The centerpiece should enhance, not dominate, the table setting. Avoid large arrangements that obstruct conversation or create a visual barrier.
- **Scent**—Strong scents and perfumes may irritate or trigger allergies in some guests. In addition, strong scents may overpower the aromas of food and beverages.
- **Color coordination and seasonality**—Fresh and dried flowers and artificial arrangements should complement the décor and reflect the season.
- **Caution**—Dried and artificial arrangements may pose a danger if placed too close to candles. Be aware of local fire ordinances that may restrict their use.

TABLE ACCESSORIES

Table accessories include a variety of items that make serving convenient and dining more enjoyable for guests. Ashtrays and matches; salt and pepper shakers; and condiments such as vinegar or ketchup, sugar, and creamers are considered table accessories. In a fine-dining environment, these should be kept to a minimum, but in high-volume restaurants in which servers are under severe time constraints, several accessories may be left on the table.

LINENS

Linen is considered one of the "big four" in the food service industry, along with china, flatware, and glassware. Linen is an expense that must be carefully monitored to control losses and additional costs. The high capital expense for a laundering facility is usually feasible for only those establishments that have a large volume of business and are usually associated with a hotel that can afford this expense. Because of the expense involved, many food service establishments are opting to forego the use of tablecloths and are using placemats, paper, vinyl, and glass table tops.

The style and colors of linens should reflect the environment and the atmosphere of the dining room. Linens may be 100% natural fiber, a 50-50 blend of cotton and polyester, or 100% polyester. Polyester is more easily maintained and colorfast, but cotton or other natural fiber linens are generally more attractive and tend to hold folds better. Creasing is particularly important for folded napkins and formally pleated table skirting and draping.

There are standard guidelines for purchasing tablecloths. The overhang on a square or rectangular table should be a minimum of 7 inches and a maximum of 12 inches. For round tables, the hang of the cloth should be a minimum of 10 inches. It is important to note that it is less expensive to purchase linens that are a standard size. Custom made linens cost considerably more.

Silencers and Napperons

A silencer may include a custom made pad or may simply be a linen or felt cloth that is placed on the table surface underneath the tablecloth. Its purpose is to give the linen used a richer texture and to reduce the noise level when plates are placed on the cover. Silencers also help to extend the life of linens. Some tables are manufactured with silencer pads already installed.

A napperon is a linen overlay that is placed over a table cloth for both protective and decorative purposes. It is used as a runner on a banquet table and acts as a seasonal decoration during the holiday season.

Skirting

Skirting refers to the specialized linen used for draping tables. Skirting provides a uniform appearance, is more economical than tablecloths, and requires less labor to maintain. Clips, pins, or tapes are used to attach skirting to a table. *See 3.25.*

3.25 Modern Velcro skirting with matching clips

3.26 An air pot brewer with a single decanter

Skirting is available in three types of pleating: sheer, accordion, and box. Sheer pleating is used for lace and other sheer fabrics in overlays. The accordion pleat is a closed pleat; the box pleat is an open pleat that is often used with more substantial fabrics.

Doilies

A **doily** is an intricately patterned lace mat that was traditionally made of cotton or linen thread and is named after Doily, a seventeenth century London draper. Today, doilies are made of paper and are a standard fixture in most restaurants. They are designed for use in between 2 pieces of china when the base of the upper piece does not fit directly into the well of the piece it is on. They may also be used on trays for hors d'oeuvres or small bite sized pastries to embellish the presentation. Doilies come in a variety of standard sizes such as 4, 6, 8, 10 and 12 inch rounds. A common service mistake is to use a doily under a coffee or soup cup when a saucer is properly sized for it.

COFFEE MAKERS

There are many types and brands of coffee makers. There are those machines that make only regular grind coffee, and those that create only espresso and cappuccino. The mechanical features of these makers vary as do the procedures for their usage and maintenance. Most establishments lease coffee makers from the company that is supplying the coffee. The advantage to leasing is a reduction in capital expenditures and free maintenance that is provided by the company in a timely manner.

The most important determinant in the selection of coffee makers is the volume of fresh brewed coffee the machines typically serve. For amounts of less than 3 gallons (11.36 l) of coffee per hour, a French press or a single pot brewer is appropriate. For 3–6 gallons (11.36–22.71 l) per hour, an air pot brewing system gives the best results. An amount of more than 6 gallons (22.71 l) per hour requires either a modular system or an automatic urn system.

Although French presses are more costly to maintain and more labor intensive, many upscale establishments use them to ensure the freshest and most flavorful coffee. French presses come in 10- to 20-ounce (296- to 591-ml) sizes and use medium grind coffee at a rate of 1–1 1/2 ounces (30–44 ml) per 20 ounces (591 ml) of boiling water.

Pour the coffee into the French press pot, and add boiling water. The grounds will float to the top. Then stir the grounds rapidly 2 or 3 times and cover the pot. Wait for 3 minutes before slowly pressing the plunger.

Single pot brewers yield 60 ounces (1.77 l), or 12 5-ounce (148-ml) servings, and may be pour-through or plumbed systems. Each pot requires 3 ounces (89 ml) of ground coffee.

Air pot brewers dispense brewed coffee into an insulated serving decanter that holds the product at 185°F (85°C) for an hour. Because additional heat is not applied, the flavor of the coffee does not deteriorate as it does in single pot brewers. Most air pots hold 75 ounces, (2.22 l) or 15 5-ounce (148-ml) servings, and use 3 1/2 ounces (104 ml) of coffee. *See 3.26*

High volume food service operations generally use an automatic urn that yields 60 5-ounce (148-ml) servings of coffee, brewed with 2 1/2 gallons (9.46 l) of water to one pound (.45 kg) of coarse-ground coffee. Unless the urn is equipped with an automatic mixing device, draw the stronger coffee from the bottom of the urn, and pour it back into the brew (but not through the grounds) to ensure uniform strength.

Modular brewers combine a fixed-location brewing module (the heating and volume control) with mobile brewed coffee containers of various capacities (5, 10, and 20 l). Heating systems keep coffee at 185°F (85°C). Most brewers, except the French press, use paper filters that eliminate soluble solids to keep coffee clear. Because paper filters are thrown away after each use, sanitation is easier with these brewers; however, filters can pick up odors that affect the coffee's flavor if stored near aromatic foods.

ICE MAKERS AND BINS

Ice is a key component of drinks that is often overlooked. An ice machine should be able to produce ice in a quantity that the establishment needs over the course of a day and should be able to fully recover the maximum quantity for the next business day. Unfortunately, many icemakers produce both thin and hollow or semi-hollow ice that melts too quickly. Ice machines must be properly maintained and kept clean and free of mold. Ice scoops should be stored in a holster attached to the ice machine, which drains properly. Many health inspectors consider ice to be a food and beverage product that must be monitored for food safety.

SODA SYSTEMS

Soda can be dispensed using a dispensing system with a soda gun. *See 3.27.* There are two types of containers that are currently used on the market: the soda tank and the bag-in-a-box. The tank system is slowly becoming obsolete. The bag-in-a-box system has a single line flowing from a container of syrup to a pump that enables the syrup to travel to the soda dispenser known as a soda gun. A protective cap must first be removed for the line to be properly connected and snapped into place. Some upscale restaurants and bars have recently replaced these systems with high quality bottled mixers that lack convenience and add to the cost.

3.27 Soda dispensed through a soda gun system

BREAD WARMERS

The bread warmer should be turned on ahead of time (approximately 1 hour) so that it is properly heated before use. For soft rolls or breads, place a small cup containing a water-soaked clean napkin in each drawer to keep the rolls moist and to prevent them from becoming dry and hard. This procedure is unnecessary for hard rolls and crusty breads.

At the end of each shift:
- Turn off the warmer.
- Remove the water cups.
- Remove the drawer and empty the contents, and wipe it clean. Return the bread and rolls to the kitchen for use as bread crumbs.
- Replace the drawer.

Note: Refrigerated or frozen rolls need to be re-baked in an oven prior to storing them in the bread warmer.

TOASTER

The conveyor toaster is most common in the food service industry. Some toasters use a timer-setting method to ensure proper toasting, while others use a rotisserie cycle span.

To clean a toaster:
- Shut the toaster off and unplug.
- Remove the grills and the crumb catch pans from the unit.
- Clean the crumbs and burnt products.
- Reassemble the toaster.

4. The Server

In this chapter, we will examine the positions available and the skills that today's professional servers need to be successful. The server's role may vary from establishment to establishment depending on the style of service. As it is a controllable variable cost, management must balance server cost with the needs of guests, the service requirements of the menu, and the cost of training as it relates to food and beverage sales pricing. Most restaurants employ single server systems that are supported by limited assistance. The server is responsible for service that begins with greeting the guest and continues to the farewell. Establishments that use modified team service employ bussers or server assistants. More elaborate and fine dining establishments usually employ a full-service team, which includes a brigade of servers who have different levels of experience and knowledge.

The Brigade

Dining rooms using the brigade system, or full-service team, may be made up of as many as seven positions.

DINING ROOM MANAGER/MAÎTRE D'

The **dining room manager/maître d'** should be in close contact with every department of the restaurant and should know all aspects of the business. The manager has the ultimate responsibility for the success of the dining room.

SOMMELIER

The **sommelier** is a wine steward who must have extensive knowledge of wines, spirits, and beverages. This individual is in charge of purchasing, service, sales training, and the control of beverages.

HOST/HOSTESS

The **host** or **hostess's** role may be assumed by the dining room manager but is frequently filled by another charming and inviting personality who can focus on greeting and seating guests using proper etiquette and protocol. This position also includes the task of ensuring the smooth flow of seating by managing the reservation system so that the seating capacity is maximized with few delays for guests who are waiting to be seated. The host or hostess should not delay seating guests if the entire party has yet to appear. Single diners should also be made to feel welcome and asked if they would prefer dining at the bar.

CAPTAIN

The **captain** supervises and organizes every service detail for his or her station or room, including taking orders and synchronizing service for the station.

WAITER OR FRONT WAITER

The **front waiter** assists the captain and should be able to perform all duties in the absence of the captain. The front waiter's primary responsibilities include the service of food and beverages to guests.

BACK WAITER

The **back waiter** serves as a bridge between the brigade and the kitchen and has the primary responsibility of placing and picking up orders from the kitchen. The individual with this title is sometimes referred to as a runner, especially in a banquet department.

BUSSER

The **busser,** or server assistant position is usually an entry-level position. This person is primarily responsible for clearing and grooming the table. Transitory employees such as high school or college students commonly fill this position.

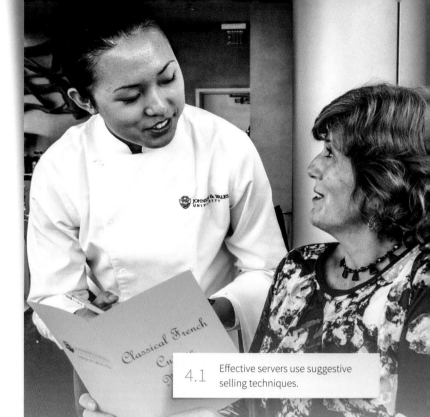

4.1   Effective servers use suggestive selling techniques.

Server Attributes

Quality service cannot be left to chance; it requires training that is refined through practice and experience. A professional server becomes the restaurant's representative and salesperson, as well as a skilled server.

SERVER AS REPRESENTATIVE

Because the server has more contact with guests than any other restaurant employee, the server is the restaurant's ambassador. This individual sets the mood in the dining room by making guests feel welcome, relaxed, and secure that their needs will be met. Courtesy, friendliness, and superior interpersonal skills are the hallmarks of a professional server.

SERVER AS SALESPERSON

A successful restaurant server is a skilled salesperson who helps guests experience a satisfying dining experience by explaining menu options, describing specials in detail, suggesting wines or other beverages to complement the food, and helping tailor choices to meet the diner's needs and expectations.

Successful selling entails making guests feel pampered, as well as adding to the revenue of both the restaurant and the server. Effective servers encourage guests to add to their original orders by guiding them to new, unusual, or premium items. *See 4.1.* This process, known as **suggestive selling**, incorporates highlighting, assumptive selling, and upselling.

Highlighting Drawing a guest's attention to particular menu items is called **highlighting**. By using vivid and enthusiastic descriptions, guests are encouraged to try specials or to order items that the chef is eager to sell. If the kitchen staff is backed up, a good server may suggest items that require less preparation and provide guests' service.

Assumptive selling The sales technique known as **assumptive selling** uses open-ended questions to guide guests in making their choices. The server might ask the guest for a wine preference, implying that a particular wine would complement the menu selection. Not only does this technique increase sales, but it also makes guests feel that their needs are being addressed.

Upselling Sales can be increased by **upselling**: a technique that promotes the sale of items of a better quality or of a larger size than what was originally contemplated. Taking an order for scotch, for example, might involve suggesting Dewar's® or Chivas Regal®, which are higher-quality and priced alternatives to bar scotch. Although the technique is not always successful, upselling consistently increases the establishment's sales and the server's income.

4.2 The uniform plays a role in creating both the ambiance and the perceived professionalism of employees in a restaurant.

THE SERVER AS A SKILLED PROFESSIONAL

The members of a restaurant's service team (busser/runner, server, captain, sommelier, bartender, host, and maître d' or manager) should strive for the following attributes:
1. Positive attitude
2. Good appearance
3. Good communication skills
4. Thorough job knowledge
5. Timeliness and the ability to prioritize

Positive Attitude

A positive attitude is essential when dealing with the public. Attitudes need to be differentiated from behaviors. Behaviors are the physical expression of a mental process. They may be learned, adjusted, and manipulated by an individual or by management, but the sincerity of the behavior can come into question when the underlying attitude that drives the behavior is absent. When we discuss the behavioral skills associated with the front of the house employees, we must first identify the correct attitude or willingness to please the guest at all times. Without such an attitude or willingness, servers with all the manual skills in the world will not succeed in their responsibilities.

Guests should not be able to read anything into a server's behavior that might detract from a positive dining experience. The server should never be judgmental about a guest or the potential to upsell and build a higher check total. Servers need to be flexible and able to adapt to personalities and circumstances.

Appearance

Servers who make a good appearance present guests with a favorable first impression of an establishment. Good personal hygiene, neat attire, and professional body language are the elements that are most important.

Personal Hygiene:
- Hair that is longer than collar length must be properly restrained.
- Hands must remain clean, which requires frequent washing, especially after using the rest room as required by law.
- Fingernails must be kept trimmed and clean.
- Teeth should be clean and breath should be fresh.
- Servers should pay attention to body odor and use deodorant as needed.
- Colognes and perfumes should not be worn as they detract from the aromas of the food and wine.

Attire. *See 4.2:*
- Jewelry should be kept to a minimum, e.g., wedding bands.
- Uniforms should be kept clean and well pressed.
- Uniforms should fit properly.
- Shoes should be clean and shined.
- Shirts and blouses should be pressed, free of stains, and not frayed.

Body Language:
Servers must be aware of physical mannerisms that might reflect poor sanitary standards or a poor attitude. **The following behaviors should be observed:**
- Make eye contact with the guest and smile.
- Maintain good posture.
- Do not slouch or lean on walls. "If you have time to lean, you have time to clean."
- Be careful about touching your hair, face, mouth, or nose, especially in view of the guests.
- Never curse or use poor language in earshot of a guest.
- Do not chatter with other servers in view of guests.
- Do not stand around with the hands in pockets.
- Smoking, drinking, chewing gum, or eating during service are never permitted.
- Do not wipe the brow or nose with the jacket sleeve.
- Do not sneeze in your bare hands.
- Never produce flatware or a napkin from one of your pockets.
- Stand erect and do not lean on or hold on to the back of a customer's chair. It suggests familiarity with the customer and is unprofessional.
- Maintain a height advantage at the table. It will help you sell.

Communication Skills

It is imperative that management train the front-of-the-house personnel in good communication skills. The people with whom the server must learn to communicate are guests, kitchen and bar personnel, and fellow dining room personnel (servers, bussers, hosts, maîtres d'). The server must recognize that communication takes place in three ways:

Written Transmit information that can be read by another person or persons. *See 4.3.* Computer assisted communication falls into this category. Take care to write orders clearly if the establishment does not use a computerized ordering system. Guest checks should be clear and accurate.

Verbal Communicate directly to the person by speaking. Do not address guests as "you guys," which undermines the guest's perception of the server as a professional. Address guests and fellow staff members professionally. Keep communications with customers friendly, but not familiar.

Non-verbal Nonverbal body language is used to communicate attitudes and feelings knowingly and sometimes unknowingly. Servers should have good eye contact with guests, use facial expressions such as smiling, but should avoid touching guests.

4.3 Written checks communicate guest needs to the kitchen.

Job Knowledge

Job knowledge includes a thorough understanding of the work-place: the layout, flow, equipment, communication between departments, familiarity with the food, wine, and beverage menus. It is essential to be able to make recommendations and to answer customers' questions about local events or landmarks, or to deal with customer complaints or problems. A complete understanding of a server's responsibility in serving alcohol is also a key element, and is further discussed in Chapter 9: "Mixology". A thorough knowledge of the manual skills of serving and clearing tables and a familiarity with using a computerized point-of-sale system are equally important.

Timeliness and the ability to prioritize

Typically servers are responsible for the service at more than one table. This group of tables (usually three or four tables) is called a **station** or **section**. *See 4.4 Three Station Layout.* The level of service within a station depends on the quality of service as well as the speed with which the server can work accurately and safely. To perform effectively, servers must be well organized and be able to prioritize their work load and execute it with an economy of movement, including but not limited to trips to and from the kitchen.

Three Station Layout

4.4   A three station layout for the dining room

Server Skills

A mastery of equipment use, a food and beverage knowledge, and a demonstration of manual dexterity to provide service seemingly effortlessly are all hallmarks of a true dining room professional. These server skills are at the heart of the profession.

SETTING THE STATION

In order to set a station of tables (or an entire dining room), there are specific steps to follow to insure the room or station is set in a timely manner. The first step is to bring the mise en place needed to set each table, and place it at one location at each table. The mise en place should include everything that is needed on the table once it is ready for guests to be seated. It would include all plateware, flatware, glassware or stemware, condiments, flower vases, candles, and guests' napkins. The mise en place is then polished at each table until the entire station is ready to set. At that point the tables are set with the required covers, the glassware lined up, and the folded napkin finishes each cover.

SETTING TABLES

Prior to setting a table, the server should check that the table is free of wobbling and correctly positioned so as not to block the flow of traffic. *See 4.5.* It is too late to adjust tables once the dining room is full of guests. Nothing is more annoying to guests than having servers bump into their chairs or tables as they walk by during service.

Whether setting a table with paper placemats or fine linen, the server must ensure that the tabletop, the chairs, the benches, and the area around each table are clean. Constant inspection of the table should take place during service, particularly when tables are being reset. When using a placemat, whether paper, vinyl or linen, it should

4.5 A well-set table begins with attention to the room layout.

4.6 Table cloths should be placed evenly across the table top.

be centered on the cover or at the guest's position, about 1 inch from the edge of the table. A paper or cloth napkin may be placed to the left side of the mat or in the center. Placement of flatware, vases, condiments, salt and pepper shakers, and any other item should be consistent and uniform on all tables.

When using tablecloths, it is important to remember that the sewn seam should always be on the under side and not visible to the guest. The cloth should be placed so it falls evenly on all sides, and ideally, should not fall below the surface or cushion of the seats. *See 4.6.* When setting a round table with four legs, as opposed to a round table with a pedestal, the tablecloth should be laid to allow the corners of the cloth to hide the legs of the table. Cloths that are stained, torn, frayed, or contain burn marks or holes should be sent for repairs or converted into rags. Never attempt to hide stains or holes by placing vases or ashtrays over them. These cloths should be neatly folded and tagged so they are separated from the inventory. Cloth napkins should be placed in the center of the setting or the center of the show plate or charger. *See 4.7.* The napkin may also be placed to the side of the place setting, possibly on the B&B plate, or as a decorative fold in the water glass.

Note: The undersides of table tops should always be checked for any chewing gum that may have been placed there by a guest.

Place Settings

Whether setting flatware for breakfast, lunch, dinner, or banquet service, it is essential to follow certain rules:
- Place the show plate or napkin at the center of each place setting first.
- The place setting should allow adequate space for placing a large service or show plate in the center without requiring the movement of utensils when serving.
- Forks are set on the left side of the cover with tines facing up.
- Knives and spoons are set on the right side of the cover.
- Knives are set with the cutting edge toward the center of the place setting.
- Flatware should be placed so that it does not hang over the edge of the table: one inch from the edge of the table is standard.
- All other flatware is placed parallel to the entrée knife and the fork. The flatware may be staggered or placed with the handles at the same distance from the edge of the table.
- All flatware is set from the outside in, following the sequence of use.
- Do not place flatware to the inside of the entrée knife or fork.
- The dessert fork and spoon are placed at the top of the cover, perpendicular to the other flatware, with the spoon on top of the fork.
- Bread and butter plates are set on the left, next to or above the forks.

4.7 A show plate or charger adds to the table décor and the ambiance.

- The water glass is set above the tip of the dinner knife, and wine glasses are set from the outside following the sequence of use. All glassware should be polished prior to service.
- If several wine glasses are pre-set in a flight, or row, the water glass may be set directly above the place setting or off to the right. The wine glass furthest to the right would be used for the first wine served, the second glass for the second wine, etc.
- When coffee or tea cups are pre-set, they are placed to the right of the knives and spoons, with the handle at the four o'clock position.
- China, flatware, and glassware should not touch each other.
- On rectangular, square or round tables with an even number of settings, all flatware items on one place setting should be aligned with those on the opposite side, in a straight line.
- If each cover includes an entrée knife and fork and is set directly across from another cover, the knife is placed directly across from the fork.
- Establishments require different settings that best suit the needs of their menus.
- A decorative centerpiece or "candlelight" should be placed in the center of the table with a set of filled salt and pepper shakers placed to one side. This should be uniform for all tables so that the salt shaker is, for example, on the left of the pepper shaker at all tables.

GREETING THE GUEST

Because first impressions are lasting, it is critical that the initial greeting is warm, relaxed, and hospitable. Greeting guests is usually the responsibility of the dining room host or hostess or maître d', although all front-of-the-house employees should be trained to greet guests properly. **Rules for greeting guests include:**
- Opening and holding the door open for guests if possible.
- Greeting guests with a warm smile.
- Making good eye contact and using an appropriate welcoming remark such as, "Good evening," "Good afternoon," or "How are the two of you this evening?" Never use language such as, "How are you guys tonight?" This is not a professional greeting from anyone in the foodservice business.
- Advising guests where they can check or hang their coats.
- Helping to remove coats whenever possible

(Note: Many restaurants dissuade their employees from checking in customers' coats because of liability issues. Any well-managed establishment will have proper controls in place to avoid any potential loss of property.)

- Inquiring if the guests have made a reservation. If so, ask for their name.
- Being honest with guests if there is a waiting period or list. Nothing irritates guests more than to be misled as to how long the wait will be.
- If there is a long delay for a party with a reservation, it is a good restaurant policy to offer a free drink or appetizer.

SEATING THE GUEST AND PRESENTING THE MENU

It is usually the responsibility of the manager or host /hostess to lead guests to their table and to ensure that they are seated comfortably. According to protocol, the host leads the party to the table and is followed by the men in the party who are then in a position to assist ladies with their chairs. If the aisles are wide enough, gentlemen escort ladies on their right side. Unfortunately, there is frequently insufficient space in dining rooms to walk side by side.

The host is responsible for:

• Checking that the menus are presentable and contain all additional inserts.
• Personalizing the way the party is addressed; for example, "Your table is right this way," or "May I show you to your table?"
• Using the guests' surnames whenever possible.
• Leading guests to the table at a pace that does not make them feel rushed.
• Pulling chairs out for the guests, ladies first.
• Presenting menus and wine lists if it is the restaurant's standard operating procedure for the maître d' to do so.
• Presenting the menus to women first and the host of the dining party last from the right side of the guest.
• Relaying any special request concerning the guests to the server.
• Removing any extra place settings.

Note: The host should never rush guests to make them feel unwelcome.

When servers are expected to help with seating, they should be familiar with the interplay between the chair and the floor treatment as it affects the way in which they can assist guests. The server may have to lift the chair slightly and may also need to use a knee to assist with pushing in the chair.

GREETING BY THE SERVER

Allow guests to relax and settle into their seats for a few moments before approaching the table. Welcome the guests to the restaurant, and possibly introduce yourself only if it is the establishment's policy to do so. More formal restaurants choose to create a greater degree of formality by not having servers introduce themselves by name.

Servers should remember to:

• Maintain good eye contact with each guest at the table.
• Stand upright at the table with your shoulders square rather than bend down.
• Maintain a certain distance between the guest and themselves by creating a buffer that allows one to hear and be heard, while not intruding on the guest's space. The noisier the dining room, the closer one has to stand to the guest.
• Even if in a hurry, never appear rushed at the table.
• Observe the guests' comfort level along with their body language, and be aware of the type of occasion that has brought them to the restaurant.

Note: The restaurant host or manager should try to determine which guest is the host of the party as well as who the guest of honor might be if there is one, and inform the server.

NAPKIN HANDLING

Once guests have been seated, it is the policy of some establishments to have servers assist with guests' napkins. However, it is contrary to guest etiquette to place the napkin on one's lap before everyone is seated, as it indicates that the meal has already begun. Other establishments have policies where the server should handle the guest's napkin as little as possible and should only do so when absolutely necessary. If a napkin fold is placed in a glass, the server should request that the guest remove it if it remains in the glass when water service occurs. If the guest leaves the table, the server should either leave the napkin where it is or bring a new napkin, and remove the used one. If the guest drops their napkin on the floor, the server should first bring a new one, then pick up the used napkin from the floor, and proceed to wash his or her hands.

THE BEVERAGE ORDER

Servers should have knowledge of popular drinks and of the brands of liquor, beers, and wines available by the glass. It is essential that beverage service is correctly performed because it is the first point of service. Servers should use appropriate sales techniques to ask guests what they would like to drink. **Servers should:**

• Take the guest of honor's order first, then those of the women, men, and finally that of the host.
• Use position numbers to ensure that the beverages are served to the appropriate guest.
• Clarify the guests' preferences regarding the preparation of drinks (e.g.: straight up or on the rocks, an olive or a twist of lemon?).
• Repeat the order to each guest if in doubt.
• Serve beverages, whenever possible, from the right side with the right hand and with the right foot forward.
• Serve the guest of honor first, then the women going in a clockwise direction before serving the men and the host last.
• Avoid reaching in front of guests.
• Handle stemmed glasses by the stem and base glasses by the base.
• Check back for a second round of beverages when the drinks are nearly consumed, using responsible alcohol practices.
• Be sure that it is the intention of all guests to have another drink if a customer orders a second round of beverages.
• Remove the empty glass before serving a fresh drink. Empty glasses should not accumulate on the table.
• Use the same procedure for reordering beverages. Refer to the original order to avoid asking again what each guest is drinking.
• Ask the guest if you may remove a glass, unless it is empty.

BEVERAGE TRAY HANDLING

General rules for the use of a beverage tray follow:

• The tray should be clean and dry before it is used at a table.
• Glasses or cups should be placed as close to the center of gravity as possible and should be repositioned as the service from the tray proceeds.

- The tray should be carried in the left hand and at a level between the chest and the waist. *See 4.8.*
- Trays should never be held between the server and the guest, or between the server and the table.
- Care should be taken not to tilt the beverage tray at an angle when placing the beverage onto the table.

(Note: If you tuck your left elbow into your side, you are less likely to tip the tray.)

- The tray should be held with the left hand under the center of the tray and not held by the edge. *See 4.9.*
- When removing glassware from a beverage tray, always hold the glasses from the base or by the stem with the fingers away from the rim of the glassware. *See 4.10.*
- Never allow a guest to remove items from a beverage tray held by a server.
- The tray should always be carried as prescribed above regardless if the tray is full or empty.

COLD BEVERAGE SERVICE

Cold beverage service includes the service of water, soft drinks, ready to drink beverages, juices, milk, liquor, beer, and wine. Glasses should be carried on a beverage, cocktail, or hand tray during service, though clean stemmed glasses may be safely and most efficiently carried by hand to save time when setting up or resetting a table. This technique prevents contact with the bowl of the glass. Glasses are placed upside down, with the stem between the fingers and the bowls of the glasses touching one another.

Water Service

Many restaurants in the United States automatically serve water to guests. Establishments that do not serve water often prefer to promote the sale of bottled water or of other beverages. Servers should not say: "bottled or just tap water". Establishments that are becoming more environmentally aware are reducing or eliminating the sale of bottled water unless the water is spring fed, flavored, and a popular request. **When serving water:**
- Pre-set water glasses to the right of the guest's cover or place setting, usually above and in line with the entrée knife. *See 4.11.*
- Bring a pitcher filled with ice water to the table.
- Use a neatly folded service towel or STP to catch any drips when pouring water into the water glass, being careful not to overfill. The glass should be about three-fourths full.
- Refill the glass as needed, never allowing the glass to be less than one-fourth full. Water service in the United States requires constant attention. Don't refill every two minutes.
- If the water pitcher has an insufficiently wide spout or lacks an ice guard, it may be necessary to remove the glass from the table and pour water behind the guest to avoid spills on the table. *See 4.12.*

4.9 Balance the tray on the fingers.

4.8 The beverage tray should be carried in the left hand.

4.10 Handle glassware by the base or stem.

4.11 Pouring water at the table

4.12 An assortment of water pitcher styles

Mineral Water

Mineral water should be served cold and poured into a glass that may be shaped differently from the water goblet for easier identification. Avoid adding ice unless requested by the guest. Guests often order mineral water because they dislike the taste of tap water. Melting ice will add tap water flavors to the mineral water.

Other Cold Beverages

When serving beverages such as soft drinks, milk, and iced tea, use an appropriately sized glass. If using garnishes, ensure that they are appropriate and fresh. Service of some beverages such as iced tea accompanied by a long spoon may be enhanced by placing the glass on a doilied B&B plate. Place the beverage to the right of the guest's cover.

When serving bottled beverages, place the appropriate glass before the guest, and proceed to fill the glass no more than two-thirds of the way to the top. Leave the bottle to the guest's right with the label facing the guest. If there is no tablecloth on the table, a cocktail napkin should be placed under both the bottle and the glass.

Beer Service

There are several factors that determine quality beer service. The first is the correct service temperature of beer. Pilsners and lagers are usually served at 44°F–50°F (7°C–10°C), ales at 50°F–57°F (10°C–14°C), and porters and stouts at 60°F–65°F (16°C–18°C). Secondly, a clear unfrosted glass is the optimal serving choice for beer to display color and clarity. The glass must be thoroughly cleaned and properly rinsed. Any detergent residue will collapse the foam, decrease carbonation, and adversely impact flavor. "**Beer clean**" is a term that refers to the highest standard of cleanliness for serving glasses. The third factor relates to the shape of the glass, which potentially enhances the appearance, flavor, and taste of beer by the way it retains the head or foam of the beer. The head helps to retain the aromas. Frosted glasses may have a place in sports bars, but the frosted condensation reduces the "head."

When serving bottled or canned beer, allow the glass to remain on a flat surface. Pour the beer so that the stream flows straight into the center of the glass. Do not tilt the glass or pour down its side. Place the bottle to the right of the glass with the label facing the customer.

If drawing from a tap, hold the glass at a 45° angle about 1 inch below the tap and open it fully. As the glass becomes half full, let the beer pour straight down the middle. It may take 2 to 3 minutes to properly serve beer from taps, especially stout beers. Close the tap when the beer head has risen slightly above the rim.

Draft beer should remain cold at 40°F–50°F (4°C–10°C), because it is not always pasteurized. Draft beer lines must be cleaned on a frequent and regular basis to avoid bacterial contamination that will negatively impact the flavor of all beer served through the unclean lines. Some states have specific laws governing how frequently draft beer lines are to be cleaned. Carbon dioxide pressure must be monitored and controlled to maintain consistent carbonation and an even distribution rate. A carbon dioxide regulator is usually connected to the tap system to accomplish this.

WINE SERVICE

A familiarity with an establishment's wine list and the basic principles of pairing wine with food is critical to a server's success. Before suggesting a wine to guests, ask about the kinds of wines they like to avoid making pointless suggestions. Be aware of any wines that may not be available or that may have a different vintage year than the one stated on the wine list. **Use the following tips to help guests select wines:**

- Take the wine order either by name or bin number. The guest ordering the wine becomes the "host" of the wine service. This guest should also be the one who will taste the wine. In some cases, this guest may not be the host of the entire meal.
- Check the wine label and vintage for accuracy before presenting the bottle to the guest. *See 4.13.*
- Pre-set the appropriate wine glasses by handling the stems only, and bring the bucket, or chiller to the table if serving a white wine. In formal settings, an additional tasting glass may be brought for the host to taste the wine. *See 4.14.*
- Determine who will be having wine, and ensure that all guests are of legal drinking age.
- Present the wine to the host for verification, and repeat the wine's brand, variety or classification, appellation, and vintage. *See 4.15.*
- Determine when the guests want their wine poured.
- Pour 1 ounce (30 ml) of wine for the host for tasting purposes. If the wine is refused, determine the reason and find the sommelier

4.16 Pour wine at the guest's right.

4.13 Check the wine label to insure accuracy before serving it to the guest.

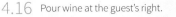

4.14 Mark the table with glassware before opening the wine.

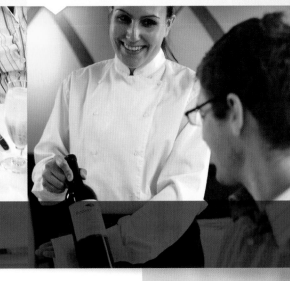

4.15 Presenting the wine before opening it allows the wine host to verify that the correct wine is being served.

Tips to help guests
select wines

or manager. A faulty cork occasionally compromises the flavor of wine. In that event, the manager may replace the wine with another bottle.

- Avoid reaching in front of the guest to pour. Delicately pour wine in a continuous flow for each person from the right side and with the right hand, twisting the bottle at the end of each pour to avoid drips. *See 4.16.*
- Serve the guest of honor first, and moving clockwise, serve the ladies first.
- Return the wine to the wine bucket or chiller, or place it on the bread and butter plate/coaster on the table with the label facing the host.
- Avoid overpouring wine.
- Discreetly allow the host to know when the bottle is empty, and determine whether another bottle is desired. If the host orders another bottle of wine, bring a clean glass for tasting, even if it is the same wine.
- If guests switch to a different wine, bring clean and appropriate wine glasses.
- When guests have finished the bottle and do not require another, remove it from the table before removing the wine glasses.

Opening Procedures for White, Rosé, and Dessert Wines

Follow these procedures when opening white, rosé, and dessert wines:
- **Ask the guest if they prefer the wine in an ice bucket as they may not.**
- **If using a wine bucket, fill it three-quarters of the way with equal amounts of ice and water. Place it in either a wine bucket stand, or if using a chiller, place it on the table to the right of the host. A chiller is pre-chilled and does not require ice and water. *See 4.17.***

- Present the wine from the right side with the label facing the host. Read the wine's primary identification: the vintage, the brand, variety, classification, the appellation in that order.
- Then place the wine bottle in the chiller or in the bucket, draping a service napkin in the form of a collar around the neck of the bottle. When opening it, rest the bottle on the side of the bucket for additional support.
- When a table is small and does not allow the server to open the bottle on the table's surface, the server must be adept at opening the bottle in the hands.
- If using the blade of a corkscrew, remove the top of the capsule by cutting it below the lip or bulge of the wine bottle. *See 4.18.* If using a foil cutter to attain a perfectly neat edge, cut above the lip. If the capsule is torn, remove it from the bottle entirely and put it in your pocket. If the bottle has an exaggerated lip at its top with a small seal affixed to the surface of the cork, perforate the seal with the worm of the corkscrew before proceeding to remove the cork.
- Wipe the top of the bottle with a clean service napkin to remove any mold or debris.
- Insert the worm of the corkscrew into the center of the cork, understanding that the point of a wine screw is not the center of the worm itself, and twist until four or five turns of the worm are in the cork. *See 4.19.* Place the corkscrew lever onto the lip of the bottle, and pull the cork straight out, using the lever. If necessary, use a delicate wriggling motion to completely remove the cork. Unscrew the cork from the corkscrew.

- Again, use a clean napkin to wipe any particles from the mouth of the bottle, making sure that your hands do not come in contact with it.
- Present the cork to the host's right side by placing it on a plate with a doily (The host may wish to examine the condition of the cork to determine the authenticity and storage conditions of the wine.) Remove the plate and cork from the table after the guest has been served the wine.
- Remove the bottle from the chiller or bucket, holding the bottle over the long folded portion of the service towel collar, and leave the label exposed to the guests' view.
- Pour about 1 ounce (30 ml) of the wine into a tasting glass for the host's approval. Do not allow the bottle to touch the glass.
- After the wine has been approved, pour wine for the other guests, serving the host last.
- After pouring the wine in 3- or 4-ounce servings (89- or 118-ml), place the bottle back into the ice bucket or chiller, and fold a service towel over the top of the bucket.
- Avoid pouring more than 3 or 4 ounces (89 or 118 ml) of wine at a time to prevent warming that may impair the flavor. Pouring smaller servings is especially important with dessert wines, which are often consumed more slowly as they are either sweeter, higher in alcohol, or both.

Note: Today's servers encounter fine wines with a variety of closures. These include glass stoppers, synthetic corks, and stelvin capsules or screw caps. The procedures recommended may be modified, especially for screw caps.

Various opening procedures for **white, rosé,** and **dessert wines**

4.17 The mise en place for white wine service.

4.18 Cut below the lip, moving the knife around the neck of the bottle.

4.19 Position the sharp point of the cork screw at the center of the cork.

4.20 A doilied bread-and-butter plate acts as the underliner to the wine bottle.

4.21 Cut below the lip, moving the knife around the neck of the bottle.

4.22a Set the notched end of the lever onto the lip of the bottle.

4.22b Support the lever while lifting the cork out of the bottle.

4.23 When the bottle is opened the wine host should be offered the cork to inspect it.

Opening Procedures for Red Wine

Red wine is not generally chilled in an ice bucket or chiller, so the procedures for opening red wine differ from those used for chilled wines:

- Bring a wine coaster or doilied bread-and-butter plate to the table along with the bottle of wine. *See 4.20.*
- Present the wine bottle from the right side, with the label facing the host.
- Place the bottle on the coaster or the doilied bread-and-butter plate, and remove the top portion of the seal as previously described. *See 4.21.*
- Use the same opening procedures described above, and use the doilied plate to present the cork to the host. *See 4.22a, 4.22b, and 4.23.*
- After approval, pour 4–6 ounces (118–177 ml) of the wine, depending on the style of glass used, and use standard rules of protocol. *See 4.24.*
- Place the bottle on the coaster or doilied bread-and-butter plate toward the center of the table, with the label facing the host.
- Remove and pocket the cork.

4.24 Pour the host a taste.

Decanting Red Wine

Red wines are decanted for three reasons:

- **Decanting** allows some wines to "breathe" so the full aromatic bouquet may be revealed.
- Careful decanting removes the wine and leaves any accumulated sediment in the bottle.
- Decanting allows wines from a cellar to reach their proper serving temperatures more rapidly, a process called chambréing.

Do not begin decanting red wine more than a half-hour before it is to be served unless requested by the guest. *See 4.25.* Pour the wine from the bottle carefully into a glass or crystal decanter (33-ounce, or 1-liter, minimum) in a slow but steady stream along the inside of the glass. *See 4.26.* If decanting an old wine, pour it slowly and continuously so as not to loosen the sediment. Stop pouring as soon as you see sediment approaching the neck of the bottle.

Young red wines such as young claret from Bordeaux, may be high in tannins. Aerating such a wine by decanting it allows the hard tannins to seem less astringent and makes the wine more palatable. Avoid decanting more delicate red wines such as a Pinot Noir.

Older red wines (10 years or more), particularly those made from thick-skinned grapes such as Cabernet Sauvignon, ideally need to stand upright for 24 to 48 hours prior to serving. If the bottle has just been brought from the cellar; however, place it in a cradle or wine basket and open it with the bottle at a 20-30° angle, taking care not to disturb any sediment. When serving from a wine cradle, a lighted candle on a plate or a flashlight should be placed to the right of the decanter so the server can clearly observe the flow of wine down the neck of the bottle. Stop pouring as soon as the sediment approaches the neck, and do not interrupt the flow because this will loosen the sediment and allow it to spread through the wine. For very expensive older red wines, the guest might choose to be served the remaining wine, regardless of the sediment. *See 4.27.* In that case, use a special silver funnel with a strainer to pour this wine into a decanter or separate glass. *See 4.28.*

White wines may also be decanted, especially those made biodynamically with little or no chemical intervention.

Chambréing Wine

Chambré is a French word meaning "brought to service temperature." Although all wines should be stored in a cool cellar at 50°F (10°C), red wines should be served at warmer temperatures, up to 65°F (18°C). Using a warm decanter is the most effective way of bringing wines to their optimum serving temperature.

4.25 Carefully open wines to be decanted to avoid disturbing any sediment.

4.26 Pour the wine slowly down the inside neck of the decanter.

4.27 Sediment, or a wine's color and tannin molecules, forms in older red wines.

4.28 A silver wine funnel may be used to decant wine.

Decanting
red wine

4.29 Twist the cage tab counter clockwise to loosen it.

4.30 Holding the cork in a napkin, twist from the bottom of the bottle.

4.31 Present the cork to the wine host.

4.32 Slowly pour a 1 ounce taste in the glass.

4.33 Fill the glasses of all the guests three-fourths full before finishing the host's pour.

Opening Procedures for Sparkling Wines

Sparkling wines should be chilled at 40°F–45°F (4°C–7°C) before opening. The most efficient way to chill sparkling wines is with a sparkling wine bucket, which is taller than a conventional wine bucket. Chilling the wine from storage temperature to serving temperature should take about 20 minutes. Insufficient chilling may cause the cork to exit the bottle explosively, cause the wine to overflow, and force a loss of carbonation. **The steps that follow are suggested for the service of sparkling wines:**

- At the table, remove the sparkling wine from the ice bucket, and wipe it dry with a service towel.
- Holding the bottle at chest height at a 45° angle, find the perforation or wire loop, and pull it out from under the foil.
- Remove the top part of the foil, and twist the wire loop counterclockwise about 5 1/2 times until the wire cage can be lifted from the lip of the bottle. Leave the cage (aggraffe) on the cork or put it in your pocket. *See 4.29.*
- While still holding the bottle at a 45° angle, grasp the cork in your left hand, and twist the bottle counterclockwise with your right hand. Do not twist the cork, which may break.
- As the cork is being expelled from the bottle, carefully counterbalance the pressure by gently holding it in and tilting it toward yourself. Allow the slightest amount of gas to escape to help preserve the bubbly character of the wine. The guests should hear a soft hiss rather than a loud pop. *See 4.30.*
- Continue to hold the bottle at a 45° angle for several seconds to equalize the pressure.
- Present the cork on a doilied plate to the guest. *See 4.31.*
- Wrap a service towel around the neck of the bottle. Pour a 1-ounce (30-ml) taste for the host's approval. If the bottle being served is a "Magnum" or greater, the bottle is held with the thumb of the right hand in the punt (indentation at the bottom of the bottle) and the bottom of the bottle resting in the four fingers of the same hand. The neck of the bottle is then rested on a service napkin placed over the left wrist and poured using both arms. *See 4.32.*
- After the wine is approved, pour it for each of the guests. Pour the wine down the center of an appropriate fluted or tulip glass, waiting for the foam to subside. Continue to pour until the glass is three-fourths full. *See 4.33.*
- After pouring, put the bottle back into the bucket with a service towel draped over it.

Service Temperatures of Wine

Serving wine at its appropriate temperature is important. Neglecting this aspect will, at very least, diminish the guest's appreciation of the wine, and at worst, destroy the wine's character and balance.

The senses of taste and smell are important to the appreciation of wine. The volatile compounds of red wine are released at higher temperatures than those of white wine, so the aromas of red wines are easier to detect at 60°F–65°F (16°C–18°C). White wines should be chilled so their acidity is less pronounced. As a general guideline, the higher the acidity in wine, the lower the serving temperature should be to preserve the balance of the wine on the palate. If red wine is served too warm, the alcohol will become too pronounced and taste less refreshing.

Dessert and Sparkling Wines
40°F–45°F (4°C–7°C)

White Wines, Rosés, Sherries, Best Champagnes
45°F–50°F (7°C–10°C)

Best Quality Dry Whites, Light Reds
(Beaujolais Nouveau, for Example)
50°F–55°F (10°C–13°C)

This is also the storage temperature for all wines.

Light Reds, Ordinary Bordeaux, Chianti
55°F–60°F (13°C–16°C)

Full-Bodied Reds
60°F–65°F (16°C–18°C)

HOT BEVERAGE SERVICE

The quality of hot beverage service is critical because it is often a guest's first or final impression of a dining experience. Coffee or tea may be served as a one-step or two-step procedure, depending on the number of guests at the table, but it is designed so the server pours at the table. Pouring at the table prevents spilling on the way to the table, and allows guests to see if the cup is clean and the amount of coffee poured is satisfactory.

One-step service means that the warmed cups and saucers, spoons, and condiments are brought to the table on a beverage tray at the same time as the coffee or teapot. The serviceware and condiments are placed appropriately on the table first, and the server proceeds to pour coffee into the cup. A two-step service requires that the server bring and place the preset on the table, and then return with the coffee or teapot to pour it into the cups. **Proper coffee or tea service requires that:**

- The coffee or teapots and cups are warmed prior to service. *See 4.34.*
- When using a beverage tray, the lip of the cup and the spoons should not come into direct contact with the tray's surface.
- The cup and saucer are placed to the right of the cover at the same time, with the handle at a 4 o'clock position. The spoon is placed to the right or above the cup on the saucer or directly on the table to the right of the cup and saucer. *See 4.35.*
- Cream, half-and-half, or milk are kept refrigerated and poured into a creamer just before service. (In upscale restaurants, the cream or milk might be heated.)
- When unwrapped sugar cubes are used, tongs are provided. The creamer and sugar bowl are placed in front of the guest of honor or the women at the table. *See 4.36.*

4.34 To quickly warm a hot beverage cup fill it with hot water.

4.35 Mark the course before serving a hot beverage.

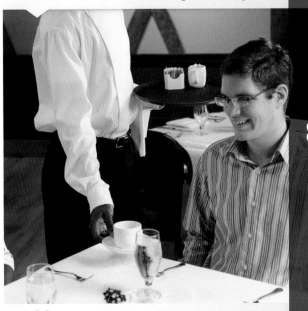

4.36 Sugar caddies and creamers are placed nearest the guest of honor or close to the women seated at the table.

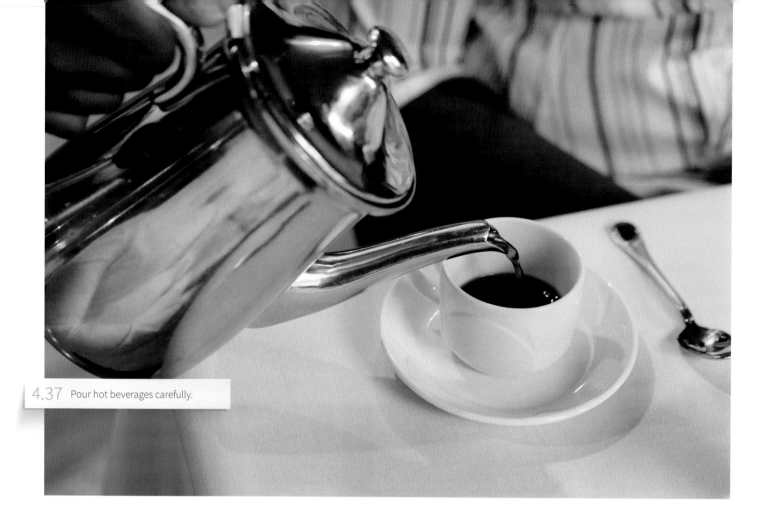

4.37 Pour hot beverages carefully.

Coffee Service

Depending on the style of meal, coffee cups may be preset on the table or brought to the table when the guests order coffee. Breakfast service often requires presetting coffee cups, saucers, spoons, and sugar and sweeteners. **Here are the fundamentals of coffee service:**

- While pouring, catch drips with a service towel or STP.
- Pour the coffee into each cup at the table until it is only three-fourths full, unless the guest has specified "black" coffee. *See 4.37.*
- When using individual pots, place the pot to the right of the guest.
- If a guest orders more coffee after a considerable time has passed, replace the cup with a new one.
- If a French press is offered, ask the guests whether they prefer to press the plunger and serve themselves.

Fundamentals for Brewing Coffee

There are five fundamentals for brewing the perfect cup of coffee: proportion, grind, water, freshness, and equipment.

Proportion The proportion of coffee to water must be accurately measured. The recommended formula is 1 ounce (30 ml) of coffee to 20 ounces (591 ml) of fresh, cold water. Prepackaged coffee packs are designed for a specific brewing capacity.

Grind Coffee beans can be ground from coarse to fine, which will determine, along with the roast level and blend, the intensity and balance of taste and flavors. The brew cycle of the coffee machine determines the grind. Fine grind requires 1–4 minutes, drip/medium grind requires 4–6 minutes, and regular/coarse grind requires 6–8 minutes.

Water The quality and temperature of the water helps to determine the flavor and the quality of coffee. Unless the water is hard, purification is usually not necessary.

Freshness Coffee beans lose essential oils and aroma when exposed to air, light, heat, and moisture. To preserve freshness, keep coffee sealed and in a dark cool storage area. Grinding coffee beans immediately before brewing ensures that they are at their best.

Equipment The cleaner the equipment, the better the taste of the coffee. Clean the grinder, dispenser, coffeemaker, filter devices, spray heads, and brewing containers thoroughly at the end of each shift. Coffee is brewed at temperatures between 195°F–205°F (90°C–96°C).

SPECIALTY COFFEE SERVICE

Consumers have become much more sophisticated and aware of coffee services that heighten both the flavors and "the coffee experience." Today's servers need to master such techniques.

French Presses

Although French presses are more costly to maintain and more labor intensive, many upscale establishments use them to ensure the freshest and most flavorful coffee. French presses come in 10- to 20-ounce sizes (296- to 591-ml) and use medium grind coffee at a rate of 1–1 1/2 ounces (30 ml–44 ml) per 20 ounces (591 ml) of boiling water.

Pour the coffee into the French press pot, and add boiling water. The grounds will float to the top. Stir the grounds rapidly 2 or 3 times and cover the pot. Wait for 3 minutes before slowly pressing the plunger or allowing the consumer to do so if desired.

Turkish or Arabic Coffee

Coffee drinking was introduced to Europe by the Turks, and the oldest method of coffee preparation was borrowed from the Arabs. Using a long handled narrow necked boiling pot sometimes called an ibriq, finely ground coffee and sugar are blended with water and brought to a boil over a low flame. Each time the solution comes to a boil, the pot is removed from heat momentarily and then reheated twice more before being poured into small demitasse cups.

Moka

Moka is a common European form of home coffee preparation that is frequently used in the United States. The moka method for brewing coffee is a steam percolation system. It uses a stove top specialized pot to make an espresso style coffee. Steam is created and forces water to travel from a lower chamber up a funnel that is part of the filter that holds finely ground coffee. The steamed water is then blended with the grounds and forced up to an upper chamber that has a filter that prevents grounds from getting into the final solution and a funnel where the coffee solution ultimately ends up. There is a safety valve on the machine to prevent excess pressure.

Espresso

Espresso is a hot coffee beverage as well as a very specific Italian experience that needs to be authentic to be fully appreciated. It is a very complex beverage that requires the use of excellent quality beans produced and roasted to exacting specifications and further prepared with highly skilled service. The perfect espresso is a balance between a rich texture created by oils that coat the tongue and prevent a perception of bitterness and acidity to create a sweet roast of intense coffee flavor. A great espresso should have a lingering taste on the palate that lasts up to a half-hour. Brewed by quickly passing steamed pressurized water at 195° F (91°C) through finely ground coffee, espresso is so named because of the speed at which a 1 ounce (30 ml) espresso can be made from 7 grams of coffee with an espresso machine in 25–30 seconds. Although the process is swift, the flavor captures the essence of the coffee bean.

4.38   A demitasse cup and saucer

Traditionally served in a warm **demitasse**, or half cup, espresso is accompanied by a demitasse spoon and sugar. *See 4.38.* **The following steps are used to brew espresso:**

- Make sure the demitasse and portafilter are warm by storing them on the heated surface of the machine. The **portafilter,** also known as the filter holder, is where the espresso grind is held once dispensed.
- Grind the coffee to order, and hold it for no longer than a few minutes before brewing so it does not oxidize and lose flavor.
- Place the portafilter under the **doser,** *see 4.39,* which measures out the precise portion, and pull the lever or press the button to release the grounds into the portafilter. Then, with the portafilter on the countertop, tamp the grounds firmly, and wipe any excess grounds from the rim. *See 4.40.*

- Insert the portafilter into the "group" of the machine, and press the button to pour the shot. (Be sure to use the shot within 30 seconds to a minute, or the espresso will no longer be hot.) *See 4.41.*
- After the espresso is served, remove the portafilter, knock out the grounds, and brush or rinse the portafilter under hot water. *See 4.42.*

Espresso uses a specific blend of freshly ground roasted beans to yield a concentrated beverage consisting of a heart, body, and crema. **Crema** is a complex suspension of emulsified coffee oils, carbon dioxide bubbles, and suspended particles that float on the surface of freshly brewed espresso. *See 4.43.* It should be hazelnut in color. An espresso that is pale in color indicates overextraction, and one that is dark brown indicates underextraction. Ideally, the good crema will have a visible pattern of thin lines referred to as **tiger stripes.** Espresso machines usually brew only one or two demitasses at a time. A shot of espresso is critical in drink recipes for caffé latte, café mocha, caffé latte based drinks, and cappuccino. Further discussion of a variety of espresso based recipes is found in Chapter 6, "The Beverage World."

Keeping coffee equipment clean is also key to a well-made espresso or cup of coffee. There should be a daily regimen and weekly schedule for side duties such as: wiping the doser with a brush, cleaning out the espresso machine by using a 'blind' in the portafilter with a cleaning solution, wiping the spray heads of a coffee machine, and presoaking coffee and tea cups in an approved solution to prevent build up of stains.

Steps for brewing espresso

4.39   The doser portions the ground coffee into the portafilter.

4.40   Tamp the grounds firmly.

4.41   The portafilter attaches to the group head for brewing.

4.42   The portafilter is emptied into a knockbox after brewing.

4.43   Crema, the amber foam of a well-made espresso

Green Tea

Steeped at 160°F–180°F
(71°C–82°C) for 2–3 minutes

Oolong Tea

Steeped at 195°F–212°F
(91°C–100°C) for 3–4 minutes

Black Tea

Steeped at 200°F–212°F
(93°C–100°C) for 4–5 minutes

TEA SERVICE

The term "tea" generally refers to a beverage that is made from an infusion of the leaves of Camellia sinensis prepared in boiling water. There are, however, a number of herbal blends that also fall into this category. **The following fundamentals are essential to steeping the perfect cup of tea:**

Proportion The proportion of tea to the volume of water will determine the final taste. Depending on the type and quality of tea leaves, 1 rounded teaspoon of tea is required for 6 ounces (177 ml) of water.

Water Trace chemicals and minerals in tap water may alter the flavors in tea. For that reason, many restaurants use bottled spring water, distilled water, or filtered water for steeping tea.

Freshness Light, temperature, humidity, and oxygen all affect tea leaves, so it is essential to store tea in a sealed container.

INFUSION

The two factors to consider when infusing tea in fresh water are temperature and steeping time.

Temperature Tea must be infused in water ranging from 160°F (71°C) to the boiling point temperature in order to release all its aromas and flavors. Generally, the greater the fermentation of the tea, the higher the required temperature of the water.

Steeping time The time needed to steep tea leaves is also based on their level of fermentation or oxidation. Greater levels of oxidation require more steeping time. Teas may be steeped more than once, but later infusion requires more time. Avoid using color as a determining factor when infusing tea because color does not necessarily correspond to flavor.

A wide variety of equipment is appropriate for steeping tea including teapots, teacups, and kettles. Regardless of the kind of equipment, it must be spotless. Constant use of the same equipment leads to a buildup of mineral deposits from the water and tea that may create off-flavors.

Most establishments use commercial-grade bagged tea because it is convenient, although higher-quality loose teas are often preferred in fine dining establishments.

Use the following procedures when serving tea:

• When a guest requests tea, bring a selection of the available teas for the guest's perusal.

• After the guest selects a tea, place the packet on a doilied bread-and-butter plate, or put the loose tea in a tea strainer or specially designed tea bag.

• Pre-set a warm cup on a saucer, a spoon on the table to the right of the guest, sugar and sweeteners, and lemon wedges or a creamer with milk, depending on the guest's request.

• If using a teabag, the guest may determine how strong or weak the tea should be. Place the teapot with the teabag propped against it on a doilied bread-and-butter plate to the right of the cup.

• For service using loose-leaf tea, place the tea in a warmed teapot, and fill the pot with boiling water. After the tea has steeped for the required time, strain the tea into the cup through a tea strainer. It is also considered proper to bring a second pot of boiling water so that guests may dilute the strength of their tea.

HIGH TEA SERVICE

Afternoon, or "high" tea is a light, midday meal that bridges the gap between early-morning breakfast and late-evening dinner. It is a Victorian tradition, which has gained a renewed popularity in recent years, and many cosmopolitan hotels and restaurants offer afternoon tea service. It provides an opportunity to sell light foods and beverages when the demand for full-service meals is low. High tea includes a loose tea selection with more detailed service and food accompaniments such as finger sandwiches, tartlets, scones, cookies, or cakes.

ICED TEA

More than 80% of the tea consumed in the United States is iced. Iced tea can be prepared from powdered tea concentrate, a commercial liquid tea concentrate, or a concentrate made on the premises.

To make iced tea from a liquid concentrate, steep the tea for about ten minutes in a quarter of the quantity of boiling water needed for fresh hot tea. Remove the tea bags, or strain loose-leaf tea. If desired, dissolve sugar or other sweetener in the hot concentrate. To serve, blend one part concentrate and two parts fresh water, and serve in a highball glass or tall goblet filled with ice and accompanied by a long handled iced teaspoon.

SELLING THE MENU AND SPECIALS

Describing the menu by providing clear, accurate, and appealing descriptions of menu items not only helps guests to decide on their food orders but also provides an opportunity for additional selling. Begin by offering a confident explanation of any daily or specials additions to the presented menu. Using descriptive adjectives, appropriate hand gestures, and good eye contact with guests, increases their comfort level and helps steer their selections. Food descriptions should follow a specific method of describing the item so that the guest understands the contents of the item and the presentation. **Describing an item should include the following accordingly:**

1. The raw product/s used
2. The method/s of preparation
3. The method/s of cooking (brased, baked, saute'd etc.)
4. The finish, sauce, garnish

Each type of food may include different descriptive details. For example, soup descriptions generally include the major ingredients, the stock, the texture, and if appropriate, the temperature ("chilled gazpacho" for example). Salad descriptions might identify whether the salad is tossed or arranged, whether cooked ingredients are served warm or cold, and the kind or kinds of dressings available. Entrées, on the other hand, include descriptions of the ingredients, such as the cut of meat; the type of preparation, such as sautéed or braised; and the fashion in which the entrée is served, such as with a specific kind of sauce. If a menu item is sold out, be sure to provide the guest with this information prior to taking the meal order.

After the guest chooses the food items, suggest a range of wines, beer or other beverages to complement the food, and describe any dessert item that must be pre-ordered due to preparation time. Describe the selections with as much appeal as possible, but take care to avoid misrepresentation. When asked a question to which the server does not know the answer, the response should be: "I don't know, but I will find out."

TAKING THE ORDER

In most restaurants, tables and seats are numbered to simplify taking the order and organizing the workflow. Each server is responsible for a specific group of tables, called a station. Depending on the level of service, a station may be as small as 12 seats or as large as 30 seats. Remember that, the numbering of tables and seats in a dining room are critical to the process of taking orders.

THE POSITION OF THE SERVER

Carefully gauge when a party is ready to order, although this is not always an easy task. Similarly, evaluate whether the guest has made a choice or needs assistance in making a selection.

When taking an order at the table, stand to the right of each guest when possible. If there is a guest of honor, take that person's order first followed by the orders of children, women, men, and finally the host's order. Collect all the specifics necessary from each guest and remove the menu before moving on to take the next person's order. When appropriate, ask about the cooking temperatures, such as the degree of doneness for a steak or eggs. Repeating the order to the guest helps to avoid mistakes. If a guest has special requests, be sure to check with the chef before the order is taken to see whether the request can be honored. Timing is equally important in determining exactly when to take the order and when to transmit it to the kitchen so as not to overburden the kitchen staff.

The position of the server and the type of service will differ slightly when serving guests at a booth or banquette.

Booth Style Tables In establishments with booths—tables that rest against a wall with high-backed and bench like seats—guests are numbered clockwise around the booth for the purpose of organizing the kitchen order and food service. Service begins with the guest seated farthest away from the server. When clearing the tableware, the service staff starts with the guests seated closest to the server.

Banquette Style Tables In a banquette, guests are seated facing the server with their backs to the wall. As with booth service, the server should number the guests clockwise from the focal point when taking food and beverage orders. Serving should be done as unobtrusively as possible, serving with the hand farthest from the guest.

WRITING THE ORDER

In traditional service, a cold item is served before a hot one, and a liquid item precedes the service of one that is solid. **In the United States, courses are generally served in the following sequence:**
1. Appetizer,
2. Soup,
3. Salad,
4. Intermezzo,
5. Entrée,
6. Cheese,
7. Dessert,
8. Coffee.

The exact sequencing depends somewhat on the order placed by each guest. Assume; for example, the first guest at a table orders an appetizer, a soup, and a salad; the second guest orders only soup; and the third orders only a salad. Using the system described, bring the first guest an appetizer. After clearing the appetizer, bring soup for the first and second guests. Once the soup has been cleared, bring the salad for the first and third guests.

Orders should be written in the correct sequence on a small order pad or a guest check or entered into a point-of-sale (POS) computer system. *See 4.44.* Beverage orders are commonly recorded on the back of the check. The seat position of each guest should be written next to the order, and the women's seat numbers should be circled for quick identification. Servers generally use a type of "shorthand" to note information and to communicate with the kitchen staff and among themselves.

TRANSMITTING THE ORDER TO THE KITCHEN

Orders are transmitted to the kitchen verbally with a written order form or by a computerized point-of-sale (POS) system. *See 4.45.* Waitstaff should be familiar with handwritten checks and able to understand check-writing principles in case a computerized system crashes.

To begin preparing a guest check, fill out the information at the top of each check in the boxes provided for the date, server number or initials, table number, and the number of guests. In the far left column, list the quantity of each item ordered. In the center column, write the item ordered and next to it, the number of each guest's position.

Prepare the check by transferring the order from the order pad to a guest check. Begin by determining whether there are more items in a single course, such as appetizers, than there are guests. Two people might, for example, order three appetizers. Also, check to see whether the same guest number appears twice for one course as in a situation when one guest orders two appetizers while another orders none.

Copy the order pad onto the guest check the way it is written, leaving a space between the courses. For example, if a guest selects an appetizer as an entrée, list the appetizer with the entrées of the other guests.

4.44 Orders should be written in the service sequence of the meal.

4.45 A computer or POS system can transmit an order to the kitchen.

A verbal ordering system is the least reliable and has very limited application in the industry. A computerized POS (Point of Sale system) is the most widely used as it is the most accurate, accountable, and efficient form of communication. Each server is given an identity code to prevent confusion or any fraudulent use of the computer. The most popular way of entering information into the computer is a touch-screen system. The advantage to this system is that it is very easy to master. Many leading restaurant chains employ handheld systems replacing handwriting entirely. **It is important to remember these points:**

- If handwritten, the top copy or dupe of the check is given to the chef, coordinator, or kitchen expediter. *See 4.46.*
- Servers should be as quiet and unobtrusive as possible in the kitchen.
- Request the course by table number rather than asking for the specific item whenever requesting food from the kitchen ("Chef, may I pick up the soups for table 213?").

- Servers of many establishments may be required to "fire" (instruct the kitchen to begin cooking) the next course they wish to pick up. The process of firing is the server's way of controlling the timing of service. This may be done verbally or transmitted by POS.
- Never serve a course until all the items for that course are ready to be served.
- As a representative of the guest in the kitchen, it is the server's responsibility to ensure that the guests receive exactly what they order. It is at this point of pick-up that servers should verify the order is correct. *See 4.47.*
- If the order is not correct and a presentation or temperature problem emerges at this time, it should be resolved in the kitchen. The customer's needs should be the first concern.
- Servers should be aware of where each guest's order is located on the tray. This will ensure that the service of the course is presented in a timely and professional manner. *See 4.48.*

Communication is essential to the success of an establishment. Taking orders correctly and transmitting them to the kitchen is imperative. Good verbal communication skills facilitate this process as well. *See 4.49 Kitchen Short Hand and 4.50 Service Slang.*

4.47 The server is the last individual who verifies the order before the guest is served.

4.48 Organize the food tray by seat position to insure that the guest receives the correct order.

4.46 A three-part hand written guest check

4.49 Kitchen "Shorthand"

Blkn or B&B	Black and blue
R	Rare
M/R	Medium rare
M	Medium
M/W	Medium well
86	Sold out of item
68	Item is again available
SOS	Sauce on the side
LOS	Light on sauce
Hold	Chef waits to prepare until server discusses the item

4.50 Service Slang

deuce	a party of 2
4 top	a party of 4
fire	to request to begin cooking an order
split	divide item in two

4.51 Properly polishing all service equipment insures quality.

4.52 Carry flatware on a serviette or STP.

4.53 The blade of the knife faces in toward the center of the setting.

4.54a The CORRECT method of handling flatware

4.54b An INCORRECT method of handling flatware

HANDLING FLATWARE

When handling flatware and cutlery in the dining room, the following guidelines should be followed:

- Use a clean side towel to wipe all flatware before placing it on the table. *See 4.51.*
- Carry flatware through a dining room on a serviette or STP. *See 4.52.*
- Place flatware on the appropriate side of the guest's cover.
- Forks to the left.
- Knives with blades facing in and spoons to the right except for dessert silverware (on top of the cover), and the bread and butter knife on the butter plate. *See 4.53.*
- Handle flatware by the "waist" or mid section. Fingers should not come in contact with the end of the utensil that goes into the customer's mouth. Also, avoid leaving fingerprints on the handles. *See 4.54a and 4.54b.*
- Place most flatware parallel one to another and perpendicular to the table. On round tables, the flatware should not follow the contour of the table's edge.
- Pre-set dessert forks and spoons horizontally at the top of the cover with the spoon above the fork.

Cleaning, sanitizing, and storing flatware and cutlery Flatware and cutlery should be washed and rinsed at high temperatures in the dishwasher and allowed to dry before being stored. The pieces should be organized by type and size in appropriately lined drawers that have washable air mats.

PROPER USE OF A STANDARD TRANSPORT PLATE (STP) OR SERVIETTE

A Standard Transport Plate or serviette is a napkin-lined dinner plate used for the purpose of carrying clean flatware to the table. Flatware should not be placed in a napkin pocket fold when using an STP but merely laid on top of a square napkin fold. The flatware should be organized by group or category depending on the size of the party being served. *See 4.55 and 4.56.*

MARKING THE TABLE

"Marking a table" is restaurant jargon for adjusting flatware. A key aspect of service, especially in an à la carte environment, involves adjusting flatware to suit the service order before each course arrives and then clearing it after each course. Flatware should be readjusted after each course is cleared, and missing or used flatware should be replaced. Clean flatware should be carried on a serviette or STP.

If the server notices a utensil on the table from a preceding course, it should be collected and placed in the fingers holding the STP and treated as a used utensil.

4.55 The grouping method of marking, organized by seat position

4.56 The categorizing method of marking, organized by the type of flatware

SERVING PLATED FOOD

The key to serving plated food is to ensure that the presentation remains as the chef intended: for example, sauces are not flowing onto the rim of the plate, the food arrives at the right temperature, and orders are delivered to the correct guest without being auctioned off.

Plate Carrying

Plate carrying refers to carrying and presenting a plated course to the guest in the manner that the chef intended. Carrying multiple plates either from the kitchen or the service tray to the table ensures that the food arrives to the guests quickly and at an appropriate temperature. Generally, a maximum of three plates are held in one hand/arm and a fourth is held in the other hand. *See 4.57a.* This technique does require practice. There are different techniques that may be used based on the size of the plates as well as the dexterity of the server. *See 4.57b.* If serving from the left, use the right hand/arm to hold three plates and hold one in the left hand. Conversely, if serving from the right, hold three plates on the left hand/arm and one in the right hand. It is always most important to serve while being open to the guest. *See 4.58.*

Use of Food Trays

Most à la carte restaurants and banquet establishments have oval service trays to allow servers to carry either large or heavy loads expeditiously to and from the dining room. Some establishments, especially hotels with room service, have staff transport food on rectangular trays that usually limit how much may be transported at one time. Usually the server will carry the tray by its handles and at waist level. Trays without handles are carried on the shoulder, as are oval trays.

Service Tray Handling

Basic handling of a tray involves these techniques:

- A service tray should be carried in the server's left hand above the shoulder. This is done to enable the server to proceed through a doorway without the door swinging back and hitting the tray. *See 4.59.*
- The tray should always be placed on a tray stand with the length of the tray crossing the bars of the tray stand.
- Distribute items on the tray so the tray is as evenly balanced as possible. *See 4.60.*
- Place tall or heavier items in the center of the tray.
- Never stack plates on top of food when clearing a guest's table.
- Remove all flatware from plates and place off to the side on the tray, separating it by type.
- When setting up the tray, do not place it close to the guest's table. (It is not part of the guest's dining experience.)
- Always carry the food tray over the shoulder, never at the side of the body, even if the tray is empty.
- Signal a server in front of you by saying "behind you" to prevent collisions.
- Be particularly alert when walking behind guests in case they stop suddenly.
- Be careful when carrying glassware on a food tray as there is a propensity to overload the tray, and this may result in significant breakage. Glasses should ideally be carried on a beverage tray.
- After clearing a guest's table, cover the tray with a service towel before carrying it from the dining room.
- Never leave unsightly trays in the dining room. As soon as the table is cleared, remove the tray from the dining room.
- Carry the tray on the palm or fingertips, depending on its weight.
- Use the left shoulder to help balance the tray, if need be.
- Carry the tray stand in the collapsed position on your right when walking in the dining room.
- Extend the right arm, which holds the tray stand, and flick the wrist so the support legs separate, bringing the tray stand to an upright position. The legs should be parallel to the body.
- Turn to the right, bend the knee, and lower the tray in a horizontal position until it sits on the support frame. Slide the tray across the top of the frame so its weight is evenly distributed.

4.57a A four-plate carry

4.57b A two-plate clearing carry

4.58 Serving an entrée while being open to the guest

- When picking up or placing down a loaded tray, keep the back straight, and bend and lift with the knees and legs. *See 4.61.*
- When removing the tray, reverse the process. Collapse the tray stand against the right hip, while holding the tray level.

Stackable Plate Covers

Stackable plate covers are specifically sized to plates so they remain firmly in place and allow the server to carry as many as 12 to 16 entrées on an oval service tray at one time into the dining room. They also enable the kitchen staff to plate hot entrées in a warming oven immediately prior to service. When removing a plate cover, invert it, and stack each of the remaining covers on top of it.

Plate Domes

Cloche is the French word for a bell and refers to the bell-shaped domes that are used as sophisticated and impressive plate covers at fine dining restaurants. In contrast to stackable plate covers, the server would have all guests' entrées served sous cloches (under the covers) simultaneously by enlisting the help of other members of the service team. The bell-shaped covers are removed in unison to add drama and to heighten the guests' dining experience.

The Pince Technique

The pince technique is used by a server to transfer appropriately sized and shaped food from a platter, breadbasket, or other serving dish to the guest's plate. The technique requires a large serving spoon and fork, called a serving set. The serving set is held in a single hand (generally the right) with the spoon facing up and is placed under the fork that has its tines pointing upwards. This allows the server to hold the serving platter or basket in one hand, close to the guest's plate, while serving the food using the other hand. This technique is also used for transferring bread from the bread warmer to a bread basket to avoid hand contact. Using a service set in this way is most often used when performing a Russian style of service.

4.59   The food tray is carried on the left hand.

4.60   Food trays should be organized to maximize balance.

4.61   Use the leg muscles when lifting or landing a loaded tray.

The Bread and Butter Course

The sequence of bread service varies from restaurant to restaurant, but typically bread is served as a welcoming gesture after water has been poured or after the food order has been taken. Bread and butter may be served in a number of ways, from the less formal family style method to formal Russian or English service using the pincing technique. *See 4.62 (A through C)* shows three bread service methods.

The pincing technique involves:

1. Lining a small breadbasket with a clean, folded napkin.
2. Using tongs or a service set to place the bread in the center of the fold and never handling the bread or rolls with bare hands. *See 4.63.*
3. Allowing 1 1/2 rolls of bread per guest for the initial serving.
4. Placing the breadbasket in the center of the table and the fresh butter where it is most convenient for the women at the table, when serving family style.
5. Replenishing bread and butter as well.

Butter Butter may be served in the form of wrapped patties, chips, curls, balls, florets, whipped, or compounded forms in a ramekin, dish, or specialty butter cup. The butter should be served near room temperature so that it is easy to spread. *See 4.64.*

Olive oil As Italian-style cuisine dominates much of the restaurant industry, olive oil has become a much more visible alternative accompaniment to bread. It should be served directly from the bottle if the container is elegant and 600 ml or less. Otherwise, it should be served from a cruet or small handled pitcher such as a creamer or monkey dish that is integrated into the décor of the room. A teaspoon and doilied underliner should also accompany the monkey dish.

4.62a Classic or Family Bread Service

4.62b Pince Bread Service

4.62c Banquet or Pre-set Bread Service

4.63 The service spoon and fork work together to pince bread.

4.64 Simple butter cuts, compound or flavored butter, and seasoned olive oil

The Appetizer Course

Some fine-dining restaurants provide a complimentary bite-sized hors d'oeuvre at the start of a meal called an "amuse-bouche" or "amuse-gueule". This should serve as both an appetite stimulant and reflect the chef's cuisine. The server should be certain to provide the guest with a list all the ingredients in case a guest has food allergies.

Appetizers are small food presentations that sometimes replace soup or salad and also present the chef an opportunity to display some creativity. They may be served hot or cold. **The general guidelines for serving appetizers follow:**

1. When a guest orders both hot and cold appetizers, serve the cold appetizer first, unless the guest requests otherwise.
2. If an appetizer is shared, divide it skillfully, if possible, at the table.
3. Adjust any specialized flatware before serving the appetizer, and remove after clearing the appetizer.
4. Provide fingerbowls if necessary, either before or immediately after clearing the appetizer.

The Soup Course

Soups fall into two distinct categories: clear soups (such as consommé) and thick or cream soups (including chowder). Clear soups are served in a warmed soup cup with a bouillon spoon. Thick soups are best served in a warmed bowl or soup plate with a soup or potage spoon. *See 4.65.* In both cases, an underliner or doilied plate under the cup/bowl helps to prevent accidents. If soups are carried on a food tray into the dining room, assemble the cups and bowls onto the liners in the dining room, not in the kitchen, to avoid soup spills onto the liners. The rim of a soup plate should also be wiped clean, if necessary, before it is placed in front of the guest. When clearing soups, make sure the soup spoon has been placed onto the underliner before removing it.

Using a Tureen

When soup is ordered, tureen service may be used for both practical reasons as well as to give the guest the impression of added service. *See 4.66.* Pre-set warmed soup plates or bowls on underliners in front of the guests. Before it leaves the kitchen, the soup tureen should be placed on a STP/serviette underliner with a ladle in it or beside it. Remove the cover before approaching the table. With the tureen in the left hand, approach and serve guests from the left, drawing the handle of the soup ladle toward yourself, using the right hand to avoid spillage. Return the ladle to the tureen before serving the next guest. Service proceeds counterclockwise around the table. Tureens may also be used for French style service where the server portions the soup onto the cups or bowls on a guéridon before presenting them to the guests.

THE SALAD COURSE

Salads may be served before or after the entrée. In the United States, the convention is to serve the salad before the entrée, while in France, tradition dictates that the salad is served following the entrée.

Cold salads should be served on chilled plates with a salad knife and fork that may also be chilled. If requested, salad oil and vinegar should be presented in clean, filled cruets. When freshly ground pepper is available, it should be offered to the guest when serving the salad. The salad course also provides the waitstaff person a good opportunity to attend to the table for replenishing bread and pouring wine.

The Intermezzo

An **intermezzo** is a pause or intermission between two courses. Usually a sorbet, sherbet, or granita is served to cleanse the palate between two courses of very different flavors. Serve the intermezzo as quickly as possible. **This is a very short course, usually lasting no longer than five minutes.**

The Entrée Course

Entrée service depends on the establishment's style of service. **There are, however, some general guidelines that apply:**

- Hot entrées should be served on a hot plate. Use a clean, folded service towel for handling hot plates, and inform the guest that the plate is hot.
- Be aware of the intended presentation, and serve the plate so that the guest can appreciate the full effect of the chef's efforts. *See 4.67.*
- Whether using a tray or carrying plates by hand, hold them as level as possible to prevent spoiling the presentation.
- Allow about an inch between the plate's edge and the table edge to lessen the risk of spilling food on the guest's clothing.
- If the guest leaves the table after the entrée has been served, keep the food warm by either taking the plate back to the kitchen or covering it with a plate cover until the guest returns.
- Within a couple of minutes of serving entrées, ask the guests if everything has been prepared to their liking. If there is a problem, handle it quickly, efficiently, and apologetically. Inform the manager as soon as possible.
- When clearing the entrée course, remove the empty wine glasses, the salt and pepper shakers, and the bread-and-butter plates and knives unless guests are opting for a salad or cheese course after the entrée.

4.67 Serve all plates as the chef intended.

SERVING FROM A PLATTER

When a chef prepares and places food on a platter in the kitchen, this is known as **platter service.** Warmed plates are preset in front of the guests before the food is presented.

With platters held on the left forearm and hand, the platter is held parallel to the table to the left of the guest but without touching the table. Using the pince technique, a portion is placed onto the guest's plate. *See 4.68.* Each platter requires a clean service set. Sauces are generally served separately, or there is a separate serving spoon for the sauce. The server proceeds to serve counterclockwise.

4.65 Thick soup served in a rimmed soup bowl with a doilied underliner.

4.66 The guest is served tableside from a soup tureen.

4.68 Platter entrée service, pinced tableside

SERVING FROM A CASSEROLE DISH

When serving from a casserole, the dinner plate and any accompaniments are preset on the table from the guest's right side. Holding the casserole dish in the left hand and a service set in the right, the contents of the casserole are served from the left of the guest and as close to the plate as possible. Casserole service can also be performed tableside using only a service spoon and leaving the remainder of the casserole for the guest to plate. *See 4.69.*

4.69   Tableside casserole service

TABLESIDE SERVICE (FRENCH STYLE OF SERVICE)

Tableside preparation is generally associated with fine dining, but other dining environments including banquet and catering have also adapted tableside preparation as an enhancement of the dining experience. *See 4.70.* The four general types of tableside service include assembling, saucing and garnishing, sautéing and flambéing, and carving and deboning.

Assembling Salads and other dishes that involve a quick and simple assembly of ingredients may be completed tableside. Examples include the preparation of Caesar Salad and Steak Tartare.

Saucing and garnishing Servers may put the finishing touches of saucing and garnishing on dishes that have been prepared in the kitchen.

Sautéing and flambéing Both sautéing and flambéing are used for items that can be quickly cooked tableside or hot beverages or desserts that are flamed as part of the preparation.

Carving and deboning Fish, poultry, game, and meats may be carved or deboned at the table. Carving also includes peeling and slicing fruits and cheese to make them more manageable for guests.

Food safety In the dining room, as in every part of an operation, it is critical to follow food safety guidelines and HACCP procedures.

4.70   Tableside preparations are often executed on a guéridon or service cart

Preparing Caesar Salad

The best Caesar Salads are prepared tableside not only for dramatic presentation but also because the lettuce remains crisp.

To prepare Caesar Salad tableside, follow these steps:

1. Attractively arrange mise en place on a guéridon.

2. Use the tines of two forks to mash the garlic and to season the bow A little kosher salt may also be added if desired.

3. Add anchovy and continue to mash using a spoon.

4. Add pasteurized raw egg yolk, and blend with the garlic and anchovy. Add Dijon mustard.

5. Drizzle olive oil into the egg mixture, stirring constantly to maintain an emulsion.

6. Blend in lemon juice, freshly ground black pepper, and wine vinegar if desired.

7. Add romaine lettuce, using a napkin to break it into appropriately sized pieces.

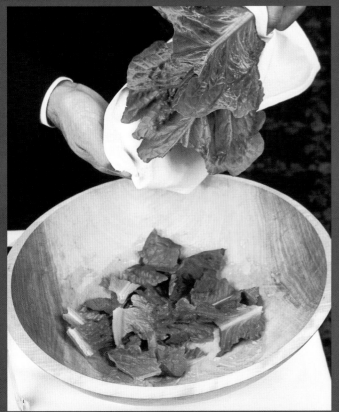

8. Toss the salad with a serving set, and add croutons and grated Parmigiano Reggiano cheese.

9. Plate the salad attractively, using the serving set.

10. Add additional freshly grated cheese and freshly ground black pepper to the customer's taste.

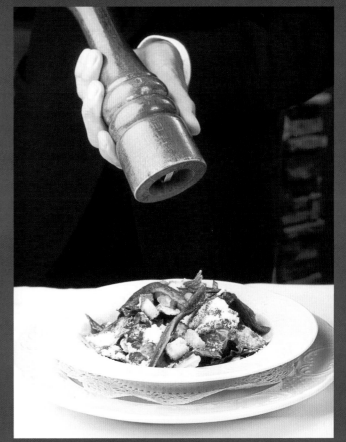

Preparing
Banana Flambé

Banana Flambé is a dessert that may be prepared tableside with flair and drama.

To prepare Banana Flambé, follow these steps:

1. Arrange mise en place attractively on a guéridon.

2. Slice the ends of a banana and cut the banana in half lengthwise using a fork to keep the banana steady.

3. Remove the skin using the service set. Cut the banana into quarters.

4. Melt butter and brown sugar in a preheated pan.

5. Use a lemon to stir the mixture. The lemon prevents the caramelized sugar from sticking to the utensil and allows the server to caramelize the sugar without it hardening.

6. Place banana quarters in the pan with the sliced side down. Lightly brown the bananas and turn over.

7. Remove the pan from the heat and add liqueur.

8. Place the pan back over the heat and flambé, tilting the pan and drawing it towards you as the sauce gently simmers.

9. Plate the bananas over ice cream in a decorative fashion and nappé with the caramel sauce.

Carving a Duck Tableside

Carving duck, poultry, and other meats requires dexterity and skill particularly in the dining room.

To carve a duck tableside, follow these steps:

1. Present the duck to the guests on a decorated platter.

2. Transfer the whole duck to a carving board without piercing the skin.

3. Remove the leg section by separating the thigh from the backbone.

4. Separate the drumstick from the thigh.

5. Remove the breast by cutting lengthwise down the keel bone and sliding the knife along the breast bone. Slice the breast into even slices. Repeat the process to remove the other breast.

6. Place the duck on a warm plate along with accompaniments.

Boning and Serving a Whole Trout

Boning fish tableside also requires dexterity and speed so guests may enjoy the food without bones while it is still warm.

For an elegant tableside presentation of trout, follow these steps:

1. Present the trout to the guests on a decorated platter.

2. Use a fork and fish knife to remove the fins.

3. Slide the fish knife under the skin and peel the skin towards the tail.

4. Gently remove the fillets by pushing them away from the bones.

5. Insert the tines of the fork into the backbone and lift the head while separating the bottom fillets.

6. Delicately plate the fillets with the service set.

Caesar Salad

Yield 1 serving   Serving size 11 ounces

Ingredients	U.S. Standard	Metric
Garlic, peeled and cut in half	1 large clove	1 large clove
Salt	1 teaspoon	1 teaspoon
Anchovy fillet	1 large	1 large
Dijon mustard	1 teaspoon	1 teaspoon
Olive oil	1 ounce	30 ml
White wine vinegar	1/2 teaspoon	1/2 teaspoon
Lemon juice, freshly squeezed	1 ounce	30 ml
Egg yolk, pasteurized	1 each	1 each
Black pepper, ground	1 teaspoon	1 teaspoon
Romaine lettuce, washed, dried, torn into pieces	4 ounces	115 grams
Croutons	4 ounces	115 grams
Parmesan cheese, grated	1 tablespoon	1 tablespoon

Method of Preparation

1. Gather all the ingredients and equipment.
2. Season the bowl with garlic, using salt as an abrasive, and then discard the garlic pieces.
3. Add anchovy, and mash with a fork. Move the anchovy to one side of the bowl, and add the mustard.
4. Blend oil into the mustard, slowly and steadily.
5. Add the wine vinegar, lemon juice, egg yolk, and pepper. Mix well.
6. Add romaine, and toss lettuce. Toss all the above by rotating service spoon and fork from back to front of bowl until lettuce is fully coated.
7. Add croutons, and toss.
8. Add cheese, and toss. Serve immediately.

Banana Flambé

Yield 2 servings   Serving size 7 ounces

Ingredients	U.S. Standard	Metric
Sugar, granulated	2 tablespoons	2 tablespoons
Butter	1 ounce	28 grams
Bananas, split in half lengthwise and crosswise	2 each	2 each
Dark rum (preferably Myers®)	1 1/2 ounces	45 ml
Cinnamon-sugar mixture	1/2 teaspoon	1/2 teaspoon
Banana liqueur	1 1/2 ounces	45 ml
Vanilla ice cream (about 2 scoops)	4 ounces	115 grams

Method of Preparation

1. Gather all the ingredients and equipment.
2. Heat Suzette pan, and add sugar and butter.
3. Lightly caramelize; then add bananas, and coat with caramel.
4. Remove the pan from the réchaud, and add rum. Return the pan to the réchaud, and flame.
5. While still flaming, sprinkle cinnamon-sugar over the pan.
6. Lower the flame and remove the pan from heat. Add banana liqueur, and return the pan to the réchaud. Allow the sauce to reduce.
7. Arrange four quarters of banana around the ice cream, and nappé with sauce, covering the ice cream.

Crêpes Suzette

Yield 2 servings   Serving size 2 crêpes each about 5 oz.

Ingredients	U.S. Standard	Metric
Sugar, granulated	2 tablespoons	2 tablespoons
Butter	1 ounce	28 grams
Oranges, zest	2 each	2 each
Lemon, zest	1 each	1 each
Grand Marnier®	2 ounces	60 ml
Orange juice	4 ounces	120 ml
Crêpes	4 each	4 each
Cognac	1 ounce	30 ml

Method of Preparation

1. Gather all the ingredients and equipment.
2. Heat the Suzette pan, and add sugar. Add butter, and mix until all the sugar is dissolved.
3. While the sugar is dissolving, add the zest of one orange and the lemon.
4. Remove the pan from heat and add Grand Marnier®.
5. Add orange juice. (If sugar caramelizes too quickly, add juice to the pan while zesting.)
6. Return the pan to the heat, but do not flambé. Dip crêpes in the sauce, one at a time; then fold into quarters. Move crêpes to the side of the pan.
7. When all the crêpes are folded, remove the pan from the heat, and add Cognac; return the pan to the heat, and flame.
8. Heat the sauce to a boil. Serve two crêpes on a preheated plate, and nappé with sauce.
9. Garnish with additional orange zest.

THE CHEESE COURSE

Cheeses are best when served at room temperature. Semi-firm and firm cheeses take an hour to warm to room temperature, while soft and semi-soft cheeses usually need a half hour. Large pieces of cheese need more time.

When serving cheeses, arrange them on a marble or wooden cheese board, trays, or a cheese cart so they may be easily cut. The cheese should be cut according to its shape so the rind is evenly distributed. A separate and appropriate cutting knife should be provided with each cheese. Bread or toast should accompany the cheese course, and if fruit is served, ensure that it is washed, dried, and cut into bite-sized portions.

THE DESSERT COURSE

The dessert course can be both the guests' most anticipated course and the kitchen's last chance to impress the guests. Some restaurants use rolling pastry carts or display desserts at their entrance to tempt guests. Other upscale, white-tablecloth restaurants offer made-to-order desserts, which require that customers select a dessert at the same time as they place the meal order.

Dessert service procedures may vary with service styles and the type of dessert. However, the fork should always be placed to the left of the cover and the spoon to the right. If the dessert fork and spoon are a part of the place setting, the spoon is placed above the fork on top of the cover with the respective handles pointed toward the appropriate side.

BUFFETIERING

In addition to the servers, buffets require a buffetier, whose responsibilities include a familiarity with, and the ability to describe all the ingredients and methods of preparation for each food item. A detailed description of the buffetier's responsibilities is described in Chapter 5, "Styles and Sequences of Service."

CLEARING A GUEST'S TABLE

There are different philosophies regarding how much a table server should clear at one time. Some fine-dining establishments limit clearing two plates only at one time and do not allow stacking. As time and efficiency are key elements to good service, others including Johnson & Wales University, train servers to clear and stack as need be, as long as guests remain uninterrupted by the scraping sounds or unsightliness. If a guest has a large amount of food left on the plate, the server should inquire if anything was the matter. Once the reason is ascertained, the server should inform the manager and clear that plate first.

When clearing a table, first make sure that all guests have finished a course. *See 4.71.* The exception is when a guest has moved his/her used plate away from the cover. Clear from the right side, but avoid reaching across the table. Walk around the table clockwise, keeping the cleared plates in the left hand and to the backs of the guests, and avoid overstacking them on your arm. When using food service trays, separate the flatware from the serviceware according to type, and ensure that the

tray is properly balanced by placing the heavier items at the center of the tray. *See 4.72.* Glassware should be cleared separately onto beverage trays to avoid excessive breakage. Clearing the table should be conducted as quietly and unobtrusively as possible.

CRUMBING THE TABLE

As the name implies, **crumbing** is the procedure for clearing the table of crumbs and other food particles. *See 4.73.* It should be done between the entrée and dessert courses as needed and as quickly, quietly, and unobtrusively as possible.

To clear the table of crumbs and other food particles between courses, follow these steps:

1. Move the glasses or utensils, if necessary, to ensure that the table is clean.
2. Crumb from the center of the table outward, away from the guest, and at a diagonal to an open corner.
3. Use a crumbing utensil such as a special brush, if available, or a folded service towel to sweep the crumbs onto a plate or small pan.

PRESENTATION OF THE CHECK

Presenting the guest check can be a challenge for servers especially if they do not know which guest in the party is paying or if they are in a hurry to turn the table. In the United States, it is perfectly acceptable protocol for a server to present the check before it is requested. One of the greatest failings of a server can be the delay of either presenting or collecting payment of a check. Once a guest has decided that it is time to leave, every minute counts and poor check handling can sour the entire dining experience. There are cues to servers that indicate when guests are ready for the check such as: making eye contact with the server, writing figuratively in the air or against the palms as if signing a check, moving the remaining serviceware away from the cover, folding the napkin and placing it on the table, or placing the wallet or credit card on the table. The server must not only continue to maintain vigilance over the assigned tables, but must also double-check the guest check to guarantee that it is accurate.

Servers may also encounter situations when two or more guests at a table ask for the guest check. In most situations, guests indicate to servers upon entering the restaurant that they would like the check. If uncertain, servers can strategically place the check between two guests. If one of the guests is a regular or is known to be the host of the party at the restaurant, the check is presented to that individual. Once the check has been presented, avoid hovering over the guest waiting for payment, but keep a close eye on the check folder for either a credit card or cash payment, and pick it up as soon as possible. Always be discreet, tactful, and gracious.

HANDLING PAYMENT

Checks are commonly paid either by credit card or cash, although guests may sometimes have a gift certificate or other voucher for the meal. If the guest is paying by credit card, check the card for the cardholder's signature and the expiration date. Process the card appropriately and according to restaurant policy. Return the card with the check and voucher to the guest, along with a pen for signing the voucher.

After the transaction is completed, remove the check to ensure the credit card voucher has been signed and the voucher has been left in the check folder. Occasionally, an authorization issue occurs with the credit card. If there is a problem, draw the cardholder aside and explain that there is a problem processing the card. Avoid embarrassing the cardholder in front of guests.

If the guest is paying with cash, ensure that you receive the correct amount, and return any change with a selection of bills to ensure flexibility in leaving a tip. It is inappropriate to ask the guest whether change is needed or to mention the tip unless asked. Some restaurants have a policy of automatically adding a service charge for large parties of 8 or more. Guests should be alerted even though the policy must be stated on the written menu. The check folder should be left on the table until the guests' departure, unless it is handed back to the server.

THE FAREWELL

When guests are ready to leave, assist them with their chairs and coats. Check the table to ensure that guests have not left any belongings behind such as a credit card or a purse, and thank them for their patronage. It is not appropriate to ask guests how they enjoyed their experience as it is the job of restaurant personnel to know what kind of experience their guests have had. But, it is most appropriate to thank them for coming and expressing a desire to see them again soon at the establishment.

RE-SETTING THE TABLE

After the guests have departed, clear the table, and place any accessories such as flowers or candles on a tray, not on a chair. Change the table linens, neatly folding the soiled linens, and taking care not to spill crumbs on the floor. Avoid allowing the surface of the table to be revealed during service.

In re-setting a tablecloth, use the following guidelines:
- The hem of the cloth should be face down.
- The corners of the cloth should line up with the corners of the table.
- If a base cloth is used, the corners of the decorative cloth should line up with the corners of the base cloth.
- The center crease of the cloth should be centered on the table and point upward.
- Use the backs of the hands to smooth the cloth.
- Replace the accessories; place folded napkins at each place setting; and reset flatware, glassware, and any other serviceware according to the establishment's specifications.

4.71 The server INCORRECTLY clears while a guest is still eating.

4.72 Organize the food tray when clearing to insure good balance and safe transport.

4.73 Crumb the table onto a bread & butter plate.

5. Styles *and* Sequence *of* Service

Western styles of service have evolved and have become formalized over the last three centuries. They generally reflect social and gastronomic developments in Europe as well as in the United States.

The terms used to describe the major styles of service may be confusing, and they are interpreted differently in the United States and in Europe. The terms French, Russian, and English services have very different meanings in Europe than they do in the United States. The descriptions that follow are those used in the United States.

Traditional Service Styles

Historically, French service was a ritual of placing elaborate platters of food for each course directly onto a table that was lined with several layers of tablecloths. Guests helped themselves from these platters. In aristocratic society, food presentations were artistic and required enormous resources and skill. These food displays were represented by famous chefs such as Marie-Antoine Carême. Dining in this manner had disadvantages: a diner could only enjoy what was placed within arm's length, and hot food was rarely eaten warm. It was also considered bad form or impolite to reach in front of someone else, just as it is today. After each course was removed from the table along with the top table cloth, the table was reset entirely with the silverware, plates, and the next food course or met. The entremets course was served on the side buffets between each course. The word **entremets** is French for "between courses," an refers today to a small course, such as a sorbet or a small dessert, which is served between courses. The Italian word intermezzo is a term that is commonly used on menus in the United States.

In the nineteenth century, French service began to incorporate elements of **Russian service,** or *service à la russe*. In traditional Russian service, the food was carried from the kitchen, presented, and then finished and served to the guest. This formal protocol was exported to France in the mid-1800s by Prince Alexander Kourakine, where it was incorporated into French service. It was further popularized by English society. This blended service allowed all the guests at the table to enjoy a particular dish that was served. A disadvantage of this service was that guests who did not care for a particular dish, were obliged to partake at the risk of insulting the host. Advantages include simplifying the chef's job and better controlling food cost. A lack of grandiose food showpieces led to the evolution of extremely fancy hollowware such as tureens and casseroles, which were made primarily of silver and porcelain.

Today, American, or plated service (known as "*à l'assiette*" service in France), is the most popular service around the world. It is simple and quick because all the food is plated in the kitchen. It enables a chef to demonstrate and highlight creativity and artistry in the presentation of a dish and permits serving food at the best possible serving temperature. This style has evolved to accommodate many types of dining establishments, from upscale fine-dining to bistros.

Although most restaurants rely on plated service, many also incorporate elements from other techniques.

Major service techniques include:
• American or Plated
• Family-style
• French
• Russian/English
• Butler

PLATED SERVICE

Plated service or American Service was at first most widely adopted in America, but it is now used internationally. This service is popular, as it requires fewer and less extensively trained dining room personnel than other services. It is theorized that this service became popular in the United States because Americans consumed more beverages than Europeans during a meal, and by serving food from the left, a guest is less likely to be interrupted. Today, little emphasis is placed on the side from which food is served as long as the guest is minimally impacted. At Johnson & Wales University, students are taught that service and clearing are performed from the right unless the server is left handed, or it is intrusive to the guest

when these tasks are conducted from the right. It is important to be consistent at the table and if serving from the right, the server would continue clockwise around a free standing table and if from the left, would proceed counter clockwise. **Plated service** is defined as the presentation of food that is completely prepared, plated, and garnished in the kitchen. Servers carefully and respectfully place dishes in front of the guest making sure the plate is properly positioned so the guest perceives the dish as the chef intended. Service is more streamlined and allows for greater speed and efficiency. The server has time to focus on sales and to be more attentive to guests' needs. The net effect is an overall savings in labor cost that is beneficial to both management and the guest. Savings may be passed on to the guest in the form of more reasonable menu prices.

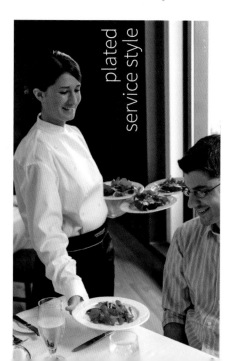

plated service style

As previously discussed, the sequence of service is predicated on a long evolution. The normal sequence of service in the United States is 1. appetizer, 2. soup, 3. salad, 4. entrée, 5. coffee, and 6. dessert. If the appetizer is hot, it follows the soup. If an intermezzo is served, it precedes the entrée.

General Rules of Plated Service

Beverages are always served to the right side of the guest with the server's right hand and right foot forward unless the guest chooses to place the glassware to his/her left. The server should then accommodate the guest. Also, if the guest's glass is unreachable at a booth table or because the guest's positioning makes it inaccessible, the server may then wish to pick up the glass rather than inconvenience the guest.

If serving to the right of a guest, proceed to the next guest in a clockwise direction. When serving to the left of a guest, proceed to the next guest counter-clockwise. Clearing is performed from the right with the right hand and the right foot forward except for items placed to the guest's left, such as the bread-and-butter plate.

PLATED SERVICE IN A BANQUET SETTING

A banquet is a predetermined meal for a group of guests. There are basically three types of banquet functions: the first is a private or personal family event such as a wedding reception; the second is a business or corporate event such as a retirement dinner or a breakfast, or a luncheon or dinner during an annual corporate meeting; and the third is a civic event, which includes proms, rotary club award dinners, political fund raisers, and holiday celebrations. A banquet may be for a few guests or for as many as 3000. Events include stand up receptions, cocktail parties, dances and simple breakfasts to elaborate dinners with white-gloved service.

Most banquet meals in this country use plated service. The servers are required to act in unison so that the guests are served each course at approximately the same time. Servers are assigned a station of 20 to 30 guests, depending on the number of courses. For example, a breakfast would usually only require one food course, juice, and coffee service. However, a typical dinner would have a soup, an appetizer, a salad, an entrée, coffee, and a dessert.

Standard rules of protocol are followed when serving a banquet:

- Always pay attention to the maître d'/captain who sets the pace of service.
- Serve the guest of honor's table first.
- If there is a split menu that offers a choice of entrées, it is imperative that the proper order is communicated to the kitchen. Note: There are a number of systems that an establishment may employ to assist customers in remembering their orders (such as coded cards which are placed in front of each guest).
- Serve the entire table at the same time for each course.
- Do not carry more than the number of covers at a table, or usually a maximum of 12 entrées on a service tray.

Advantages American service has several advantages. Service is generally quite fast. The service staff needs less training because the service is easier to master. Equipment costs are limited and less space is required between tables, so more guests can be seated if need be. Chefs also have greater control of costs and presentation under this system.

Disadvantages American service lacks the elegance of French or Russian/English service, and the theatrical presentation that makes the dining experience memorable. Also, guests cannot choose their own portion sizes.

FAMILY-STYLE SERVICE

In **family-style service,** the chef prepares the dishes in the kitchen, and then servers place the prepared platters, casseroles, or tureens in the center of the guests' table with the appropriate serving utensils. Guests serve themselves using plates that servers place in front of them. The platters, casseroles, utensils, etc. should be cleared when emptied. Clearing the guest's covers follows the protocol for American service. This service style may also be used for select courses in any other style of service.

Advantages Family-style service minimizes the costs of dining room labor and helps to create a warm, familial atmosphere. Guests may decide on the portion size they want, and the meal is perceived as a good value for customers.

Disadvantages The lack of portion control can result in considerable food waste, and there is no control over plate presentation. Some guests may miss the personalized service provided by other serving styles.

FRENCH SERVICE

French service is usually associated with elegant settings when expense is not a determining factor. Because a key element of **French service** is tableside preparation and/or plating, servers prepare and plate special dishes tableside in full view of the guest. In order to deliver such elaborate and labor-intensive service, a restaurant generally requires a team of highly skilled and knowledgeable servers called a brigade, who need to work together closely.

General Rules of French Service

As with plated service, food and beverages are served from the right with the right hand. With the exception of bread-and-butter plates and knives, all dishes are cleared from the right with the right hand, and servers move clockwise around the table whenever possible.

Food is prepared tableside or plated on a **guéridon,** or side stand, and then served.

PLATING THE GUEST'S COURSE IN FRENCH SERVICE

The plating performed by the Captain of a Brigade is performed using the **service set** with the spoon in the right hand and the service fork in the left. Unlike Russian Service, the Service Set is held in both hands and not together in the right.

The plating is performed from left to right (from the platter to the plate). The starch and vegetables should be plated first, followed by the protein. If the meat has to be carved, this is done after plating the other items. This allows the protein to remain warm, and the juices will not drain out. If the item is prepared for two or more guests, each guest's plate should look the same. Upon completion, the guéridon is pulled back from the guest's table to enable the commis de rang (Front Server) to serve the guests. The guéridon is then removed to the side of the station.

See 5.1. Today, as restaurants blend service techniques, styles of service can be combined. For example, some plates are prepared and plated in the kitchen, while others are not. The serving of these dishes must be coordinated with the tableside items as they are completed, so all plates can be presented to the guests at the same time.

Because French service is associated with elegant restaurants, specifically designed flatware may be used for particular courses. A fish knife and fish fork might be set in restaurants using this type of service. Most flatware producers no longer manufacture these specialty pieces due to lack of demand.

5.1 Proper mise en place is essential when preparing foods tableside.

french service style

Show plates for decorative purposes are preset on the cover, and if removed, may be replaced by service plates after the guest has ordered. A **Service Plate** is used as an underliner for all courses other than the entrée. If one guest decides not to join others at the table in selecting a course, the guest has a service or show plate placed in front of him or her. Plates that are prepared in the kitchen may be served **sous cloche,** or "under a bell." These large, domed plate covers are removed by servers simultaneously in front of the guests to add to the drama of dining.

Sequence of Service

The generally accepted rule for the sequence of service is that cold food precedes hot food, and liquids are served before solids. If serving a cold soup such as Vichysoisse, the soup is always served first. When the soup is served hot, and an appetizer such as smoked salmon is served cold, the soup follows the cold fish. When both the soup and appetizer are hot, the soup is served first. The appetizer may then be followed by a fish course or an intermezzo prior to the entrée. Salads are served after the entrée and may be followed by a cheese course. Desserts are then served prior to coffee service. The meal may end with small petit fours, bonbons, or chocolate truffles.

The Brigade

Elaborate service requires a team or **brigade** of service personnel who can work together as one. The brigade system is not limited to French Service as its complexity is a reflection of the menu being served. A typical brigade is made up of the following individuals: the dining room manager, captain, front waiter, back waiter, waiter's assistant or busperson, and wine steward.

The Dining Room Manager, Maître d', or Chef de Service, or Chef de Salle The dining room manager must be in close contact with every department and know all aspects of the business: dining room, banquet facilities, service bar, front bar, kitchen, dishwashing area, and the front office. **The responsibilities of this individual include the following:**
- Hires and trains the dining room staff.
- Ensures the proper setup of the dining room.
- Inventories all dining room equipment.
- Requisitions the necessary supplies.
- Supervises the reservation system.
- Schedules the dining room staff.
- Opens and closes the dining room each day.
- Seats guests.
- Solves all customer issues or complaints.
- Is responsible for check reconciliations and cash reconciliation at the end of each shift.

The Captain The station captain (chef de rang) has the responsibility of supervising and organizing all the service aspects in an assigned station. **Responsibilities include:**
- Ensuring that the tables are correctly positioned and set.

- Ensuring that all equipment needed is ready.
- Observing all guests within the station at all times.
- Being attentive to all verbal and non-verbal guest communication.
- Suggestively selling food and beverages.
- Accurately taking all orders.
- Answering all questions regarding ingredients and the preparation of food and beverages.
- Preparing and portioning foods tableside.
- Synchronizing service within the brigade system.
- Overseeing all tables to ensure guest satisfaction.
- Accurately totaling each check and collecting payment.
- Being accountable for all check reconciliations for the assigned station.

The Front Waiter The front waiter (commis de rang) assists the captain and should serve the food. In the captain's absence, the front server must be able to perform all the captain's duties. **Responsibilities of the front waiter include:**
- Serving food and beverages to the guest.
- Marking the guests' table based on the order given.
- Serving beverages immediately upon receiving the order from the captain.
- Serving food once the course is plated by the captain.
- Opening and serving all bottled wine ordered by the captain unless the wine steward or sommelier is performing this service.
- Providing assistance to the back waiter and busser in clearing the guests' table.
- Ensuring that the table is properly marked and flatware is properly adjusted.

Note: All food items should be taken from the right side of the guéridon with the waiter's right hand and presented to the guest.

The Back Waiter The back waiter (commis de suite) brings all food orders from the kitchen to the service area and serves as the link between the brigade and the kitchen staff. **The back waiter's responsibilities consist of:**
- Managing the timing and "firing" of food orders.
- Placing and picking up all orders, service equipment, and utensils from the kitchen and bringing them to the dining room.
- Presenting platters prepared by the kitchen to the guest prior to plating.
- Assisting in the clearing of both the guéridon and the guests' table.
- Delivering the necessary ingredients for the preparation of tableside dishes.
- Providing all equipment and utensils for the plating of items (plates, service sets).
- Knowing the ingredients and methods of preparation and garnishes.
- Being aware of the stage of service at each table in the station.
- Coordinating efforts with the captain, the chef in the kitchen, and other members of the brigade.

The Waiter's Assistant or Busser The waiters' assistant or busser (commis de débarrassage) is usually an entry level position in an apprentice system. **Responsibilities of the waiter's assistant include:**
- Serving bread, butter, and water and replenishing these when necessary.
- Clearing the table after each course.
- Cleaning the table after the guests have departed.
- Resetting each table.
- Making sure a supply of clean linens and flatware is on hand.
- Performing any other duties necessary to keep the dining room in smooth running order.

Note: In some European countries, bread and water are served only if ordered.

The Wine Steward or Sommelier The **wine steward** or **sommelier** must have extensive knowledge of wines and spirits and may be in charge of the purchasing and service of wine. In Europe, the sommelier may be wearing the taste-vin cup; a silver cup hanging on a chain around the neck. This custom evolved in the caves or dimly lit tasting cellars of Burgundy. The silver cups refracted the limited light, and due to the dimpling of the cup, it enhanced the light to enable the cellar master to determine the condition of the wine when it was poured. Today, wearing the tastevin is more symbolic and is rarely used as it was originally intended. **Responsibilities of the sommelier include:**
- Selling and serving bottled wines. Assisting guests in making wine selections based on their selection of food.
- Directing the training of front of the house staff in wine and spirits.
- Developing wine lists.
- Establishing the pricing of wines.
- Developing wine programs to augment sales in the restaurant; for example, wine dinners or the sale of wines by the glass.
- Maintaining the wine inventory.
- Maintaining the correct storage and the cellaring of all wines.

Advantages French service, as a full-service, is elegant, stylish, and highly personalized. It is ideal for presenting certain dishes tableside such as Dover sole or for carving meats. Tableside service allows for the presentation of foods at the best maintained temperatures.

Disadvantages French service takes much longer than American service, reducing the ability to turn tables. Equipment such as guéridons and specialty carts require floor space, limiting the number of tables in a restaurant. The cost of equipment needed and the highly skilled servers required push menu prices higher as well.

RUSSIAN, ENGLISH, OR SILVER SERVICE

In Europe, **English service** refers to a service in which the server spoons or plates portions directly onto a dish that is in front of the guest. In the United States, this type of service is often called Russian service, or sometimes silver service. Regardless of how it is labeled, there are general principles that must be followed. The term English Service is also used when a host or hostess performs the same tasks of carving and plating each guest's portion and having a server serve the accompaniments.

General Rules of Russian/ English-Silver Service

When using silver service, all food is prepared, portioned, and garnished before being placed on platters, tureens, or service plates. Unlike French service, silver service can involve a single server or a team of servers. All servers, however, have a clean service towel, usually draped over the left forearm.

Beverages, plates, and bowls on underliners are set in front of the guest from the right side, and food items are served with the right hand from the left side of the guest proceeding clockwise. Service proceeds counterclockwise around the table. Service sets are used to transfer food (pincing) from the platter to the guest's plate.

Russian Service of Soup

When soup is ordered, a **tureen** is a part of Russian service. Warmed soup plates or bowls on underliners are placed in front of the guests from their right side with the server's right hand. Before leaving the kitchen, the soup tureen is placed on a STP/serviette underliner with a ladle in or beside the tureen. The cover is removed before approaching the table. With the tureen in the left hand, approach and serve guests from the left with the tureen just above the guest's bowl, drawing the handle of the soup ladle toward yourself, using the right hand to avoid spillage. Return the ladle to the tureen before serving the next guest. If the soup is accompanied by a garnish, the garnish is served from a side dish next to the tureen with an appropriate utensil. Service proceeds counterclockwise around the table.

Russian Platter Service

Another aspect of this service is the use of a platter to serve guests' solid food items. The chef prepares and places food on a platter in the kitchen. Warmed plates are preset in front of the guests from their right side before the food is presented. With platters held on the left forearm and hand, position the platter parallel to the table to the left of the guest, without touching the table. Using the pince technique, place the portion onto the guest's plate. Each platter requires a clean service set. Sauces are generally served separately, or there is a separate serving spoon for the sauce. The server proceeds counterclockwise.

Russian Casserole Service

In casserole or cocotte service, the dinner plate and any accompaniments are preset on the table from the guest's right side. Hold the casserole dish in the left hand and a service set in the right. The contents of the casserole are served from the left of the guest and as close to the plate as possible. Clearing is done from the guest's right, with the server using the right hand.

Advantages Russian (English, silver) service is faster than French service and requires fewer extensively trained staff. It allows guests to determine their own portion size and gives the chef greater quality control.

Disadvantages Initial costs for equipment used in Russian service are high, and servers need to be skilled in using service sets. More space is needed between guests for server access. Additionally, there can be considerable temperature loss in foods served on a platter. Finally, the last guests served may receive the food from a platter with an unappetizing appearance.

BUTLER SERVICE

Butler service is similar to Russian service but allows for the guest to select the food portion from the platter or tureen. This type of service is used most often at receptions, with servers carrying trays of hors d'oeuvres from which guests make a selection. It is important that cocktail napkins are offered to the guest in a convenient manner. There should be trays placed conveniently about the room for guests to dispose of frill picks, used napkins, and any other such items.

Butler service can also be used to serve guests seated at a dining room table. The server would present an item on a tray or platter or a soup in a Tureen from the guests' left side, and the guests would serve themselves. The server would proceed in a counterclockwise direction around the table.

Advantages At a full service meal, the handles of the utensils for the platters must be directed toward the guests for their convenience. When the course is presented a second time, new service utensils should be used. The advantages of this type of service are that guests may choose their own portion size, and items can be creatively displayed on trays. Serving guests at stand-up receptions is also cost-efficient.

Disadvantages Butler service has several disadvantages. Portion control is difficult. If guests choose not to serve themselves, the host may be embarrassed. If guests are not dexterous, the presentation of food on their plates may not be appealing. More space is also needed between chairs to allow server access.

BUFFET SERVICE

Providing a buffet for guests can be conducted in an à la carte or banquet environment. It has become a popular dining option because it is relatively efficient and economical. Although the menu may be limited, guests may select from a variety of options and choose the quantity and combinations they prefer.

With the exception of the kitchen staff, buffets often require a limited service staff. A buffet table is used to display both hot and cold prepared foods. Cold food platters are kept chilled, and hot dishes are kept warm in chafing pans. Hot and cold foods are held at their appropriate temperatures to ensure food safety and appetizing flavors. Today, there are three common types of buffet service: simple, modified deluxe, and deluxe.

STYLES OF BUFFETS

The Simple Buffet

A simple buffet is basically unstaffed. Customers serve themselves, and the server is responsible only for setting tables, replenishing food items, clearing tables, presenting checks, and breaking down the buffet table. The simple buffet is commonly used in conference centers and hotels, where the buffet table can be wheeled into a meeting room so guests may serve themselves without disrupting the meeting.

The Modified Deluxe Buffet

Although customers select soups, appetizers, salads, entrées, and possibly desserts from a buffet table using the modified deluxe buffet service, staff members serve beverages and assist at the buffet at various levels, depending on the establishment. In more elaborate environments, the buffet may be partially plated or entirely plated by *buffetiers*, while in casual restaurants, the guests serve themselves. A chef often assists at the carving station. Large parties, such as an office Christmas party or an anniversary celebration, often use this type of service.

The Deluxe Buffet

The deluxe buffet provides the most extensive service. With the exception of the entrée, all courses are plated and served. In a buffet service, the server invites guests to the buffet table, or in an à la carte environment, informs guests of the choices available, and makes recommendations. The server is responsible for serving and clearing beverages and serving any plated course using American service. As needed, the server clears and replaces soiled plates and flatware. The buffetiers

supervise the correct positioning of the buffet tables and the organization of the display. Cold items are displayed first and hot items last. The buffetier also estimates the number of guests a buffet table can accommodate and oversees all the details for the comfort and safety of the guests.

Buffetiers are responsible for the smooth operation of the buffet and the safe handling of the food. They ensure that the food is at the correct temperature. Hot foods are placed in a chafing pan. The insert pan should be at least one-third full of hot water, using at least two heat sources, unless an electric heating element is used. The buffet surface and plates must be checked for cleanliness (including both sides of the plates). Cold buffet foods must be protected by sneeze guards. Chilled plates are available for appetizers and salads. Dinner plates are heated so they are warm, but not hot to the touch. Service utensils must have clean handles; those with soiled handles are replaced. Chafing pans are kept covered when guests are not using them. Hinged chafers have the hinged side away from the guests.

Any pan with shingled food items has the first piece on top of, rather than under the piece behind it. For two-sided buffets, food is shingled in two opposite lines. Food is reordered when a pan is one-third full and replaced before the pan is empty or when the appearance of the food has diminished because it has been in the pan too long. Food should not be transferred from one pan to another in the dining room. Accompaniments and condiments are placed near the appropriate item with the correct

service ware; salad dressing choices, for example, are found near the salads with the appropriate serving utensils.

Plates and bowls are replaced before they are all used but are never stacked more than 30 plates high. Hot pans are removed safely by using two servers, one to remove the used pan and the other to replace a full one. Used pans are not removed until a replacement is ready because the steaming pans pose a risk to guests. Guests are cautioned before the staff approaches the buffet with a hot pan, and chafing pans are changed using service towels. The buffet is broken down safely by discarding leftover food, wiping the table clean, covering chafing pans, extinguishing all canned fuel containers before moving them, and safely discarding the hot water.

Advantages Buffet service minimizes dining room labor costs, and customers have a wider selection of food from which to choose. Guests may also determine their own portions. Buffets can present an impressive display of food, and if properly managed, reduce service time.

Disadvantages Buffets produce a considerable amount of food waste and leftovers. Because of the lag time between when the first table of guests is invited to the buffet table and when the last are summoned, the buffet table may look less attractive for later guests unless it is well maintained. Guests may have to wait in long lines, and individuals with physical disabilities may also be at a disadvantage at buffets. There is also a potential for food contamination and cross-contamination, unless the buffet is carefully managed and supervised.

6. *The* Beverage World

The beverage world has never been as exciting as it is today. In every category, there is innovation, diversity, and a renewed focus on quality. Humans have enjoyed beverages and have transformed them into an essential part of social interaction. Professor Patrick McGovern, an archeochemist at the University of Pennsylvania, uncovered the existence of fermented beverages dating back to 7000 B.C. McGovern concluded that the earliest fermented beverages in Jiahu, China were derived from fruits and grains, which sometimes included botanicals. Others believe that one of the earliest alcoholic beverages was koumis—fermented mare's milk— a drink that is still enjoyed today by the Mongols. The evolution of non-alcoholic beverages, such as tea, coffee, and other infusions came later. Regardless of the beverage, consumption of both alcoholic and non-alcoholic beverages has become a social ritual in every part of the world and has even been identified as a social "lubricant."

The earliest known taverns existed in ancient Sumer in Mesopotamia (modern Iraq) around 3500 B.C. Over thousands of years, various protocols and etiquette for serving beverages evolved into the more modern forms of teahouses, cafés, and taverns, which became prominent in England during the 16th and 17th centuries. These establishments were then brought to Western shores by the Puritans and early colonists.

In Asia, early civilizations learned to make tea, while in the Americas, Mayan and Aztec rulers sipped drinks made from chocolate. Coffee growing developed in Ethiopia and was brought to Arabia, Turkey, Central and South America, and the Pacific Islands. Although many beverages have been revered or condemned because they had psychotropic or stimulant properties, beverages today are an important part of restaurant service and a considerable profit center.

The Beverage Industry

Over the past two decades there has been an explosion of beverage choices for consumers. The number of breweries has grown from 70 to over 2,800, the number of wineries in the U.S. alone exceeds 8,300, the availability of bottled waters spans from Iceland to Fiji, dozens of single variety coffees are served by professional coffee baristas at all kinds of cafés, 2,500 teahouses offer a wide assortment of teas including vintage and flowering teas, and a cocktail renaissance has occurred with an emphasis on craft versus volume.

Americans are seeking to replicate experiences they have enjoyed during their travels abroad, and consistent marketing efforts are piquing interests in a variety of brands. Since one in three meals is eaten away from the home, Americans have become more sophisticated in their taste experiences than ever, and are also expecting that servers in the food and beverage industry have knowledge of new products.

BEVERAGE PROFITABILITY

It is important to realize that when analyzing beverage sales in restaurants, non-alcoholic beverages such as bottled water, tea, coffee, juices, and milk are considered part of food sales and food cost. Beverage sales are key to the profitability of most full-service restaurants: overall beverage costs traditionally run between 22% and 28% of beverage sales in a full-service restaurant. All beverages do not have equal cost percentages. For example, wines are usually priced so that they run at a 40% to 45% cost in fine-dining restaurants, while the cost of sales of spirits may run as low as 12% in bars and taverns. In fine-dining restaurants, the sales of beverages may contribute to more than 75% of the establishment's total net profit. In addition to increased sales, research shows that enjoying a great beverage also increases the satisfaction rating of a diner's entire restaurant experience.

THE ROLE OF BEVERAGE PERSONNEL

6.1 Beverage Consumption shows that there are numerous opportunities for servers to sell many types of beverages. Studies suggest that up to 62% of drink orders are influenced by servers and bartenders who have visible and innovative programs. Without training, servers may not realize the opportunities that exist to upsell and to provide their customers the option to experience something new. In Chapter 9, "Mixology" we examine the specific roles of the beverage manager, head bartender, bartender, bar back, and cocktail server as it applies to serving alcoholic beverages. Without proper beverage training for employees, the success of a full-service restaurant is questionable.

Personnel must also be knowledgeable about other beverages that are related to food costs such as coffee. Restaurants rarely expend the energy and resources on nonalcoholic beverage training even though the profit potential is high with the cost of teas, coffees, and sodas and bottled water as low as 8%. But why should servers lack knowledge of these products when an establishment is attempting to maximize the guest's experience, the restaurant's profitability, and the server's income?

6.1 Beverage Consumption

Beverage Consumption in the U.S. in 2013 in millions of gallons according to Next Level Marketing :

Coffee	13,100
Soft Drinks	8,730
Bottled Water	9,350
Milk	6,760
Beer	6,342
Tea	2,305
Juices	1,495
Wine	774
Distilled Spirits	499
Cider	37

Coffee

There are over 110 million Americans who enjoy coffee in one form or another. Sixty-three percent of Americans start the day with a cup of coffee, and thirty-one percent drink specialty coffees such as lattes, espressos, or cappuccinos. In fact, coffee is the third most popular beverage in the world after water and tea. There are over 144 million 60 kg bags of coffee produced in 70 countries around the world, with Brazil as the largest producer. Coffee is the world's second most traded commodity after oil. Worldwide, there are about 20 million coffee farming families, and approximately 100 million people depend on coffee for their livelihoods. Its export value alone is immense, and as such, it plays a crucial role in the economies of several tropical countries.

THE COFFEE PLANT

Coffee trees produce berries that resemble cherries. The berries, bright red when ripe, usually contain two seeds, or beans, which are processed, roasted, ground, and brewed into liquid coffee. Although more than 25 wild species of coffee trees have been identified, only two, C. arabica and C. robusta (now reclassified as C. canephora), are cultivated for commercial use.

Initially planted from nursery-grown seedlings, the coffee tree begins producing fruit in four to six years and continues to do so for about 40 years. A self-pollinating evergreen, the coffee tree blooms with fragrant white flowers and produces between 2,500 and 4,000 berries—enough to produce a pound and a half of roasted coffee beans. Most growing regions have a single yearly harvest, but regions with two distinct rainy seasons have two harvests.

Coffea arabica About 62% of the world's coffee production comes from *C. arabica* plants. **Arabica,** the highest-quality coffee, grows best in a narrow band on either side of the equator at altitudes ranging from 2,000 to 6,000 feet (610 to 1,829 m). In Central and South America and East Africa, where the majority of coffee grows, year-round temperatures of about 70°F (21°C) and abundant rainfall provide the plants with ideal conditions. Most arabica fruits ripen at different times on the same plant and grow in rugged terrain, so harvesting is labor-intensive. Only ripe berries yield superior coffee and must generally be picked by hand. Arabica is lower-yielding and more susceptible to disease than robusta. Consumers willingly pay a higher price for arabica's sweet aroma and winy, fresh, and slightly acid taste.

Coffea robusta *Coffea canephora,* or **robusta,** is hardier than Arabica and grows well at lower altitudes in wet valleys and tropical forest climates. It has a significantly higher percentage of caffeine than arabica. Like arabica, a robusta plant begins to mature four to six years after it is transplanted. It is also easier to cultivate, and growers often use machines to harvest it. Large coffee roasters often use these less expensive robusta beans as a supplement in their blends and for use in instant coffees. Robusta's heavy, earthy aroma and flavor provide a heavier body with a characteristically thicker viscosity.

Varietal and specialty coffees About 10% of the world's coffee bean crop is classified as gourmet or specialty quality coffee. A **varietal coffee** is a coffee that comes from a single varietal or **cultivar** from a single growing region. Guatemalan, Antigua, Jamaican Blue Mountain, Hawaiian Kona, Costa Rican Tarrazu, Kenyan AA, Ethiopian Yergachev, or Sumatran Gayo Mountain are all examples of varietal coffees. Specialty coffees are often blended by the roaster from two or more varieties of beans that complement one another. Roasters who blend coffees generally do so using their own judgment, and their blends often define their image.

Certified organic coffee
The market for organically grown and processed products has expanded considerably in the last few years. There is, however, a difference between products that claim to be "organic" and those that are "certified organic." Certified organic coffees have been endorsed by an accredited, independent, third-party inspection. Detailed record keeping must demonstrate that the coffee has at least 95% certified organic ingredients, which are grown without the use of synthetic fertilizers or pesticides. The grower must also practice shade-tree canopy preservation to provide habitats for migratory birds so the coffee may be designated as "bird friendly." Finally, certified organic coffee must be kept separate from all other coffee throughout its production and processing.

FAIR TRADE CERTIFIED COFFEE

Over 100 companies in the U.S. market their coffees as "Fair Trade Certified." Coffee is one of the most price volatile commodities in the world. Coffee prices have been as low as $0.60 per pound, as was the case in 2009. "Fair Trade" agreements support a livable income of $1.61 per pound for the coffee of small growers and support organic farming in shade grown areas by offering further premium pricing.

COFFEE PRODUCTION

A number of conditions determine which of three methods growers use to harvest coffee. Where the terrain is too rugged for mechanical harvesting, growers use the most expensive **selective method,** picking only ripe berries from the tree by hand. For varieties that ripen their berries at the same time, one swift movement sweeps the branches clean of berries using the **strip method.** The **mechanical method** of harvesting is most common on coffee plantations where the trees are planted on relatively flat terrain in even rows. In this method, the harvester straddles the row and agitates the trees to cause the beans to fall onto a conveyor belt.

PROCESSING

As with growing and harvesting techniques, processing methods depend on the kinds of beans and the conditions where the trees grow. Where sufficient water is available, a wet method of processing is used, mostly for arabica coffees. Both the kind of bean and the method of processing give the arabica variety its characteristic high quality. In areas where water is not plentiful, processors use the dry method. In the 1990s a third process known as the pulped natural method, which is a hybrid of the two, evolved in Brazil.

The wet method Using the **wet method,** coffee processors first depulp the berries mechanically. Depulping exposes the parchment-covered beans, which then soak in tanks of water until fermentation softens the mucilage layer for easy removal. Timing is critical because fermentation must not affect the bean itself. The beans are then washed to remove the fermented layer and are spread in the sun on drying patios for 7 to 21 days. More modern drying methods include drum dryers that tumble the beans for two to three days at temperatures from 122°–140°F (50°–60°C). Through the drying process, the moisture content of the beans drops from approximately 70% to about 11%. After a rest period of 20 to 30 days, the parchment and silver skin are peeled off by a hulling machine before the coffee is roasted to fill orders. High-quality beans that are processed by the wet method generally have cleaner flavors, few if any undesirable characteristics, and a more acid taste.

There are a couple of specialty coffees that have reached the market place and generated considerable faddish interest given the unusual 'wet method' of processing and the prices they command. The first is Kopi Luwak made from Arabica beans that have been processed by the gut of the palm civet in Sumatra. The second is similarly processed by elephants in Thailand and marketed as Black Ivory coffee and retails for $75 a cup. The animals digest the cherry, parchment, and silver skin leaving a deposit including the beans that can then be roasted. Both are said to have a less acidic and smoother taste.

The dry method In areas where water is scarce, processors use the **dry method** of processing to produce sweet, smooth, complex coffee tastes. This method is used primarily in areas such as Yemen or Ethiopia where robusta is the dominant coffee crop. It may also be used for arabicas if water supplies are insufficient.

Processors using this method allow the coffee cherries to dry partially on the tree and spread them to dry in the sun for 14 to 21 days. Mechanical huskers then remove the dry pulp and parchment. Beans that have been prepared by the dry method have a heavier body but may sometimes develop off flavors.

The pulped natural method Coffee cherries are pulped and the beans are dried without going through a fermentation stage to remove the mucilage in the **pulped natural method.** Excellent coffee can be produced in this way with characteristics of both the dried and wet methods, including a full body.

SORTING AND GRADING

Dried beans are graded by size, density, and color. Size grading uses screens to separate beans according to their diameter. A number 10 bean, for example, has a diameter of 10/64 inch (4 mm). The beans are sized by passing them through the appropriate screens. Density is determined by subjecting the beans to an air jet that is calibrated to separate heavier beans from lighter ones. Color sorting is usually accomplished by hand, but some processors color-sort electronically. Finally, the beans are packed in burlap or plastic bags and shipped to roasters across the world.

The sorting and grading process varies from country to country. In general though, coffee beans come in six export grades. The top grade is known as SHB, or strictly hard beans. These are grown at a high altitude of at least 4,000 feet (1.2 km) above sea level.

COFFEE CLASSIFICATIONS

The dried, but still green coffee beans are classified according to botanical variety, processing method, and altitude of growth. The International Coffee Organization has classified green coffee beans, for example as: Colombian milds, other mild arabicas, Brazilian, other arabicas, and robustas. In recent decades the organization has lost its standing, and the above classifications are no longer as readily accepted. They do, however, provide useful descriptions of the wide variability of coffees.

Colombian milds Grown primarily in Colombia, Kenya, and Tanzania, these coffees constitute 16% of the world's production and are graded principally on bean size. These beans produce sweet, highly aromatic brewed coffee with a thick body.

Other mild arabicas This classification encompasses most of the arabicas grown in Central and South America. Accounting for about 26% of the world's production, these beans are graded according to growing altitude, density, color, and the number of defects. Their taste is winy to sour, with moderate aromatics and a smooth body, which is typical of medium-altitude coffee, grown at 2,000–4,000 feet (610–1,220 m).

Brazilian and other arabicas Grown in Brazil and Ethiopia, these beans make up about 37% of the world's coffee production. They are graded by the growing area, which determines the taste characteristics and the number of imperfections. The brewed coffee made from these beans has a winy-to-sour taste, moderate aromatics, and a smooth body.

Robustas Accounting for 39% of global coffee production, robustas are graded on density, size, and the number of defects. These beans produce a brew with a neutral-to-sharp taste, pungent aromatics, and a heavy body. Because robustas are 10% to 40% less expensive than arabicas, they are often used as filler in blended coffees.

THE ROASTING PROCESS

Roasting coffee beans brings out their full flavor and aroma. Their flavors depend on the degree to which the beans are caramelized during the roasting process. *See 6.2 Levels of Roasting.* Many complex chemical changes take place during roasting, which generally takes from 8 to 16 minutes at temperatures of approximately 350°–500°F (180°–260°C). As they reach a temperature of about 400°F (204°C), the beans begin to turn brown, and the oils, called coffee essence, start to emerge. This process, called **pyrolosis,** produces the distinctive flavor and aroma of the coffee.

ESPRESSO AND ESPRESSO BEVERAGES

Properly made espresso is thick, dark, and intensely fragrant, with a bittersweet taste. It is topped with creamy golden foam called "crema." A single demitasse, or half-size cup serving contains only 1–1 1/4 ounces (30–37 ml) and is served immediately after brewing. Espresso may be combined with ice, cold milk, steamed milk, whipped cream, mocha, and other flavorings to create a wide range of recipes.

There are several popular espresso-based drinks served in food service operations:

- **Americano**—Americano is a single shot of espresso with 6 to 8 ounces (177 to 237 ml) of hot water added.
- **Caffè latte**—Caffè latte is a single shot of espresso topped with steamed skim milk and a layer of frothed skim milk.
- **Cappuccino**—Cappuccino is a single shot of espresso, topped with 4 1/2 ounces (133 ml) of thick foam of steamed emulsified milk served in a 6- to 8-ounce (177- to 237-ml) cup or glass with sugar on the side.
- **Caffè breve (brief)**—A caffè breve consists of a single shot of espresso and 4 ounces (118 ml) of steamed half-and-half, served in a 6-ounce (177-ml) cup with sugar on the side.
- **Corretto (corrected)**—A corretto is made of a single shot of espresso with a 1-ounce (30 ml) shot of liqueur served in a demitasse.
- **Doppio (double)**—A double shot of espresso served with sugar on the side, makes up a doppio.
- **Espresso macchiato (marked)**—An espresso macchiato is a single or double shot of espresso topped with a heaping teaspoon of steamed milk.
- **Lungo (long)**—A lungo is a single shot of espresso served in a demitasse with sugar on the side.
- **Ristretto (restricted)**—A shot of espresso, served in a demitasse with sugar to the side and a "water-back" composes a ristretto.

Five common but imprecise levels of roasting give different "roasts" their distinctive flavors and aromas.

Cinnamon roast

Cinnamon roast is the lightest commercially available roast. These beans have no visible oils on their surface, and the flavor and body are light.

Full City roast

Full City roast is a medium roast.

Vienna roast

Vienna roast describes both a medium roast that is chocolate brown with dark speckles and a particular blend of different roasts.

French roast

Sometimes called New Orleans roast, French roast is heavily roasted to bring out a strong, characteristically bitter flavor and aroma.

Italian roast

Italian roast is the darkest stage of roasting. The beans become carbonized and coated with a film of oil. These beans are usually reserved for espressos made by large producers, but great espressos may also be made with beans roasted to a much less carbonized level.

DECAFFEINATED COFFEE

Caffeine, a nitrogen compound found in plants, is a mild stimulant that may increase the heart rate and cause sleeplessness in some people. As little as 10 milligrams may cause discomfort.

The Food and Drug Administration (FDA) guidelines state that coffee labeled *decaffeinated* must have 97% of the caffeine removed from the green coffee bean prior to roasting, so decaffeinated coffee has about two to five milligrams of caffeine per serving. Three main processes are employed to decaffeinate coffee beans. Because caffeine is water-soluble, each process begins with moistened green coffee beans.

The conventional water method In this process, the green beans are treated with steam and water to open their cellular structure. They are then flushed with a decaffeinating agent such as methylene chloride or ethyl acetate. The beans are further treated with steam and water to evaporate all remaining traces of the decaffeinating agent. No traceable amount of the agent is left in the beans.

Swiss water processing Swiss water processing is similar to the water method but uses charcoal filtration rather than chemicals.

Supercritical carbon dioxide decaffeination This method uses carbon dioxide as the solvent agent. The carbon dioxide is passed through the coffee beans under tremendous pressure (250–300 times atmospheric pressure), typically extracting 96%–98% of the caffeine. Although expensive, this method is popular because carbon dioxide is abundant and reusable.

The **Origins** of **Espresso**

In 1903 Luigi Bezzera, an Italian manufacturer, was unhappy about the amount of time his workers spent on their coffee breaks. He thought that by shortening the brewing process, which took as long as 20 minutes, he could shorten the breaks.

Bezzera decided to brew the coffee under pressure. He invented a machine he called the "Fast Coffee Machine." Not only did Bezzera's machine reduce the brew time to a mere 20 seconds, but it also made a better cup of coffee than traditional methods made. The quick brewing time extracted the coffee's best qualities while leaving behind the unfavorable qualities, such as bitterness.

Later Achilles Gaggia, a barkeeper, decided to improve on the basic espresso machine by adding a lever and piston that produced more pressure in the brew chamber. Today, Gaggia espresso machines and related equipment are familiar sights behind the counters of the world's coffee bars.

DEGASSING AND PACKAGING COFFEE

Preserving the maximum flavor, freshness, and aroma of coffee while packaging it for distribution is a complex problem. After coffee beans are roasted, they produce carbon dioxide gas equal to about three times their volume. If the carbon dioxide is not released prior to most commercial packaging, the pressure of the escaping gas will cause the package to burst. Unfortunately, when the carbon dioxide dissipates, the beans can absorb oxygen and become somewhat stale.

Packers have developed ingenious packaging solutions to resolve the gas problem. Greaseproof, moisture-proof, resealable bags are nitrogen-flushed to displace oxygen. A one-way valve allows carbon dioxide to pass out of the bag while preventing air from entering it. After packages have been opened; however, storage conditions have an important effect on the coffee's flavor and quality. One leading producer, Illy, developed another ingenious system that best preserves the aromas of whole beans by packaging the beans in a canister that expands with the CO2. The container is actually filled with additional carbon dioxide to force the aromatic compounds back into the beans themselves to extend their flavor.

STORING COFFEE

To keep coffee's taste and aroma from dissipating, store it away from air, moisture, and heat. *See 6.3.* Buy smaller quantities of whole beans, and store the coffee in tightly sealed containers. Unopened proportioned nitrogen-flushed coffee packs generally have a "use by" date and can be stored in a cool room. Coffee should not be stored under refrigeration.

TASTING TERMS

Humans perceive taste through receptors on taste buds located primarily on the tongue. But taste is also affected by texture and mouthfeel. Although taste is a somewhat subjective sensation, people have generally agreed on the meaning of several taste descriptors: sweet, sour, bitter, mellow, bland, fresh, and sharp, for example. *See 6.4.* Coffee tasters also have an agreed-upon vocabulary.

Acidity This desirable characteristic refers to the lively, palate-cleansing tartness of coffee. It is a characteristic of arabica from high-altitude growing regions. Acidity should not be confused with bitterness.

Body Body refers to the sense of heaviness or thickness of a coffee. Descriptors for this sensation range from thin, light, and watery to buttery, heavy, and thick. Sumatran can be the heaviest coffee, and Mexican and Ethiopian coffees tend to be the lightest. Several factors, such as the type of grind, the amount of water used, and the brewing method, can also affect the coffee's body.

Flavor Flavor is the most important tasting term, which refers to the overall impression of aromas, flavors, and body. Coffee can often be described as mellow or harsh, grassy or earthy. The terms "chocolaty" or "winy" (winelike) may also be used to describe a coffee's flavor.

6.3 Coffee should be stored away from air, moisture, and heat.

6.4 Professional coffee tasters use a technique called "cupping" to evaluate different coffees and to create blenc

History of Coffee

circa a.d. 1000
The practice of roasting coffee beans begins in Yemen.

A decoction is first made from the dried hulls and beans of the coffee plant.

circa late 1200s
Muslim pilgrims spread the practice of drinking coffee throughout the Near East, Middle East, and North Africa.

circa late 1400s

circa 1599
Although the Roman Catholic Church initially calls it "Satan's latest trap to catch Christian souls," coffee gains widespread popularity throughout Europe.

1616
The Dutch begin cultivating coffee in Ceylon and Java.

1720

1740
Gabriel Mathieu de Clieu, a French naval officer, smuggles a coffee seedling into Martinique. The plant is the ancestor of most of the arabica beans cultivated around the world.

1773
Coffee becomes America's patriotic beverage following the Boston Tea Party.

London has more than 2,000 coffeehouses.

1971
Starbucks® opens its first store in Seattle's Pike Place Market, and freshly roasted whole beans, gourmet blends, and specialty coffees become trendy.

Present
Today, coffee is brewed and served in more ways, to more people, than at any other time in history.

Crema Crema is the amber foam that floats on top of a well-made espresso. The amber foam should have *'tiger stripes'* created by oils and colloids—suspended coffee particles and carbon dioxide. This mixture not only gives espresso a rich, full mouth feel but coats the tongue to prevent the bitterness of the coffee from being perceived. *See 6.5.*

6.5 A well-formed crema adds to the enjoyment of a cup of espresso.

Mocha Named for the Yemen port of Moka on the Red Sea, from which coffee was first traded, mocha was a term used to describe coffee in Europe during the sixteenth century. When chocolate was brought from the Americas to Europe, Europeans believed that it had a flavor similar to that of coffee. Mocha is a term now used to describe a blend of coffee and chocolate and is not to be confused with Moka brewing, which was discussed in Chapter 3: "The Restaurant Environment."

THE FUTURE OF COFFEE CONSUMPTION

Despite a continuous increase for instant coffee consumption in countries like India and China where tea has always been the predominant choice of hot beverage, the market for gourmet coffee is on the rise as well. From greater transparency in coffee sourcing to roasting green beans at home, coffee drinking, for many consumers, is now more about the experience. Consumers are now eager to know how their coffee was grown, who grew it, how it was grown, and how it was processed.

Baristas and shops for specifically roasting coffee are focusing more on the *terroir* of coffee and investing heavily on the latest brewing technology to bring the ultimate coffee to the consumer.

The results are stunning new coffee brewers, like the Ratio Eight and the Steampunk brewing system from Alpha Dominche, and sleek new tools like the Acaia brewing scale. The hallmarks of these new machines are precision crafting, fine materials, and an elevated sense of style.

The **Steampunk**, for example, is a revolutionary coffee and tea brewing system that unlocks flavor profiles that are hidden by other machines using a touch-screen computer that allows the barista to input recipes for each type of coffee. The craft comes in as the recipes are developed: the barista can customize the temperature, brew time, and how the grounds are agitated, tweaking the recipe to bring out more fruit or acidity in the coffee. Once a recipe is programmed, the coffee will come out the same each time it's brewed.

Tea

Legend has it that a Chinese emperor discovered tea in 2737 B.C. when a fragrant leaf or two from a nearby camellia tree blew into some water he was boiling. Tasting the brew, he declared it delectable, and thus was born the cultivation of tea. However, it was not until the Ming dynasty (A.D. 1368–1644) that tea consumption became a part of everyday life in China.

By the 1600s, explorers and traders were importing tea to Europe and then further abroad to America. Tea drinking soon became fashionable among British aristocrats. In the late 1700s, afternoon tea became an everyday ritual among members of English society. Tea among the upper classes included not only the hot beverage but also delicate, crustless sandwiches and pastries. These offerings soon expanded to include toasted bread with jam as well as scones and crumpets. The working classes soon developed their own ritual, with "high tea" consisting of meats, cheese, and breads taken as their principal evening meal.

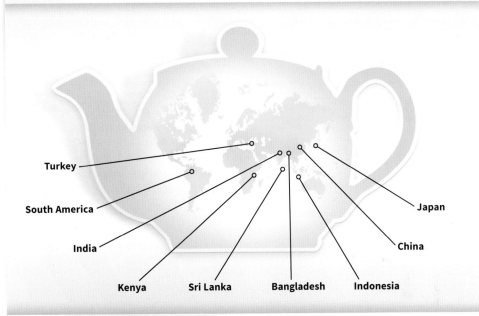

TEA PRODUCTION

Today, tea is the most popular beverage in the world after water. It is available in a wide variety of forms, ranging from the modest inexpensive tea bag, to extremely rare and proportionately expensive herbs that are gathered by hand in remote regions of the world.

Tea is processed from the leaves of **Camellia sinensis**, a tree or shrub that grows best at higher altitudes under damp, tropical conditions. The leaves are hand-harvested or plucked from the plants' youngest shoots, called the first and second flush. About 4,200 pounds (1,905 kg) of fresh tea leaves produce 1,000 pounds (454 kg) of finished tea.

Although tea grows in many other regions, India, China, Sri Lanka, Indonesia, and Kenya account for most of the world's commercial production and exports. Teas often take their names from the regions in which they are grown.

TEA CLASSIFICATION

Although all tea comes from basically the same plant species, there are approximately 1,500 grades and 2,000 different blends of teas. Four general classifications of tea define the level of enzymatic oxidation that leaves undergo during processing.

White Tea

White tea is unoxidized and silvery in color with the highest concentration of caffeine. It is made from the youngest shoots or buds of specific tea varietal plants. There are several white teas of note particularly in the Fujian province of China. It is also harvested in small quantities in Assam and Darjeeling in India and in Sri Lanka.

Green Tea

Green tea is also unoxidized and yellowish-green with a slightly bitter flavor. Steaming or heating the leaves immediately after picking prevents enzymatic oxidation that turns tea leaves into black tea. After heating, the leaves are rolled and dried. Green teas need to be properly stored and served fresh. Green teas are produced primarily in China, Taiwan, and Japan.

Examples of green tea include:
- **Gyokuro**—the finest grade of exported Japanese tea
- **Tencha**—the powdered tea used in Japanese tea ceremonies
- **Sencha**—the most common Japanese tea, which is popular in restaurants and sushi bars.
- **Gunpowder**—the highest Chinese grade, which is rolled into tiny balls
- **Imperial**—a grade from Sri Lanka, China, or India
- **Shou Mei**—a Chinese green tea known as "old man's eyebrows"

Oolong Tea

Oolong tea combines the characteristics of black and green teas. The leaves are partially oxidized, the process is interrupted, and the leaves are rolled and dried. Oolong is often flavored with scented agents such as jasmine flowers. It is also graded by leaf size and age.

Examples of oolong tea include:
- **Formosa Oolong**—a delicate, large-leafed oolong tea with a taste reminiscent of ripe peaches. Unique and expensive, it is suited for breakfast or afternoon tea.
- **Black Dragon**—a kind of tea from Taiwan.
- **Pouchong**—a tea grown both in China and Taiwan.

Black Tea

When steeped, **black tea** is strongly flavored and amber or coppery brown. The color and flavor result from plucked leaves that are dried, or withered, and then rolled in special machines to release the enzymes that give the tea its color, specific taste, and aroma. The leaves are then "fired," or heated and compressed to their final shape.

Teas are also sorted by leaf size and according to their brewing time. Larger leaves take longer to brew than smaller leaves. Size classifications include souchong, or large-leaf tea; pekoe, or medium-leaf tea; and orange pekoe, or the smallest whole-leaf tea.

Broken tea leaves are categorized as either fannings or dust and are used for tea bags. Broken orange pekoe is of a high-quality and generally produces a darker brew of the kind most commonly steeped from tea bags. Black teas are the best known and most popular in the West, but most teas sold in the United States are blends. Even the same tea blend or type of tea will taste different from blender to blender. **Some of the most popular types of teas are:**
- **Assam**—a rich, black tea from Northern India, valued as a breakfast tea by connoisseurs.
- **Ceylon**—a full-flavored black tea with a delicate fragrance, ideal for iced tea because it does not turn cloudy when cold.
- **Darjeeling**—a full-bodied, black tea with a Muscat flavor, grown in the foothills of the Himalayas.
- **Earl Grey**—a popular choice for afternoon tea, Earl Grey is flavored with oil of bergamot.
- **English Breakfast**—a full-bodied, robust blend of Indian and Sri Lankan teas.
- **Lapsang Souchong**—a tarry, smoky flavor and aroma, best for afternoon tea or as a dinner beverage.

ICED TEA AND TEA BAGS

Iced tea and the tea bag have "happy accidents" in common. Iced tea was invented at the 1904 World's Fair in St. Louis, Missouri, when the temperature soared and fairgoers were ignoring the hot brew. Tea merchant Richard Blechynden decided to dump a load of ice into the tea and to serve it cold to attract business.

In 1908, New York tea merchant, Thomas Sullivan, carefully wrapped samples of his product in muslin bags for restaurant managers to test. When he realized that the restaurants were brewing his samples in the bag to avoid the mess of tea leaves, the tea bag was born. It is at about the same time that Thomas Lipton, a British merchant and owner of several tea plantations, began marketing his high-quality tea blend in convenient, inexpensive boxes that were affordable to middle- and working-class people.

By 2008, according to the Tea Council, tea sales reached $7 billion with only a little more than 1% of the tea brewed in the United States prepared from loose tea. Approximately 80% of tea is served cold. The remaining tea is made from instant tea.

Many other "teas" are produced by infusing roots, stems, seeds, berries, flowers, leaves, herbs, and spices in water. Infusion involves steeping flavoring agents in water. The following list contains a summary of different types of infusions:

Scented teas Scented teas are made by blending aromatic petals from flowers such as jasmine, lavender, gardenias, or magnolias with tea leaves.

Flavored teas Flavored teas gain their distinct character by the addition of the essence of citrus fruits, berries, vanilla, or other flavoring components to tea leaves.

Spiced teas Blending flavoring agents such as cinnamon, nutmeg, coriander, and cloves with tea leaves produces spiced teas. The most well known example is *chai* (which is the Hindi word for tea). The chai that is most commonly marketed in the U.S. is *masala chai* which is a spiced tea. Most chais are traditionally prepared with black teas, spices, and hot milk and are sweetened.

Herbal teas Herbal teas, or tisanes, are infusions made from herbs such as chamomile, spearmint, ginseng, and lemon balm. One traditional infusion from South America called *yerba mate* is gaining popularity in the U.S.. It is typically infused with hot water and served in a gourd with a silver straw. These beverages do not contain any real tea at all; however, they are prepared in the same way as tea infusions.

Bottled Water

Bottled water consumption has doubled in the last 5 years and has reached sales of 8.6 billion gallons, of which 25% is purified municipal water rather than sourced from springs, lakes, rivers, and aquafers. Bottled water cost between $0.25 and $2.00, while municipal water cost a penny or two to produce. While sales continue to increase, there are critics that point out that bottled water is not regulated to the extent that municipal waters are and may pose some health issues due to the lack of fluoride and a greater concentration of chemicals. Most taste tests demonstrate that consumers cannot differentiate between bottled purified water and municipal water. Sales of bottled waters in restaurants can provide added sales, but there are affiliated costs such as storage and disposal costs.

Mineral waters have flavors and tastes that provide consumers with a different experience. They are defined by the U.S. Food and Drug Administration as containing a minimum of 250 per million of total dissolved solids and come from a specific protected source. They are either carbonated or uncarbonated, and their characteristics can impact the tastes of accompanying foods or beverages such as wines. The tasting terminology of waters is similar to that of other beverages with the addition of the term **"sapidity,"** which reflects the minerality present in the water. Highly mineralized waters are often described as being hard, while those lacking such intensity are described as soft.

Soft Drinks

Soft drinks are so described due to the absence of (hard) alcohol. Non-carbonated soft drinks were first marketed in France in the 17th century. Joseph Priestly, an English clergyman and scientist, first carbonated drinks artificially and may be credited as the forefather of carbonated soda drinks. This novel and refreshing idea was commercialized in the U.S. by Benjamin Silliman, the first professor of chemistry at Yale University.

It was in the U.S., that soda water with additives, whether fruit juices or botanicals such as sarsaparilla, were first commercially marketed and sold. By the mid 19th century, soda fountains had become a fixture. It is no surprise that once the crown cap seal was invented and the bottling of sodas was industrialized, this category of beverage not only became preeminent in the U.S., but also became a fixture in all four corners of the world. The most famous of these beverages came from research done by a John Pemberton who developed a drink called French Wine Coca, which was an alcoholic concoction that included the coca leaf, a known stimulant from South America. He adapted this formula by including a West African kola nut extract that also contained 2% caffeine. He had to change the recipe to conform to prohibition laws that were passed in Georgia in 1886. The drink's name was based on the new recipe's two primary ingredients: coca and kola, and total soft drink sales of this beverage at that time neared $74 billion with continued trends toward diet sugar-free products.

Ready *to* Drink Market

The ready to drink market includes some of the beverages already discussed as well as flavored iced teas, chais, iced coffees, coconut waters, vitamin waters, and highly caffeinated drinks such as Red Bull TM. Establishments need to be aware of the changing market and trends so as to satisfy their guests' needs. At dinner-house and fine dining establishments, bartenders should be able to create unique alcohol free drinks to meet or exceed guests' expectations.

7. Beer

Beer is the number one category of alcoholic beverage in the world today in terms of both volume and dollar amounts. Beer is brewed and consumed in every country on every continent on the planet,* and more people consume beer than any other category of alcoholic beverage. A large proportion of profit in restaurant alcohol sales is from beer, with a gross profit margin of anywhere from 80% to 95% in a typical draft portion and even more for Brew Pubs.

In some parts of the world beer production has seen dramatic growth, especially Brazil and China, which is now the world's largest beer-producing country. Meanwhile beer production in North America and other areas has been gradually falling for many years, but demand for craft beer continues to grow by double digits every year. Craft beers offer a greater diversity of flavor and many are locally produced, which appeals to today's more savvy consumers. A restaurant's alcoholic beverage program must include a wider array of beer styles to be competitive today, and its service staff must be well educated in proper beer service and sales to maximize profits.

*Production and consumption of alcoholic beverages in public is officially prohibited in many Islamic countries, yet still occurs albeit on a smaller scale.

IN THE BREWERY.

WAIFS AND STRAYS.

Ancient History *of* Beer

Recent archaeological research has proven that it was the discovery of beer by our nomadic ancestors that prompted them to begin farming and to build homes, thus forming the foundations for human civilization. These early peoples discovered that wild barley and other grains, when allowed to soak in water, created a type of frothy, tangy liquid bread with mysterious intoxicating effects. The resulting beverage was probably cloudy, brown, and very different from many of today's commercial beers, although its consumption evoked the same feelings of contentment and relaxation that it does today. Ancient civilizations recognized this process as a type of divine transformation, which not only made the grains more nutritious, but also allowed them to be stored for longer periods of time.

According to clay tablets found in Mesopotamia (today's Iraq) dating back to about 6000 B.C., the earliest known recipe of any kind is one for making beer, known as the Hymn to **Ninkasi,** the goddess of beer. Ancient Egyptians also employed beer brewing methods that resulted in the production of Tetracycline, a potent antibiotic that helped to fight disease. Royal family members were entombed with entire miniature breweries to supply them with this crucial drink in the afterlife, and beer was used as a form of currency and payment to the workers who built the Great Pyramids.

By about 4000 B.C., Sumerians, considered the master brewers of the ancient world, boasted over 200 varieties of beer, often enhancing its flavor by adding such ingredients as dates and honey. Egyptians added their own flavorings, such as herbs and fruits, and passed their brewing knowledge on to the Greeks and Romans.

EUROPEAN BREWING DEVELOPS

Throughout the dark ages, beer brewing was a part of a woman's daily household duties, and beer was a staple item in the diet because the boiling during the brewing process eliminated disease-causing bacteria that often contaminated water. Widows who made ends meet by selling their beers were known as **Alewives** or **Brewsters.**

From the 9th century onward, the primary land owner and thus governing body throughout Europe was the Catholic Church, which also filled the medical, educational, and judicial roles. Commercial beer brewing was done by license from the church granting the use of a proprietary blend of herbs and roots (known as gruit) which acted as a preservative. Brewers would pay their taxes by purchasing membership and required supplies of **gruit** from the church. Thus, the Catholic Church was able to control and profit from brewing within their territories. The monastic orders throughout Europe were the primary brewers of the rural areas, and many of these are still brewing and selling their beers today (see Belgian Beers).

THE RISE OF HOPS

Both secular and religious forces sought to break free of the church's control during the Middle Ages. The feudal (non-religious land holders) built their own estate breweries to retake the brewing from the monastic orders, and city burghers built their own commercial breweries in the towns. These city and feudal brewers refused to purchase gruit from the church and instead added their own blends of herbs and spices, including poison ivy, as a means of preservation.

Then the Reformation (or rise of Protestantism) in northeast Europe made the break official and sought to eliminate some of the toxic beers on the market. In 1487, Albert IV, Duke of Bavaria (southern Germany, today), passed the German beer purity law *(Reinheitsgebot),* which is still in effect today. This law prohibited the use of gruit and only allowed for the use of three ingredients in beer: malted grains, water, and **hops** — the ingredients were taxed by the Bavarian government. (Later this law was revised to include yeast, upon its discovery by Louis Pasteur, see "Yeast"). In 1516, this Reinheitsgebot was amended by Duke Wilhelm V to include selling price restrictions and to reduce competition for cereal grains with the bread bakers.

In areas still under Catholic control, such as England, the use of hops in beer brewing was prohibited. Brewers, however, recognized the superior preservative abilities of hops over gruit, which enabled them to use less grain and make lower alcohol beers. So many used wild hops and crafted malty beer styles to hide the hop flavors.

THE EVOLUTION OF LAGERS

A revision to the Reinheitsgebot in 1587 prohibited the home brewing of beer during the summer months and only allowed commercial brewing. The law recognized that the hot continental summers of central Europe were not conducive to quality beer brewing. To ensure an adequate supply, home brewers brewed an extra supply in the spring and stored (or lagered) their beer in cellars throughout the summer. These Märzen beers (named after the month of March in which they were often brewed), were then released in the early fall during the many festivals that marked the beginning of the brewing season, the most famous of which is Munich's Oktoberfest. Ice-packed caves in Bohemia (today's Czech Republic) and southern Germany's Bavarian Alps allowed commercial brewers to continue to brew, store, and preserve beers year round. The yeast strains to mutate into our slow-acting lager yeasts of today, thus creating new beer styles.

The most famous of lager styles was created in the Czech city of Pilzn where the Pilsner style was developed. Many lighter American beers were originally modeled upon this type of beer.

THE BEGINNING OF AMERICAN BEER

From the earliest Puritan settlements in the United States, the dominant beer styles were ales. The English colonists used a variety of local ingredients in their beer styles, such as pumpkins and spruce tips, to create a diverse array of beers. Most beer brewing was done in the home, and ciders were also popular. Once populations began to move to the cities, urban breweries arose to replace home brewing, and commercial brewing became dominant. An influx of German immigrants in the mid-1800s introduced lagers and set up large-scale commercial brewing centers near the lakes and rivers of the Midwest where they had a reliable supply of ice year round. The growth of these new mega breweries changed the industry and prompted the creation of commercial refrigeration in 1860, pasteurization in 1876, and the subsequent railroad distribution system.

As of 1880 about 2,300 breweries were scattered across the United States. But by the turn of the century, industry consolidation had already begun. Mega breweries owned and managed their own saloons, flooding the market and driving prices down, forcing saloon managers to rely upon illegal activities (gambling, prostitution) to subsidize revenue. The proliferation of these undesirable establishments prompted the rise of the Anti-Saloon League, led by Carrie Nation, who fought to ban all alcohol sales.

The beer industry was all but destroyed by national Prohibition in 1919; the only breweries that survived did so by producing malt sodas, "near beer" (under 2% ABV), cheeses, and ice cream. Even though it was legal to make wine at home during prohibition, home brewing was strictly forbidden, as it was thought that beers would automatically be made into whiskies. After Prohibition was repealed in 1933, there were only a handful of breweries left, and America had developed a taste for liquor in the form of cocktails and mixed drinks. The Great Depression and Dust Bowl of the mid-1930s prevented the beer industry from bouncing back. Then the grain rationing of World War II led brewers to resort to cheaper ingredients and lighter styles of beer. By the 1950s, only four breweries, Anheuser-Busch®, Miller®, Coors®, and Stroh's®, dominated the market, with a combined 97% share of total sales.

CRAFT AND MICROBREWERIES

In 1978, President Jimmy Carter signed a law that finally legalized the brewing of beer in the home. The last 2 states to legalize home brewing (Mississippi and Alabama) did so as recently as 2013. The American Homebrewers' Association, founded in 1978, helped to promote a generation of home brewers and beer drinkers with more adventurous tastes. Americans also began to develop a taste for imported beers, even though the long voyage gave many of them off flavors before they reached the consumer. (See 'beer faults') Nevertheless, the movement towards greater variety and fuller flavors had begun.

American craft brewing managed to survive throughout this time, with small local producers like Yuengling in Pennsylvania and Anchor in California. But the rise of local craft breweries in the 1980s and 1990s was a result of the growth of the homebrew industry and pioneers like Ken Grossman of Sierra Nevada in California. This was helped by the passage of legislation that granted tax advantages to microbreweries.

Today, the United States has more breweries than any other country in the world, with the craft brewing movement spreading across the globe to other countries as well. The majority of craft breweries in the US are Brew Pubs (See Sidebar The Rise of the Brew Pub). As craft beer sales have soared, sales of the light corn- and rice-based American flagship lagers has fallen, prompting the major brewers to expand their portfolios of products by purchasing smaller craft brewery brands and promoting their own mass-produced 'faux craft' brands to compete. *See 7.1.* Many have also begun to re-purpose their brands with new flavors or even added flavors to try to appeal to a younger market.

The Rise of the Brew Pub

A large portion of the breweries in the U.S. today are **Brew Pubs.** According to the Brewers' Association, a Brew Pub is defined as *"A restaurant-brewery that sells 25 percent or more of its beer on site. The beer is brewed primarily for sale in the restaurant and bar. The beer is often dispensed directly from the brewery's storage tanks."* Where a typical restaurant can make about 90-95% profit from draft beer sales, a brew pub can earn 98% or better. Serving from storage tanks also means that there are no packaging costs, and the beer is always fresh. Brewpubs can also get direct feedback from their customers about new or seasonal styles and brew only as much of each style as they want.

By crafting menus that utilize beer in the dishes and pairing beers with the food, Brew Pubs can appeal to today's beer-savvy consumers.

7.1 A modern brewery using traditional technology

Becoming Beer

Across the globe, the types of beer styles seem infinite. Although almost all beers are made up of four main ingredients – water, malted grains, hops and yeast – the subtle differences in variations of these ingredients create many possible recipes. Combine that with the potential addition of other ingredients, changes in brewing techniques, and aging, the possibilities are endless. *See 7.2.*

Brewing Beer

Beer Ingredients

Water Characteristics of local water sources defined many beer styles

Malted Grains Provides starch (sugar), and body, flavor and color

Hops Main preservative, adds crisp bitterness, flavor and aroma

Yeast Many types, converts sugars to alcohol, creates variety of flavors

Adjuncts Unmalted grains, or additional spices, fruits, or other flavorings

Brewing Process

Malting Sprouting then drying grain to create enzymes, flavors, sometimes colors

Milling Crushing the grains into a Grist, or coarse meal

Mashing Combining Grist and warm Liquor (brewing water) to reactivate enzymes

Lautering Using grain husks as a filter to clarify the wort

Sparging Using warm liquor and gravity to rinse the wort from the grain husks

Kettling Boiling process, the actual 'Brewing' of the beer, sterilizes and much more

Circulation Separating the Green Beer from the Trub, or protein residues

Chilling Bringing the hot Green Beer down to yeast-friendly temperatures

Fermentation Yeast consumes sugars, creates alcohol, CO_2 and flavors

Conditioning Time for flavors to evolve and soften, can happen in bottle, cask or tank

Priming Adding additional sugars for carbonation, usually only bottle-fermented beers

7.2 The Brewing Process

WATER

All beverages are composed mainly of water, but unlike the water used in wine, the water used in brewing is added during the process. Water comprises 90% to 96% of beer's volume, and its mineral composition greatly affects the beer's quality and style. Brewers refer to their brewing-quality water as **"liquor."** A variety of ions and dissolved minerals will affect enzyme activity during mashing (see below), clarity, color and/or hop extraction rates, body and fermentation, and of course, flavors.

Throughout Europe, many of the classic beer styles were developed as a direct result of their local water type. Burton-on-Trent in England produces its famous "Burton" pale ales, which have a distinct taste profile that comes from a particularly high mineral concentration in the water (See IPA). The famous lagers of Munich and Pilzn, and the dark rich stouts of Dublin, are also examples of beer styles that evolved as a result of their local water source. Today's technology allows the brewer to manipulate the mineral composition of the water source to craft a variety of classic beer styles in one location.

MALTED BARLEY

Barley, the most significant solid ingredient in brewing, provides enzymes for starch conversion; nutrients for yeast; and contributes body, flavor, and color to beer. *See 7.3.* Although other cereal grains (either malted or unmalted)—such as wheat, oats, rye, sorghum and millet – may also be brewed into beer; barley is by far the most popular and practical for malting.

Malting has five steps: steeping, germinating, drying, kilning, and conditioning. First, the grains are soaked in warm water until they reach a moisture content of 46%. Then they are warmed and aerated and spread out on the drying floor to germinate for about five days. During this time the barley is turned or raked constantly to allow it to sprout evenly. During sprouting, the barley forms many enzymes needed for brewing. The most important of these are **maltase,** alpha, and beta **amylases,** which will later convert starch to the sugars needed for fermentation. After germination, the malt is dried at 100° F to halt germination. Then afterwards, the malt may be kilned or roasted to gaain color and flavor, but this kilning also destroys enzymes. The last step, conditioning, allows the flavors in the malt to develop and soften, which usually takes several weeks.

There are 5 main types of malt:

- **Pale Malts** are the base for all beers and have relatively neutral flavors but a considerable amount of starch and enzymes. Two-Row barley is used for craft beers, where six-row barley (thus called due to six rows of smaller grains on the stalk) is used for beers with a high degree of unmalted adjuncts.
- **Toasted Malts** are lightly kilned and have flavors reminiscent of crackers or bread. These also have starches and enzymes.
- **Crystal or Caramel Malts** go through a process known as **"wet kilning,"** where the germinating grains are slowly brought up to kilning temperature without drying. This allows the enzymes to convert some of the starches and proteins, which are then caramelized in the kiln, creating complex honey or caramel flavors. Crystal malts can range in color from very light to very dark and have considerable flavor but no usable enzymes or starches.
- **Roasted Malts** are the darkest of malts and often have roasted or even burnt flavors. Even a small amount of these in a grain bill (recipe) will create a dark colored beer.
- **Other Malts** include malts made from other grains such as rye or wheat and smoked malts. Unmalted grains of any type are considered **adjuncts.**

MILLING

Before brewing, the malted barley needs to be milled, or ground into a coarse meal called **grist,** to expose the interior starches to the brewing water. **Milling** is best done just before brewing to preserve freshness and flavor. The grist must be of the proper consistency to allow full exposure of starches for greater efficiency, while keeping the husks intact to prevent tannin extraction and to later act as a filter (See "Lautering".)

MASHING

The grist and the warm liquor are gradually combined in a large heated and/or insulated container called a mash tun. This process is known as **dough in.** Enzymes in the grist are reactivated at various temperature levels or destroyed at others. So carefully controlling the temperature of the mash will determine which enzymes are allowed to work. Each temperature and time variation is known as a **rest** or step.

During the protein rest, enzymes such as peptidase and proteinase break down proteins into soluble amino acids for the yeast to use during fermentation, and glucanase breaks down tough cell walls. A protein rest is generally only needed for unmalted grains or under-modified malts. At higher temperature ranges, the maltase and amylase enzymes will break down the starches into fermentable and non-fermentable sugars (**dextrins**). This process is called **saccharification** or **conversion.** Between 130° F and 152° F, Beta Amylase will produce only fermentable sugars, resulting in a dry, higher-alcohol beer. Between 148° F and 165° F, Alpha Amylase will create a combination of fermentable sugars and dextrins, resulting in a sweeter or more full-bodied beer. A single-step infusion will bring the mash to around 150° F for about an hour, where both Beta and Alpha Amylase can work concurrently.

At the end of the mashing process, the sweet, sticky liquid is known as **wort** and the left-over grain husks, known as **spent grains.**

7.3 Malted barley is the heart and soul of beer. It determines its color, flavor, and aroma.

LAUTERING

Also known as Vorlauf, **lautering** is the process of filtering the wort through the spent grain husks to prepare the liquid for the kettle. During lautering, the wort is gently pumped and recirculated over the grain bed, forcing the husks to sink to the bottom of the vessel and form a compact filter bed. Once the wort begins to run clear, it is time for **sparging.**

SPARGING

To separate the sweet, sticky wort from the grain husks, warm liquor is used to displace the wort. The warm water is sprayed over the top of the mash tun as the wort is slowly pulled out and sent to the kettle. Since the water is lighter (less dense) than the wort, it slowly replaces the wort in the grains and rinses any remaining sugars off of the husks.

KETTLING

During **kettling,** the wort is brought to a full, rolling boil for about 1 hour. **During this time, several things occur:**

1. Wort is **sterilized** by boiling, and any remaining enzymes are deactivated.

2. **Clarification** occurs when dissolved proteins coagulate and form floating chunks. This process is also known as **hot break.**

3. Caramelization of sugars makes the liquid slightly darker. This is why very light beers are difficult to make.

4. Evaporation condenses the wort and concentrates sugars.

5. Grain-derived aromatic compounds are also driven off during the open boil, preventing any later formation of off-flavors in the beer.

6. Lastly, the **isomerization** of hop compounds occurs when these molecules change shape and become soluble. Hops are added in stages throughout the boil, depending on the purpose and type of hops used (see below).

HOPS

Hops have been used for medicinal purposes for thousands of years, but their use in beer was not documented until the 10th century. Hops (humulus lupulus) are a perennial vine that grows over 20 feet tall in hop yards in cooler, dry climates. The main hop-growing areas of the world include Germany, The United States, China, the Czech Republic, Poland, Slovenia, North Korea, The United Kingdom, Albania, and New Zealand.

The cone-shaped flowers of the hop vine contain a variety of oils and resins and are added to beer for several reasons:

1. Hops are antimicrobial but do not impact brewer's yeast, so they help preserve beer.

2. If added at the beginning of the kettling process, their bitterness (measured in **alpha acids**) will balance the sweetness of the malt and give a characteristic crispness to the beer's finish.

3. If they are added toward the end of the boil, they will not give bitterness to the beer, but rather their aromas and flavors. The aromas of hops vary from herbal or piney to earthy, spicy and tobacco-like, to even citrusy and floral, depending on the variety. (See "Noble Hops.")

4. Hops are also important in aiding clarification of the wort, helping to coagulate proteins. Hops also help beer to retain the head or the foam that forms when beer is poured. A beer with more hops, such as an IPA, will tend to have more foam.

CIRCULATION

After the kettling is completed, the **"green beer,"** as it is now known, must be prepared for fermentation. First, the green beer undergoes a whirlpool circulation to separate the protein deposits and hop residues, now known as **trub.** This can be achieved by moving the liquid to a separate vessel, called a centrifuge, to spin the liquid and remove the solids. Another method is to create a whirlpool within the kettle, using a pump or by manually stirring. A third method is the use of a **"hop back,"** or separate vessel packed full of fresh hops. The hot wort is run into the hop back through an offset inlet to create a whirlpool. As the hops help to collect and filter out the trub, they add even more hop aromas to the green beer.

What are "Noble Hops"?

Many brewers talk about their use of Noble hop varieties in their marketing. There are many hop varieties that are considered "Noble". These varieties have three things in common. First, they have a mild, pleasant aroma. Secondly, they are low in alpha acids, or bittering compounds. And thirdly, they are identified by their terroir, or the unique conditions of the place where they are grown.

Although there is some disagreement, the following varieties are widely considered to be the 4 Noble hop varieties:

• Hallertauer Mittelfreu (Germany)

• Tettnang (Germany)

• Saaz (Czech Republic)

• Spalt (Germany)

CHILLING

Once the green beer is clear and the trub removed, it needs to be chilled down to a yeast-friendly 70-80° F. Commercial brewers may use a heat exchanger, or device where cold water and hot green beer pass through a series of thin metal pipes, and passively exchange heat without touching in the same way a radiator heats a room. Smaller producers may also use immersion chillers or other means. With any method, it is crucial that the green beer and everything that comes in contact with it be perfectly sterile. During this time, the green beer is often oxygenated to allow the yeast to quickly begin fermentation. Oxygen is added using either an in-line injection type or bubbling apparatus in the fermenter. Alternatively, a healthy yeast starter can accelerate the time of fermentation and eliminate the need for oxygenation of the green beer, which risks creating oxidized flavors in the final beer.

FERMENTING

The green beer is transferred to a sterile, temperature-controlled fermenting tank. The appropriate yeast culture is added, or pitched into the green beer. Within 48 hours, primary fermentation begins and will last anywhere from 1 to 3 weeks, depending on the fermentation temperatures, the style of beer, and the amount of available sugars for the yeast.

YEAST

Yeast is a single-celled fungus that is essential to fermentation. Brewers will say that "Brewers don't make beer, yeast does. Unhappy yeast means bad beer." Yeast cells produce alcohol and added natural carbonation to beer. Although the results of yeast growth have long been appreciated in bread making and brewing, it was not until 1876 that Louis Pasteur first described the role of yeast in fermentation.

Yeast reproduce by budding, or cloning themselves. As a result, yeast cultures will change, or "drift" over time, changing the flavors of the beer. For this reason, commercial brewers will preserve pure versions of their yeasts in secure locations to refresh their yeast cultures at regular intervals.

To a great degree, the strain of yeast in brewing determines the type and style of beer. **The choice of yeast strain used is based upon several factors:**
- Preferred fermentation temperature range
- Degree of **attenuation,** or how much of the sugar will be converted to alcohol, versus how much will be left as the body of the beer
- Flavors produced by the yeast, including **esters, phenols,** and other flavors
- How well the yeast **flocculates,** or settles out of the beer after fermentation. Certain styles of beer are meant to be hazy, while others are meant to be clear.

Although there are innumerable variations and strains, beer yeasts are generally classified into three categories: ales (Saccharomyces cerevisiae, lagers (Saccharomyces carlsbergensis), and wild (various strains of Brettanomyces).
- **Ale yeasts** work quickly (7-10 days) at warmer temperatures (between 50° and 70° F), thus the carbon dioxide is less dissolved and tends to push the yeast to the top of the tank. *See 7.4.* This creates a floating bubbling mass of yeast that protects the fermenting wort from oxygen and bacteria, allowing for the traditional open vat fermentations. Ale breweries would then harvest, or crop this yeast from the vessel to use for future batches. Ale yeasts tend to produce fruity esters (aromatic compounds reminiscent of bananas or bubble gum) in the beer.

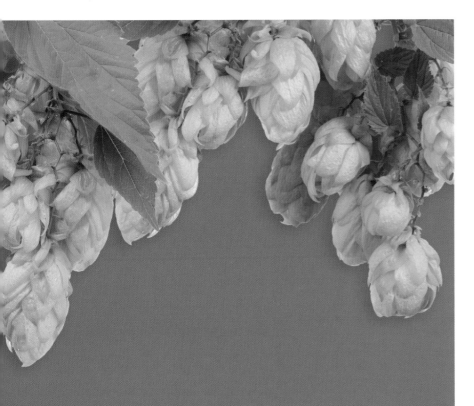

Other varieties, often considered Noble include:
- Fuggles (UK)
- Kent Goldings (UK)
- Liberty (US)
- Mt. Hood (US)

7.4 Yeast + sugar = alcohol + CO2
Note the froth from the fermentation's CO2.

Real **Ales**

In the UK and now across the U.S., craft brewers often produce what are known as **Real Ales,** which are **cask-conditioned.** These ales complete their fermentation in a 9-gallon cask (known as a **Firkin**), although they can also be found in other containers *(see 'Beer Packaging').* They are served either from above by gravity or by a siphon pump called a **beer engine** that gently pumps the ale leaving a thick, creamy head. *(See Styles of Beer)* These ales are served unfiltered, and with only the gentle natural carbonation from fermentation. The relatively short shelf life (3 -5 days after tapping) makes these Cask Ales a beer lover's treat. Traditional styles served in Cask include the lower-alcohol **"Session Beers",** like Mild (a Brown ale) or Ordinary Bitter (a Pale Ale). Today; however, a variety of styles are served in this method. For more information on the many festivals that feature cask ales in the UK and across the U.S., visit the site for CAMRA (The Campaign for Real Ale).

- **Lager yeasts** ferment at cooler temperatures (40-50° F) and thus ferment more slowly. A period of 2-3 weeks for primary fermentation is common, during which time the yeast consumes more thoroughly, leaving a cleaner beer with no esters or yeast-derived flavors.
- **Wild yeasts,** such as **Brettanomyces,** generally work in conjunction with bacteria such as Lactobacillus and Pediococcus, commonly used for other fermented foods like chocolate, soy, or kimchi. The flavors of wild yeast cultures are very much a part of the terroir of specific beers, such as the famous Belgian Lambics. Sour and Barrel-aged beers are now becoming popular across the world, with many craft breweries making exceptional examples. The acids and flavors created by these yeast cultures give the finished beer a tanginess that makes it easy to pair with foods.

LAGERING AND CONDITIONING

At the end of fermentation, the beer is chilled, causing the yeast to flocculate at the bottom of the tank. It is then racked to a bright beer tank, which allows the beer to further clarify and permits its flavors to subtly combine known as conditioning. In the secondary tank, or bright beer tank, gravity helps to further clarify ales. For lagers, the conditioning process occurs at a cold temperature, around 40° F and is known as **lagering,** during which time the lager yeast scavenges remaining sugars and other compounds. This process may last for several weeks to several months, which makes lager beer more expensive and time-consuming to produce for small brewers.

Many beers are bottle-conditioned where they undergo a slight secondary fermentation for carbonation and leave a small yeast sediment visible in the bottle. These beers must be served carefully so as not to rouse the sediment.

PRIMING

The process of adding additional sugars to a beer to induce a secondary fermentation is known as priming. Most commercially produced beers, including craft beers, generally do not undergo priming but instead are filtered and force carbonated before packaging. Priming with corn sugar (dextrose) or other sugar sources is most commonly done with bottle-conditioned beers *(see above).*

Some traditional lager brewers **kräusen** their beers: a process in which sweet unfermented green beer is added to the lagering beer to cause a secondary fermentation and refresh the supply of nutrients for the yeast. This also allows for more consistency from batch to batch but requires that the brewer make the same style of beer from batch to batch.

Beer Labeling

Draft/Draught; If a malt beverage label contains this on the label, it means the product has not been pasteurized or some other method of removing or inhibiting the growth of bacteria has been done.

Brand Name: This name must not be misleading in any way as to the age, origin, identity, or characteristics of the malt beverage.

Lite/Low-Carb/Light; A malt beverage can be labeled with caloric representation or low carbohydrate as long as a statement of average analysis appears on the label.

Government Warning: Required to be on all beverages sold in the United States that contain alcohol.

Class Designation; The brand label must say the class designation of the malt beverage product. See section on Beer Styles for examples.

Alcohol Content; Each state varies on its laws pertaining to the requirements.

Country of Origin; As regulated by the U.S. Customs and Border Protection, a County of Origin state is required on containers of imported Malt Beverage.

The name and address of the bottler and/or the importer

Net Content: Must be displayed in English units of measure.

Beer **Packaging**

Beer production in the U.S. is measured in a unit called a barrel, or 31 U.S. gallons, but consumers cannot buy a **barrel** of beer. Instead, beer is commonly sold in 12-ounce cans and bottles, as well as the following formats:

- A **Keg** is a half-barrel, or 15.5 gallons (1984 ounces, or about 165 12-ounce servings)
- A **Half-Keg** is a quarter barrel, or 7.75 gallons
- The **Firkin** is the traditional 9-gallon cask used for cask-conditioned ales
- Soda Kegs/Cornelius Kegs/**Logs** are the straight 5-gallon kegs used by home brewers and now craft breweries, due to their space-saving features and ease of transport.
- **Growlers** are the half-gallon (64 oz.) glass jugs traditionally sold at Brew Pubs and craft breweries and filled fresh from the tap. Recently, some states have allowed for growlers to be filled at retail stores as well.
- **Bombers** are the 22 oz. bottles becoming popular for specialty beers and bottle-conditioned ales.

The **Beer Can**

The first use of cans to package beer was in 1933, by the Kreuger Beer Company, quickly followed by Pabst and others. The use of cans for beer took decades to develop, due to reactions of the beer with the metal, which required designing a special lining and the need to contain up to 80 lbs. of pressure of carbonation. Since then, beer cans have become widespread, as the package offers great savings in shipping weight and storage, as well as a larger surface area for marketing than a typical bottle label. Cans also give 100% protection from light, less oxygenation, and less breakage than glass bottles. When craft beers first hit the market, brown bottles (to protect hop flavors from light) were perceived as indicating higher quality beers, and cans were seen as identifying cheap beers. But now, much in the same way that screw cap closures are seen on high-quality wines, many craft breweries have opted to can some or all of their production to preserve quality, and consumers are recognizing the many benefits of canned beer.

Beer Styles

A beer style *(See 7.5 Styles of Beer)* is comprised of a set of objectively-measurable parameters (such as color and alcohol content) as well as commonly perceived descriptors for aroma, flavor and mouthfeel. Other aspects of a style's definition include ingredients and traditional production methods. Although many beers will label themselves as one style or another, the world-recognized standard for these definitions is by far the Beer Judge Certification Program, or BJCP. Their published guidelines (newly-revised in 2014) are used as a basis for comparison for beers in competition and are referred to for legal labeling parameters. Their full guidelines can be accessed for free on their website at www.bjcp.org.

The Bock Story

Legend has it that a duke from Saxony brought an especially strong malty lager beer to Bavaria (southern Germany) from Einbeck. In the local Bavarian accent, "Einbecker" sounded like "Einbock", or "one goat". The name was eventually shortened to **Bock,** and these stronger styles of beer usually carry the symbol of the goat on their label.

Monks began brewing this strong Bock style as "liquid bread" to sustain them during Lent. Double-strength beers were called Doppelbocks and carry two goats on their label. In the city of Munich, the monks in the order of St. Francis of Paula founded the Paulaner brewery in 1634, and named their Bock beer "Salvator" or "The Saviour", in reference to its sustaining qualities. Other brands may now feature the "-ator" ending on their names in reference to this classic beer.

The Bock family of styles has several members:

- **Bock** is a slightly stronger and maltier version of a lager, very smooth with no hop flavor.

- **Doppelbock** is stronger, darker and maltier, and often sweeter and more full-bodied.

- **Tripelbock** is lighter in color and body than a Doppelbock but higher in alcohol.

- **Weizenbock** is a type of Bavarian wheat-based beer with the richness of a bock.

- **Maibock** is lighter in body, amber in color and higher in alcohol.

- **Eisbock** is created by first brewing a Doppelbock, and then freezing and removing the water content, to create a very high-alcohol brew indeed.

ALES

BROWN ALES

Brown Ales are the oldest style of beer, since early malting practices were imprecise, resulting in mostly darker malts. Brown styles of ales include Porters and Nut Brown Ales. Porters were named after the dock workers who drank this full-bodied malty style with their everyday staple food, oysters. Nut Brown Ales contain no nuts, as the name refers to its color, and they are lighter bodied than their Porter cousins.

PALE ALES

Pale Ales became popular when the use of glass drinking vessels by the wealthy allowed them to see their beers. Thus, paler malts and Pale Ales became fashionable. The category of Bitters (Ordinary, Standard and Extra Special Bitter) are examples of pale ales that are more malt-focused but with a hint of hop crispness on the finish. India Pale Ale (see Sidebar) has become the most popular of the Pale Ale styles.

STOUTS

Stouts are a family of dark brown to black styles that were originally just a darker version of Porters. Today; however, they range from the light-bodied Dry Stout,to the lactose-enhanced Sweet/Milk Stout, to the cookie-like Oatmeal Stout, and the high-alcohol intensely-flavored Russian Imperial Stout.

WHEAT ALES

Wheat Ales, often called White Ales, are made with a 25-75% wheat base and tend to be lighter in color. Styles include the Bavarian Hefeweizen, which is an unfiltered wheat beer with strong banana and clove esters from the yeast. American Wheat beers range in flavor, generally lack these banana and clove esters, and may have moderate to strong hop aromas. They are often sold as Summer Ales and have fruit flavors added. The German Berliner Weisse is a sour, low-alcohol wheat beer that is served with the addition of fruit syrups to balance the natural acidity. Belgian Wit is made with unmalted wheat, coriander, and orange peel (See Belgian Beers).

BELGIAN

Belgium has a long history of brewing unique, flavorful beers. Located at a cultural crossroads, Belgium shares bits of its language, architecture and cuisine with all of its neighbors – England, France, Germany and Holland. Their brewing traditions and beer styles also draw on a variety of influences yet remain uniquely Belgian. Unlike England and Germany, Belgian beer laws do not restrict the type or quantities of ingredients used in brewing, control brewing methods, or regulate labeling terms or style definitions. As a result, Belgian brewers craft a plethora of one-of-a-kind beers as part of their gastronomy.

BIÈRE DE GARDE

As the name suggests, this style is most common in the southern Wallonia province, nearer to France. Literally "Beer for Keeping", these are rather strong, intensely flavored beers that improve with bottle age. Many are vintage-dated and sought by collectors. Also known as "Farmhouse Ales", this is more of a 'catch-all' style, since most of these beers are unique to the brewery and vary greatly.

WIT

A style of Wheat beer that uses unmalted wheat and adjunct flavorings of coriander, orange peel, and other such spices and herbs and sometimes known as "Belgian Wheat." Although this style is often copied in the US, the authentic Belgian version is more subtle.

SAISON

The name means "season" and applies to the summer season for which they are designed. The wheat base makes them crisp and refreshing, but the deceptively high alcohol (due to candi sugar additions) allows them to withstand the warmer storage conditions. Spices and fruits of all sorts can be added for variety, and this style is also widely copied in the U.S.

SOUR

Sour beer styles are brewed around the world, but Belgium has the greatest diversity of traditional sour styles. Utilizing wild (feral) yeast strains and souring bacteria, these styles require months and even years of aging before bottling and continue to improve in bottle.

FLEMISH RED ALES

From the northern area around Flanders, these barrel-aged specialties have very complex malt flavors and improve with age.

OUD BRUIN (FLEMISH BROWN)

Unlike the red version, the brown is not barrel aged but instead features earthy, roasty malt character.

LAMBICS

Named after the Belgian town of Lembeek, the Lambic family of sour beers are fermented for over a year in oak casks. Most are packaged with a cork and cage, like Champagne.

STRAIGHT LAMBIC

This unblended style is very sour and is generally served in local brasseries, often blended to balance the acid.

FRUIT LAMBIC

After primary fermentation in a barrel, fresh fruits are added to the casks for a second fermentation, giving the beer their acidity, flavor, and color, while boosting the alcohol level. This style is very appealing to wine drinkers, is now readily available in the U.S., and is an easy partner with many rich foods. Common flavors include Framboise (raspberry), Kriek (sour cherry), Cassis (black currant), and Pêche (peach). Geuze—This is a fractionally-blended style of Lambic where new beer is added to older beer to increase the acidity and alcohol. The result is an extremely sour style with the flavors of both a Fino Sherry and Champagne.

LAGERS

PILSNER

Pilsner hails from the Czech city of Pilzn, where the soft, neutral ground-water allows the delicate Moravian malts and Saaz hops to shine through. A similar style, German Pils, uses German malts and either Tettnang or Hallertau hops. American Pilsner was all but lost after Prohibition but has now been resurrected by many craft brewers across the country, utilizing American malts and hop varieties.

AMERICAN LIGHT LAGERS

American Light Lagers contain a high-proportion of unmalted adjunct grains, like corn and rice. Little to no hop flavors are used, and thus must be served cold to be refreshing. Although they are light in body and flavor, they typically contain more calories than a Dry Stout, which makes the lightest versions even more appealing. Malt Liquor is a higher alcohol version that uses corn sugars to boost alcohol cheaply.

OKTOBERFEST

Oktoberfest is both a style of lager beer and an enormous annual event in Munich (see History page 83). The style is complex and malty with a hint of Hallertau hops and a refreshing, clean finish. Like Kölsch (see below), the Oktoberfest name can only be used by the breweries found within the Munich city limits. Similar styles from outside this area are labeled as Märzen (brewed in March) or simply Festbier. Vienna is a similar style but usually lighter bodied and slightly roastier. Ironically, the Vienna style is rarely brewed in Vienna anymore and is more likely to be found in Mexican breweries like Negra Modelo.

BOCK

Bock is a family of beer styles described in detail in the sidebar, page 90.

SCHWARZBIER

Schwarzbier is also known as Black Lager and has the roasty flavors of a stout without the bitterness, paired with the clean light body of a lager.

RAUCHBIER

Rauchbier is a unique style from the German city of Bamberg, where Beech-smoked malts are used to brew a malty Märzen style that has the intense smokiness of bacon.

HYBRID STYLES OF BEER

ALT BIER

The German word *Alt* means "Old" and refers to ales produced before the evolution of lagers. Alt is made with an ale yeast fermented at lager temperatures, which results in a lighter, smoother beer with no fruity esters.

KÖLSCH

According to the World Trade Organization, is a beer can only bear the name if it originates in the German city of Cologne. This style, however, is very popular among American craft brewers, since it is lighter and crisper than an alt. Both Alt and Kolsch are ale yeasts fermented at lager temperatures.

CALIFORNIA COMMON

This is an American invention made famous by Anchor Brewing Company in San Francisco. Their "Steam Beer" is brewed with a lager yeast fermented at ale temperatures because during the times of the Gold Rush, German immigrants did not have artificial refrigeration in the California Sierras. The beer's name is derived from the observation of the high carbonation levels, or misty "steam" that arose from a freshly-opened cask.

CREAM ALE

Once a very popular style among American brewers, Cream Ales fell by the wayside, survived only by Genessee. Today craft brewers have resurrected the style, which features a light lager beer augmented with a little bit of stock ale for body and smoothness. It contains no cream or lactose and is not an ale, thus the name can be misleading.

What is a
Trappist beer?

Trappists are Franciscan monks who produce and sell a variety of agricultural products – cheese, wool —
to support their monasteries. Although many beers will call themselves "Abbey style", six of these breweries
are in Belgium, one in Austria, one in France, two in the Netherlands, and as of 2013, one in the United States.

The styles of beer vary but most are made with candi sugar additions, which result in high-alcohol styles for
aging. They include a **Belgian Blonde Ale, Dubbel** (malty and dark), **Tripel** (lighter color, but higher alcohol),
and **Belgian Golden Strong** and **Belgian Dark Strong,** as well as many unique specialty beers like **Quadrupels.**
These Trappist beers are some of the most highly sought after and expensive beers in the world.

Sensory Analysis *of* Beer

Beer judges must be able to describe what is present in a sample as well as what is absent, as the lack of many taste and flavor compounds can be strong indicators of a beer style. In addition, a beer judge must be well versed in the intricacies of the brewing process, as every twist and turn can be tasted in the final product. Beer analysis also requires detailed description of the textural, or tactile aspects, especially carbonation. As a result, professional beer tasters do not expectorate (spit); however, the lower alcohol levels of most beers mean that there is less interference upon the taster's judgment than with wine. (At Johnson & Wales University, students are required to expectorate at all in-class tastings).

SETTING UP FOR TASTING BEER

Analysis should be in a bright, well-lit room, preferably with ample amounts of natural light rather than fluorescent. Many professional tasters will also bring their own small flashlight to help assess the clarity of some very dark samples.

The room should be clean and free of any distracting noise or ambient aromas, with either white tablecloths or large sheets of white paper on the table. Sensory analysis forms should be clear and easy to read, and mechanical pencils are preferred to standard ones to prevent the smell of the graphite from interfering with the tasting process.

A dump bucket in the center of the table is also used when opening samples in case of any excess foaming or gushing and for disposing of leftover samples. Clean napkins or towels should also be on hand in case of spills, and neutral bread or crackers should be used between samples to cleanse the palate.

Beer glassware comes in a wide variety of shapes and sizes, each meant to accentuate the particular virtues of a specific style. These traditional glasses are key to the enjoyment of a beer, *see 7.6,* and one should never consume beer straight from a bottle or can, as that would eliminate the perception of aromas and flavors. But, since any glassware is rarely "beer clean" (see Beer Service), professional beer tasters and judges at competitions always use clear, rigid, sterile disposable plastic cups, to ensure that no detergent or other residues interfere with the samples.

THE TASTING PROCESS

Beer tasting begins with a sniff. This is because many of beer's aromas can be fleeting, and the professional taster or judge needs to glean as much information from the sample as possible. With a quick sniff, tasters will assess the intensity of the aromas and distinguish the amount and type of malt and hop aromas. Ales may have estery aromas from the yeast, and some beers will have spicy or smoky phenols, **diacetyl** (buttery) aromas, and more. Many aged beers may have dried fruit or candied aromas and toasty, roasty or nutty aromas from malt. And hop aromas – ranging from spicy and floral, to zesty, citrusy and fruity, to earthy, woodsy or herbal – can help to identify the origin and style of a beer.

Next, the taster will assess the appearance of the sample. Colors of beers range from whitish to dark black and are generally described on a scale of 1-50, according to **SRM** (Standard Reference Method). The color should correspond to the stated style of beer. Clarity is noted, and some styles, such as bottle-conditioned or wheat-based beers, are normally hazy. The head should also be examined for the color, texture, and persistence of the foam. Insufficient head may indicate a flat or stale beer, a higher-alcohol sample, or unclean glassware *See 7.7*. The level of carbonation should also be visible and will vary according to the style of beer.

7.6 The right glass for a beer enhances flavor, aroma, and appearance.

7.7 A head of foam is an inviting sight, which also keeps the beer fresher longer.

Unlike wine, two sips are needed to assess a beer. The first sip should be used to identify flavors, such as the amount and type of malt and hop flavors, as well as any esters, diacetyl, or other flavors. Tasters should note any sweetness or bitterness, as well as the balance, character, and length of the finish. Acidity is more noticeable in wheat-based beers, but in all styles of beers, it adds to the refreshing quality of the beer's finish.

A second sip will be used to assess the mouthfeel or texture of the sample, including the body or weight of the sample, the effervescence or carbonation level, and hop **astringency**. Hop bitterness is commonly stated on a label in **IBUs**, or international bittering units. But this is in relation to Gravity Units, or sugar levels. **Creaminess** and **warmth** levels should also be noted.

Finally, overall impressions include general drinking pleasure, trueness to style (if known), potential food pairings, and comparisons to other styles or brands. The quality level is often difficult for beginners to assess, but with experience, tasters can determine the relative value of samples as well. In this section, judges will also make recommendations to the brewer on ways to improve the recipe or brewing process to better fit the indicated style or to achieve better balance of flavor.

STORING BEER

There is a myth that all beer is highly perishable and must be consumed as fresh as possible, in the same way that there is a myth that all wine improves with age. The truth is for beers, wines, and more, age and maturity are related but separate things.

Most beer is ready to be consumed as soon as it is released by the brewery and will taste best as close to that date as possible. Pasteurized beer has a shelf life of about three months. Certain styles, however, such as the highly-hopped India Pale Ales or bottle conditioned beers with yeast sediment can last longer. IPAs will lose their hoppy aromas and flavors over time, becoming more subtle and malty. Higher-alcohol styles - such as Doppelbocks, Barleywines or Bière de Garde - can actually improve with age for a year or more.

Although dark bottles are preferred to minimize the effects of UV light, a dark storage container or environment is even better. High temperatures, or temperature fluctuations will also reduce the beer's shelf life and lead to oxidized or stale beer with a cooked flavor. Ideal temperature ranges are between 50°F–55°F (10°C–13°C).

Serving beer using a draft system can save a restaurant a considerable amount of money in terms of profitability and storage space but requires diligence in sanitation of the draft system and glassware. The use of draft systems, however, can limit the number of offerings due to the size of the kegs and need for more refrigeration space. Unpasteurized and draft beers keep only two or three weeks and must be kept refrigerated at all times. Once a keg or cask of beer has been tapped, it should be consumed within a few days. For styles that are less popular, restaurateurs should use smaller kegs, or only serve bottles.

Beer **Faults**

Identifying off aromas and flavors in beer can be tricky, as what may be appropriate in one style of beer would be considered a fault in another.

Here are some of the more common beer faults:

Skunkiness occurs when isomerized hop compounds in a finished beer are exposed to blue light, such as sunlight or fluorescent lights and change into sulfury skunk aromas. Light colored beers, or those in clear or green glass bottles are very susceptible to becoming "light struck". For many years, American consumers mistakenly thought that all European lagers were supposed to taste skunky because they inevitably were subjected to poor shipping and storage conditions. Dark-colored beer, or dark glass bottles or cans, offer good protection. Many large domestic brewers use only hop extracts with no hop aroma for their light beers if packaged in clear glass.

Oxidation can occur at various points in the brewing process, and brewers are careful to avoid it. But oxidation can also happen in finished beer in package. Faulty packaging is one source of oxidation, but age is the usual culprit. If a beer oxidized, it may smell like cardboard or wet paper, and it may be darker in color than it should be.

Vegetal aromas, such as cabbage or broccoli are undesirable and usually indicate the use of stale hops. It may also indicate poor sanitation in the packaging process.

Diacetyl or buttery aromas and flavors can be acceptable in certain beer styles in small amounts. If it is a pronounced buttery flavor, then it is likely due to contamination during the packaging process. The most common source of uncharacteristic buttery flavors is unclean tap lines, which remain a problem throughout the industry.

DMS (Dimethyl Sulfide) is the flavor and aroma of creamed corn. It is usually a result of stale or low-quality grains or improper kettling techniques. It can be avoided by (ideally) choosing fresh high-quality ingredients, undertaking a multiple-step mash, and/or ensuring that the wort remains at a full rolling boil, uncovered, throughout the kettling process.

Acetic Acid is produced by acetic bacteria, which are present in the air around us. These bacteria consume alcohol and convert it to acetic acid, more commonly known as vinegar. Acetic acid is highly volatile and thus can be detected easily by smell. It is usually a result of contamination during fermentation and/or packaging.

Brettanomyces is the wild yeast family that is used to produce the famous sour Lambics of Belgium and many other sour beers worldwide. In those beers, it can add a complexity and subtleness, but in styles where it is inappropriate, it may smell or taste like smokiness or earthiness.

Serving Beer

There are five aspects of a well-served beer: serving temperature, appropriate glassware, sanitation of glassware and tap lines, proper pouring techniques, and appropriate representation and sales description.

Temperature Each beer style has an appropriate serving temperature to maximize its enjoyment. Contrary to popular belief, ice-cold beer is designed to numb the palate to prevent tasting the beer, not to enhance it. Typical serving temperatures for light-bodied lagers and wheat ales are around 40° F. Serving temperatures for malty, English ales are usually around 50° F, or cellar temp. Certain full-bodied or higher-alcohol styles can be served even warmer, depending on the season and food accompaniment.

Glassware Traditional glassware choices for certain styles of beer are based upon several criteria. The volume of the glass should match the alcohol content of the beer. A 12% ABV Barleywine, for instance, does not belong in a 16 oz. pint but would be better served in a 6 oz. snifter. And the wide mouth of a stemmed goblet for an Abbey Dubbel allows the taster to enjoy the delicate complexity of the aromas, while avoiding warming from the drinker's hands. A smaller size glass is also used for the Kölsch style, called a 'stange', to keep the beer cold, crisp, and refreshing.

A narrow type of glass is also designed to support the delicate head of light styles of beer, such as Pilsner. The Hefeweizen Vase is very tall with a wide mouth to hold the large frothy head of this unfiltered style. The dimpled glass stein, used for Munich Dunkel or Oktoberfest, is made of thick glass (not stone, as the name implies) to hold the temperature of the beer. The dimples in the glass help to accentuate the colors of the beer as well.

Sanitation In the same way that you would never serve food on a dirty plate, all glassware for beer service must be **"beer clean,"** or free of any detergent, oil residues, or scratches of any kind. Glasses for beer service should never be washed with plates or other dishes or in standard ware washing machines. Instead, all beer glasses should be washed in a separate machine or hand-washed and air-dried. A quick rinse before service with cold water or a small amount of the beer to be served may also be appropriate.

There are several ways to test for "beer clean" glasses. First, visually inspect the glass for food particles, lipstick, or other debris. Once the beer is poured into the glass, there should be no bubbles forming on the inside of the glass. If there are, this indicates the presence of scratches or debris inside the glass that may have been invisible. Filling and emptying the glass with water is called the sheeting test. If there are spots inside the glass where the water does not sheet, this indicates contamination. The salt test will show any greasy deposits. First rinse the glass with water, and then coat the inside with salt. If there are spots where the salt does not stick, then they contain oils or detergents. Finally, when drinking a beer, you can conduct the lace test. With each sip, a thin even ring of foam should be left around the inside of the glass. If not, then the glass is not clean.

Draft Maintenance Proper design is the first step to maintaining a clean, efficient draft system. Draft lines, which run between the keg and the tap should be relatively short. Every foot of draft line contains only up to an ounce or so of beer, depending on the diameter of the line. This small amount of beer will get flushed out with each cleaning. But each foot of line represents 12 inches of potential bacteria and contamination that can cost gallons of wasted beer in the form of foam down the drain and unhappy customers. In some states, the owner is required to pay a licensed contractor to come in at regular intervals to clean and tag the draft lines. In other states, the distributor is required to perform this task. However, it is ultimately the owner's responsibility to ensure that the system is functioning efficiently and cleanly.

Pouring Techniques How a beer is poured, whether from tap or bottle, will affect your customer's enjoyment. When pouring from a tap, the faucet handle should be grasped at the base and pulled fully open. The glass should be held at a 45° angle ½ inch below the level of the spout. The tip of the spout should never come in contact with the beer. Once the glass is half full, turn the glass upright and continue to fill the glass, so there will be ½ inch to 1 inch of foam on the top. Highly carbonated and unfiltered beers will have more foam, and the pour should be adjusted accordingly. When serving beer from the bottle, the server should ask customers if they would like to pour it themselves. If the server is pouring, most beers can be poured straight down the center of the glass and should produce the correct amount of foam. Certain styles (IPA, Hefeweizen) may need additional care as these have more foam.

For bottle conditioned beers, pour gradually, and leave the last half-ounce of sediment behind in the bottle. For larger format (22 oz. or larger) bottle conditioned beers, pour all servings at the same time without lifting the bottle between pours, as this would rouse the sediment.

Sales More than ever, having an educated sales staff is critical to success with beer, whether on- or off-premise. Your service staff must be able to accurately describe and recommend beers to your customers. Any menus or lists also need to be accurate and helpful to the customer. "Progressive" beer lists, which arrange the selections by style or flavor instead of origin, are becoming more common for this reason but do not replace the need for trained employees. Many distributors will offer staff training programs for their customers, but these will be based on the offerings of that distributor. Professional organizations, such as the Cicerone© program, are gaining recognition worldwide for their training and certifications.

Send it Back!!!

A customer may send back a beer for a variety of reasons. If the beer was served at the wrong temperature or in a dirty glass, it should automatically be sent back. If a visual inspection shows any haze or cloudiness in a style for which it is not appropriate, this likely means contamination. A beer that has any off aromas (see Beer Faults) should also be sent back immediately. If dirty tap lines are suspected, try looking at the bottled selections for a replacement. Excessive foaming (gushing) or lack of foam are also indicators of poor beer handling and/or sanitation. And if the beer is not as the server or menu described it, replace it with something else. Many restaurants and bars also serve flights of beer to allow the guest to sample 4- 8 different styles in smaller portions.

The Role *of* Beer *in* Cuisine

Beer has been an integral component in many cuisines throughout history, and it still is today. Beer was served throughout the day, considered healthful and nutritious, and was served with any meal for any occasion. In addition, beer was a staple item in the kitchen and a useful and tasty addition to many recipes.

PAIRING BEER WITH FOOD

Pairing beer and food is not a new idea, as witnessed by thousands of years of human history. Today, more restaurants are offering beer pairing dinners to meet the increasing demand, and employers are seeking candidates with beer and food pairing knowledge and experience.

The growing variety of beers available on the market provides consumers with a world of choices and combinations to explore. Even though the success of any particular pairing is always a matter of personal taste, there are some guidelines that can help one find a successful pairing.

First, look at historical pairings for inspiration. Oftentimes, these pairings evolved over many years of trial and error and can form a good basis to start from. Seasonal pairings are also a great clue. Understanding the principles that make that pairing work will assist in finding new matches.

Here are some factors to consider:
- The **body of the beer** should complement the weight of the food. A heavy, malty barkeywine has no place next to a stuffed fillet of sole.
- Although all beer is acidic, and carbonation is a natural palate cleanser, **sour or acidic** beers can cut through fatty or rich foods like stews or foie gras, or rinse away salty foods like bacon, or hold up to acidic foods such as a boulliabase.
- **Dominant flavors** of the beer should marry (not dominate, compete, or mirror) the flavors of the food. Having a very smoky Rauchbier with a smoky barbecue obscures the best features of each. A creamy mild cheese, on the other hand, or a cassoulet will benefit from the contrasting smokiness of the beer.
- **Alcohol content** is also a factor to keep in mind, especially as it relates to the occasion. A Double IPA would not be a good choice for a luncheon pairing. Higher-alcohol beers can also emphasize spicy flavors in food.

- **Hop bitterness** in a beer is surprisingly easily tamed by many fatty foods, and herbal or citrusy hop flavors can pair nicely with fresh vegetables. But beware - the heat of chili peppers or curry is amplified by hop bitterness, making for an exciting pairing indeed.
- **Malt bitterness** in a stout, for instance, can be tamed in either of two ways. A match with chocolate cake emphasizes the malt flavors and lowers the bitterness. Alternatively, salty foods such as cheddar cheese or oysters will enhance the sweetness of the malt, offsetting any bitterness.
- **Dominant flavors,** especially those of adjuncts like blueberries or chipotle peppers, should always be considered.

More Fermented Beverages

There have been, and still are, many other fermented beverages that have evolved over the millennia, from **tej** in Ethiopia, to **chicha** in the Amazon, to **pulque** in Central America, or **kvass** in Russia and Ukraine.

Some of these historical fermented beverages have found a niche in the US, especially among the younger generation and the urban hipster crowd. But still other categories – gluten-free beers, ciders and perries, sakes and meads – are growing very rapidly, and the demand shows no sign of slowing.

GLUTEN-FREE BEER

With the rising rates of Celiac's Disease, gluten sensitivity, and people choosing to eat a **gluten-free** diet, there is a growing demand and a booming market for gluten-Free beers. Although there are many ways to ferment gluten-free ingredients, getting them to taste like beer is the real challenge brewers face. Another is cross contamination from their conventional brewing equipment and ingredients. For this reason, more gluten-free **contract breweries** have opened allowing craft brewers to add a gluten-free option to their lineup of beers without investing in the additional equipment and facilities.

Gluten-free beers are made around the world and also tend to be quite expensive ranging in price from $10 per 6-pack to $6 per bottle. Ingredients used for these 'beers' include spelt, malted buckwheat (which is a legume, not a grain), chestnuts, sorghum, rice, corn, and cane sugar. The inclusion of hops varies, as ingredients such as buckwheat already have a natural bitterness, so hop bitterness is not desired. Many other gluten-free brews add fruit flavors to make them more appealing. All ingredients including amylase enzyme and any yeast strain must be certified gluten-free as well.

Some products are also labeled as **"gluten reduced,"** but not gluten-free. This is achieved by the use of a clarifying agent that removed suspended proteins, including gluten proteins, from a finished beer. In this way, the brewer simply follows a standard beer recipe and removes gluten afterwards. Whether or not these gluten-reduced beers are safe for an individual, however, is not part of the brewer's realm. Thus, consumers should consult their doctors before consumption if they are not sure.

CIDERS AND PERRIES

In America, the term **cider** usually refers to unfiltered, non-fermented apple juice. In traditional Europe; however, the term cider refers to the fermented apple beverage. If pears are used, the product will be called a **perry.** Since ciders are made from apples, they are technically a type of wine and are naturally gluten-free. Many ciders, however, are relatively low in alcohol, refreshing, and served on draft in pubs and restaurants. Ciders and perries are also usually packaged in 12 oz.

bottles and sold in 6-packs, which is why they are often marketed and displayed alongside beers.

Many craft breweries are now producing ciders as part of their product line, and these can be found across the country during any season. There is also a growing variety of imported ciders available in bottles and on draft. Due to the acidity, ciders make excellent partners with many foods, especially fall flavors.

During the early days of colonial America, cider was the principal drink made at local orchards and farms. Colonial cider consumption is estimated to have been over 35 gallons per capita annually, approximately 10 times our current wine consumption. Once populations began to center in cities, the market for fresh ciders was eventually replaced by beer, which could be freshly brewed in the cities. During Prohibition, Americans lost many of our heirloom apple varieties that were grown specifically for cider production, because entire orchards were cut down for fear that they would be used for fermented ciders.

There are many different styles of ciders and perries. They can be still or sparkling, dry, medium or sweet, and range in alcohol levels from 4.5% to 14.5% in a New England style cider.

Flavors can range from fruity to austere and smoky, and many also feature the tannic aspects of the skins. They can bear the name of the variety of apple or pear or have spices or other fruits blended in. Some even undergo a double Champagne-style fermentation, while others are aged in used Bourbon barrels or fortified with molasses or brown sugar.

SAKE

Sake is a fermented rice beverage most often associated with Japan, although versions are found throughout the Far East. Documented history of Sake brewing goes back to 2000 BCE, and traditional sake-drinking customs are still an important part of the Shinto religion. Commonly called 'rice wine', sake is actually a form of beer because it is made from grain. Unlike beers; however, sake does not use barley or hops, only rice, water and yeast. A similar beverage from Korea, **Soju,** can be made with all rice but sometimes includes tapioca or sweet potato and can be very smooth and refreshing.

Like beer brewing, traditional sake production starts with the water. Many small towns and villages in Japan were home to several sake breweries due to their exceptional water quality. The type of water from a specific region or town will affect the flavors and qualities of the sake much in the way dissolved mineral content in water will impact the style of beer.

The second ingredient is rice, and there are several types of rice that can be used for making sake, including some red rice varieties. This rice is polished to remove the outer layers, which contain fats and tannins from the husk. The finest sakes are made from rice that is milled down to less than half of its original size and use only the very heart of the rice kernel.

Since rice is a grain that does not malt, the starches are converted to fermentable sugars in a different way. First the milled rice is washed and soaked to absorb water. It is then transferred to racks to drain any excess water, and then steamed in a large steamer. The hot rice is removed and spread out with a small rake on cheesecloth and bamboo racks to cool. When it has cooled somewhat, the rice is divided into three portions – koji, shubo and moromi – and each is cooled at the correct temperature.

The koji portion is called such because a type of mold is added to it called **koji** (*aspergillus orizae*), which will break down the starches into fermentable sugars. The koji culturing occurs in the separate koji room at 75-80° F where the rice is turned and the temperature maintained to encourage the mold's growth.

The shubo portion of the steamed rice will have water and yeast added to it as well as some of the koji mixture. It is then stirred and fermentation begins as the yeast culture multiplies.

Finally, the moromi is made when more water, steamed rice, and koji are mixed together and shubo is added. With vigorous stirring, the koji breaks down starch into sugar, and the shubo yeasts will convert sugars to alcohol. Repeated additions of koji and shubo refresh the culture until the alcohol content gradually and naturally builds up to 16%.

When fermentation is complete, the free liquid is drained and the rice is pressed in the traditional "shushibori" method, where in cheesecloth bags of wet rice are stacked on top of each other, allowed to drain, and then restacked. This method is similar to the cheddaring process for cheese. The resulting liquid is known as "funaku-chi". After bottling, it is heat pasteurized to destroy any remaining enzymes and to stabilize the product.

There are many types of sake on the market today, but the highest-quality sakes are perishable, do not travel well, and must be purchased as fresh as possible. These "Junmai" sakes are 100% rice and are graded according to the level of milling of the rice, with Junmai Daigingo having the highest quality rating. Some fine sakes are pink from the use of red rice; unfiltered with a heavy, creamy, cloudy sediment; or even aged in cedar barrels. Fine sakes should be served slightly chilled and sipped slowly to savor their complexities. There are now a growing number of high-quality sake producers in the US. Most Americans, however, are still more familiar with the low-grade sakes. Cheap sake (Honjozu Ginjo) types are made by machine and with the addition of grain alcohol. These are very common in hibachi and sushi restaurants and are served very warm to mask their harsh flavor.

MEAD

The oldest documented fermented beverage in the world is **mead**. Early cave paintings show its accidental discovery and enjoyment. Although mead making can and has been done in all parts of the world, the most northerly climates have the most deeply entrenched mead-drinking traditions. For instance, the term **"Honeymoon"** is derived from the Viking tradition of encouraging newlywed couples to consume mead for the first month, or lunar cycle after marriage, thus (it was observed) ensuring conception.

Once relatively obscure in the United States, mead making has now exploded onto the scene, with **meaderies** opening across the country and specialty craft meads being featured on more and more restaurant lists. Today, meads are quickly being rediscovered by connoisseurs as complex, delicious drinks, and high-quality meads command higher prices, too. Since the primary fermentable ingredient in mead is neither grain nor fruit, but honey, mead is neither a beer nor a wine but in a class of its own.

Mead is produced by diluting honey with clean water to the appropriate consistency or sugar content. The origin of the honey is extremely important, as the types of flowers that are used by bees to produce the honey will have a great impact on the flavor of the fermented mead. Water quality is also of the utmost importance, as it is with beer. Selecting the appropriate yeast strain as well as providing additional yeast nutrients, is key to a healthy fermentation.

Meads come in a wide variety of styles and flavors – sweet or very dry, still, petillant or sparkling, and low to high alcohol. Some will even designate a variety of honey. Other common types of mead include **Melomels,** or meads with additional fruits added. If that fruit is apple, it is known as a **cyser.** If wine grapes are used, it is called a **pyment.** If spices are added, it is known as a **metheglin,** and if malt sugars are used, it becomes a mead/ale hybrid known as a **braggot.**

8. Spirits *and* Liqueurs

Spirits and liqueurs play a key role in the profitability of a food and beverage establishment. They offer both chefs and mixologists the ingredients to create flavorful food or drink recipes for the enjoyment of guests.

Spirits *and* Liqueurs Defined

A **spirit** is a highly alcoholic beverage produced by both fermentation and distillation. Alcoholic distillation is the process by which the alcohol from a fermented liquid is evaporated, captured, and cooled to liquid form. Spirits are made from fermented products such as grapes, sugarcane, apples, potatoes, and grains. The fermented liquids are then distilled to create such spirits as whiskey, brandy, tequila, vodka, and rum.

Liqueurs, also known as **cordials,** are highly refined, sweet spirits to which flavorings such as fruits, nuts, herbs, or spices have been added. They are often enjoyed before dining as apéritifs or after dinner as digestifs. They are also essential parts of many cocktails. Most liqueurs contain between 17% and 30% alcohol by volume, and some may contain as much as 50%.

LIQUOR AND LIQUEURS IN HISTORY

It is not known for sure who discovered the method of distillation or exactly when it occurred. Many experts speculate that the Chinese used distillation as early as 3000 B.C., and this technology traveled the Silk Road to India around 2000 B.C. The ancient Sanskrit texts include a variety of terms for high strength alcoholic beverages. The science of distillation was also known to the Ancient Greeks. Aristotle described distilling seawater to capture freshwater in about 400 B.C., but the first recorded distillation of alcoholic beverages in Europe did not occur until circa 900 A.D.

Culinary Relevance

Cocktails and apéritifs traditionally accompany canapés before dinner, and brandies and liqueurs are served with coffee after dinner. Spirits and liqueurs are indispensable parts of dining for many people.

Unlike wine and beer, spirits are not usually prominent features in the preparation of savory foods, though they are sometimes used as an ingredient in marinades or basting sauces. For tableside dessert preparations and for pastry chefs; however, liquors and liqueurs are invaluable flavoring agents.

THE DISTILLATION PROCESS

Monks and alchemists improved on the process of distillation over the centuries. In 1205, Arnaud de Villeneuve became the first person to distill wine in France. In Great Britain, with the dissolution of the monasteries in the sixteenth century, monks began to share their knowledge with distillers. Over the years, the distillation process has been refined, although the essential process remains basically the same.

Distilling spirits is possible because water and ethyl alcohol, the two primary components of a fermented beverage, have different boiling points. *See 8.1.* Because alcohol and water boil at different temperatures, a distiller can heat a fermented

8.1 A Charentais Pot Still is used in making eau de vie that will become Cognac.

beverage to the boiling point for ethyl alcohol (173°F/78°C), capture the vapor, and then cool it to condense it into liquid alcohol. Water is left behind because of its higher boiling point of 212°F (100°C). The alcohol is vaporized and then recondensed in an apparatus called a still.

All alcoholic beverages fall into one of three categories:
- Fermented beverages made from products such as grains and fruits with alcoholic strengths ranging from 3.2%–15%
- Distilled spirits resulting from a distillation of fermented beverages.
- **Compounded beverages** made by combining either a fermented beverage or spirit with a flavoring agent.

PRODUCTION PROCESSES

There are five potential steps in the production of distilled spirits: mashing (for use with grains), fermenting, distilling, aging or filtering, and blending. For a flavored spirit or liqueur, there is an additional step of compounding.

Mashing

Corn, barley, and rye are the principal grains used in making beverage-quality alcohol. The process begins with milling the grains to break down the hull and to free the starch that will eventually convert to alcohol. The next step is to turn the grain starch into grain sugar by mixing the grain meal with water to form a mash. Barley malt is then added, and the end result is maltose, or grain sugar.

Fermenting

Fermentation begins when yeast is added to the mash. As the yeast grows, it digests the sugar and releases alcohol and carbon dioxide. The yeast multiplies to create grain alcohol, and the alcohol mixes with congeners, or flavoring compounds.

Distilling

When the fermented liquid is heated to vaporize the alcohol, some water and some **congeners** (flavor and aroma compounds) are left behind. When the alcohol vapor is cooled, it condenses into clear ethyl alcohol. When a pot still is used, a **single batch distillation** is not sufficient enough to concentrate the wash into a desirable and potable spirit. *See 8.2.* Therefore, the majority of pot still spirits are redistilled multiple times. It is during the second distillation that the "**heart**" of the spirit is separated from the "**heads**" and "**tails**."

- **Heads** compounds first released at the lowest boiling point; volatile and harmful
- **Heart** middle compounds
- **Potable spirit** ethyl alcohol
- **Tails** compounds released last at higher boiling points

Heads are released at the lowest boiling point (they come off first), while tails release only when the temperatures are at their highest. **Continuous distillation** utilizes a variety of **column stills** fashioned after the Coffey Still was invented in 1827. *See 8.3.* The Coffey Still is comprised of two tall linked columns known as an **analyser** and a **rectifier.** These columns contain a number of perforated plates located at differing heights. The fermented liquid, referred to as the **wash,** is fed into the rectifier column and flows to the analyser column where it is sprayed out over the top plate. Simultaneously, hot steam pumped from the bottom of the analyser rises and strips the alcohol from the wash. The vapor then passes from the top of the analyser to the bottom of the rectifier where it starts to rise through the perforated plates and is fractioned or separated in a continuous motion. This type of distillation produces high proof, highly rectified spirits. At higher proof levels, fewer flavor components called congeners remain and produce a rather harsh neutral spirit.

Aging or Filtering

To mellow the harshness of this clear spirit, the liquid is either aged or filtered. Aging takes place in charred oak barrels that give color and flavor to the spirit, absorb impurities, and mellow the harshness. *See 8.4.* The character of the spirit depends on the aging time. Clear spirits, such as vodka, are filtered in activated charcoal or other systems to mellow them. Higher-quality clear spirits are filtered as many as four or more times.

Blending

After the aging or filtering is completed, the spirits are reduced in **proof,** or percentage of alcohol by volume, to the desired concentration by the addition of demineralized water. In the blending process, spirits of different ages and sometimes from different grains are blended into the final product, which is then bottled and packaged for sale. Once bottled, the product ceases to age or change. *See 8.5.*

The Pot Still

The Continuous or Column Still

Analyser

Rectifier

Heads

Wash

Cold Wash

Vapor

Spirits (liquid)

Steam

Tails

Compounding

The process of compounding blends spirits with other flavorings, including sweeteners. Compounding is achieved through **infusion,** which involves steeping flavoring agents using heat; **maceration,** which steeps them by using a cold method; or **percolation,** which allows the spirit to trickle through a flavoring agent much in the way water trickles through ground coffee, except the process is repeated. Compounding may also be achieved by **redistillation,** which involves distilling a spirit with a flavoring agent; gin, for example, is redistilled with juniper berries. Cold Compounding is adding flavoring to neutral spirits and is the least expensive method for flavoring a spirit.

8.4 Barrels are manufactured from French and American oak staves.

8.5 After aging, whiskeys are blended for uniformity.

QUALITY AND BRANDING

There are basically four sales categories of alcohol beverage products: **generic or value brands, premium brands, high end brands,** and **super-premium or luxury brands.** The price range usually varies by category. For example, Cognacs would fall under the super-premium category even though there is great disparity in pricing between a VS Cognac and a XO Cognac. A greater variation by category exists within American whiskies.

Generic or value brands A category such as "coffee brandy" is a general category of coffee liqueur that any number of companies can produce. A **proprietary brand** such as Kahlúa® is a trademarked name that no one else can replicate. When discussing a spirit such as rum, white rum is the generic category while Bacardi® is proprietary. The pricing of this category tends to be the lowest at under $12.00.

Premium brands Premium brands of spirits or liqueurs are proprietary brands, both domestic and imported, which fall into a higher price range based on their perceived quality and brand recognition. The price range is approximately $12.00 to $18.00 per liter bottle.

High end brands This alcohol category is based on brand recognition and has a price range that is approximately $18.00 - $30.00 per liter bottle.

Super Premium or luxury brands Alcohol brand categories in the greater than $30.00 per liter bottle price range are typically considered the highest quality brands.

AMERICAN WHISKIES

The U.S. government requires that all **whiskies** are made from a grain mash, are distilled at 90% alcohol by volume (ABV) or less, and are reduced to no more than 62.5% ABV (125 proof) before aging in oak barrels. (The exception is corn whiskey, which does not have to be aged in oak.) Whiskies must have the aroma, taste, and characteristics that are generally attributed to whiskey and must be bottled at no less than 40% ABV (80 proof). The eight designations that follow are rigidly defined by law and regulated accordingly.

Straight

Straight whiskey is unblended and contains no neutral spirits. It must be aged at least two years but is generally aged four years in new charred oak. Old Charter® (10 years old) is an example.

Bourbon

Bourbon whiskey must contain a minimum of 51% corn; must be produced in the U.S., distilled at less than 80% ABV (160 proof), and aged for a minimum of two years in new charred oak barrels, although most are aged longer. This straight whiskey has seen a renaissance with the introduction of single batch and single barrel high-end bourbons. Examples of these include Maker's Mark®, Jim Beam® 80 proof, Early Times®, and Old Grand-Dad® 86 proof. Single batch bourbons include Basil Hayden's®, Booker's®, and Knob Creek®.

Corn

Corn whiskey must contain at least 80% corn, be distilled at less than 80% ABV (160 proof), and be aged for a minimum of two years in new or used uncharred barrels. Old Gristmill®, Virginia Lightning®, and Georgia Moon® are examples of corn whiskies.

Sour Mash

Sour mash is the result of the fermentation process, in which the mash is soured with a lactic culture such as that used for sourdough bread. Examples include Jim Beam® Black Label 90 proof and Chester Graves® 90 proof.

Tennessee

Tennessee whiskey differs from bourbon only in that the distillate is leached or filtered through sugar maple charcoal in mellowing vats before it is diluted with demineralized water and aged in charred oak barrels. One of the more popular examples is Jack Daniel's® Black Label 90 proof.

Blended

Blended whiskeys are light bodied with at least a 20% straight whiskey content blended with unaged neutral spirits. Seagram's 7 Crown® 80 proof and Corby's Reserve® 80 proof are examples of blended whiskies.

Bottled in Bond

Bottled in bond is a straight whiskey produced by one distiller. It must be aged at least four years, bottled at 100 proof, and stored in bonded warehouses under government supervision. Examples include Old Forrester® 100 proof, Beam's® 100 proof, and Old Grand-Dad® B/B 100 proof.

Rye

By definition, rye whiskey must be produced from a grain mash containing at least 51% rye grain. It may not be distilled at higher than 160 proof and must be aged in new charred oak barrels. Examples include Jim Beam Rye®, which is 86 proof, Rittenhouse Rye® and Ri®.

IMPORTED WHISKIES

A variety of imported whiskies are available in the United States for consumption, including Canadian, Irish, Scotch, and Japanese whiskies.

Canadian

Virtually all Canadian whisky is six years old or older. Anything aged for less time must be labeled as such. All Canadian whisky is aged in oak casks for at least three years, but most are typically aged from six to eight years.

By U.S. law, imported Canadian whisky must be produced in Canada and must contain no distilled spirits fewer than three years old. This whisky is often simply referred to as rye whiskey or rye even though it contains more corn and other grains. Examples include Seagram's VO®, Canadian Club®, and Seagram's Crown Royal®.

Irish Whiskies

Irish whiskey must be produced in Ireland; is typically triple-distilled, usually in pot stills from Irish grain; aged in wooden casks for greater than three years; and bottled at not less than 40% ABV. Its base is barley with oats and other grains added for additional flavor. The soft mineral content of the water and triple distillation give Irish whiskey a heavier and smoother character than its Scottish counterpart. Examples include Jameson® 80 proof, Bushmills®, Murphy Irish® 86 proof, and Dunphy's Irish®.

Scotch Whiskies

Scotch whiskies include blended Scotch whisky, single malt whisky, and blended malt whisky. The smoky flavor of Scotch whisky is quite distinctive due to the use of peat smoked sprouted barley in the malting process.

Blended Scotch This whisky consists of a mixture of grain whisky and malt whisky and may contain as many as 40 different malt whiskies. Examples include Cutty Sark®, J&B®, Dewar's®, Johnnie Walker Red®, Johnnie Walker Black® 12 years old, and Chivas Regal® 12 years old.

Single malt Single malt is a whisky distilled from one particular Scottish distillery. It is a scotch made from 100% malted barley and is double pot distilled. Scotland has more than 100 distilleries, each of which produces a distinctive single malt whisky.

Blended malts Malted scotches or pure malt scotches are blends from more than one distillery. Vatted malts cannot be made from other grain whiskies. It is also a term that has been discontinued and renamed "blended malts". Examples include Johnnie Walker® Green Label and Hogshead® Vatted Malt.

Highland malts Highland malts vary greatly in character. Examples include The Balvenie® 15 year, The Macallan® 12 year, Dalmore® 12 year Single Highland, Highland Park® 18 year old, and Glenfiddich® 12 year old.

Lowland malts Lowland malts are generally softer and lighter in nature. There are fewer differences among them than there are among malts from other regions. Examples include Glenkinchie® 12 year old and Auchentoshan® 21 year old.

Islay malts Islay malts can be the most pungent and heavily peaty of all the malts. They take their characteristics from the peat that is used to dry the barley and from their closeness to the sea. Examples include Bowmore® 12 year old, Laphroaig® Cask Strength 10 year old, Ardbeg® 10 year old, and Lagavulin® 16 year old.

Speyside and Campbeltown single malts These malts have a distinctive, briny taste. The two distilleries in this region produce three single malts, each with its own character. Examples include Cragganmore® 12 year old, The Balvenie® 12 year old Double Wood Speyside, Springbank® 100 proof 10 year old, Hazel bam® 8 years old, and Glen Scotia® 12 years old.

GIN AND GENEVER

Gin is unaged liquor made from grains such as barley, corn, or rye and is flavored with juniper berries, coriander, and other herbs and spices. Gin is valued for its ability to blend harmoniously with other mixers. Examples of classic gin recipes include the martini (with dry vermouth), or the gin and tonic.

Most English gins are London Dry gins in style and are similar to American gin. They are generally distilled at a lower proof than Dutch or Genever gin and because they are dry, are conducive to blending with a mixer that is off-dry.

Plymouth Gin and Old Tom Gin are styles that were common in the 19th Century and are today regaining popularity. Plymouth Gin is a Protected Geographic Appellation and is defined by a smooth juniper taste. Old Tom is fuller bodied and sweeter. Genever, the original gin from Holland, is much more highly flavored and fuller-bodied than English gin. Examples of English gins include Beefeater®, Boodles®, Tanqueray®, Bombay®, and Bombay Sapphire®.

VODKA

Vodka is produced primarily from grain, potatoes, molasses, or beets. Russian vodkas are typically made from wheat, while Polish vodkas are created from rye or potatoes. In the U.S., domestic vodka is defined as a "neutral spirit," which is refined to be without a distinctive taste, aroma, color, or other characteristics. As a neutral spirit, vodka lends itself well to mixing with other beverages or fortifying other spirits and is preeminent in the U.S. market. The super premium vodkas are triple or quadruple distilled and demand higher prices because they are less harsh and have a lower, congener content. Examples of leading brands in the U.S. are: Smirnoff®, Belvedere®, Absolut®, Stolichnaya®, Skye®, Wyborowa® (Vee-ba-rova), Grey Goose®.

RUM

Most **rum** is made from fermented sugar juice, sugarcane syrup, sugarcane molasses, and other sugarcane by-products. Rum is produced wherever sugarcane grows—primarily in the Caribbean on the islands of Puerto Rico, the Virgin Islands, Jamaica, Barbados, Trinidad, Martinique, and Haiti. Rums are classified as white, golden, or dark.

While classifications of rum primarily reflect the length of aging, there are three distinct styles based on colonial experience. The lighter, molasses-based style that is most popular in the U.S. is from Puerto Rico, the Dominican Republic, Cuba, and Central and South America. The second style is reflected by the heavier and darker English styles from Barbados, Bermuda, Jamaica, and Guyana. The third style is the Rhum Agricole from Martinique, Guadeloupe, and Haiti.

White rum White rums are generally highest in alcohol content and are light-bodied and clear with a subtle flavor. If they are aged in oak casks, they are usually filtered to remove any color. Primarily used as mixers, white rums blend particularly well with fruit flavors. The world's leading brand is Bacardi® Superior, but there are many other producers such as Cruzan Estate® Light, and 10 Cane®.

Golden rum Golden, or amber rum is medium bodied, and usually aged for at least three years in oak casks. Its taste is smooth and mellow. Examples include Flor de Cana®, Barcardi® Gold, Appleton Estate®, and Gossling's® Bermuda Gold.

Dark rum Dark rum is the traditional, full-bodied, rich rum, dominated by overtones of caramel. The best are produced in pot stills and are usually aged for a minimum of six years in oak barrels. The best of these rums are consumed straight up. Examples include Bacardi® 8 year, Myer's Dark®, Gossling's® Black Seal, Mount Gay® Extra Old, Flor de Cana® 21 year old, and Zacapa® 23 year old.

Spiced rum Rums infused with spices are known and sold as spiced rums. They are either made with dark rums or colored with caramel and are used in hot drinks and pastry preparations. Examples include Captain Morgan® and Sailor Jerry's® Navy®.

Rhum Agricole Rhum Agricole is a style of rum produced from sugar cane juice rather than molasses. It is produced primarily in the French-owned islands of Martinique, Guadeloupe, and La Réunion. It has a lighter more vegetal character and is produced by using a continuous still. Examples of producers include Clément® and Depaz®.

CACHAÇA

Cachaça is the spirit of Brazil. Brazil produces most of the world's sugar cane and cachaça. Like Rhum Agricole, it is produced from sugar cane juice and shows distinctive vegetal notes. Some traditional distillers use a maize starter in the fermentation that restricts the EU rum designation. Cachaça is the second most widely produced spirit in the world after shoju or soju, a rice based spirit primarily from China, Korea, and Japan. While there are over 40,000 Cachaça distillers in Brazil, the dominant imported label is Leblon®.

BRANDY

The word **brandy** has its roots in the Dutch word brandewijn, which means "distilled wine." Dutch traders distilled the highly acidic white wines of the Cognac region to limit taxes (ten barrels of wine produce only one barrel of Cognac). People soon discovered the longer the distilled beverage aged, the better it tasted. Other brandies are distilled from fruit wines and pulp. Although many countries produce brandies, the best known, such as Cognac and Armagnac, are distilled from grape wine.

Cognacs are among the world's elite brandies. Their high quality stems from the kinds of grapes from which they are distilled, the soil and climate of the Cognac region, and the skill of the distillers.

Cognac is distilled twice in pure copper alembic stills soon after the base wine (made from Ugni Blanc, Colombard, and Folle Blanche grapes) has finished fermenting. The first distillation produces a 30% alcoholic liquid called the *brouillis*, which is redistilled to make the *bonne chauffe*. Then the brandy is aged in Limousin and Tronçais oak barrels, in which a slow oxidative reduction gives the cognac its distinctive flavor. The resulting evaporation is called "the angels' share."

The soil's impact is codified into the appellation laws. The more chalk, the better the appellation. The best area, in the heart of Cognac, is Grande Champagne followed by Petite Champagne. The other subdivisions include: Borderie, Fins Bois, Bon Bois, and Bois Ordinaire. Labels with "Fine Champagne" are a blend of Grande and Petite Champagne Cognacs with a minimum of 50% Grande Champagne in the blend.

Like all spirits and brandies, Cognac ages only as long as it remains in wood, but after 25 years, there are diminished returns. The most notable houses for Cognac include Martell®, Hennessy®, Rémy Martin®, Courvoisier®, Otard-Dupuy®, Camus®, Hine®, Delamain®, Salignac®, and Castillon®.

Cognac Labeling Designations: *See 8.6.*
- **VS** Very Special is aged no less than 2 years in oak.
- **VSOP** Very Special Old Pale cannot be aged less than 4 years.
- **XO** Extra Old or Extra Ordinary are house blends that must be aged at least 6 years but are usually aged 12 or more years. The minimum aging for XO cognac is expected to increase to 10 years beginning in 2018.
- **Vintage** Vintage Cognacs are allowed since 1988 under special control procedures.

Armagnac

Armagnac brandy is the oldest French brandy. Documented references to the spirit go back to the fifteenth century. Armagnac is mostly produced in the unique alembic armagnaçais, a type of column still, which dates back to the earliest days of brandy production. Although Armagnac shares Cognac's high standards, the two brandies are very different. Armagnac is an Appellation Contrôlée French grape brandy from Gascony, which is produced under strict controls and inspection procedures.

Three growing zones—Bas-Armagnac, Ténarèze, and Haut-Armagnac—are allowed to use the appellation on their label. Like Cognac, Armagnac's unique character comes from a combination of climate, soil, and grape varieties. Also like Cognac, most Armagnacs are blends, although some single vintages or single vineyard varieties are available. Blended Armagnacs generally have a higher proportion of older vintages than Cognac and are frequently a better value. Most Armagnacs shipped to the United States are classified as: 3 Star, which are aged no less than 2 years in oak; V.S.O.P aged more than 4 years in oak; or Hors d'Age aged more than 10 years in oak. There are also the vintage Armagnacs that are prized as the very best. These must also be aged at least 10 years in wood, although they are frequently aged longer. Armagnacs have a prune, violet, or spice aroma and tend to be drier and more rustic than cognacs. Leading imported brands include Darroze®, Marquis de Montesquieu®, and Clés des Ducs®.

8.6 Distinct labeling terms highlight a Cognac's aging.

American Brandies

Most brandies produced in the United States may not enjoy the reputation of their French counterparts, but brandies made by artisans such as RMS®, Germain-Robin®, and Jepson® stand up to the very best France has to offer. For cocktail and culinary use, E & J Gallo Brandy® or Christian Brothers Brandy® are ideal.

Pomace Brandies

Pomace brandies are made from the pressed skin, pulp, seeds, and stems of grapes that remain after wine pressing. They are seldom aged and are usually harsh and raw, although they may have a fruity aroma that is generally missing from more refined brandies. Many regard pomace brandy as an acquired taste.

Marc Marc is the pomace brandy that is produced in all wine-producing regions of France. It is generally consumed locally and very little is exported to the U.S.

Grappa Grappa, produced primarily in Italy, has been called the "firewater style" of pomace. In recent years; however, some single variety grappas have been produced with smoother, more elegant results.

Pisco Pisco is the specialty brandy of Peru, Chile, and to a lesser degree, Bolivia. It was very popular in San Francisco in the nineteenth century and has found renewed interest in the United States. Chilean Pisco is pot distilled from Moscatél de Alejandria, Torontel, and Pedro Ximénez grape varities. It is a clear brandy with little or no aging. Peruvian Pisco is made primarily from the black Quebranta grape and the Muscat grape and is pot distilled to bottle strength. The best examples of Pisco are aromatic spirits reminiscent of jasmine and orange blossom. Pisco that are primarily imported are Peru's Pisco Porton® and Chile's Capel®.

Serving Brandies

Traditionally, brandy is served in a short, squat, tulip-shaped glass called a snifter. The shape of the glass concentrates and emphasizes the brandy's bouquet. The brandy should be at room temperature when it is poured. The glass does not need to be heated because the heat of the hand should be enough to release the aromatic qualities of a good brandy.

TEQUILA

Tequila is a distillate made from the fermented and distilled juice of the blue agave plant. This cactus-shaped plant related to the lily takes nine years to develop a large bulbous core, called a **piña,** which weighs up to 170 pounds (77 kg). The pressure-cooked and shredded piña is made into mash, fermented, and then distilled into tequila. Tequila has its own appellation, *Denominación de Origen,* which delineates growing regions and specifies ingredient content. The production of tequila is strictly regulated by the CRT *(Consejo Regulador del Tequila),* whose symbol appears on every label of tequila. Tequila is produced in and around the Mexican state of Jalisco. There are two types of tequila permitted: 100% Agave and Tequila Mixto. The latter allows up to 49% of other fermentable sugars to be added to the fermentation.

White Tequila Labeled blanco or plata (silver), it is unaged or slightly aged and filtered to remove color.

Gold Tequila This tequila is the same as blanco but has caramel added for color.

Reposado Tequila Aged 2 to 11 months, **reposado** must be made from 100% blue agave.

Añejo tequila This tequila is aged for a minimum of one year in small barrels less than 600 litres.

Extra Añejo Extra añejo is a new category that signifies that a 100% agave tequila has been aged for three years or more.

Tequila has become extremely popular in the U.S., with 75% of it poured for margaritas, which is the number one called drink. There are now hundreds of imported brands of Tequila. Some of the most notable include Herradura®, Sauza®, Don Eduardo®, Patrón®, and José Cuervo®.

Mescal, an agave based distillate, is made primarily in the state of Oaxaca. Mescal is made from a variety of agaves. The piñas are first roasted in pits or clay ovens then crushed in a mill and put into fermenters. Mescals are typically unaged and have a distinct smokey character. Notable producers include Del Maguey®and Monte Alban.

AQUAVIT

Aquavit is distilled liquor from Scandinavia. It ranges from 42% to 45% ABV. Distilled from a fermented potato or grain mash, it is usually flavored with caraway or cumin seeds but may also be flavored with citrus peel, cardamom, aniseed, or fennel. Aquavit is traditionally served chilled, often straight out of the freezer, in small glasses that are emptied in one shot. It is not typically mixed with any other beverage.

BITTERS

As the name suggests, **bitters** are a very bitter, or bittersweet liquids distilled from various herbs and roots. Bitters, though an essential element in many cocktails, are used sparingly in cocktails and cooking to add a dry zest. Because they are both a digestive aid and an appetite stimulant, bitters are used in both before- and after-dinner mixed drinks. Bitters are highly alcoholic and should not be used in non-alcoholic drinks. Most notable producers include Campari®, Fernet Branca, Angostura®, Peychaud's®, and Fee Brothers®.

Liqueurs

Liqueurs still retain the mystique of secret elixirs and potions concocted by monks and alchemists—most often in secret. Benedictine and Chartreuse, for example, are herbal blends developed by ancient religious orders. The Benedictine order first made its famous liqueur in 1510 by mixing herbs, plant parts, and spices into a Cognac base. The recipes for Chartreuse predates the American Revolution and is such a secret that only five monks at a time are permitted to know the 130-ingredient recipe.

LIQUEUR PRODUCTION PROCESSES

Production methods of liqueurs vary widely from one liqueur to another. In some cases, the exact manner of production is also a carefully guarded secret. But in general, there are five basic methods of production.

Infusion

Infusions are made by steeping flavoring agents in a hot liquid, usually water or fruit juice, much like steeping tea. The resulting "tea" must be strong enough to impart flavor to the entire blended liqueur; however, the infusion is generally much stronger than tea.

Maceration

When an aromatic or flavoring agent is immersed in the base spirit until the spirit absorbs the flavoring or aroma, the process is called maceration. A maker might, for example, macerate fresh strawberries in a spirit to avoid losing the aroma, flavor, and color of the berries. Because heating can cause evaporation of both the alcohol and esters, maceration is a cool process that can take up to a year. The final result is called a tincture and is the basis of the liqueur.

Percolation

In percolation, the flavoring agents are placed in a container above the base liquor, which is then bubbled up through it. This process can take weeks to absorb the flavors and to form a product called an extract.

Redistillation

Redistillation, which is used mostly for flavoring agents such as seeds, citrus peel, or mint employs an extraction method. The flavoring agent is steeped in spirits for several days and then placed in a still with other spirits to be distilled. A vacuum is used to permit the distillation to occur at lower temperatures so more of the flavors are retained.

Cold Compounding

Cold compounding is a simple method of flavoring liqueurs by blending in essences and concentrates to the base spirit. This method is used for the least expensive liqueurs.

PROPRIETARY BRANDS

There are two general types of liqueurs: generics and proprietaries. Generics are liqueurs such as crème de menthe or crème de cacao that are not proprietary and may therefore be produced by any producer. Proprietaries are trademarked liqueurs that are made according to specific, usually highly secret recipes. Examples include Grand Marnier®, Southern Comfort®, or Benedictine®.

Flavor Classifications

Although liqueurs come in a great variety of flavors, they generally fall into these classifications:

- **Fruit-flavored** These liqueurs are popular and bear a label that identifies the fruit that flavors the liqueur, such as Midori®, made with melon.
- **Seed-based** Although one seed predominates in the liqueur, the beverage is usually made from several kinds of seeds.

- **Herbs** Among the most complex, herbal liqueurs may contain a dozen or a hundred herbs (except for mint or anise seed). Herbal flavors do not usually dominate the liqueur.
- **Crème** Called crème liqueurs for their creamy texture and sweet taste, crèmes take their name from the dominant flavoring ingredient, such as a fruit (crème de banane).
- **Peels** The most frequently used peels are those in the citrus family, such as orange or lemon. *See 8.7.*

Popular Brands of Liqueurs and Cordials

Alizé®
From France; a blend of passion fruit, or other flavors and cognac; a variety of colors

Amaretto
Aromatic liqueur made from apricots and almonds steeped in aquavit (fusion of alcohol); brown color

Amaretto di Saronno®
Brand name of Amaretto; brown color

Anisette
Sweet, mild, liqueur with licorice-like flavor; clear

B&B Liqueur D.O.M.®
Delicate finesse of Benedictine D.O.M. with drier cognac; amber color

Benedictine D.O.M.®
Classic French herbal liqueur; amber color

Boggs Cranberry Liqueur®
Tart, tangy taste of juice of cranberries; red color

Campari®
Italian bittersweet spirit apéritif; infusion of aromatic and bitter herbs; light ruby red color

Chambord Liqueur Royale de France®
From France; rich aroma and taste of framboises (small black raspberries) and other fruits and herbs combined with honey; dark purple color

Chartreuse®
Classic herb liqueur with subtle flavor and aroma drawn from 130 wild mountain herbs distilled and blended in brandy; yellow or green color

Cointreau®
Classic French specialty orange liqueur; fragrant, mellow bouquet with subtle hint of orange; blends sweet and bitter Mediterranean and tropical orange peels; clear

Cream Liqueurs
Bailey's® (dominant brand), Carolans®, Emmets®, Leroux®, Myers®, O'Darby's®
Fresh cream blended with spirits and natural flavorings; Irish whiskey is the most widely used spirit; brandy, cordials, rum, and vodka are also used; creamy brown color

Crème de Banane
Flavor of fresh, ripe bananas; yellow color

Crème de Cacao (Brown)
Rich, creamy, deep chocolate flavor drawn from cocoa and vanilla beans with hint of spices; brown color

Crème de Cacao (White)
Less intense chocolate flavor; clear

Crème de Cassis
Full, rich, flavor of black currants; very dark purple color

Crème de Framboise
Raspberry-flavored liqueur; dark purple color

Crème de Menthe (Green)
Refreshing, tangy, natural mint flavor; cool, clean; green color

Crème de Menthe (White)
Virtually identical to green crème de menthe; lack of color makes it useful in more drink recipes

Curaçao
From the island of Curaçao in the Netherlands Antilles; clear amber color; similar to Triple Sec but sweeter and more subtle; lower proof; clear, orange, or blue color

Domaine de Canton®
A sweet liqueur made from Vietnamese baby ginger and VSOP Cognac; emerald in color

Drambuie®
Old Scotch whiskey, delicately honeyed and spiced; amber color

Frangelico®
Wild hazelnuts (filberts) blended with spirits, berries, and herbs; amber color

Fruit-Flavored Brandies
Flavor and aroma of fresh, ripe fruit defined by product name (apricot, blackberry, and so on); higher proof and drier than fruit liqueurs; color varies

Fruit-Flavored Liqueurs
Flavor and aroma of fresh, ripe fruit, defined by product name (apricot, blackberry, and so on); lower proof and sweeter than fruit brandies; color varies

Goldwasser
Flavor blend of herbs, seeds, roots, and citrus peels; tiny flakes of gold imperceptible to the tongue that shimmer in this clear liqueur

Grand Marnier®
From France; classic cognac-based orange liqueur; flavor and bouquet from peels of wild bitter oranges; amber color

Irish Mist®
From Ireland; flavor blend of four whiskeys, honeys from heather, clover; essence of a dozen herbs; amber color

Jägermeister®
Distinctive flavor blend of 56 roots, herbs, and fruits; dark brown color

Kahlúa®
Flavor aroma of choicest coffees; dark brown color

Kahlúa Royale®
Blends Kahlúa, fine brandy, a hint of chocolate, and oranges; dark brown color

Kümmel
One of the world's oldest liqueurs; fairly dry and usually 70 proof or more; essential flavor is caraway with a hint of cumin seed and anise; clear

8.7 Orange peels from Haiti are an essential flavor to the liqueur Grand Marnier®.

- **Fruit brandies** These fall into three general groups: brandies flavored with apples and pears; those using stone fruits such as plums, peaches, or apricots; and those flavored with berries, such as blackberries or elderberries.
- **Nut liqueurs** Among these liqueurs, there are favorites such as Amaretto (almonds) and Frangelico® (hazelnuts).

Serving Liqueurs

Liqueurs or cordials are sweet, potent, and contain essential oils that may aid in digestion. They are popular as after-dinner drinks. Due to their sweet flavors, they add smoothness, texture, and palatability to many cocktails. In France, certain liqueurs are used in the form of highballs. Crème de cassis, for example, is mixed with wine to make Kir Frappés. A popular way of serving liqueurs is by filling a small stem glass with shaved ice and pouring the liqueur over it.

Liquore Galliano®
From Italy; natural golden liqueur; distinctive flavor of anise and vanilla; rich, sweet, palatable; natural flavorings of seeds, herbs, and spices; yellow color

Liquore Strega®
From Italy; rich, fragrant, golden liqueur with flavors of more than 70 herbs; yellow color

Lochan ora®
From Scotland; distinctive scotch-based liqueur with subtle flavors drawn from Curaçao and Ceylon; gold color

Malibu®
From Canada; flavor blend of white rum and coconut; clear

Mandarine Napoléon®
From Belgium; a tangerine liqueur; flavor and bouquet of ripe Andalusian tangerines and cognac; orange color

Maraschino
From Italy; made from cracked Maraschino cherry stones and mixed with elderberries; clear

Metaxa®
From Greece; brandy-like liqueur from grape base, slightly sweet with distinctive flavor; amber in color

Midori®
From Japan; light, refreshing taste of fresh honeydew melon; green color

Monte teca®
From Mexico; tequila-based liqueur; rich, golden taste; clear in color

Opal nera®
From Italy; anise and elderflower flavor with hint of lemon; color of black opal

Ouzo
From Greece; sweet, white liqueur; licorice-like anise flavor, slightly drier and stronger proof than anisette; when water or ice is added, it turns milky white

Pear William
From Loire Valley in France; delicate flavor of Anjou pears; clear

Pernod®
From France; blends select anise seed, special flavorings, and natural herbs with spirits; light pastel green color

Peter Heering®
From Denmark; famous cherry flavored liqueur produced since 1818; formerly known as Cherry Heering®; dark red color

Pimm's Cup®
From England; tall "sling" drinks (Pimm's Cup No. 1 is the gin sling); red color

Praline Liqueur®
Rich, mellow vanilla- and pecan based flavor of the original New Orleans praline confection; caramel color

Ricard®
From France; anise and herb liqueur; pastel green color

Rock and Rye
Whiskey-based liqueur containing crystals of rock candy, flavored with fruits (sometimes has pieces); amber color

Sabra®
From Israel; flavors of orange and chocolate; dark chocolate color

Sambuca Romano®
Liqueur flavored with elderberry and anise; clear

Schnapps
Apple Barrel®, Aspen Glacial® (peppermint), Cool Mint®, Cristal® (anise), DeKuyper Peachtree® (peach), Dr. McGillicuddy® (menthol mint), Rumple Minze® (peppermint), Silver Schnapps® (100-proof, peppermint), Steel® (85-proof peppermint) Predominantly for after-dinner sipping; often too sweet and syrupy for straight drinking; good with many mixers; various colors

Sloe Gin
Bouquet and tangy fruity flavor resembling wild cherries; made from fresh fruit of the sloe berry; red color

Southern Comfort®
From America; high-proof, peach flavored liqueur with a bourbon whiskey base; coppery amber color

St. Germain®
An artisanal liqueur made with fresh elder flowers from France; light yellow color

Tia Maria®
From Jamaica; coffee-flavored liqueur; dark brown color

Triple Sec
Crystal-clear orange flavor; like curaçao but drier and higher proof; flavor blends peels of tangy, bittersweet green curaçao and sweet oranges; clear

Truffles®
Combination of spirits and imported chocolate; chocolate color

Tuaca®
From Italy; brandy base with a hint of herbs, vanilla, and fruit peels; golden color

Vandermint®
From Holland; Dutch chocolate with a hint of mint; chocolate cream color

Yukon Jack®
100-proof blend of sweetened Canadian whiskies; amber color

Wild Turkey Liqueur®
Bourbon base; herbs, spices, and other natural; amber color

9. Mixology

Humans have combined various alcoholic beverages since the earliest of times. In this country, the Puritans and early settlers brought with them "strong waters", a reference most likely to Dutch Gin or Genever. They were also familiar with the social aspects of taverns and mixed drink recipes that were consumed in both England and France as well. These recipes included or evolved into punches, crustas, shrubs, flips, caliboguses, bounces, sangarees, and syllabubs to name but a few.

The history of social drinking in the U.S., and the art of mixing specific various distilled spirits with a variety of mixtures and ice are said to be uniquely American. The birth of the cocktail is truly an American cultural product. The basic principles, techniques, recipes, and tools may be traced as far back as the early 1800s. Many today salute the immortal Jerry Thomas as the forefather of today's modern mixologist. **Mixology** is the study of cocktails, mixed drinks, and their ingredients. Those who study mixology—mixologists or bartenders—are highly skilled professionals who must understand complex local, state, and federal laws; possess a working knowledge of psychology and current events; and master hundreds of beverage recipes and techniques. Bartenders generally work in restaurants, bars, hotels, private clubs and resorts, and on cruise lines.

Profits generated from beverage sales may account for 75% of the profit margin in the fine dining segment of the restaurant industry. In the last five years there has been a trend in mixology with a renaissance of crafted cocktails, which are based upon classic recipes that emphasize the use of fresh and top quality ingredients. Most establishments continue to operate cost effective, high volume operations by using less expensive commercially prepared ingredients such as sodas from a bag-in-a-box and generic spirits. Each environment has its own challenges, but all share some basic principles for setting up and managing an efficient and profitable operation.

The Beverage Profession

The beverage profession offers a number of career track job opportunities. In the past, these opportunities depended on an apprenticeship. Today, those interested in climbing the career ladder of beverage opportunities must have a beverage and managerial knowledge as well as hands-on experience. Internationally recognized education and certifications that validate such knowledge and experience have become crucial to quality job placement.

THE BEVERAGE MANAGER

The beverage manager or beverage director position is often a senior management position within high-volume establishments, hotels, clubs, casinos, cruise lines and restaurants, which have extensive or complex wine lists and liquor inventories. A beverage manager must be knowledgeable in, and oversee all aspects of beverages including: beer, wine, spirits, and non-alcoholic offerings. The position involves purchasing, receiving, storing, requisitioning, costing, and inventory control. Responsibilities may include but are not limited to, interviewing, hiring, training and supervising all beverage personnel, menu development, purchasing equipment, developing and maintaining standards, and ensuring profitability.

BAR MANAGER OR HEAD BARTENDER

Multiple and single unit restaurants, and even hotels with multiple beverage outlets usually have a manager who is in charge of bar operations. This complex management position requires the expertise of an individual who exercises many qualities to oversee the daily bar business. It is the bar manager's responsibility to achieve the goals established by the owner or upper management and to run an efficient and profitable operation while catering to the needs of the guest. Management responsibilities may include: hiring and firing, training, forecasting and budgeting, scheduling, purchasing, inventory and costing, merchandising and promotional sales, quality control, and implementing standards.

THE BARTENDER

Good **bartenders** share a common set of traits and follow certain guidelines that spell success or failure for the bar operation. They must be friendly, hospitable and customer focused, have expertise in mixology, and must have a thorough knowledge of and adhere to state sanitation and alcohol service laws. Professional bartenders must be knowledgeable about an expansive range of alcoholic and non-alcoholic products and be skillful in marketing and selling to the guest. They should possess good organizational skills and practice effective cost control. The ability to recognize behavioral cues that indicate levels of intoxication is also critical to an establishment's survival in today's society.

The Good Bartender's Guidelines
- Offer a friendly greeting.
- Develop a memory for recognizing regular customers and drink preferences.
- Never hurry the customers.
- Step back after serving the guest.
- Handle complaints courteously.
- Cooperate with and be helpful to other employees; avoid employee conflicts.
- Utilize good telephone etiquette.
- Prepare drinks on the rail or bar in front of the customer.
- Return bottles to their proper places immediately to keep the bar neat and organized.
- Use the appropriate glass and garnish for each drink.
- Handle all glassware according to sanitation guidelines. *See 9.1.*
- Use a fresh sundry for each drink.
- Use a fresh glass for every drink unless the customer specifies otherwise.
- Follow standardized recipes or house recipes.
- Use a consistent measure for drinks. *See 9.2.*
- Avoid overfilling a glass; one-quarter inch from the rim is a good rule of thumb. *See 9.3.*
- When pouring two identical drinks, prepare a double recipe and half-fill each glass. Then pour additional liquid until the glasses are evenly filled.
- Ring drinks on the guest check, and place the check face down in front of the customer.
- Never sit, eat, or smoke at the bar, even when off duty.
- Remain professional at all times.

9.1 The correct procedure for handling stemware and baseware

9.2 A jigger pour

THE BARBACK

Barbacks assist and support bartenders by performing various tasks during the set up, service, and break down of the bar area. Barbacks support the work of bartenders by cutting fruit, preparing juice and mixers, filling ice bins, setting up sundries, washing and replacing glassware, and stocking product. Barbacks help the bartender in keeping the work area clean during operating hours. Opening and closing duties may vary depending on the bar operation. Typically, a barback relieves the bartender of duties other than preparing drinks and taking care of customers and payment. Many barback positions are apprenticeships for becoming a bartender.

THE COCKTAIL SERVER

Cocktail servers are usually employed to support service to customers in large establishments such as nightclubs, casinos, and banquet facilities, so that guests need not travel to and from their seats or location. They are responsible for the sales and service of cocktails and beverages to guests. Cocktail servers, generally ring drinks through the POS system and order and pick up drinks from bartenders who may be located at a service bar. Cocktail servers should be familiar with the drink families, appropriate glassware, the sequence of drink orders (call order), and the appropriate garnishes for each drink. Drinks should be delivered and cleared using a beverage tray, and cocktail tables should be monitored for cleanliness and sanitation.

9.3 All drinks should allow for a 1/4 inch margin from the rim.

Cocktails *and* Mixed Drinks

The terms cocktail and mixed drink are often used as though they were synonymous. There are, however, several important differences between these two terms. A **cocktail** is a fairly short drink, made by mixing liquor or wine with fruit juices, eggs, and/or bitters. Cocktails are created by mixing two or more ingredients together to make a new flavor that is both pleasing and palatable. Unless the drink is made to the specifications of a particular customer, no single ingredient should overpower the others. Although cocktails are stirred or shaken with ice in bar glasses or cocktail shakers, they are generally served up or without ice in stemmed glasses. If the guest prefers, the cocktail may be served on the rocks or with ice.

Mixed drinks, on the other hand, are tall drinks served over ice. Mixed drinks combine liquor with a mixer—one as simple as club soda or as complex as several kinds of fruit juices, various carbonated beverages, and even puréed fruits. Generally served in a base glass, mixed drinks are served with ice.

HISTORY OF COCKTAILS AND MIXED DRINKS

Experts differ on the origins of the word cocktail. Everyone does agree, however, that the cocktail, like jazz, was born in America. New York Times' restaurant critic William Grimes writes, "other countries can copy the cocktail, but seldom improve it." One of the first uses of the word cocktail as a reference to an alcoholic beverage appeared in the 1806 publication of New York's Hudson Valley The Balance and Columbian Repository. Here a reference is made to the cocktail as a "stimulating liquor, composed of spirits of any kind, sugar, water, and bitters. It is vulgarly called a bittered sling and is supposed to be an excellent electioneering potion, in as much as it renders the heart stout and bold, at the same time that it fuddles the head." By 1889, the Century Dictionary had formalized the term, defining the cocktail as "an American drink, strong, stimulating, and cold."

Most researchers agree that the origin of the cocktail dates back to the time of the American Revolution when Americans were unable to import rum and other spirits from Great Britain. Americans began distilling their own whiskey, although some of it was of a dubious quality. Mixing this whiskey with sugar and bitters improved the taste, and the cocktail was born. As the distillers' skills improved; however, distinctive and high-quality whiskies, such as Kentucky Bourbon, began to develop. Eventually whiskey found its way into one of America's earliest classic cocktails, the mint julep.

The first recorded reference to the julep is in 1787 when the drink was described as a combination of rum, water, and sugar. By the 1830s; however, the julep recipe had acquired mint and ice. Juleps were served ice cold but were created differently depending on social class preferences. The wealthy made them with expensive brandy, while common folk used whiskey.

KEY INGREDIENTS

Key ingredients with which bartenders work, include the spirit or liqueur, ice and mixers, juices, simple syrups, bitters, and garnishes. Bartenders, like chefs, can only create great cocktails or mixed drinks if all the ingredients are of the highest quality.

Spirits

The quality of the finished drink reflects the quality level of the spirit. Generic spirits generally have more congeners and lack a smooth alcoholic finish. The flavors of each have attributes that allow them to uniquely integrate with different mixers and create countless variations. **The general standard alcohol contents of each of the spirit categories are:**

- Vodka–40% to 50%
- Gin–40% to 47%
- Blended Whiskies and Bourbon–40% to 45%
- Scotch–40% to 62%
- Rum–40%
- Tequila–40%
- Brandy–40%
- Liqueurs–40% to 45%
- Aperitifs–16% to 30%.

Cocktails may be distinguished from **mixed drinks** by the following **characteristics:**

1. **Presentation:** Cocktails are short and served "up" unless called for "on the rocks." Mixed drinks are tall and are served with ice.

2. **Procedure:** Cocktails are stirred or shaken, while mixed drinks are served ice down-pour or speed-shaken.

3. **Glassware:** Cocktails are served in a stemmed glass, and mixed drinks are served in a tall base glass.

Ice

It was ice that transformed the barkeeper from host and server to juggler, conjuror, and artist. Throughout the 1830s clean ice from New England was available even during the hottest months, and ordinary people acquired a taste for it. Crafting drinks with fresh ingredients shaken or stirred over ice was a common practice throughout the 1850s and 60s. Tools and techniques became more elaborate as did the drinks. Ice is the common ingredient in today's cocktails and mixed drinks. Perhaps no bar ingredient has generated more discussion in quality bar programs than ice shape, density, style, and quality. Today's mixologists use a variety of ice styles including, shaved, cubed, crushed, sphered, or smoked. The goal is to obtain the perfect drink temperature without excessive dilution of the drink. Quality ice must be made from quality water, and filtration is recommended. Large, dense cubes may be best when serving spirits on the rocks or in highballs, while cracked ice works best with very sweet drinks, juices and soft drinks. Inferior ice, such as small hollow cubes, often fails to chill a beverage without over diluting it.

Garnishes, Juices, Mixers, Simple Syrup, and Bitters

Cocktails created after the 1950s became the victims of artificial ingredients and mass production techniques. Today, many bar operators are able to include fresh produce including fruits, vegetables and herbs in syrups, tinctures, bitters, infusions, and fruit purees. With the return of the crafted cocktail, numerous recipes may require fresh juices, culinary ingredients, and an array of garnishes. Only fresh, seasonal, quality fruits, herbs, and vegetables should be used at the bar to make the best juices and garnishes.

All fresh juices should be refrigerated with strict rotation and date guidelines, and garnishes should be kept at the appropriate temperature to guarantee freshness and eye appeal. Some fresh juices degrade within hours. Garnishes are intended to add color and flavor to a drink.

Refrigeration or temperature control garnish boxes may be used to store ready to use garnish.

The addition of mixers to today's recipes varies from bottled sodas, house charged waters, homemade infusions, and crafted sodas and sours to prepared mixes and packaged products. *See 9.4.* For consumers, this means there are always interesting new cocktails. Many of today's cocktail recipes have replaced the sugars with gum syrup or simple syrup. **Simple syrup** can be prepared in advance by dissolving superfine sugar with equal parts water. Rich simple syrup increases the ratio to 2:1, sugar to water. The infusion of syrups with herbs, spices and natural flavorings can increase the bartender's arsenal of flavor additions. Cocktail bitters such as Angostura®, Peychaud's®, and Fee Brothers® brands have an alcohol base. *See 9.5.* When added by the drop they do not affect the alcohol content of a drink but rather enhance the flavor and balance. Prepared or house made bitters can come in a variety of flavors including fruits, herbs, botanicals, and spices.

9.5 Cocktail bitters enhance the balance and flavor of a drink.

9.4 Emphasis should be placed on fresh ingredients.

Bar Glassware

Today's glassware is available in a variety of shapes and sizes. *See 9.6.* Consider durability, size, and balance when purchasing glassware. One should always use an appropriate glass for each drink. It is recommended to closely match the glass size with the correct proportion of ingredients. When handling glassware, strict sanitary guidelines should be followed. Pick up glasses by the stem or base only; never pick up a glass by the rim or put fingers in the glass, and never scoop ice into a glass by using the glass as the scoop.

9.6 Glassware is available in a variety of shapes and sizes.

BAR OPERATIONS

The layout of a bar must be carefully planned and laid out. A bartender should have almost all tools and ingredients within easy reach to allow for taking no more than a step or two in any direction. The bartender should build drinks on the bar rail within clear view of the guest so that the guest may see the preparation of ingredients and the skill/expertise of the bartender. *See 9.7.*

Bar Opening Procedures

Follow appropriate procedures for opening the bar to ensure efficiency. Evening bartenders should also adhere to proper bar closing procedures to guarantee a quick and efficient opening the following day. Develop and use checklists to make sure that each task is completed every time the bar is opened. **To open a bar, follow these steps:**

1. Begin by checking the cash register, and ensure that the previous shift has been closed out properly. Then count the bank, or cash that has been issued in the presence of a manager, and ensure that it is correct. Make sure that there are ample quantities of guest checks or paper for the POS printer.

2. Turn on the glass washer, or fill the three-compartment sink: (1) wash, (2) rinse, (3) sanitize. Wash any soiled glasses, and leave them on the drain board until dry. *See 9.8.*

3. Check bottled drinks: rotate and restock them according to established bar stocks. Restock liquor issued for the day, and turn in empty bottles for inventory control.

4. Clean the soda gun. Check soda levels and the carbon dioxide pressure.

5. Check fruit garnishes, fruit juices, cream, and other bar mixes. Wash containers, refill, and refrigerate.

6. Prepare sufficient garnishes for one shift.

7. Check all sundry supplies and bar implements.

8. Wash and polish the bar counter, drain and wash sinks and ice bins, and wipe the neck of each bottle on the back bar. Line up the bottles with labels and pourers facing in the same direction.

9. Visit the rest room to check your appearance.

10. Have a manager watch over your bar should you need to leave.

11. Open the bar on time. All mise en place should be complete, and the bar should be fully stocked and ready for business.

Key Bar Tools

A bartender's tools are a critical component in making drinks accurately and consistently. The following tools are the minimum required tools needed to successfully concoct non-frozen drink recipes.

Mixing Glass, Metal Shaker, Speed Shaker, Hawthorne/Spring Strainer, Jigger, Long Stirring Spoon, Channel Knife

Muddler, Ice Tongs, Zester, Steel Muddler

Bottle/Can Opener, Fine Mesh Strainer, Flat Bottle Opener, Specialty Bottle Opener, Hand Juicer, Wine Opener

9.7 The bar rail acts as the bartender's stage.

9.8 The three basin sink—wash, rinse, sanitize

9.9 Air mats allow air flow around bar glassware.

Hand-Washing Glasses

It is especially important to keep glasses clean and sanitized. **Here is the proper method for hand-washing glasses:**

1. Wash glasses in the first compartment of the sink. Use warm water (at least 110°F–120°F/43°C–49°C), a washing compound, and a brush.

2. Use the second compartment to immerse the glasses in clean, warm water of at least 110°F (43°C). Change the rinse water often. Never rinse glasses in dirty water.

3. Sanitize the glasses in the third sink compartment using water containing a chemical sanitizer. The water temperature and immersion time vary depending on the chemical compound used.

4. Drain and air-dry glasses. Store them inverted on shelving lined with air mats. *See 9.9.*

Use of Chemicals

Several chemical solutions are available for sanitizing hand-washed glasses, including the following:

- A solution of water and at least 50 to 100 parts per million (ppm) of available chlorine. Temperature: not less than 55°F (13°C) Time: at least 7 seconds
- A solution of water and at least 220 ppm of a quaternary ammonium compound (quats), (or follow manufacturer's instructions). Temperature: not less than 75°F (24°C) Time: at least 30 seconds
- A solution of water and at least 12.5 to 25 ppm of available iodine in a solution with a pH not less than 5.0. Temperature: not less than 75°F (24°C) Time: at least 30 seconds

A field test kit should be used to measure the chemical concentration at any time.

Automatic Glass Washer Procedures

In most states, legal requirements call for the use of automatic glass washers in new commercial operations. Properties with automatic washers should have a dump box in which to discard sundries, garnishes, and ice. A **dump box** is a receptacle with a screen over a drain that allows ice or water to drain without allowing garnishes and sundries to clog the plumbing. The temperatures of the glass washer cycle should be checked to ensure that a minimum temperature of 180°F (82°C) for the final rinse is reached.

Bar Closing Procedures

Closing the bar properly helps to ensure efficient operation. **To close the bar:**

1. Wipe and thoroughly clean the speed rack; wipe bottles and replace.

2. Sanitize empty shelves for clean glasses.

3. Collect all used glassware, and place it on the counter above the sink area. Wash hands.

4. Wash glassware, one type at a time, washing cream-drink glasses last. Replace glasses on the shelf that is covered with air mats.

5. Rinse and wash sinks, and dry them to prevent scaling.

6. Wash and polish the drain board and other parts of the sink.

7. Clean out the ice bin, and wipe dry.

8. Sweep the floor, and remove the trash container.

9. Wrap or store fruit garnishes appropriately, and refrigerate them for the next day.

10. Refrigerate all perishable mixers, label, and date. Wash and store empty containers.

11. Fill in the day's requisition for liquor, wine, and beer.

12. Stock coolers for the next shift, rotating all products (FIFO).

13. Run appropriate closing procedures on the POS system. If using a manual system, count the guest checks and correlate them with the issue register. Note any unused checks. Close out the cash register according to the house policy.

14. Check security, and inform management when ready for inspection.

BAR SET-UP

Good bartenders need to ensure that they have properly set up their mise en place of ingredients. Bottles should be enticingly gleaming with labels facing guests. Back up bottles of the most commonly used or near empty products should be stored within easy reach. The bar mats should be placed on the rail with bar tools such as shakers, mixing glasses, and speed shakers inverted and ready for use. **Bar sundries** refer to non-edible supplies such as sip sticks, beverage straws, sword picks, and cocktail napkins that are needed for bartending. Salt and pepper, sugar, commonly used spices and sauces such as Tabasco®, and Lea & Perrins® Worcestershire sauce should also be near at hand.

Fixed versus Portable Bars

Fixed bars are permanently established with running potable water and proper glass washing capabilities. Portable bars may be used in banquet halls and off–premise catering operations to allow for flexibility of location. Portable bars have certain disadvantages that may reduce the number of products, displays, glassware, and the techniques that a bartender may use.

The Speed Rack (The Well)

Bar set-ups vary enormously based on the type, size, and the targeted bar audience. Most bars are set up with **speed racks** that are located in the **well,** which is mounted to the sinks and the ice bin. They are designed for bartenders to easily access the most commonly used spirits and mixers. At a high end bar, one might find all spirits in the speed rack or well to be "call" or proprietary brands such as Smirnoff® Vodka rather than a generic brand of vodka. The set-up of the speed rack varies from house to house. The following is an example of a speed rack set-up from left to right: Rose's® Lime Juice and Grenadine, Vodka, Gin, Blended Whiskey, Scotch, Rum, Brandy, Dry Vermouth, and Sweet Vermouth.

The Back Bar

The **back bar** should be set up to display bottles in an attractive way to promote sales and to market premium, super-premium, and ultra-premium brands. The arrangement will depend on the type of bar, the space available, and the beverage menu focus. It should also be functional for the bartender.

The following list (although not inclusive), contains the High End and Super Premium **Brands that are currently significant in the U.S. market:**

Irish Whisky

- Bushmills®
- Jameson®

Scotch Whiskies

- Ballantine's®
- Glenlivet®
- Chivas Regal®
- Johnnie Walker®
- Dewars®
- Laphroaig®
- Glenfiddich®

Canadian Whisky

- Canadian Club®
- Seagram's 7®
- Crown Royal®
- Seagram's VO®

Vodka

- Absolut®
- Ketel One®
- Belvedere®
- Smirnoff®
- Chopin®
- Stolichnaya®

Gin

- Beefeater®
- Grey Goose®
- Bols Genever®
- Plymouth®
- Bombay®
- Tanqueray®
- Boodles®

Blended Whiskies and Bourbons

- Baker's®
- Knob Creek®
- Basil Hayden's®
- Ri-®
- Heaven Hill®
- Rittenhouse Rye®
- Jack Daniel's®
- Wild Turkey®
- Jim Beam®

Rum

- Bacardi® light rum
- Captain Morgan® Spiced Rum
- Depaz® Rhum Agricole
- Mount Gay® gold rum
- Myer's® dark rum

Tequila

- Cabo Wabo®
- Milagro®
- Gran Centenario®
- Patron®
- Herradura®
- Sauza®
- José Cuervo®

Cognacs

- Camus®
- Hine®
- Courvoisier®
- Martell®
- Delamain®
- Otard-Dupuy®
- Hennessy®
- Rémy Martin®

Liqueurs

In addition to premium category spirits, the back bar usually displays liqueurs that may be served as cordials or used in recipes for cocktails and mixed drinks. Liqueurs are also categorized by price and quality. **The following list includes both generic and proprietary brands that might be incorporated into a fully stocked bar:**

- Apricot-flavored brandy
- Crème de banane
- Crème de cacao (dark)
- Crème de cacao (light)
- Crème de cassis
- Crème de menthe (green)
- Crème de menthe (white)
- Curaçao (blue)
- Curaçao (orange)
- Peach schnapps
- Peppermint schnapps
- Triple sec

Propietary Brands

- Amaretto di Saronno®
- Bailey's Irish Cream®
- Benedictine D.O.M.®
- Campari®
- Chartreuse®
- Cointreau®
- Drambuie®
- Frangelico®
- Galliano®
- Grand Marnier®
- Kahlúa®
- Maraschino®
- Midori®
- Navan®
- Peter Heering®
- Southern Comfort®
- St. Germain®

Bar Terminology

The **jigger** is a legal measure of 1.5 ounces (45 ml). A jigger is also the commonly used name for a bar tool used to measure ounces or fractions of ounces in making alcoholic beverages. Jiggers can be found in a variety of shapes and sizes. A double-sided stainless steel cup, the most common jigger measures 1½ ounces on one side, and ¾ of an ounce on the other, but many sizes are available. Note: one ounce of liquid equals 30 ml.

Other terms include:

- **Back** A chaser on the side.
- **Float** The final liquid ingredient added to the drink after the usual procedure is performed; a float finds its own space and should not be incorporated into the drink.
- **Free-pour** Pouring spirits or liqueurs without using a measuring device, such as a jigger. This is less professional, as exact measurements are critical in professional bartending for balanced drinks.
- **Hold/no garnish** Served without garnishes.
- **Light** A drink containing a reduced amount of liquor but the normal amount of mixer.
- **On the rocks** Served on ice, usually in a rocks glass.
- **Shot** A measure of liquid (quantity determined by the house) served straight up
- **Straight up or neat** Served without ice; the drink never comes into contact with ice.
- **Tall/Long** A drink served in an 8- to 16-ounce (240- to 500-ml) highball or zombie glass; the amount of the mixer is increased, not the amount of liquor.
- **Up** Prepared with ice to chill but served strained from the ice in a stemmed glass.

Making Cocktails *and* Mixed Drinks

Four basic procedures are used in making cocktails and mixed drinks. These are the stir, shake, ice down-pour, or speed-shake methods. Unless otherwise specified, cocktails are usually served up when ordered. *See 9.10 Cocktails Procedure* and *9.11 Mixed Drink Procedure.*

For cocktails served up:

- **Stir procedure** Gently agitate with ice to chill and blend the cocktail ingredients.
- **Shake procedure** Agitate energetically with ice to disperse or incorporate heavy ingredients.

For mixed drinks or cocktails requested on the rocks:

- **Ice down-pour procedure** Build by placing ice in a service glass, then add liquor and the mixer; serve as is.
- **Speed-shake procedure** In a service glass, agitate with ice to disperse or incorporate heavier ingredients.

Vermouth Base (Served Up)

Name of Drink	Procedure	Glass
Gibson	Stir	Cocktail
Manhattan	Stir	Cocktail
Martini	Stir	Cocktail
Negroni	Stir	Cocktail
Rob Roy	Stir	Cocktail

Short Sours (Served Up)

Name of Drink	Procedure	Glass
All sours (i.e. whiskey)	Shake	Sour
Bacardi® Cocktail	Shake	Cocktail
Between the Sheets	Shake	Cocktail
Cosmopolitan	Shake	Cocktail
Daiquiri	Shake	Cocktail
Gimlet	Shake	Cocktail
Jack Rose Cocktail	Shake	Cocktail
Kamikaze	Shake	Cocktail
Margarita	Shake	Coupe
Pisco Sour	Shake	Cocktail
Sidecar	Shake	Cocktail
Ward 8	Shake	Cocktail

Short Cream Base (Served Up)

Name of Drink	Procedure	Glass
Brandy Alexander	Shake	Coupe
Grasshopper	Shake	Coupe
Pink Squirrel	Shake	Coupe

Vermouth Base (Served on the Rocks)

Name of Drink	Procedure	Glass
Gibson	Ice down-pour	Rocks
Manhattan	Ice down-pour	Rocks
Martini	Ice down-pour	Rocks
Negroni	Ice down-pour	Rocks
Rob Roy	Ice down-pour	Rocks

Short Sours (Served on the Rocks)

Name of Drink	Procedure	Glass
All sours (whiskey)	Speed-shake	Rocks
Bacardi® Cocktail	Speed-shake	Rocks
Between the Sheets	Speed-shake	Rocks
Cosmopolitan	Speed-shake	Rocks
Daiquiri	Speed-shake	Rocks
Gimlet	Speed-shake	Rocks
Jack Rose Cocktail	Speed-shake	Rocks
Kamikaze	Speed-shake	Rocks
Margarita	Speed-shake	Rocks
Pisco Sour	Speed-shake	Rocks
Sidecar	Speed-shake	Rocks

Short Cream Base (Served on the Rocks)

Name of Drink	Procedure	Glass
Brandy Alexander	Speed-shake	Rocks
Grasshopper	Speed-shake	Rocks
Pink Squirrel	Speed-shake	Rocks

Long Cream Base

Name of Drink	Procedure	Glass
Girl Scout Cookie	Speed-shake	Highball
Orgasm	Speed-shake	Highball
Toasted Almond Bar	Speed-shake	Highball
White Russian	Speed-shake	Highball

Long Sours

Name of Drink	Procedure	Glass
Long Island Iced Tea	Speed-shake	Sling/zombie
Sloe Gin Fizz	Speed-shake	Collins
Singapore Sling	Speed-shake	Sling/zombie
(Tom) Collins	Speed-shake	Collins

Tropical-Polynesian

Name of Drink	Procedure	Glass
Mai Tai	Speed-shake	Collins
Piña Colada	Speed-shake	Sling/zombie
Planter's Punch	Speed-shake	Collins
Zombie	Speed-shake	Sling/zombie

Highball

Name of Drink	Procedure	Glass
Juice Highball*	Ice down-pour	Highball
Soda Highball	Ice down-pour	Highball

Cordials

Name of Drink	Procedure	Glass
All Cordials	Ice down-pour	Rocks

*Exception to the rule for juice-based drinks: speed-shake juice-based highballs that have a liqueur with a juice mixer.

Performing the Stir Procedure

Drinks prepared using the stir procedure are served cold, but the ice is strained out to prevent diluting the liquor and mixer. Drinks prepared this way are usually served with a garnish.

To perform the stir procedure, follow these steps:

1. Chill a stemmed glass by filling it with ice, and place it on the rail.

2. Put ice into a mixing glass until it is one third full.

3. Pour the base into the mixing glass.

4. Add the liquor.

5. Hold the mixing glass with the fingers closed at the base and stir. Holding the bar spoon by its helix, roll it back and forth between the thumb and index finger until well chilled. Gently remove the bar spoon.

6. Remove the ice from the chilled serving glass.

7. Using a Hawthorne/spring strainer over the mouth of the glass, strain ingredients into the serving glass.

8. Garnish and serve.

EIGHT BASES FOR ALCOHOLIC BEVERAGES

It is important to be familiar with the types of alcohol that are used as the bases for many cocktails and mixed drinks. Note that the base ingredient or mixer for both mixed drinks and cocktails does not change, but the liquor changes according to the name of the drink. *See 9.12 Bases for Alcoholic Beverages.*

9.12 Bases for Alcoholic Beverages

Vermouth

Cocktails

Sours

Short sours–cocktails
Long sours–mixed drinks

Creams

Short creams–cocktails
Long creams–mixed drinks

Cordials (Liqueurs)

Two-liquor drinks

Carbonated Highballs

Mixed drinks

Juice-Based Highballs

Mixed drinks

Polynesian or Tropicals

Mixed drinks

Wines and Punches Specialties

Cream- and ice cream-based drinks; coffees mixed with spirits

Performing the Shake Procedure

Mixologists use the shake procedure to more fully incorporate spirits and mixer ingredients. The ice is strained from the drink before serving it. The key to a well-shaken drink is that it is vigorously shaken. This can best be done by holding the shake/mixing glass combination over the right or left shoulder. Shaking too long dilutes the drink. A fifteen second shake adds one-half to three-quarters of an ounce of additional liquid to the drink. This dilution makes a cocktail taste balanced and less alcoholic on the palate. The shake procedure also incorporates air bubbles that change the texture and lighten the drink.

To perform the shake procedure, follow these steps:

1. Put ice into a mixing glass until it is one-third full.

2. Add spirit(s) and/or liqueur(s).

3. Add mixer and/or base ingredient(s).

4. Place a metal cup or base over the top of the mixing glass, making sure that the metal cup is sitting evenly, not at an angle.

5. Give the top (bottom of the metal shaker) a light tap to create a vacuum.

6. Pick up the whole unit from the bar, and flip it over so the metal is facing down, and the glass is near your shoulder.

7. In a quick, even movement, shake vigorously moving the unit back and forth in rapid succession for fifteen seconds.

8. With the metal shaker still on the bottom, hold the unit in the left hand for balance. Press the index finger against the glass mixer. Make a fist with the right hand.

9. Locate the frost line on the metal shaker, and strike the side to break the vacuum.

10. Twist off the mixing glass, and strain the liquid through the spring strainer into a glass.

Performing the Ice Down-Pour Procedure

For mixed drinks and cocktails requested on the rocks, the ice down-pour procedure is used. These drinks are served cold over ice.

To perform the ice down-pour procedure, follow these steps:

1. Fill the base glass to the rim with ice, always using an ice scoop.

3. Garnish.

2. Add measured liquor(s) and/or liqueur(s).

4. Add the stirrer or sip stick, and serve.

Performing the Speed-Shake Procedure

The speed-shake procedure is appropriate for mixing spirits and heavier mixers. Drinks that are speed shaken are generally served tall with ice.

To perform the speed-shake procedure, follow these steps:

1. Place a base glass filled to the rim with ice on the bar or rail.

2. Pour liquor(s) and/or liqueur(s).

3. Add the mixer and/or the base ingredient(s).

4. Place the metal speed shaker over the glass.

5. Pick up the unit; flip it ensuring that the metal speed shaker is on the bottom, and shake the container back and forth in quick, even movements until well incorporated.

6. Pour the drink from the speed shaker into the chilled glass, garnish, and add a sip stick.

Vermouth-Based
Drinks

The Martini remains a universally popular cocktail. It is a dry, sharp, appetite-whetting drink that has become progressively drier (less vermouth) over the years. There is no Martini recipe on which all bartenders agree. By the time it came to be called a Martini, the drink had become a mixture of equal parts gin and dry vermouth.

The Manhattan was named for Manhattan, New York, where bartenders in speakeasies cut the harshness of bootlegged liquor with syrups and aromatic flavorings. In addition to whiskey or bourbon, the original Manhattan contained bitters, sugar, and much more vermouth than today's recipe. Although the recipe for a basic Manhattan is sweet vermouth and whiskey, using dry vermouth creates a Dry Manhattan. Using both sweet and dry vermouth makes the drink a Perfect Manhattan.

In Rob Roys, Scotch replaces the whiskey or bourbon used in the Manhattan recipe. Like regular Manhattans, Dry Rob Roys and Perfect Rob Roys vary according to the type of vermouth used in their preparation.

Vermouth-based cocktails are served up in cocktail glasses and are stirred, unless a customer requests the cocktail on the rocks. For an on-the-rocks version, use the ice down-pour method, and serve the drink in a rocks glass.

Garnishes Vermouth-based drinks may be garnished in a variety of ways.

• A Martini may contain either a cocktail olive or lemon zest.
• A Manhattan or a Rob Roy sports a maraschino cherry. When making a Rob Roy with dry vermouth rather than sweet vermouth, use lemon zest. When the drink contains both sweet and dry vermouth, the garnish is optional. Use either a cherry or lemon zest.
• A Negroni, which contains Campari® (a slightly bitter Italian apéritif), is garnished with an orange slice or lemon zest.
• Garnish a Gibson with a cocktail onion.

Vermouth-base stir and/or ice down-pour

martini (classic)

Gin	1 1/2 ounces
Dry vermouth	3/4 ounce
Olive or zest	garnish

dry martini

Gin	2 ounces
Dry vermouth	1/2 ounce
Olive or zest	garnish

vodka martini

Vodka	1 1/2 ounces
Dry vermouth	3/4 ounce
Olive or zest	garnish

extra-dry martini

Gin	2 1/4 ounces
Dry vermouth	1/4 ounce
Olive or zest	garnish

smoky martini or silver bullet

Gin	1 1/2 ounces
Dry vermouth	1/4 ounce
Scotch (float)	1/2 ounce
Olive or zest	garnish

gibson

Gin or vodka	1 1/2 ounces
Dry vermouth	3/4 ounce
Cocktail onions	garnish

manhattan

Bourbon or blended whiskey	1 1/2 ounces
Sweet vermouth	3/4 ounce
Cherry	garnish

Classic recipe includes a dash of bitters.

southern comfort/deluxe manhattan

Southern Comfort®	1 1/2 ounces
Dry vermouth	3/4 ounce
Cherry or zest	garnish

perfect manhattan

Bourbon or blended whiskey	1 1/2 ounces
Dry vermouth and sweet vermouth, combined	3/4 ounce
Cherry or zest	garnish

dry manhattan

Bourbon or blended whiskey	1 1/2 ounces
Dry vermouth	3/4 ounce
Zest	garnish

rob roy

Scotch	1 1/2 ounces
Sweet vermouth	3/4 ounce
Cherry	garnish

Classic recipe includes a dash of bitters.

dry rob roy

Scotch	1 1/2 ounces
Dry vermouth	3/4 ounce
Zest	garnish

perfect rob roy

Scotch	1 1/2 ounces
Dry vermouth and sweet vermouth, combined	3/4 ounce
Cherry or zest	garnish

negroni

Gin	1 ounce
Sweet vermouth	1 ounce
Campari®	1 ounce
One-half slice of orange	garnish

Build over ice in an old-fashioned glass.

Sours

Sours are drinks that use a sour base, such as lemon or lime juice. The origins of incorporating sours into drinks long predate the invention of the cocktail. They were standard ingredients of the all-popular punches of the seventeenth and eighteenth centuries. Consumption of citrus fruits was recognized by the English to be a valuable source of vitamin C, which also prevented scurvy among their navy's seamen. Limes were often preserved in rum so they could be consumed on long voyages. Laughlin Rose invented the preservation of lime juice in a non-alcoholic medium in the 1860s that led to including Rose's® Lime Juice as a naval ration. It is considered a staple of any bar.

Sours can be classified as short sours and long sours. Traditionally, bartenders have used simple syrup, lemon or lime juice, and egg whites as a **sour mix**. Today, commercially made sour mixes are commonly used. Short sours are composed of liquor(s) and/or liqueur(s) with sour mix or lime juice. Long sours contain the same ingredients, with the addition of carbonated soda to cut the sour taste. Serve a long sour in a tall glass, garnished with a cherry and an orange slice.

Use cocktail or sour glasses for short sours. The only short sours served with garnishes are sour-type cocktails, such as whiskey sours or apricot sours that are garnished with a cherry. If a customer requests the cocktail on the rocks, however, use the speed-shake procedure, and serve the cocktail in a rocks glass.

Sour Mix

Use fresh lemon and or lime juice mixed with simple syrup to create the perfect balance of sweet and sour. Sour mixes for a whiskey sour should only use lemon. Margaritas are best with only lime. Egg whites may be added to make cocktails slightly foamy and to give the drink a lighter texture.

short sours shake or speed-shake

between the sheets

Brandy	1 ounce
Lemon mix	1 ounce
Triple sec	1/2 ounce
Rum	1/2 ounce

Using the "BLT on Rye" mnemonic is a handy way to remember the ingredients of this drink, though it does not contain rye whiskey.

sidecar

Brandy	1 1/2 ounces
Triple sec	3/4 ounce
Sour mix	1 ounce

kamikaze

Gin or vodka	1 1/2 ounces
Rose's® Lime Juice	1/2 ounce
Triple sec	3/4 ounce
Lime wedge (optional)	garnish

stone sour

Apricot brandy	1 1/2 ounces
Orange juice	1 ounce
Sour mix	1 ounce
Cherry	garnish

gimlet

Gin or vodka	1 1/2 ounces
Rose's® Lime Juice	3/4 ounce
Lime wedge (optional)	garnish

cosmopolitan

Vodka	1 1/2 ounces
Cointreau	1/2 ounce
Lime juice	1/4 ounce
Cranberry juice	1 ounce
Orange	garnish

whiskey sour

Whiskey	1 1/2 ounces
Sour mix	2 ounces
Cherry	garnish

Serve in a sour glass.

daiquiri

Light rum	1 1/2 ounces
Sour Mix	2 ounces

bacardi® cocktail

Bacardi® light rum	1 1/2 ounces
Sour mix	2 ounces
Grenadine	1/2 ounce

ward 8

Whiskey	1 1/2 ounces
Sour mix	2 ounces
Grenadine	1/2 ounce
Cherry or orange slice	garnish

jack rose cocktail

Applejack	1 1/2 ounces
Grenadine	1/2 ounce
Sour mix	2 ounces

margarita

Tequila	1 1/2 ounces
Lime juice or sour mix	1 ounce
Triple sec	3/4 ounce

Rim the champagne coupe with salt. To rim or frost a glass, moisten the rim of the glass with a wedge of citrus fruit, and dip the outside of the glass into a small container of salt or sugar. Set the glass aside. Blend or shake.

pisco sour

Pisco	1 1/2 ounces
Lime juice	1 ounce
Simple syrup	1 ounce
Egg whites	1 each
Angostura® bitters	several drops

long sours speed-shake

tom collins

Gin	1 1/2 ounces
Sour mix	2 ounces
Club soda and 7UP®	to fill
Cherry and one-half orange slice	garnish

Also known as a John Collins
Speed-shake—Collins

Variations

Mike Collins—whiskey
Pedro Collins—rum
Joe or Ivan Collins—vodka
Sandy Collins—scotch

singapore sling

Gin	1 1/2 ounces
Sour mix	2 ounces
Club soda and 7UP®	equal parts to fill
Cherry flavored brandy or liqueur (float)	1/2 ounce

Classic recipe includes 1 dash of Angostura® bitters
Speed-shake—Sling/Zombie

sloe gin fizz

Sloe gin	1 1/2 ounces
Sour mix	2 ounces
Club soda	to fill
Cherry and one-half orange slice	garnish

Speed-shake—Collins

long island iced tea

Vodka	1/2 ounce
Gin	1/2 ounce
Rum	1/2 ounce
Tequila	1/2 ounce
Triple sec	1/2 ounce
Sour mix	4 ounces
Coke® (float)	1 ounce
Lemon wheel	garnish

Speed-shake––Sling/Zombie

Cream- and Ice Cream-Based Drinks

Cream drinks are usually very sweet, smooth, and pleasing to the palate. They are perfect after-dinner drinks, and many customers order them instead of dessert.

All cream-based drinks may use ice cream instead of cream. Usually, vanilla ice cream is the flavor of choice, but any flavor that blends well with the liqueur's flavor will work, including coffee, strawberry, peach, or chocolate. Sherbets may also be used to make freezes, or frozen drinks. Prepare cream drinks by using either a shake or a blend procedure. The blend procedure uses a blender to mix the ingredients more thoroughly and to give the drink a creamier, frothier texture.

The **blend procedure** is appropriate for any drink that is shaken, but it should always be used when incorporating ice or solids, such as strawberries in a Strawberry Daiquiri. **To use the blend procedure:**

1. Place the ice in the blender 1/4 full; add the remaining ingredients.

2. The blender container should be one-fourth full; the ice should be covered with the other ingredients.

3. When using a two-speed blender, blend for 3 seconds on low and then 7–10 seconds on high.

4. Using a cocktail spoon to maintain an even flow, pour the blended ingredients into an appropriate glass.

Short cream drinks Serve short cream drinks in a Champagne coupe. The only cream-based drink that has a garnish is the Alexander, which requires a sprinkle of nutmeg.

Long cream drinks Long cream drinks are generally prepared using the speed-shake procedure and are served in a highball glass; they receive no garnish.

frozen cream-based drinks
blend or shake or speed-shake

summer rum freeze

Bacardi® rum	1 1/2 ounces
Lime sherbet	2 scoops
Pineapple juice	3 ounces
Cream or milk	3/4 ounce
Pineapple spear or lime wheel	garnish

Place ingredients in the blender. Blend until creamy. Pour into a tall goblet.

short-creams blend or shake

brandy alexander

Brandy	1 ounce
Dark crème de cacao	1 ounce
Cream or milk	1 ounce
Nutmeg	garnish

grasshopper

Light crème de cacao	1 ounce
Green crème de menthe	1 ounce
Cream or milk	1 ounce

pink squirrel

Light crème de cacao	1 ounce
Crème de Noyaux® or Crème d' Amande	1 ounce
Cream or milk	1 ounce

long-creams speed-shake

orgasm

Amaretto	1 ounce
Vodka	1/2 ounce
Kahlúa®	1/2 ounce
Cream or milk	4 ounces

Classic recipe: short cream with Bailey's® Irish Cream instead of milk.

white russian

Vodka	1 1/2 ounces
Kahlúa®	1/2 ounce
Cream or milk	4 ounces

Traditionally a layered drink with half-and-half cream set on top of a Black Russian. Today, prepare using speed-shake, serve tall.

girl scout cookie

Peppermint schnapps	1 ounce
Dark crème de cacao	1 ounce
Milk	4 ounces

toasted almond bar

Amaretto	1 ounce
Dark crème de cacao	1 ounce
Milk	4 ounces

Cordials or Two-Liquor Drinks

Cordials are sweet alcoholic beverages in which two-liquor drinks are combined with a distilled spirit or brandy. The spirit helps cut the pronounced sweetness of the cordial. Except for drinks such as the Mud Slide, which requires the speed-shake procedure, two-liquor drinks are served on the rocks in a rocks glass, using the ice downpour procedure with the spirits poured in first. Cordials that are considered layered drinks must be carefully poured into the glass so the ingredients do not mix but rather remain in layers.

The cordial *pousse-café*, French for "coffee-pusher," requires a very steady hand to layer the different colored liqueurs, one on top of the other, in a pony glass. Each layer is created by pouring individual liqueurs into the glass over the back of a cocktail spoon. Generally, the last ingredient is flamed to add drama. As many as 56 different ingredients can be used to make a pousse-café. Knowing the specific gravity of each ingredient allows bartenders to pour the densest liqueur first and the least dense last.

cordials ice down-pour

black russian
Vodka	1 1/2 ounces
Kahlúa®	3/4 ounce

godfather
Scotch	1 1/2 ounces
Amaretto	3/4 ounce

sicilian kiss
Southern Comfort®	1 1/2 ounces
Amaretto	3/4 ounce

mud slide
Vodka	3/4 ounce
Kahlúa®	3/4 ounce
Bailey's Irish Cream®	3/4 ounce

Speed-shake

after 5
Kahlúa®	1/3 ounce
Bailey's® Irish Cream	1/3 ounce
Peppermint schnapps	1/3 ounce

Layered in order

stinger
Brandy	1 1/2 ounces
White crème de menthe	3/4 ounce

godmother
Vodka	1 1/2 ounces
Amaretto	3/4 ounce

rusty nail or queen anne
Scotch	1 1/2 ounces
Drambuie®	3/4 ounce

b-52
Kahlúa®	1/3 ounce
Bailey's® Irish Cream	1/3 ounce
Grand Marnier®	1/3 ounce

Highballs

Highballs consist of carbonated mixers, water or juices, and the appropriate liquor served tall in highball glasses on ice. Highballs with carbonated mixers or water require only the ice downpour procedure to have their ingredients fully incorporated. Highballs made with liqueurs are speed-shaken to incorporate their ingredients. The basic recipe, however, is the same: 1 1/2 ounces of liquor (or customer preference), and 4 ounces of soda or other mixer. Pour the liquor over ice cubes in a highball glass, top with any flavored soda, and serve.

Highball history Mixed drinks and highballs have origins as fabled as those of the cocktail and the cordial. Many were created by individuals in different occupations and locations based on practicality or culture.

One of the first mixed drinks was called Gin and Tonic by British troops in the late 1800s. Like many of the original cordials, the drink grew out of the desire to add "a spoon full of sugar" to help the "medicine go down." Required to take daily doses of bitter quinine, a medicine used to ward off malaria; British soldiers in India began adding sugar and water to the dose. Before long, they discovered that adding gin, their favorite liquor, made the medicine go down even better, and so the Gin and Tonic was born.

Highballs were named by railroaders in the 1800s who typically placed a ball on a high pole to indicate to oncoming trains that the track was clear and they could maintain their speed. When the men had time enough to stop for a fast drink of whiskey and ginger ale, they coined the term "highball" as a name for their drink. The popular Screwdriver was also named by Americans while working in Iran's oil fields where alcohol is forbidden. They began using screwdrivers to secretly mix drinks made from vodka and orange juice.

carbonated and juice-based highballs
ice down-pour

Today's highball is made of many different combinations of liquors and flavored sodas. Water may also be a base for a highball. Regardless of the combination, the basic recipe is as follows:

Liquor	1 1/2 ounces
Soda	4 ounces

highball

Whiskey	1 1/2 ounces
Ginger ale	4 ounces

Variations

Presbyterian—whiskey, ginger ale, and club soda
Cuba Libre—Rum and Coke, lime garnish
7 and 7—Seagram's® 7 and 7UP®
Jack and Coke—Jack Daniel's® and Cola

comfortable screw

Southern Comfort®	1 1/2 ounces
Orange juice	4 ounces
Orange slice	garnish

Speed-shake

bocce ball

Amaretto di Saronno®	1 1/2 ounces
Orange juice	4 ounces
Club soda	(float)

Speed-shake

cape codder

Vodka	1 1/2 ounces
Cranberry juice	4 ounces
Lime wedge	garnish

harvey wallbanger

Vodka	1 1/2 ounces
Orange juice	4 ounces
Galliano® (float)	1/2 ounce
Orange slice and cherry	garnish

tequila sunrise

Tequila	1 1/2 ounces
Orange juice	4 ounces
Grenadine (float)	1/2 ounce
Orange slice and cherry	garnish

madras

Vodka	1 1/2 ounces
Cranberry juice	2 ounces
Orange juice	2 ounces

salty dog

Vodka	1 1/2 ounces
Grapefruit juice	4 ounces

Rim glass with salt.

pearl harbor

Midori®	1 ounce
Vodka	1/2 ounce
Pineapple juice	4 ounces

Speed-shake

classic mixed drink

woo-woo

Peachtree® Schnapps	1 ounce
Vodka	1/2 ounce
Cranberry juice	4 ounces

Speed-shake

basic bloody mary mix

Vodka	1 1/2 ounces
Tomato juice	4 ounces
Salt and pepper	dash
Lea & Perrins® Worcestershire sauce	dash
Tabasco® sauce	dash
Lemon mix	dash
Horseradish (optional)	1 teaspoon
Celery salt (optional)	dash
Celery stalk or lime wedge	garnish

Speed-shake; serve in a goblet.

Variations

Bloody Maria—tequila

Bloody Jane or Red Snapper—gin

Bloody Caesar—Vodka and Clamato Juice salt & pepper rim

Virgin Mary—non-alcoholic Bloody Mary

alabama slammer

Sloe gin	1/2 ounce
Banana liqueur	1/2 ounce
Orange juice	4 ounces
Southern Comfort® (float)	1/2 ounce

Speed-shake

sex on the beach

Peachtree® schnapps	1 ounce
Vodka	1 ounce
Orange juice	2 ounces
Cranberry juice	2 ounces

Speed-shake

sea breeze

Vodka	1 1/2 ounces
Grapefruit juice	2 ounces
Cranberry juice	2 ounces

scarlet o'hara

Southern Comfort®	1 1/2 ounces
Cranberry juice	4 ounces

Speed-shake

fuzzy navel

Peachtree® schnapps	1 1/2 ounces
Orange juice	4 ounces

Speed-shake

old fashioned

Sugar	1 package
Bitters	2 or 3 dashes
Club soda	splash
Stemless cherry or orange slice	garnish

Muddle or crush with a muddler, the ingredients to release the oils and juice of the fruit. Then add 2 ounces of blended whiskey or bourbon and a splash of club soda. Serve on the rocks. Garnish with an orange slice and cherry.

mojito

Fresh mint	2 sprigs
Simple syrup	1 ounce
Lime juice	3/4 ounce
Bacardi Silver® Rum	1 1/2 ounces
Angostura® bitters (optional)	2 dashes
Club soda	To fill

Muddle mint, simple syrup, and lime juice together in a mixing glass. Add the remaining ingredients and shake with ice. Strain into a highball glass with fresh ice and top with club soda. Garnish with a fresh mint sprig.

sazerac

Ricard®	Splash
VS Cognac	1 ounce
Rye Whiskey	1 ounce
Simple syrup	1/2 ounce
Peychaud's® bitters	2 dashes
Angostura® bitters	2 dashes
Lemon peel	garnish

Fill two rocks glasses with ice. Splash the Ricard into one rocks glass, swirl and then pour it out. Add the remaining ingredients into the second rocks glass and stir. Strain the ingredients into the first chilled, seasoned rocks glass, and garnish with the lemon peel.

caiparinha

Cachaça	2 ounces
1/2 lime	quartered
Superfine sugar or (1 oz simple syrup)	2 teaspoons

Fill a rocks glass with ice. In a glass mixer, muddle lime quarters with sugar for 15 seconds. Add cachaça and ice from the rock glass and shake well. Pour contents into a rocks glass and garnish with lime.

Polynesian-
Tropicals

The Polynesian or "Tiki" bar culture in the U.S. began in the 1930s with the opening of Don the Beachcomber and Victor Bergeron's Trader Vic. The latter eventually became a worldwide chain with as many as 25 restaurants, which expanded the Polynesian/Tiki culture. Both restaurants claim to have invented the Mai Tai, and a number of tropical drinks have since followed.

The Mai Tai, Piña Colada, Zombie, and Planter's Punch are usually rum-based drinks with tropical fruit flavors such as pineapple, orange, or coconut, which add sweetness to the mix. Polynesian-Tropical drinks are generally prepared using a blender or the speed-shake procedure and are decoratively garnished with combinations of a cherry, orange slice, or pineapple chunk.

polynesian-tropicals

mai tai

Sugar or simple syrup	1/2 ounce
Orange curaçao	1/2 ounce
Myer's® rum (dark)	1 ounce
Mount Gay® rum (gold)	1 ounce
Amaretto	1/2 ounce
Lemon mix	3 ounces

piña colada

Coco Lopez®	1/2 ounce
Pineapple juice	3 ounces
Mount Gay® rum (gold)	2 ounces

planter's punch

Grenadine	1/2 ounce
Lemon mix	1 ounce
Orange juice	3 ounces
White rum	1 ounce
Myer's® rum (dark)	1 ounce
Pineapple juice	1 ounce

zombie

Grenadine	1/2 ounce
Light rum (bar)	1 ounce
Myer's® rum (dark)	1 ounce
Lemon mix	2 ounces
Orange juice	1 1/2 ounces
Orange curaçao	1 ounce

Non-alcoholic Cocktails and Mixed Drinks

Non-alcoholic cocktails or "**mocktails**" and alcohol-free alternatives are an important aspect of mixology. About 40% of the U.S. adult population does not consume alcohol. Designated drivers, abstainers from alcoholic beverages, and young people may want to take part in social occasions where others are enjoying alcoholic beverages. Diverse, quality, alcohol-free options must be available to them. The ever-expanding options of bottled water, crafted soda, tea, juice, energy drinks, alcohol-free beer, and crafted mocktails are sales opportunities not to be missed. Possibilities are endless and provide an opportunity for increasing beverage sales. The key is to create recipes and drinks with the same high standards as regular cocktails. Bartenders should use their imaginations and creativity to cater to this market.

non-alcoholic cocktails and mixed drinks

shirley temple

Ginger ale	6 ounces
Grenadine	1 ounce
Cherries	garnish

florida cocktail

Grape juice	2 ounces
Orange juice	1 ounce
Lemon mix	2 ounces
Club soda	fill to 1/4 inch from the rim
Fresh mint leaves	garnish

Speed-shake

pussyfoot

Lemon mix	2 ounces
Orange juice	2 ounces
Rose's® Lime Juice	1 ounce
Grenadine	1/2 ounce
Pasteurized egg yolk	1 ounce
Orange slice and cherry	garnish

Alcohol *and* the Law

The first liquor-control laws in America's English colonies became effective in 1733 when Georgia's governor prohibited the importation of hard liquor into that colony. Since that time, governments have passed a variety of liquor laws—some to control and deter the consumption of alcohol and others to raise money. Popularly known as "sin taxes," laws taxing such items as alcohol and tobacco are popular with legislators because they are not considered necessities.

EARLY ALCOHOL LAWS

Shortly after the United States became an independent country, a tax on alcohol prompted the first confrontation between citizens and federal troops. The 1794 Whiskey Rebellion sent Pennsylvania farmers, who found it cheaper to transport alcohol than the grain used to make it, into the streets to protest a tax on spirits. Twenty years later, Indiana prohibited the sale of liquor on Sunday, and by 1833, more than 5,000 temperance groups with more than a million members lobbied for an outright ban on the sale of alcohol. A string of controls across the country, including Maine's 1846 prohibition law, made complete prohibition of the sale of alcoholic beverages an idea growing in popularity.

PROHIBITION

On January 16, 1920, the Eighteenth Amendment, which banned the sale of liquor in the United States, became law.

Prohibition was a failure and turned many ordinary citizens into lawbreakers, paving the way for the development of organized crime, and costing the United States government approximately $1 billion each year in lost revenues and enforcement expenses. Experts estimate that about $36 billion spent for bootlegged and smuggled liquor traveled from the wallets of ordinary citizens into the pockets of criminals.

In the end, Americans opted for regulation over the expensive and largely ineffective Eighteenth Amendment. In 1933, the Twenty-first Amendment repealed Prohibition, setting up a climate for new regulations.

TTB (FORMERLY THE ATF)

Federal laws govern trade practices and the issuance of required permits. In 1972, the Bureau of Alcohol, Tobacco, and Firearms (ATF) received its charter to operate under the Department of the Treasury. However, regulatory supervisory changes were made when the **Alcohol and Tobacco Tax and Trade Bureau (TTB)** was established under the Homeland Security Act of 2002 when some of the enforcement functions of the ATF were shifted to the Department of Justice. The TTB's function is to collect taxes owed and to ensure that alcohol beverages are produced, labeled, advertised, and marketed in accordance to federal law. For example, government regulations require that distilled spirits be bottled in similar containers with affixed Internal Revenue tax stamps. The stamp must span the crevice where the bottle cap ends and the bottle begins so that upon opening the bottle the stamp tears, but a portion of the stamp still remains affixed to the opened bottle. Failure to comply with this regulation may result in a fine of up to $10,000 or imprisonment of not more than five years, or both. Federal law prohibits the use of empty liquor bottles for any reason or the marrying of contents of two or more bottles of the same liquor.

The TTB has three areas of responsibility:
- **Revenue collection** The bureau collects revenues from all producers of beverage alcohol on the basis of proof gallons.
- **Consumer protection** Alcoholic beverages must conform to the Standards of Identity and are produced, labeled, advertised, and marketed according to the federal law.
- **Trade practices** These practices promote voluntary compliance.

Producers pay excise taxes, and retail dealers who sell alcoholic beverages also pay a special federal tax. When the tax is paid in full, the dealer is issued a special tax stamp for the class of business for which the tax is paid.

LEGAL DEFINITIONS

The TTB uses specific definitions to levy taxes on alcoholic beverages:
- **Alcohol** A volatile, colorless liquid obtained through the fermentation of a liquid containing sugar.
- **Alcoholic beverage** Any potable liquid containing from 0.5% to 75.5% ethyl alcohol by volume.
- **Spirit** A potable alcoholic beverage obtained from the distillation of a liquid containing alcohol.
- **Proof (American method)** The strength of a liquor, which was at one time called "gunpowder proof."

To test the strength of liquor, distillers used to pour it on gunpowder and throw a lighted match on it. If the liquor blazed, it was too strong. When liquor was the proper strength and mixed with gunpowder, it would burn steadily with a blue flame. The addition of 50% water produced a slow, steady flame. That strength was called "100 proof." Today, regulations apply the same scale on the following basis: Pure 100% alcohol is 200 proof, and 1 degree of proof is equal to 0.5% alcohol. Dividing the proof number by 2 yields the percentage of alcohol by volume. The term proof indicates the strength.

Conversely, the proof number is always twice the percentage of the alcohol in the beverage. The remainder of the content in the beverage includes distilled water, coloring, and flavoring components.

PROOF GALLON TAXES

All alcoholic beverages, whether they are produced in the United States or imported, are subject to Internal Revenue taxes. Imported alcoholic beverages are also subject to customs' duties. The alcohol content of the beverage determines the tax rate. The standard one-gallon proof contains 100 proof, or 50%, alcohol. If a gallon contains 150 proof alcohol, it is taxed as 1.5 proof gallons. The trade term for a spirit of more than 100 proof is an overproof spirit.

A tax gallon is the measure used to determine how much tax is paid, according to the rate of taxation and/or duties, times the number of tax gallons of spirits. For beverages containing less than 100 proof alcohol, the tax is paid on the actual gallons.

The federal government taxes wines at different rates, ranging from $1.07 to $3.40 per gallon depending on the alcohol content and the degree and type of carbonation. The beer tax is $18.00 per 31 gallons and $0.05 cents on each 12-ounce can. The tax on distilled spirits is $13.50 per proof gallon. These taxes are paid by on-premise and off-premise retailers, which must track the sale of each category and maintain written records that are subject to both TTB and local government audit.

DUTIES

Import duties are imposed in addition to the federal, state, and local excise taxes charged for alcoholic beverages. Imported spirits are therefore often more expensive than domestic varieties. Negotiated trade agreements can alter the amount of duties charged on imported alcoholic beverages. Wines, in particular, are commonly available from countries all over the world, especially Mexico, Canada, the Caribbean nations, European countries, and Australia. Fifty percent of the average retail price of a bottle of spirits consists of federal, state, and local taxes.

STATE CONTROLS

With the repeal of Prohibition, the federal government turned over most alcoholic beverage sales control to the individual states. Each state has the absolute authority to control the sale of alcohol within their borders and to regulate the import and export of alcohol as well. Control of the sale of alcoholic beverages falls into two categories: open-license states and control states.

OPEN-LICENSE STATES

Open-license states grant licenses to private enterprises to operate as wholesalers of alcoholic beverages to both on- and off-premise retailers and to the retailers themselves. Strict rules may govern the manner in which both tiers of the distribution system operate. For example, tied house relationships, whereby the distributor operates or owns part interest in a retailer, may not exist. Most states also have local option laws that leave the decision to allow the sale of alcoholic beverages up to local communities.

In addition to these state controls, some states have "dry" communities where it is illegal to transport alcoholic beverages from neighboring "wet" communities. Each state and municipality may also enforce the opening and closing hours for establishments that sell liquor. Provisions may be set with respect to the number of licenses permitted in a given area, and restrictions may be enforced concerning the sale of alcohol within a designated proximity from places of worship, schools, or hospitals.

CONTROL STATES

Control states operate to varying degrees as the sole distributors of alcoholic beverages to on- and off-premise retailers. In some of these states, the state acts as the only off-premise outlet for liquor sold to consumers. In such cases, beer and certain wines may be sold through private enterprises, such as grocery stores. To prevent consumers or operators of bars and restaurants from purchasing alcoholic beverages across state lines, some control states require a special stamp or mark on each bottle to prove the item was purchased legally within the state.

State Laws

Those who work in establishments that serve alcohol must be familiar with all the state laws governing the sale of alcoholic beverages. Failure to know the law can have serious consequences for the employer and the employee. Some consequences are legal; others are a matter of conscience, especially if innocent people are injured by someone who should not have served them alcohol.

DRAM SHOP LAWS

For bars, restaurants, and their personnel, **dram shop laws** are the most critical issue affecting the sale of alcoholic beverages. Dram shop laws originated in the nineteenth century in England and were first enacted in the United States in 1873. In states with dram shop laws, restaurants, bars, and their employees are held liable for illegal acts committed by patrons under the influence of alcohol served to them in the establishment. These laws are also known as **third-party liability laws.** Lawyers began using these laws in the mid-1980s to litigate civil actions. Many such suits resulted in unprecedented multimillion-dollar awards.

NEGLIGENCE LAWS

Even in states that do not have dram shop laws, courts generally apply common law to alcohol related cases. Basing their decisions on precedents, courts usually favor the victim over the persons who served or sold the liquor. Generally, in non-dram shop states, courts base their decisions on Alcohol Beverage Control (ABC) regulations, either because state laws were violated or because sellers or servers were negligent in serving alcohol to an obviously inebriated person or to a minor.

In addition to facing third-party liability and negligence laws, the operator of a restaurant, tavern, or bar, the employees of such an establishment, or the host of a private party may be subject to criminal liability. If convicted, these persons could receive prison sentences. The establishment and its employees can also face administrative liability, whereby the state or Alcohol Control Board can levy a fine or suspend or revoke a liquor license.

DRUNKEN DRIVING LAWS

The hope of preventing thousands of deaths caused by drunk drivers has encouraged many states to strengthen drunken driving laws. In these states, offenses that are commonly referred to as DWI, driving while intoxicated, or DUI, driving under the influence, are no longer treated lightly. These offenses are punishable under per se laws, dictating that a single piece of evidence, such as the results of a Breathalyzer™ test or the refusal to take such a test, is sufficient evidence to presume guilt.

THE IMPACT OF LAWS ON INDUSTRY

As we have seen, criminal, administrative, and civil sanctions exist for servers, managers, or owners of establishments who fail to make reasonable efforts to ensure alcohol consumption occurs in a responsible and moderate fashion.

An establishment and its servers must be acquainted with all pertinent laws and regulations and must undergo alcohol awareness training to demonstrate that negligence has not occurred. Each server should know which persons cannot legally be served.

These include anyone
• who is legally intoxicated or who would become intoxicated if served an alcoholic beverage.
• who is a known alcoholic.
• with a propensity toward alcoholism.
• who is legally under age.

All states mandate only those persons who are 21 years of age or older may purchase or be served alcoholic beverages. Because forging identification has become easier with today's technology, establishments need to stay abreast of publications on identification issues, which are updated yearly.

As a precaution, a server should check the identification of anyone who looks younger than 30 years old. Some national chains have made it a policy to check the identification of all who purchase alcoholic beverages, regardless of age.

Legally acceptable forms of identification include:
• a state-issued driver's license with a photograph
• a state-issued identification card with a photograph
• a military identification card with a photograph
• a United States' passport.

An establishment's employees are not required to accept any identification issued outside the state in which the establishment is located. Some states, such as Rhode Island, require that employees have a "Minors Book" located at the bar. Anyone who presents proper identification but who appears underage or "illegal" for some reason must sign the book before being served. A good guide to follow is if there is sufficient reason to question the legal age of a patron, politely refuse to serve that person any alcoholic beverage.

The Effects
of Alcohol

Alcohol is a food product, but it is classified as an intoxicating drug that depresses the brain and other parts of the central nervous system. Although alcohol is fairly high in calories, it has little nutritional value. An ounce of pure alcohol has 210 calories; one ounce of whiskey (43% alcohol, or 86 proof) has 75 calories. A 12-ounce (355-ml) container of beer has between 120 and 210 calories. Although moderate consumption of alcohol, especially wine, may have some health benefits, long-term abuse will result in permanent damage to the liver, kidneys, and brain, as well as to the central nervous, digestive, and circulatory systems.

....

INTOXICATION/ABSORPTION RATE FACTORS

Because alcohol requires no digestion, it is absorbed and transported by the bloodstream throughout the body in a very short time. A small amount enters the capillaries in the mouth even before the beverage is swallowed. About 20% of the remaining alcohol is quickly absorbed through the stomach lining. However, the presence of food in the stomach slows the absorption of alcohol because alcohol mixes with the stomach's contents and is digested along with the food.

During the initial stage of the digestive process, the "door" between the stomach and the small intestine, called the pylorus valve, generally remains closed, trapping food and alcohol in the stomach. Too much alcohol may cause a pylorospasm, in which the alcohol-sensitive pylorus valve prevents the food and alcohol from moving through the system.

Pylorospasms trap sufficient alcohol in the stomach to cause irritation and distress. The drinker may elect to stop drinking at this point because he or she feels ill when the stomach lining secretes excess amounts of hydrochloric acid. This process is a self-protective mechanism that can prevent the overconsumption of alcohol, but not all people recognize the symptoms.

When alcohol reaches the small intestine, the remaining 80% is absorbed into the bloodstream. The faster the alcohol is absorbed, the more likely the consumer is to become intoxicated. The higher the alcohol content of the beverage, the more quickly it is absorbed into the bloodstream. Alcohol mixed with carbonated beverages is absorbed faster than alcohol of the same proof mixed with fruit juice.

Several other factors also **influence** the rate **of absorption of alcohol,** including the following:

- the **rate** of consumption
- the **gender** of the consumer
- the **height, weight,** and **physical condition** of the consumer
- the **mood** of the consumer
- the **amount of food** in the consumer's stomach
- the presence of **medications,** some of which can speed up the effects of alcohol

LEVELS OF INTOXICATION

Learning to recognize and understand the effects of alcohol will help servers determine whether to serve or continue to serve alcoholic beverages to a guest. The brain and other parts of the central nervous system are affected more quickly than are other organs of the body. When blood alcohol content is sufficient to cause intoxication, or drunkenness, it also impairs memory, motor control, and judgment. **These behavioral clues can help determine when a patron has become intoxicated:**

- **Loss of inhibitions** An intoxicated person becomes talkative, relaxed, over-friendly, and exhibits mood swings. Depending on how extreme his or her actions are the person may fall into a happy category or one of pronounced excitement.
- **Loss of judgment** An intoxicated person often exhibits erratic behavior. He or she may use foul language, become angry, or act impulsively. The person may be excited to the point of confusion.
- **Loss of reaction** An intoxicated person may easily lose his or her train of thought. He or she may exhibit unfocused eyes, slurred speech, and unsteady hands.
- **Loss of coordination** An intoxicated person may suffer loss of balance, drowsiness, and a lack of dexterity. When a drinker reaches this stage, he or she is approaching the fourth stage of intoxication.

STAGES OF INTOXICATION

The table below is based on the effects of alcohol consumption on a man weighing 150–160 pounds (68–73 kg). One drink represents 1 ounce (30 ml) of 100 proof distilled spirits, 3 ounces (90 ml) of sherry, 5 ounces (150 ml) of wine, or 12 ounces (355 ml) of beer. Note that a woman who weighs 120–130 pounds (54–60 kg) becomes intoxicated faster than a man of similar weight. This more rapid intoxication takes place because women generally have less water and more body fat than men. The higher rate of water in a man's body dilutes the alcohol, lowering the blood-alcohol level.

INDUSTRY RESPONSIBILITIES

Although the food and beverage industry cannot be responsible for all the problems associated with excess alcohol consumption, servers and establishment operators can ensure the behavior of staff members promotes responsible consumption of alcoholic beverages by:

- Checking identification as routine in every case in which there is doubt about a patron's age.
- Recognizing the signs of intoxication and refraining from serving anyone who has consumed too many drinks or who exhibits signs of intoxication.
- Declining to serve any customer who appears to have consumed excess alcohol elsewhere.
- Encouraging impaired customers to call for a cab, to contact a friend for a ride home, to offer to make the call for the patron, and persuading the customer to surrender the car keys when warranted.
- Observing responsible and reasonable standards in serving and consuming alcohol to set a good example for fellow employees and friends.

Stages of Intoxication

Stage	Drinks per Hour	Blood Alcohol	Rate to Metabolize
Happy	1	0.02	Less than 1 hour **Loss of inhibitions:** talkative, relaxed
Excited	2	0.05	Two hours **Loss of judgment:** loud, boisterous, inappropriate remarks, and behavior
Confused	4	0.10	Four hours **Loss of reactions:** slurred speech, staggering, mood swings, double vision, some loss of coordination
Stupor	8	0.20	Eight hours **Loss of coordination:** after 6 hours, still legally drunk; emotional, erratic behavior; inability to stand; loss of memory; barely conscious, approaching paralysis
Coma	1 pint	0.40–0.50	**Unable to metabolize:** comatose, and dangerously close to death; brain centers are anesthetized
Death		0.60–0.70	

10. Enology

It is little wonder that the ancient Greek god Dionysus was known as the god of wine and ecstasy. Few beverages excite as many senses as does wine. Brilliant colors, inviting aromas, complex bouquets, subtle tastes and textures—the products of the winemaker's art—have made wine an integral part of ceremonies and social and religious rituals by enhancing well-prepared meals and cementing friendships. Today, science has also revealed the long-term health benefits of moderate wine consumption.

Introduction *to* Wine

The simple definition of wine—the fermented juice of grapes—does little to explain why academics in such diverse fields as archeology, biology, chemistry, microbiology, geography, horticulture, sociology, economics, and medicine have all been fascinated with the study of wine. Perhaps the interest stems from the simple fact that from the vineyard to the table, wine is the perfect blend of art and science, a study of infinite variety and nearly endless permutations.

There are many species of grapes and thousands of varieties within each species. It is the *Vitis vinifera* species, however, that produces most wines. Of the 10,000 varieties of **Vitis vinifera** (the name means "wine bearing"), the wine market is concerned primarily with no more than 50 varieties. Because winemaking is both a science and an art form, the history of winemaking has been characterized by continual challenges for winemakers and growers alike to produce more complex wines.

THE HISTORY OF WINE

Winemaking is a natural phenomenon: grapes contain sugars that wild yeasts convert to ethyl alcohol. Winemakers of today select the varieties of grapes and the yeasts that ferment them into wines with infinite care.

Until the nineteenth century, the history of wine making may be viewed as a struggle against spoilage. Wood inadvertently became an added flavor component in wine when the Romans adopted the same standard medium for transportation and storage used by the ancient Gauls of France for beer. Wood has certain anti-microbiological elements, but without proper sanitation, wines stored in wood can become both oxidized and affected by microorganisms such as acetobacter, which turn wine into vinegar.

Modern winemakers, however, have little excuse for making faulty wines. The art and science of grape growing and winemaking are based on centuries of experimentation and learning about conditions that make for good wines—and sometimes, great ones.

Wine and religion Over the centuries, wine has been inextricably linked to religion. From the ancient Greeks and Romans to the Jewish and Christian traditions, wine has been associated with mystical and religious experiences because of the symbolism of the annual rebirth of the vine as well as the psychological effects of wine.

The earliest years The earliest traces of winemaking may date back to 7500 B.C. in Jiahu, China, although these wines were produced from native Chinese species, while the earliest traces of vinifera date back to approximately 5600 B.C. in the Caucasus region. By 4000 B.C., winemaking had spread to Mesopotamia, Babylon, and Egypt. At that time, the Egyptians also began the practice of labeling wines to indicate the place of origin, the grape, the name of the winemaker, and the vintage.

Written references to grapes appear in the Bible, which notes that Noah planted a vineyard after the great flood and said to have occurred in about 5600 B.C. When the Phoenicians or Minoans introduced winemaking to Greece circa 2000 B.C., its sale created wealth with which the Greeks built their great civilization. *See 10.1.* The Greeks spread vineyards and winemaking along the Mediterranean coast including present day Greece, France, Spain, Turkey, Italy, and the islands such as Sicily.

Winemaking technology continued to develop under the Roman Empire. Winemakers began understanding wine production and the relationships between varieties and soil, climate, aging, and storing temperatures. Later, the Romans introduced winemaking to the Gauls (modern-day French). Between 350 A.D. and 1200 A.D., some monastic orders, particularly the Benedictines, Carthusians, and Cistercians, preserved and improved winemaking knowledge in Europe. In the process, they cultivated vineyards to produce wine for sacramental and medicinal purposes, and to generate income.

Trade expands winemaking As world exploration and trade expanded in the 1400s, Europeans looked for ways to preserve wine during long trade voyages. Dutch and English traders learned to **fortify** wines from France, Portugal, and Spain by adding brandy to stabilize them for sea voyages. The Germans are said to be the first to add sulfur to wine to prevent spoilage. Although this method continues to be widely utilized to this day, it is used more judiciously. Exploration and trade also introduced winemaking to the Americas, Australia, and South Africa when Europeans began to settle in the New World.

Technology advances winemaking In the mid-1600s, glass that was strong enough for commercial bottling was developed by the English, although these bottles were not widely used until the 1700s in Europe's wine-making regions. With the increased use of bottles, the use of cork stoppers became more commonplace. *See 10.2.* These developments not only contributed considerably to the popularity of dry wines and the need for better quality control and the marketing of brands, but they also marked the beginning of wine as a modern beverage.

10.1 A clay amphora used as a wine vessel

Hybridizing vitis species to combat Phylloxera has proven to be relatively disappointing because of the inferior quality of most hybrids. A **hybrid** is a cross sometimes between muliple vitis viniferas and multiple non vitis viniferas, for example. Only a few hybrid varieties, notably Seyval Blanc and Vidal Blanc for whites, and Chambourcin and Maréchal Foche for reds, are still grown, particularly in New England and in Mid-Western states due to their hardiness and their ability to survive severe winters.

Interaction between Europe and North America resulted in another imported blight that attacked Europe's vines. When grafting began to enjoy success, huge quantities of American rootstock were imported to Europe. With them came downy mildew, a plague that weakened the vines, reduced the crops, and killed 30% of France's vines outright. It took four years for growers to learn that spraying the vines with copper sulfate could prevent this mold. The spray is still used today.

In 1920, the wine industry was again suppressed in the United States, this time with the enactment of the **Volstead Act,** which made the production for sale of alcoholic beverages illegal or prohibited. **Prohibition** devastated most wineries. Only the limited production of sacramental or medicinal wines was permitted. However, a legal loophole allowed citizens to make up to 200 gallons of wine per year for home consumption. The planting of high-yielding table grape varieties doubled grape production. When Prohibition was repealed in December of 1933, it left a legacy of second-rate wines, which would last for over 30 years. Prohibition also led to the eventual varietal labeling of wines. When U.S. producers first began to market their wines, they were unable to label them by variety as they were made for the most part from inferior blends. Later, most wines were labeled using 17 different **semi-generic labels,** which are still used today: Californian Chablis and Californian Champagne are such examples. *See 10.4.* In an attempt to differentiate better wines during the 1950s, producers in California began to label wines varietally.

Improved quality control During the 1930s, France focused on improving the quality of wines after re-establishing its vineyards. The country developed the **Appellation d'Origine Contrôlée (AOC or AC)** system, which was adopted from the regulatory governing system for the production of Roquefort cheese. This system delimited the name of a wine to a region and determined the varieties best suited to the particular environment of that region. Thus, the concept of terroir was born. The system recognized that in addition to the soil, the complete ecosystem of an area, including climate, wind, temperature, rainfall, sunlight, and topographical features, all affected a wine's distinctive quality.

10.3 Grafting vinifera onto American rootstock protects the vine from Phylloxera.

During the 1700s, Dom Pérignon, cellar master at the monastery in Hautvilliers at Épernay, France, made significant advances in the science of winemaking. He began to understand the different characteristics of varieties; the role of terroir; the cuvée, or blending of different varieties; and the role of temperature in fermentation and cellaring.

In the years following the French Revolution (1789–1815), monastic orders lost their landholdings, and their vineyards were distributed to supporters of the Revolution. The Napoleonic Code of Law granted equal inheritance rights to heirs, resulting in ever-smaller landholdings. **Négociants,** or merchants, took on an increasingly important role of not only distributing, but also "raising" the wines purchased from the owners of these small vineyards.

In 1851, *oidium,* a powdery mildew fungus, devastated many of France's vineyards, particularly in Bordeaux. Growers learned to use sulfur and lime to combat the problem, and this solution is still used today.

By 1855, wine brokers played a pivotal role in creating a list of the best wine producers for the *Paris Exposition Universelle.* The list ultimately became the foundation for the Bordeaux wine "Classification of 1855," which rated the 61 best wines, primarily of the Médoc region, and the 26 best Sauternes dessert wines. The list survives nearly unchanged to this day.

The problem of wine spoilage, however, continued to plague winemakers. In 1862, Napoleon III invited Louis Pasteur, France's premier scientist, to tackle the problem. Pasteur soon discovered that bacteria present in wine, especially **acetobacter** (the organism that turns wine to vinegar), could be controlled if the bacteria were deprived of light and oxygen. He suggested several solutions: fill wine bottles as full as possible, use colored glass to deprive bacteria of light, store wine bottles on their sides so that corks remain moist and swell to keep oxygen from seeping into the bottles, and store wine in a cool environment to retard bacterial growth. Pasteur also developed a pasteurization process for wine, which would later be used primarily to treat milk.

Biological challenges In 1862 the European wine industry faced its biggest challenge when **Phylloxera** *(now classified as Daktulosphaira vitifoliae),* a microscopic pest, was accidentally introduced to vineyards in France through the importation of American vines by the French merchant, Borty, to the Rhône Valley. By 1880, *Phylloxera* infestations had become so widespread that the pest was known as the "Blight of Europe." It was not until the 1890s that a solution was found. It is through the efforts of Jules-Emile Planchon and C.V. Riley of Missouri, who grafted the *Vitis vinifera* vines to Native American vitis species (particularly riparia and the St. George *rupestris* rootstock), that the vines achieved a resistance to this plight. *See 10.3.* Unfortunately, *Phylloxera* remained a recurring problem, which devastated California vineyards once again in the 1990s. Of the major wine producing regions, only Chile, Cyprus, and Washington State have remained free of the pest and do not graft their vinifera scion onto American rootstock.

American wines improve Ernest and Julio Gallo preserved American wine consumption from the 1930s to the 1960s by producing well-made "table wine" that was readily accessible to the American table. In the 1950s, fine winemaking was again recognized as feasible in California as a result of the action of a few creative vintners.

James Zellerback, for example, who replicated the details of a Burgundian cellar down to the type of oak used for aging, developed a Chardonnay that was reminiscent of Burgundy's best white wine. Inspired by his success, Joseph Heitz and Robert Mondavi visited Europe and came away impressed with the importance of the use of French oak for barrel aging. American winemakers began to focus on planting top-quality vines. Robert Mondavi can certainly be credited with the renaissance of the production of fine wine in California and for achieving world-wide recognition of Napa as a premier wine growing region. During this same period of time, the University of California-Davis School of Oenology became a world leader in the study of viticulture and winemaking.

A blind wine tasting held in Paris, France in 1976 resulted in French judges rating some American wines as superior to some of the best that France had to offer. Consequently, a "grape rush" occurred, especially in Napa Valley. This pivotal event, now known in the wine world as the "Judgment in Paris," also resulted in wine producers from around the world believing that they too could produce world-class wines. Tax advantages inspired heavy investments in vineyards, and led to the creation of the more than 400 wineries now operating in Napa Valley alone. Europeans and Australians have made major investments in such American wineries.

Beginning in 1980, certain geographic areas became identified as **American Viticultural Areas (AVA)** as a result of the concept and centrality of place or **terroir.** This designation, however, does not guarantee quality as does an Appellation of Origin. Some AVAs are geographically huge making the centrality of place somewhat meaningless. The first AVA was the Augusta AVA in Missouri, but it was the Napa Wine Growers Association that was actually able to make its appellation a critical marketing tool in the U.S. consumer's mind. Other regions witnessed the marketing advantages of developing their AVAs, and in 2014, there were approximately 238 AVAs in the U.S., California being home to 141 of them.

When *Phylloxera* reasserted itself in vines grafted on AxR1 rootstock that offered insufficient resistance to the pest due to its partial vinifera genes, most California vines had to be replanted in the 1990s. This disaster allowed producers to apply recently acquired knowledge to plant more appropriate clones and to realign vineyards to optimize sunlight and spacing more efficiently and more densely—all contributing to improved quality.

Despite the problems that periodically surface, areas around the world have dedicated their resources to viticulture in support of the belief that great wines are first created in the vineyard. New World wines have made great inroads in fine wine markets, offering consumers ever improving quality. Concurrently, there has been a major shift throughout the world from consuming "table" wines to enjoying premium and super-premium wines. One of the primary marketing messages of New World wine producers for the past 30 years has been an emphasis on the fruit intensity of their wines rather than a focus on the "earthy" and more "minerally" characteristics found in Old World wines. This division is not as clear at the premium quality level of wines, because Old World wines blur the lines even further with the creation of their more 'fruit forward' wines. Today, wine consumption in the U.S. has increased by 14% over the last 4 years to over 2.5 gallons per adult, still pale in comparison to the 15 gallons per adult in France. Yet, there is excitement as the U.S. is now the number one wine consuming country in the world with 13% of the market share.

Winemaking

The critical elements in producing good wines are the grapes, the climate, the viticulture or growing conditions, and the vinification or the process of winemaking.

THE GRAPE VARIETY

The essence of wine is the grape used to produce it. A thorough knowledge of the categories, the composition, and the varieties of grapes is essential to the winemaker's art.

Grape categories Grapes are generally divided into four categories: Native American Vitis species such as Labrusca, Rupestris; two subdivisions of *Vitis vinifera;* and a hybrid, or cross between non vinifera species and a *viniferas.*

- Native American *Vitis* North American wild grapes are overly acidic and typically lack the balance or subtlety of *vinifera.* They commonly have a "foxy" flavor that many associate with Concord grape juice. Wines made from these species do not generally pair well with food, although the Norton variety with its very dark color and lack of 'foxiness' is an exception.
- *Vitis vinifera* grapes, typified by varieties such as the Thompson Seedless, also known as Sultana in Europe, are primarily used as table grapes or for raisins because of their undistinguished quality, which makes them unsuitable for fine wines. Both in Europe and the United States, winemakers blend these grapes into table or jug wines, although this category is declining in importance.
- *Vitis vinifera* grapes that produce fine wines, on the other hand, have a distinct character that makes them the focus of the winemaker's art. These varieties are also highlighted in this chapter.

- French-American hybrid grapes generally produce less satisfactory wines than *vinifera* varieties, though some, such as Seyval Blanc and Vidal Blanc, may be made into palatable, if not distinctive, wines.

Grape composition The well-known adage "fine wine is created in the vineyard" recognizes the pivotal role of grape varieties in creating a fine wine. The grape captures the sun's energy, stores it as sugar, and retains the water and minerals absorbed by the vine's root system. In exceptional growing years, wines are made in which the alcohol, sweetness, acidity, **tannins** (a chemical compound found in grape skins), stems, and **pips** (seeds) are perfectly balanced, and the flavors are fully developed. The key to fine wine is always balance—and balance begins with perfectly balanced grapes. *See 10.5.*

10.5 Anatomy of a Grape

Every part of the grape contributes to the flavor and aroma of the wine.

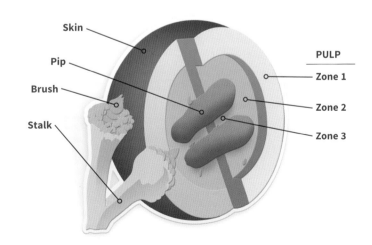

- Skin
- Pip
- Brush
- Stalk

PULP
- Zone 1
- Zone 2
- Zone 3

Grapes consist of 70%–85% water, 15%–30% sugar and extracts, 0.3%–1.8% acids, and 0%–0.2% tannins. By the time grapes are fermented, the resulting wine has developed more than 300 organic compounds, many of which are volatile aromatic compounds with distinct odors.

Aromas refer to fragrances derived from the grape itself and include compounds found in all fruits. Bouquets refer to those fragrances that result from fermentation and aging. These sometimes take years to develop as the wine slowly evolves and changes in chemical composition.

When grapes ferment into wine, the fermentation process creates alcohol from sugar stored in the grape. If the sugars are completely fermented, the wine is dry. If the sugars are not completely fermented, the wine retains varying degrees of sweetness and may be described as off-dry to very sweet. In addition, ethanol, the main form of alcohol produced by fermentation, is perceived by humans as sweet, so wines high in alcohol but without residual sugars seem to be a little sweet.

In red wines, tannins and phenolics found in the grapes' skins, stems, and pips are important to the wine's balance and mouthfeel. Tannins vary in **astringency,** creating a chalky "dried-out" feeling in the mouth to a very spicy and harsh taste. They provide significant textural components and act as a preservative in red wine. In white wines, tannins are generally negligible because the skins, stems, and seeds from which tannins are derived are removed very early in the winemaking process, although wood or oak tannins can be a factor, especially with oak aged Chardonnays. The acid component in wine not only provides balance but also allows wine to age well. Several acids—tartaric, malic, lactic, and succinic—are found in wine, each with unique characteristics.

Although the very acidic tasting tartaric acid is uncommon in most other fruits and vegetables, it is important in grapes, and therefore in wines. Because the salt in tartaric acid (potassium bitartrate) is only partially soluble in alcohol, it may precipitate from the wine. Crystals of potassium bitartrate are sometimes present on the cork or are found floating in the wine. The crystals look like glass, but they are not harmful; in fact, as a by-product of winemaking, they are sold for culinary use as cream of tartar.

The tart or acidic taste of malic acid, which is also found in green apples such as Granny Smiths, may also be detected in wine. Malic acids are partially or fully converted to lactic acid in wines that undergo malolactic fermentation. Almost all red wines undergo this secondary bacterialogical fermentation, which reduces the overall perception of the wine's acidity, making it seem "softer." Citric acid is rare in wine unless it is used for acidifying inexpensive bulk wine. Succinic acid is present in small amounts in grapes and is a byproduct of fermentation. It is mostly significant because it binds to other molecules to form esters to provide a greater concentration of flavors. Acids, however, are important to wine because they give it liveliness and balance the alcohol and/or sugars.

GRAPE VARIETIES

The world of wine owes much of its variety to the genetic instability of *vitis vinifera,* the "wine vine." More than 10,000 identified varieties, and hundreds of different clones of these varieties have resulted from this instability. Most wine connoisseurs, however, are primarily interested in only 50 or so of these, which are divided into white and black grape varieties. Most wines produced in the New World are sold using varietal names—those that identify the wine by the variety from which the wine is made. Old World wines may be made from essentially the same grape variety, although their names are most often reflective of the geographic region or appellation where they are grown rather than on the grape variety. This is because the characteristics of the soil, moisture, temperature, and orientation have profound effects on the grapes of each region. A wine labeled *Puligny-Montrachet,* for example, is a Chardonnay made in Burgundy, France. In the United States, the wine is simply labeled *Chardonnay.* However, due to pressure from the world market, Europeans are more apt to use varietal labeling to support the appellation name.

White Grape Varieties

Pertaining to grapes, the term white has a specialized meaning. White grapes are any light-skinned grapes that range from pale green to gold and even pink. White wines differ from red wines because they lack the anthocyanins or pigmented tannins found in the skins, as well as the stems and pips of black grapes, in some cases. White wines can also be fermented from black grapes if the juice does not come in extended contact with the skins. There are white and red Zinfandel wines, for example, but both are made from the same black grape.

Chardonnay Growers are particularly fond of the Chardonnay grape because it is so malleable and adaptable to different climates. The classic Old World model of wine making is used for white Burgundies such as Chablis, Montrachet, Meursault, and Pouilly-Fuissé. These wines have a moderate to high acidity, a dryness with apple or melon aromas, and vanilla and buttery notes when aged in oak. They can develop enormous complexity with bottle age.

New World wines made from Chardonnay tend to have higher alcohol levels and flavors with hints of sweetness; more peach and tropical nuances; more oak-derived notes such as coconut; and lower acidity, which may result in their somewhat reduced ability to age.

Sauvignon Blanc The principal white grape of Bordeaux and the eastern Loire Valley, Sauvignon Blanc makes a clean, dry, intense, aromatic white wine with an herbaceous, mineral-like character. In fact, the name *Sauvignon* comes from the French word *sauvage,* or "wild."

Sauvignons from South Africa often have characteristics similar to those of Old World grapes. Sauvignon Blancs are frequently blended with Sémillons to mellow the tart, herbal character of Sauvignon Blanc—a practice that is common in Bordeaux, France, as well as in other locations such as California and Australia.

New Zealand Sauvignon Blancs have their grapefruit acidity balanced by the richness of higher alcohol content while retaining their intense herbaceous flavors and tropical guava notes. In California, wine produced from Sauvignon Blanc is often referred to as Fumé Blanc, especially if oak aged, although the wines do not have a smoky character. California Sauvignon Blanc wines are more diverse than in the past: many are aged in oak and often have a more floral and a softer fig or melon characters, while others have a more New Zealand clean dry fruit and herbaceous character with a high acidity.

Some Chilean wines labeled *Sauvignon Blanc* were actually made from Sauvignon Verte or Sauvignasse grapes, a variety that is less herbal and unrelated to Sauvignon Blanc. Most of these Chilean vineyards, however, have now been replanted with Sauvignon Blanc and offer both a New World and Old World style as do the wines of South Africa.

Riesling Often identified as the most noble of the white grapes, the Riesling grape can produce wines with a searing acidity that is balanced by a residual sweetness; delicate rose aromas; and notes of peaches, apricots, and melons. These qualities, coupled with a Riesling's often low alcohol content when made into wine, are responsible for this grape's light body, delicacy, and transparency.

Produced in the classic regions of Germany such as Mosel, Riesling can develop mineral or earthy notes balanced by a delicate sweetness. Rieslings from the Alsace region of France are fuller-bodied than those from Germany, northern Austria, New York, and the Clare or Eden Valleys of Australia, which are light-bodied but complex. This is perhaps because Rieslings adapt well to the cooler growing sites these locations offer. The Rieslings grown in warmer regions in Australia and California, and those from Washington State and Oregon, are generally softer and slightly fuller, sometimes with more diffuse flavors. Riesling is one of the most versatile wines for pairing, complementing foods as diverse as smoked, cured or salty cuisine, as well as spicy Asian dishes.

Chenin Blanc Old World wines made from Chenin Blanc are vibrant, complex, long-lived, and shimmering in their acidity. These wines include the great wines from Vouvray, Savennières, and Saumur. In the Loire Valley of France, these grapes are fermented to varying degrees of sweetness from bone-dry to lusciously sweet to balance their high acidity.

In California, Chenin Blanc was once the most widely planted classic grape variety, but it has now been supplanted by Chardonnay. Chenin Blanc is grown for volume in the warm climate of California's Central Valley producing indistinct bulk wines. In South Africa, where it is also known as *Steen,* Chenin Blanc makes up 20% of the country's grape harvest. When compared with Chenin Blancs made from grapes grown in the Loire Valley of France, wine from South Africa reflects a broad spectrum of styles, although generally characterized by less acidity and with a distinct perfumed and honeyed character.

Gewürztraminer A pink-skinned native grape of Germany and Alsace, Gewürztraminer produces particularly aromatic and full-bodied white wines. The name perfectly describes the character of the grape. *Gewürz* in German means "spiced" and the wine made from these grapes has slightly tannic spicy notes. *Traminer* identifies the older grape variety from which the Gewürztraminer mutated. Wine tasters use such words as lychee nuts, gingerbread, honey, and musk to describe the flavors of wines made from these grapes, but it is their scents of jasmine and roses that make them some of the most recognized wines in the world.

The very best Gewürztraminers grow in Alsace, where the region's fine, crisp autumns produce late-picked grapes that make wines of a low acidity and a mouthfilling viscous quality with a hint of bitterness and spicy notes. Germany also produces

delicious products. One of only a few white wines with a slightly bitter finish, Gewürztraminer may be dry if produced in Austria, or off-dry when produced in Germany, California, Washington State, and Southeastern New England.

Sémillon A golden grape variety from southwest France, Sémillon is one of the principal varieties produced in Bordeaux's sweet wine-producing communes. This grape plays two roles in winemaking: one as the star and the other as an understudy. For Sauternes—those rich, complex dessert wines counted among the world's most long-lasting unfortified wines—Sémillon is the star. It produces luscious, richly honeyed wines with perfectly balanced sweetness, acidity, and alcohol, partly because its thin skin makes it particularly susceptible to *Botrytis cinerea,* or "noble rot." In its supporting role, Sémillon is blended with Sauvignon Blanc, particularly in Bordeaux and in California. In Australia, Sémillon is blended with Chardonnay to improve the balance of both the varieties.

Sémillon plays quite another role in Australia, however, especially in the Lower Hunter Valley. Hunter Valley Sémillon wines are light, acidic, dry, and unoaked, but they age very well. After about five years, this variety develops into rich wines with an intensely honeyed bouquet and an almost orange color.

Pinot Gris A natural mutation of Pinot Noir, Pinot Gris grapes come in colors as varied as the strikingly different flavors of the wines made from them. Pinot Gris (gray pinot) grapes can be bluish to silver, mauve-pink, or a gray or ash yellow. Depending on where they are grown, they produce very different wines mainly because of their different levels of alcohol and acidity. In Italy, the grapes are called Pinot Grigio, and the wine is generally crisp and light. By contrast, the Pinot Gris of Alsace, once known as Tokay-Pinot Gris, produces rich, somewhat spicy and fuller-bodied wines. In Germany, the variety is called *Grauburgunder* or *Ruländer,* and the wines have a broader flavor.

The Pinot Gris of the New World, particularly in Oregon, produces wines with flavors that some tasters compare to spice cake and pears. High quality Pinot Gris are also produced in the Russian River Valley, Sonoma Coast, Napa, and Monterey.

Viognier Viognier originated in the Rhône Valley of France, and although close to obscurity until recently, it found its best expression in the appellations of Condrieu and Château Grillet. It is planted in many different AVAs in California and has found impressive expressions in Virginia. Viognier has many characteristics of Chardonnay in that it is somewhat full-bodied, has good acidity, and is malleable. Wines produced from this variety are described as elegant and exotic with hints of honeysuckle or musky fruit and a smooth texture. Without oak, it has distinctive floral and peach aromas with a nutty almond finish.

Muscat Muscat is the many-hued grape that Pliny the Elder once called "the grape of the bees" for its attractive aroma. With four major clones in its family tree, the variety has grown around the Mediterranean Sea for centuries. Most Muscats thrive in relatively hot climates such as those of Greece, Morocco, Sicily, and Sardinia where they are made into sweet or semi-sweet wines with generally low alcohol content and a pronounced taste of the grape. In Italy, Muscat is the grape of choice for sparkling Asti.

In Alsace, however, the Muscat Blanc à Petits Grains and Muscat Ottonel branches of the family tree produce fresh and fruity wines that are always fermented to dryness. In Australia, the Muscat Gordo Blanco (most often times called the Muscat of Alexandria) is used to make "liqueur Muscats." Californian Andrew Quady produces a number of Muscat-based dessert wines, particularly in the fortified style of a French *Vin Doux Naturel* such as Beaumes-de-Venise.

Palomino Palomino grapes yield a neutral-tasting wine that oxidizes easily because of its low acidity. The variety grows prolifically in hot climates and is the grape used to make sherry in Spain.

Ugni Blanc Ugni Blanc or Trebbiano originated in Italy and is the most widely planted white grape in both France and Italy. It is the basis for Cognac and Armagnac in France as well as for traditional balsamic vinegars in Italy.

Muscadet Although the variety is technically called Melon de Bourgogne, it derives its name from the region of the Loire Valley closest to the Atlantic where it thrives—an area called Muscadet de Sèvre-et-Maine. The wine is frequently allowed to remain on the lees sediment formed during fermentation until the wine is bottled. Wine made from Muscadet develops a more defined and refreshing character with a lively spritz. Such a wine would be labeled sur lie (on the lees) and is particularly suitable to serve with seafood.

Albariño (Alvarinho) Albariño (Alvarinho) is a thick-skinned grape variety particularly adapted to damp climates. Some versions of the wines made from grapes principally grown in northwest Spain (Rías Baixas) and Portugal are characterized by delicate floral aromas and high acidity. In other versions, the wines are fuller bodied and have a greater alcohol content. Albariño is one of the few Spanish wines sold as a varietal.

Grüner Veltliner Grüner Veltliner is Austria's most planted wine grape. The variety has also spread to other areas of Eastern Europe. Although some wines produced from this grape are quite simple, those from the best growing regions are complex with tropical fruit notes and high acidity to balance the high alcohol content.

Pinot Blanc Pinot Blanc is a mutation from Pinot Noir and has characteristics similar to those of Chardonnay, although the wines made from this variety are generally not as complex in flavor, aroma, or texture. There are notable exceptions from Alsace and Germany.

Black Grape Varieties

Just as "white" grape varieties are not really white but rather green or yellow, "black" grape varieties are not really black, and their colors may range from red to purple to deep blue violet. They do share one important characteristic: black grapes are necessary to produce red wines because these wines derive their color from maceration with the skins as both white and red viniferas have white pulp.

Pinot Noir Pinot Noir is a difficult grape to grow successfully in the necessary cool growing regions, but it is responsible for France's fine red Burgundies and many Champagne wines. Connoisseurs believe that Pinot Noir produces among the finest red wines in the world. The wines are more delicate and have lower tannins and a higher acidity than varieties such as Cabernet Sauvignon. Burgundies have aromas of cherries, raspberries, mint, and herbs, but New World Pinot Noirs have more baked cherry and floral aromas. With bottle aging, the wines develop distinct earthy bouquets of leather, mushrooms, and game.

While Pinot Noir has long found a home in Germany and Austria where it is known as Spätburgunder, it was generally very light in color and body with a high acidity and a frequently fermented off dry. Due in no small measure to global warming, some of the world's best Pinot Noirs are now being produced in Germany where they have fuller body and deeper color and might easily be mistaken for a great growth from Burgundy.

The legendary silky quality of Pinot Noir has also made it a world traveler. In the late 1960s and 1970s, Pinot Noir became the wine star of Oregon due to the pioneering efforts of producers such as David Lett and Dick Erath. In the 1980s, growers in the Russian River Valley, Carneros, and Santa Barbara, California took advantage of cool growing areas to produce notable Pinot Noirs. The film 'Sideways' also put Pinot Noir in the spotlight in the U.S., and its sales increased significantly early in the 21st century. By the 1990s, New Zealand growers were also planting Pinot Noir grapes, and by 1997 the variety overtook Cabernet as the region's most-planted black grape. New Zealand Pinot Noirs, especially those from Otago, Marlborough, and Martinborough have won worldwide acclaim.

Cabernet Sauvignon Cabernet Sauvignon, a small dark purple grape that Sotheby's describes as "the noblest variety of Bordeaux," produces satiny, rich, and complex wines with proper barrel and bottle aging. Proper aging is important because the fruit's small size gives Cabernet a high ratio of skin to pulp to potentially produce a very astringent young wine. With aging; however, Cabernet's acidity allows it to mature into complex wines with blackberry, black currant, cassis, plum, mint, violet, roasted bell pepper, eucalyptus, and cedar bouquets. When less fully ripe, Cabernet Sauvignon makes wines with a more vegetal character.

The most notable Cabernet Sauvignon-based wines in the Old World come from the Médoc growers of Margaux, St.-Julien, Pauillac, and St.-Estèphe, in Bordeaux. In the New World, California growers, particularly in Rutherford and Oakville AVAs in Napa and the Alexander Valley in Sonoma County, are producing world-class Cabernets. Today Cabernet Sauvignon is widely grown in Italy, Spain, California, Washington State, Chile, and Australia. In the Médoc region of France, Cabernet is frequently blended with Merlot and Cabernet Franc to achieve mellowing and balance. Similar blends in California are sometimes called Meritage if Cabernet Sauvignon does not represent a legally required minimum percentage of 75%.

Merlot Merlot—the name means "little blackbird"—is a deep blue cousin to Cabernet Sauvignon. Merlot is the predominant variety grown in the Bordeaux region of France, especially on the right bank in St. Émilion and Pomerol. Merlot, when fully ripe, produces textures that are softer and smoother than Cabernet, with plum and blackberry character. The bouquets are more buttery and creamy, and the wine has cocoa and earthy flavors. Merlot is frequently blended with Cabernet to moderate Cabernet's astringency, particularly in Bordeaux. Because of Merlot's ripe and less tannic profile, it became a fad variety in the 1990s and is frequently offered in restaurants by the glass. Merlot responds well to heavier clay soils and is easier to ripen in cooler climates, so the variety has also become popular in Long Island's North Fork and in the southeastern part of Washington State where it produces some exceptional wines. Chile also makes exceptional Merlot, especially with grapes from the Rapel Valley, although much of the wine labeled Merlot in the past was made from a closely related variety called Carmenère, which gives the wine a different profile and an almost licorice taste.

Cabernet Franc Cabernet Franc is a parent plant of both Cabernet Sauvignon and Merlot, and is the most-commonly planted grape in the Anjou-Touraine region of the Loire Valley. It is also found to a lesser extent in Bordeaux, especially on the right bank of the Gironde River. Particularly suited to cooler, inland climates, these grapes ripen about a week earlier than the Cabernet Sauvignon variety.

Cabernet Franc grapes produce wines that are generally lighter in color, lower in tannins, and slightly more aromatic with hints of violets, blackberries, and licorice. As New World winemakers follow the Bordeaux recipe of blending with Cabernet Sauvignon, Cabernet Franc grapes are being planted in limited numbers in Australia and New Zealand.

Syrah (Shiraz) Syrah (Shiraz) is an old, black variety of grapes grown in the northern Rhône region of France, which produces rich, tannic fruits. This smaller-berried grape generally contains more phenolics, which along with anthocyanins, makes Syrah a wine that benefits from long aging in oak and in the bottle. The best French Syrah wines are from Northern Rhône appellations such as Côte Rôtie.

Richly aromatic with hints of black pepper, green olive, violets, and black currants, Syrah also forms the basis for Australia's finest red wines and has been Australia's most-planted variety, perhaps because the variety thrives in warmer climates. Recently, Australian winemakers have blended Shiraz with Cabernet Sauvignon.

Because of its recent surge in popularity, many vintners are producing Syrah in the cool Santa Rita Hills of Santa Barbara and in the Napa Valley as well as in the warmer regions of Mendocino and Sonoma County. Washington State has also developed some of the United States finest Syrah-based wines.

Gamay Gamay is a plump grape with a characteristic cherry and raspberry aroma, which is grown principally in the southern Burgundy region of Beaujolais. For the most part, simple and fruity wines made from the Gamay grape tend to be light and fresh, especially when vinified using carbonic maceration, which gives the wine fruity, almost bubble gum, banana, and mint aromas. This style of wine is generally at its best when young. Top quality Cru Beaujolais becomes more similar to good Burgundian Pinot Noir when bottle aged.

Grenache (Garnacha) Grenache (Garnacha) is grown in the southern Rhône Valley of France. The basis for many of the renowned Châteauneuf-du-Pape wines, it is also one of the principal varieties used in Spain's Rioja wines. It is currently the 7th most planted black variety in the world.

Grenache earned much of its reputation as the primary grape used in the high alcohol, dry Tavel rosé wines. Grenache has a floral and white pepper profile along with olive and licorice aromas. Grenache is also found in southeastern Australia and in Monterey County, California where it is frequently blended with other varieties.

Tempranillo Tempranillo (literally "the early grape") is the key variety in many of Spain's wines. It has good color, attractive cherry and strawberry flavors, moderate acidity, and silky tannins. It derives a spicy, leathery and tobacco leaf bouquet from its adaptability to long-term American oak barrel aging. Its expression reflects the *terroir* in which it is grown and is now in almost all regions of Spain. It is also one of the most widely planted varieties in Portugal where it is known as Tinto Roriz. There are a few notable plantings in California's Sierra Foothills and in Oregon.

Zinfandel Zinfandel, according to DNA testing, originated from the Croatian Crljenak (pronounced sirl-yen-knock) Kaštelanski and is the same variety of grape as the Italian *Primitivo*, which may have been imported from the United States. In the United States, Zinfandel grapes were first grown on the East Coast and were then brought to California. Wine made from this grape was hailed as California's claret. The variety produces its best fruits if the growing season is warm, not hot, and the vines are not allowed to overproduce. Producing wines from Zinfandel grapes is not easy. The compact bunches ripen unevenly, leaving a narrow window for harvesting. The best red Zinfandels are dry, acidic, alcoholic wines that are balanced by ripe sweet- or dried fruit character with fresh tobacco and spice notes. They are ideal accompaniments to barbecues and roast turkey. In California, this formerly predominant variety of grape has been used for making white Zinfandels.

Sangiovese Sangiovese is Italy's most famous grape and is so ancient that its name translates to "blood of Jove." It is responsible for Italy's noted Tuscan wines—Chianti, Vino Nobile di Montepulciano, and Brunello di Montalcino. Although the variety's quality varies from year to year because of its slow, late ripening and fluctuations in the weather, Sangiovese has good acidity and makes a good food wine.

Italian immigrants brought Sangiovese to the New World, but it was not until the 1980s and 1990s that Italy's reputation for high quality wines developed. Italy's wines became a ubiquitous presence on restaurant wine lists in the United States, prompting a sudden increase in the number of acres planted of this variety in California, although it was unsuccessful in challenging Tuscany's dominance.

Nebbiolo Nebbiolo, which is recognized as one of Italy's most noble grapes, grows almost exclusively in the Piedmont region of northwestern Italy. Wines made from this pale purple black grape are tannic, austere, and highly alcoholic, but they mature into remarkably fine, elegant wines. Their aromas are floral, and their bouquets have an earthy, truffle-like character.

Hybridized Grapes

Although many hybridized grapes were developed in response to *Phylloxera*, some hybrids occurred by chance, such as Catawba, which became the basis of Ohio's sparkling wine industry in the mid-1800s. Other hybrids, such as Chancellor and Baco Noir, are used in winemaking in New England, New York, and Canada where they better withstand the cold winters. For the most part, however, hybrids have not proven to be successful wine grapes as developers had originally hoped.

CLIMATE

Climate depends to a certain degree on latitude, but several other factors are also important in determining a location's general or prevailing weather patterns. Temperature is an important component of climate, which can be modified by proximity to bodies of water, prevailing wind patterns, precipitation, altitude, and the amount of sunshine in a given location. Climates can be described as belonging to 3 broad classifications: Maritime, Mediterranean, and Continental. The climate has a dominant impact on the types of diseases and pests that affect vines.

Latitude Latitude is a significant indicator of a climate's suitability for viticulture. Tropical areas are generally too hot for growing grapes, and the high latitudes are too cold. Most successful vineyards are located between the 30° and 50° north latitude and south latitude. Because latitude affects the length of days and the relative coolness of nights in a region, different varieties of grapes are often suited to particular locations in a relatively small geographic area. In cool climates, low solar exposure associated with higher latitudes or altitudes, produces the compounds responsible for the grape's distinctive aromas. *See 10.6.*

Temperature The amount of sugar and acidity that a grape variety develops as it ripens depends on the growing season of the area where it is planted. Research done by Maynard Amerine and Albert Winkler at the University of California-Davis School of Oenology demonstrated that different grape varieties need to be grown in specific climatic zones to fully ripen. To conduct their research, Amerine and Winkler developed a model using Heat Summation Areas. The method is based on the fact that vines lie dormant when aggregate temperatures remain below 50°F (10°C). For any day that the temperature averaged above 50°F (10°C), Amerine and Winkler assigned degrees based on the difference between the average temperature for that day and 50° F (10°C). For example, if the average temperature is 69°F (21°C) on April 1, that day is a 19-degree day. The Heat Summation (the sum of all the degree days between April 1 and October 31) determines the classification.

Here are the five classifications:
- Region I–Fewer than 2500°F accrued degrees
- Region II–2501°F–3000°F accrued degrees
- Region III–3001°F–3500°F accrued degrees
- Region IV–3501°F–4000°F accrued degrees
- Region V–4001°F–4500°F accrued degrees

In the Northern Hemisphere, the growing season begins around April 1, when the average temperature is high enough (above 50°F/10°C) for new shoots to develop from the dormant buds (bud-break). Flowering occurs from mid-May to June, and tiny berries appear and develop but remain green until mid-July. The onset of ripening is called **veraison** (French for "true season")

10.6 Temperature Climate Zones

Wine grapes grow best in temperate climate zones.

50°N
30°N

30°S
50°S

Climate	Characteristics	Examples
Maritime	Warm long summer, cool winters	Bordeaux, Loire, Long Island, Napa
Mediterranean	Warm long summers, warm winters	Rhône, Tuscany, Santa Barbara
Continental	Hot short summer, long cold winters	Burgundy, Germany, Austria

when the berries develop color and begin to soften. Harvest generally begins in mid-September but varies from region to region based on the weather conditions in the location and the grape variety. *See 10.7.*

Temperatures are very important to the development of grapes. Higher temperatures elevate the sugar content in the grape and cause acidity to decline more rapidly. This inverse relationship is important to the winemaker, who hopes to balance the alcohol and the acidity in wine. Varietal characteristics are also important in this process. The winemaker and the vineyard manager usually work together to harvest the grapes at their optimum quality. In areas of France, such as Burgundy, the grape may physiologically ripen before sufficient sugars have developed to make a wine with the proper alcohol and acidity balance. Winemakers may then correct an imbalanced condition with sugar prior to fermentation. This process is known as **chaptalization.** In warmer parts of coastal California, on the other hand, grapes may develop sugar ripeness before the grapes are physiologically ripe. Winemakers in these geographic areas are allowing grapes to become physiologically ripe, which explains the higher alcohol levels in their wines. They may also acidify their wines as grapes lose their acidity with longer 'hang time' on the vine.

10.7 Veraison—Grapes will complete the color change during the last stages of ripening.

Early Romans first recognized the correlations between fine wines and cooler climates when they discovered that although grapes grown in cool areas produced smaller quantities, the fruit was of a higher quality. In cooler environments, flavors and colors have a longer time to develop and the grapes retain good acidity. Acidity is the component in wine that makes it refreshing. This is also one of the reasons the world's best wines are produced from grapes that are grown in cool regions.

Bodies of water Bodies of water have a profound influence on climate. Large, deep masses of water, such as oceans, large lakes, or rivers moderate both summer and winter temperatures. Temperatures become warm later in the spring and fall frosts generally arrive later in the season. *See 10.8.*

10.8 Water helps to moderate or ease the extremes of temperature such as in the Vaud along Lake Geneva, Switzerland.

Wind In locations where strong winds cause sudden temperature fluctuations (called wind stress); growers often plant tall shrubs or fast-growing trees to act as windbreaks. Winds can hinder flowering and pollination of ripening vines and decrease their final yields by altering their ability to transpire.

Rainfall and humidity Few crops are as sensitive to rainfall or humidity as grapes. Excessive rain during the growing season can cause rot and fungal diseases in the fruit. During the summer, too much rain leads to excessive plant growth rather than to good fruit development. At harvest time, too much rain can bloat the grapes and dilute their sugar and flavor content. In winter, on the other hand, plentiful rainfall is beneficial because it provides the necessary water table for deep roots of vines to extract needed moisture and trace minerals throughout the summer growing season. Drought can lead to excessive stress and cause the plant to physiologically shut down.

Frost For grape growers, late and early frosts are a disaster. A late spring frost can seriously diminish a vine's production potential, and an early autumn frost can damage the harvest's quality and yield. Frost is one of the primary factors for planting vines on hillsides rather than on valley floors where frost first occurs.

Sunlight The process of **photosynthesis** (the formation of sugars from carbon dioxide and a source of hydrogen—such as water—in the chlorophyll-containing tissues of plants exposed to light) is essential to plant growth and development. The amount of direct sunlight the plants receive affects not only the health of the vines but also the sweetness of the grapes, and ultimately, the alcohol content of the wines made from them.

VITICULTURE

Viticulture, or the science of growing grapevines, encompasses all major fruit-growing conditions.

Terroir *Terroir* is a French term that is sometimes loosely translated as "territory," but in viticulture, terroir encompasses much more than a land location. It includes all the elements that comprise growing conditions—soil, climate, topography, geology, and hydrology.

Soil French wines have long been named according to the region where the grapes are grown because many French winemakers believe that grapes derive flavor and quality from the soil as well as from other regional growing conditions. Until recently, American and other New World winemakers have maintained that the soil is merely a support for the vine and a reservoir for water and nutrients. Climate plays the largest part in determining grape flavor and quality. Regardless of their nationality, however, viticulturists agree that grapevines grow best in well-drained soils on bench lands or slopes that encourage deep root growth. Fertility is also important to vine growth, although growers are wary of overly fertile soil that might encourage overgrowth of vines or overproduction of insipid grapes. *See 10.9.*

Irrigation Irrigation is generally not allowed in the European Union's (EU) quality wine regions after the vine is mature enough to produce yields for appellation designation (usually the fourth year). The reason is due both to the general presence of rainfall during the growing season and the need to stress the vine sufficiently to produce concentrated fruit. Many EU quality wine appellations have suffered near drought conditions in the past few years and have received permission for limited irrigation in such circumstances. In other wine producing regions where there is little or no rainfall and no limitations, drip irrigation is common. *See 10.10.*

10.9

Loam and schist from Alsace, France

Beaujolais, France with granite and schist

Burgundy, France and its limestone clay

Albariza soils of Jerez, Spain

Gravel of Médoc, France

10.10 An irrigation system waters a young vine.

Vintage The word *vintage* comes from the French word *vendange*, which means "harvest" and also designates the year in which a wine is made. Ideal weather may bring a great vintage year, but early or late frosts, hail, or heavy rains may be disastrous. Until recently, great vintage years have been the exception rather than the rule in the cool wine-growing regions of Europe. Even great growing years require a skilled winemaker to take full advantage of an exceptional grape harvest's flavor development and balance. Some wines may not have a vintage label because they contain blends of grapes of different vintages. Non-vintage champagnes, for example, are such blends and do not necessarily reflect a lower quality.

Viticultural practices Although nature plays a pivotal role in the grape's flavor and composition, nurturing the vines is also critically important. First, the selection of rootstock and clone will affect the grapes, as will the age of the vines. Vines do not provide fruit of high quality in sufficient quantity to make wine until at least their third or fourth year. Some believe that many vines do not attain peak quality until their eighth to tenth year. Although some areas have vines that are 100 years old, most vines are economically productive for 20 to 25 years.

Growers also manipulate the size and shape of the vines by training, trellising, pruning, and using a process called **canopy management.** The canopy is made up of the grape leaves that absorb sunlight for photosynthesis. New World growers, principally those in the United States and Australia, encourage leaf growth to limit yields. They also prune the vines to determine how the vine will grow and the number of buds it will have. The number of buds affects the number of clusters of grapes, or the vines' yields. The correlation between high vine density and good quality is a matter of controversy among growers. In Europe, appellation laws limit vine density, but in New World vineyards, there are no set limits— although grapevines tend to be far less densely planted than in Burgundy, for example.

Yield management The way in which growers manage yields is important to the quality of wine that is produced from grapes. Different varieties yield different quantities of grapes. High-yielding varieties such as French Colombard or Carignan generally produce undistinguished wines sold formerly as table wines in Europe. The warm areas where they thrive encourage large yields, higher alcohol, lower acidity, and less well-defined flavors.

Growers know that smaller yields and longer **"hang time"** on the vine generally produce harvests with better balance. In the European Union, quality wine regions have specific limits placed on yields. Fine wine varieties are manipulated to reduce yields through pruning and crop thinning, a process called vendange vert (green harvest). *See 10.11.* The resulting wines tend to be much more expensive but are of a considerably higher quality because up to half of the crop may be thinned and discarded.

Harvesting The point at which grapes are harvested is so important to the quality of wine that the decision is made jointly by the vineyard manager and the winemaker (when the fall weather does not dictate the timing). Growers use a refractometer to determine the Brix measurement, the name given to the scale used to measure sugar density. *See 10.12.*

The method of harvesting is also significant. Because technology has improved dramatically and the labor shortage of agricultural workers continues to rise, more grapes are mechanically harvested than ever before. Mechanical harvesting does not necessarily have a negative impact on the quality of the juice, though for top quality wines and some appellations such as Champagne, hand harvesting predominates or is legally required.

Sustainable agriculture Sustainable agriculture is perhaps one of the most important issues facing all agricultural producers. Growers have become increasingly aware of the long-term environmental effects of using chemical pesticides, herbicides, and fungicides. Sprays may drift to neighboring properties, and their residues can contaminate aquifers and impact wildlife habitats. *See 10.13.* As growers look for alternatives to chemicals, they are adopting more organic methods of sustainable agriculture. By investigating the life cycles and activities of pest species and their predators, growers are finding new ways to control pests. Birds of prey such as owls or more sophisticated technological solutions such as pheromone strips that disrupt the mating cycles of some pests are replacing chemical sprays. Vineyard managers are also moving away from the monoculture of the vine. Planting cover crops such as mustard greens between the rows of vines, for example, repels pests from the vines and also helps to reduce soil impaction. Physical barriers such as nets, which do not have a negative impact on the environment, can protect the crops from flocks of migratory birds that might otherwise consume the harvest in minutes. There are vineyards that go far beyond these measures to be certified as organic or biodynamic, which can result in wines that have greater intensity but are more expensive to produce.

VINIFICATION

Among winemakers, there is a frequently repeated adage that states: "It is easy to make a bad wine from good grapes, but you cannot make a good wine from bad grapes."

Winemakers produce wine on the basis of the quality of grapes they are able to grow. Over the past decades, science has enhanced traditional viticulture, and grape quality has generally improved with new horticultural methods. Critics charge, however, that better science has also been accompanied by a lack of diversity in the international varieties used in winemaking. Although modern wines are clean and generally consistent, they also have fewer individualistic taste profiles. Over the past decade, that concern has sparked a philosophical shift among some winemakers. Minimum treatment or intervention is becoming more common especially in the super-premium category. Although technology has provided winemakers with tools their predecessors did not have, many have come to believe that the costs

10.11 Green harvesting or crop thinning— Grape clusters are cut from the vine to reduce a vineyards yield while improving the quality.

10.12 The brix or sugar content is measured using a refractometer to help judge ripeness.

10.13 A farm worker sprays fungicide in the vineyard.

10.14 In the destemmer, spinning bars separate the grapes from their stems.

exceed the benefits. A strictly scientific approach based on chemistry alone may have led to the homogenization trend that has produced wines with less typicity and fewer subtle differences due to site and terroir.

Classification of Wines

Wines are generally organized into five classifications: table wine, dessert wine, sparkling wine, fortified wine, and aromatized wine. Part of the winemaker's art involves deciding on the class of wine that is best suited to the grapes at hand, much as a chef decides on the type and quality of ingredients to use.

Table Wine

The term *table wine* is no longer applied in the European Union replaced by the word wine (*vin, vino, vinho, wein,* etc) followed by the country of origin. In the United States, the term is used to distinguish table wines from sparkling or fortified wines. Table wines generally contain from 6.5% to 14.5% alcohol, but the normal range is from 10% to 12% alcohol. Table wines may be fermented to dryness or to off-dryness. Depending on how they are made, the wines may be white or red and range in color from pale white to amber, crimson to tile brick red, or a shade of salmony pink for rosé or blush wines.

MAKING WHITE WINES

The process used to make white wines includes: destemming ➡ crushing ➡ sulfiting ➡ pressing ➡ adjusting ➡ fermentation ➡ racking ➡ [malolactic fermentation]* ➡ blending and aging ➡ fining and adjusting ➡ finishing and bottling.

*Note: Only a few white wines, such as Chardonnay, undergo malolactic fermentation.

MAKING RED WINES

Red wines are processed by destemming and crushing ➡ sulfiting ➡ maceration and skin contact ➡ fermentation ➡ pressing ➡ racking ➡ malolactic fermentation ➡ blending and aging ➡ fining and adjusting ➡ finishing and bottling.

Destemming After grapes are harvested, the stalks and stems are generally removed in the winery by crushing/**destemming.** *See 10.14.*

Crushing Crushing is a misleading term because the process is quite gentle. Its objective is to split the skins of grapes to release freerun juice. Crushing is quite distinct from pressing, during which the juice is squeezed from the pulp that is closer to the skins of the grapes. The juice of white wine may occasionally be kept in skin contact for several hours at low temperatures to extract greater flavor. Grapes for white wines are gently pressed before fermentation, but grapes used for red wines are pressed after fermentation.

Pressing Wines are pressed and strained by various kinds of presses. The extracted juice with minimal fragments of stems, seeds, or skins is called the **must.** Some black grapes that are made into red wines may not have all the stems removed from the must if the wine to be made requires the tannins they produce. A key point is that the greater the pressure, the greater the tannin levels in the must. When winemakers make white wines,

they try to maximize the amount of must without extracting the tannins and the bitter oils contained in the pips. The first pressing may extract only about 75% of the juice and is used for better-quality wine. Subsequent pressings have more tannin and may be fermented and later blended into the wine or used to produce vinegar or an inexpensive brandy called marc, grappa, or pomace brandy in the United States.

Grapes for red wine are crushed and then fermented before being pressed so that maceration extracts the color and tannins from the grapes' skins and pips. The pressing need not be gentle because the release of tannins is desirable in red wines. *See 10.15a and 10.15b.*

Must adjustments Winemakers can make adjustments to the must before it is fermented including chaptalization or must enrichment, SO2 treatment, settling, and acidification or deacidification.

Chaptalization is the process of adding sugar to the must to increase the potential alcoholic content of a wine. Increasing the alcohol in the wine gives it a rounder, softer texture because alcohol counterbalances acidity. However, must is

10.15a A pneumatic horizontal wine press

10.15b A traditional basket press

more commonly enriched using rectified concentrated grape must, a colorless and tasteless concentrate of grape sugars including glucose and fructose. Enrichment of the must is common in the wine regions of northern Europe, especially in parts of France where it is carefully regulated. This practice is also allowed in Canada and in the northeastern United States where cool climates may prevent grapes from having enough sugar to develop sufficient alcohol to give the wine the necessary balance.

Musts are also commonly treated with sulfur dioxide to prevent oxidation, to control the growth of bacteria, and to eliminate any undesirable wild yeasts that may have been present on the grapes. If winemakers use cultured yeasts to ferment the must, they may be added at this time.

Winemakers may also need to adjust the pH, a measurement of the acidity of the must. In warm climates where grapes fail to develop sufficient acids to ensure good balance in the finished wine, winemakers may acidify the wine by adding tartaric acid. In cooler areas, it is sometimes necessary to deacidify the wine by adding calcium bicarbonate.

Maceration By definition, **maceration** involves soaking a material in liquid to separate softened parts of the material from the harder ones. When making red wines, winemakers use this process to extract the phenolics including tannins, coloring materials, anthocyanins, and other glycosides, which include flavor precursors and compounds from the grape skins and sometimes the pips or stems that are in the must.

Left untreated, the must would normally begin to ferment during maceration because the sugar and yeasts needed for this process are already present in the grapes. To macerate without fermentation, winemakers need to keep the must cold—below 48°F (9°C), the point at which yeast growth is retarded. Cold maceration may last for two or three days. It is not uncommon for high-quality red wines to undergo extended maceration (including fermentation) of up to 36 days to create longer chain tannins that will feel less astringent and taste less bitter. If the winemaker is making a blush or rosé wine, the maceration period is a few hours.

Fermentation During fermentation, yeasts in the must convert sugar to ethyl alcohol and carbon dioxide as part of their metabolic cycle and further release heat as a by-product. Violent fermentation can raise temperatures to more than 100°F (38°C) if left uncontrolled. At that temperature, the yeast dies. Conversely, if temperatures are allowed to fall below 48°F (9°C), the yeast will stop growing. Northern Europe's fermenting rooms (cuveries) are often warmed, while those in parts of California and Australia are sometimes cooled.

Fermenting white wine Although fermentation creates both white wines and red wines, each type of wine requires different fermentation conditions. One important variable in fermenting white wine is temperature. Today's winemakers control temperatures precisely by using stainless steel vats with cooling jackets, *see 10.16,* although some winemakers still use small oak barrels (Bordeaux barriques which have 59 gallons or 225 liters capacity) for certain wines such as Chardonnay, whose character can be more adapted to oak flavors.

Winemakers ferment white wines between 50°F (10°C) and 65°F (18°C) for 1–3 weeks. At those temperatures and durations, the wine is refreshing, fruity, and matures faster. At higher temperatures, fermentation is quicker, but for most wines, quality may suffer. Chardonnays can be an exception. They are fermented in oak barrels at 68°F (20°C) and higher to gain complexity and longevity.

Fermenting red wine Black grapes are fermented with their skins and pips in vats. Most vats are made of wood, but there are also concrete, stainless steel or glass-lined vats. For red wines, fermentation occurs at 68°F (20°C) to 88°F (31°C). At higher temperatures, the wine's fruitiness and delicacy may diminish.

Because the grape skins are left in the must, red wines also require additional attention during fermentation. Carbon dioxide and heat force skins and any remaining stems to the surface of the must to form a **cap.** Winemakers need to submerge this cap to prevent excessive heat buildup beneath it. Punching down the cap also prevents prolonged exposure to oxygen (allowing actobacter to turn the wine into vinegar) and creates a more uniform maceration and fermentation. Modern winemakers use several processes to ensure that the cap is submerged including punch down for more delicate reds, and pumping over the cap for more hardy reds. Fermentation ends naturally when all the fermentable sugars in the must are converted or when the alcohol level generally reaches 14% (in some cases over 15%). At that level, alcohol is toxic to the yeast, and it causes the yeast to die.

Several other conditions can also cause fermentation to stop prematurely. **Some of these are accidental, and others are deliberately created by the winemaker:**

1. Temperatures above 105°F (41°C) will kill the yeast, and cause a "stuck fermentation" to occur. Temperatures may also be brought down below 40°F, and yeast cells go dormant.

2. Adding brandy or a neutral spirit to the wine raises the alcohol level above the maximum that the yeast will tolerate, and fermentation stops. Winemakers add alcohol when they wish to leave residual sugar in the wine for sweetness.

10.16 Stainless steel, temperature controlled fermentation tanks

3. Pasteurizing, or flash-heating wine to 185°F (85°C) for one minute stops fermentation. Although pasteurization also neutralizes harmful bacteria, many believe it also strips the wine of some flavor components. Pasteurization, therefore, is not suited to wines requiring bottle aging.

4. To stop fermentation before all of the sugar is metabolized, winemakers may also add sulfur compounds.

5. Some winemakers use a centrifuge and filtration to remove yeasts from the wine. A rough filter followed by a sterile filtration prevents harmful bacteria or yeast from remaining in the wine, especially during clarification and the final bottling stages.

Racking After fermentation has occurred and the lees have precipitated to the bottom of the vessel, winemakers generally siphon the wine into a clean vat, cask, or barrel leaving the lees behind. Each time wine is racked into a new container, 2%–3% of its volume is lost. All fine wines are racked at least twice, and the finest are racked four times the first year and twice in the second year. **Racking,** a process that gives controlled exposure to air so the limited contact with oxygen can help the wines mature, not only clarifies the wine but also aerates it.

Malolactic fermentation Concurrent with or after the primary (or alcohol) fermentation is complete, almost all red wines and a few other white wines such as Chardonay, undergo a **malolactic fermentation.** Unlike the original fermentation, malolactic fermentation is not caused by yeasts but by lactobacteria that converts harsher malic acid in the wine to softer lactic acid. This fermentation has advantages and disadvantages. It can give cool-climate, acidic wines a softer more buttery character, but it can also leach out or mask the wine's fruit flavors.

Lees and bâtonnage Lees is the term for the sediment containing dead yeast and other solids that collect in the bottom of the wine tank or barrel following fermentation. Most wines are racked off the lees as part of the winemaking process. However, some wines that are fermented in barrels are left on the lees and are stirred back into the wine in a process called **bâtonnage.** Bâtonnage also allows for oxygen to be introduced preventing the creation of sulfur compounds. *See 10.17a and 10.17b.* This process contributes to **autolysis** (or the breakdown of yeast cells), which releases agents throughout the wine to reduce the bitterness from the wood tannins and to add a creamy quality and complexity to the wine.

Blending and aging Many wines develop greater complexity and better balance if they are blended with other wines. Generally speaking, wines that need blending are fermented separately and then blended before aging. Wine may also develop complexity over time through a process called aging, which normally takes place in wood. Not all wines benefit from oak aging. Winemakers age their wines in oak because the wood is tightly grained enough to store the liquid, and yet sufficiently porous to allow the slow and minute interaction of the content with oxygen. The flavors of oak should support rather than overwhelm the flavors in the wine.

The source of the oak, its treatment, age, and size all affect how the wood interacts with the wine. Oaks from different regions of France—Limousin, Tronçais, Allier, Nevers, and Vosges—generally have a tighter grain than American oak and can be split as opposed to American oak that must be sawed. The more porous American oak gives wines distinct vanillin, coconut, and tannic flavors. French oaks may cost 3 to 4 times as much as American oak varieties. *See 10.18.*

Making the oak barrels is complex. Producers called **cooperages** make barrels using carefully controlled processes. The degree to which the oak barrel is toasted affects the amount of toastiness in the wine's taste. *See 10.19.* The smaller the barrel, the more contact it has with the wine and the greater its effect on the flavor. Newer oak contributes more oak flavors than older oak. After three years of use, however, old oak barrels contribute little to the wine's flavor.

During the first few months of aging, some of the wine evaporates and some is absorbed by the wood to create an airspace called **ullage,** in the barrel. If the airspace is allowed to remain, the wine will oxidize. Winemakers therefore fill the space with additional wine of the same kind, a process known as topping off. At the point where topping off occurs, wine casks are loosely sealed with bungs (stoppers), which are later replaced with wooden bungs. During aging, impurities sink to the bottom of the cask, so the wine is racked into another cask to leave the accumulated sediment behind.

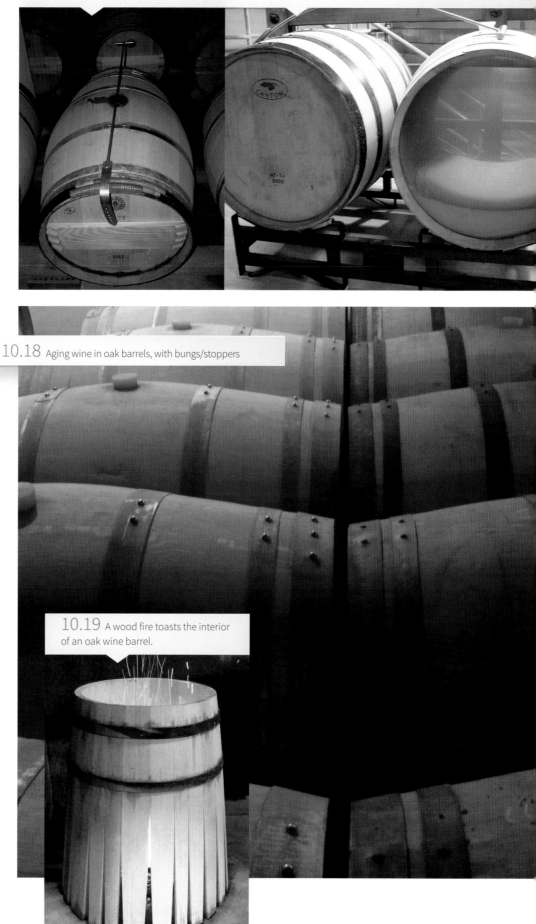

10.17a The stirring wand used for bâtonnage

10.17b The lees or dead yeast cells in the wine resting at the bottom of the barrel

10.18 Aging wine in oak barrels, with bungs/stoppers

10.19 A wood fire toasts the interior of an oak wine barrel.

Because many white wines cannot stand up to 100% oak aging, a winemaker may blend different lots of wine from the same vintage and vineyard; for example, the first may be 100% oak aged wine in new casks, the second lot aged in older wood, and yet a third lot aged in stainless steel.

Fining Fining is a clarification process used to give wines their brilliance. Although the wine eventually clarifies itself, fining saves time and expense. Fining agents include gelatin, egg whites, casein, isinglass, or bentonite clay. In addition to removing cloudiness, some fining agents may also remove some tannins to achieve a softer wine. Most commercial wines are either fined or filtered.

Finishing and bottling Before bottling, many wines are either centrifuged or filtered twice—the first is a rough filtration used soon after fermentation, and the second is a sterile filtration done immediately before bottling. Although some winemakers centrifuge their wines, the process can dilute the flavors. Consequently, the process is not used for fine wines.

Filtration is used mainly for white wines, especially those with residual sugar or those that do not undergo malolactic fermentation. Fine red wines, however, may not be filtered because the filtration process may also cause the wine to be stripped of some flavor components and complexity. These wines are sold as unfiltered and may not be as brilliant as other red wines. *See 10.20.*

10.20 The bottling line completes the wine production process.

Winemakers can also correct a wine's balance by adding ascorbic acid to finish or adjust the acidity of wine. Balancing wine with ascorbic acid is most common in warmer climates, where wines often lack acidity.

Cold stabilization Wine is bottled in sterilized bottles. After the bottle has been filled, the neck may be flushed with nitrogen or carbon dioxide to prevent oxidation. The bottle is then corked, and the wine is stored upside down to keep the cork moist. Moisture swells the cork and ensures a tight seal to prevent oxidation of the wine. Wine is not usually shipped for release until it is allowed to rest for several weeks because of the bottle shock that may occur.

Cork Cork is the bark taken from a species of oak tree common in southern Portugal and Spain. *See 10.21.* When the oak reaches 20–25 years of age, the cork bark is stripped manually from the tree. Cork may be reharvested from the same tree

10.21

Traditional cork closures

A metal screw cap closure

A modern glass cork closure

every 9–15 years. Cork provides an excellent seal because it is resistant to liquids and provides an efficient barrier to oxygen. However, cork is sometimes tainted by the organic compound TCA (trichloroanisole), created during the cleaning process, which gives off a distinctive dank wet basement smell and ruins the potential enjoyment of any fruit in the wine. The problem was recognized and addressed by cork producers within the last five years and is now less common. TCA can also be traced to other sources in the winery such as building materials and pallets. It should be noted that cork is not a perfect seal and trace amounts of oxygen that allow the wine to mature do seep into the wine.

Although the screw cap is a perfect barrier to oxygen, it has only recently begun to gain general acceptance because its image has been too closely associated with that of inexpensive jug wines. Because the screw cap can result in a lack of oxygen ingress, wines can become reductive, allowing for the development of skunky sulfur based compounds in the wine. Many screw cap closures have now been adapted to allow for trace amounts of oxygen to enter the bottle. The use of synthetic corks, however, is more controversial because they seem to be less well suited for long-term aging.

Cellar and bottle aging Almost all wines are best consumed within 1–3 years and do not improve with age. The tiny minority (less than 1%) that does benefit from bottle aging undergoes revealing changes with time. *See 10.22.*

Wines mature at different rates on the basis of individual vintage characteristics, their appellation, and vinification. The higher the level of acidity, the greater the potential for aging. Although residual sugar and tannins act as preservatives, they are also key to the evolution of flavors and balance. Without acidity, the wine's balance disintegrates. White wines generally have higher acid levels but few tannins. Fine Riesling and Loire Chenin Blanc wines evolve more slowly than do most Chardonnays. Red wines from Bordeaux that are Cabernet-based have not only the tannins but also the acidity to make them long-lived.

Storage conditions also affect the rate of aging. As a rule, warmer storage conditions accelerate aging, and cooler storage retards it. Longer bottle aging in cool (55°F) and humid (85%) conditions, however, gives the wine greater complexity and a more pleasing bouquet. Bottle size also affects aging times, with wine in smaller bottles aging faster than wine in larger ones.

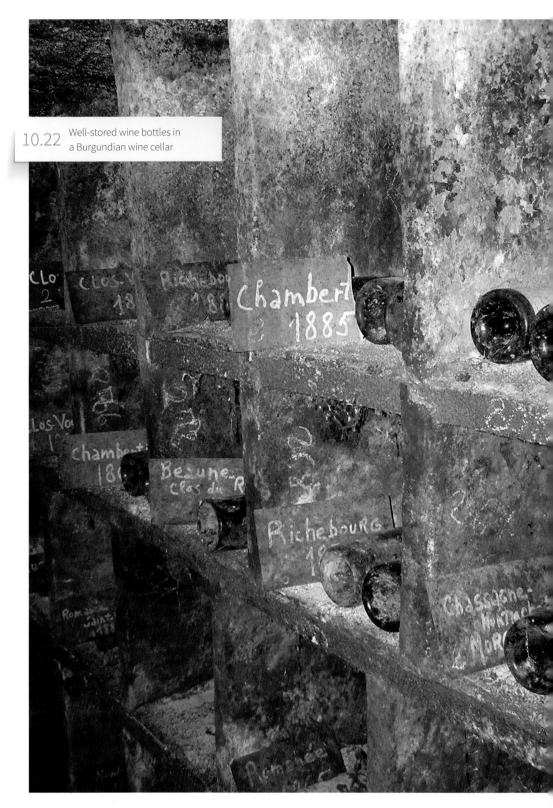

10.22 Well-stored wine bottles in a Burgundian wine cellar

Following the Steps from Grapes to Wine

From first pressing to final racking and finishing, winemaking has not changed essentially for thousands of years, although today's winemakers are rigorously scientific about the process.

Steps in vinification include:

1. The mechanical or hand harvesting that brings the grapes to the winery takes place.

2. White grapes are then pressed before fermentation to extract the must. Black grapes are pressed after fermentation to extract the wine.

3. Fermentation may take place in large open vats.

4. For more delicate red wines, the "punch down" method is preferred.

5. Racking siphons the wine from one vat or container into another, leaving the sediment behind.

6. Wine acquires additional flavors from toasted oak barrels that are used for storage and aging.

7. Fining helps to clarify the wine more quickly than the natural processes.

8. Thieving allows the winemaker to maintain quality control during aging.

SPECIAL WINEMAKING METHODS

Various methods for creating distinctive wines have evolved over the centuries.

Carbonic Maceration

Carbonic maceration is a red winemaking method common in, but not limited to, the Beaujolais region of Burgundy, France. Carbonic maceration extracts a fruity, light-bodied, aromatic wine from whole grapes such as Beaujolais Nouveau. In this process, bunches of uncrushed grapes are placed in a carbon dioxide-filled vat. When the grapes are sealed inside, they begin to ferment. The sealed grape bunches undergo an intracellular enzymatic fermentation that produces no more than 2% alcohol. After 1-2 days or up to 1 week, the grapes are crushed, and the must is macerated and fermented in the traditional way. Red wines made using carbonic macerations are ready to drink without long periods of aging because the process results in wine with little tannin and an increased fruity and mentholated aroma. These wines do not age well. This process is generally not suitable for white wines.

Dessert Winemaking

Technically, dessert wines fit into one of two categories that are designated by the Federal Standards of Identity as fortified wines. Not all dessert wines are fortified, however. Some are made using special viticultural or vinification practices. There are five primary methods for making a dessert wine.

Late harvest Late harvest wines are made from grapes that have been allowed to continue ripening for at least one week after the regular harvest. Extended ripening produces intensely sweet grapes, but waiting to harvest them is risky because the grapes are vulnerable to pest infestations or sudden changes in weather.

Botrytis cinerea *Botrytis cinerea* is a mold that causes infected grapes to dehydrate and proportionately increases their sugar and glycerol content. Botrytis is common in sites located near bodies of water where considerable humidity is created in the morning and then burned off by the midday sun. The best-known botrytized wines are: Sauternes from Bordeaux, France; Trockenbeerenauslese from Germany and the Neusiedlersee in Austria; and Tokay wines from Hungary. These wines are also made in Australia and the United States as Special Select Late Harvest wines. *See 10.23.*

Raisined grape wines Many famous wines are made from intentionally raisined grapes. These include Vin Santo from Tuscany, Umbria or Pedro Ximénez from Spain, and some of the Muscats from Samos or other Greek isles.

Ice wine Ice wine, or *eiswein* as it is known in Germany (from where it originated), is produced from grapes that have been allowed to freeze naturally on the vine before being harvested and pressed. The result is a high concentration of sugar in the must that produces an intensely sweet wine. Canada's most famous wines are its ice wines, and the best ice wines in the United States are from Washington state and New York's Finger Lakes region. There are also wines called "winter wines" that are made by artificially freezing late-harvest grapes. These can also be of a very good quality. *See 10.24.*

Mutage Mutage is generally the adding of alcohol or sometimes sulfur dioxide, to prevent the yeast from continuing to convert sugar into alcohol. Wine referred to as Vin Doux Naturel from France and Port wines are examples of such wines. *(See Fortified Wines, page 164.)*

10.23 Botrytized grapes are used to produce the sweet wines of Sauternes.

10.24 Ice wines are made from grapes harvested when frozen.

Sparkling Wines

Although many people use the term champagne as a synonym for sparkling wine, champagne is only one of many sparkling wines. Champagne takes its name from the region in France where it is produced.

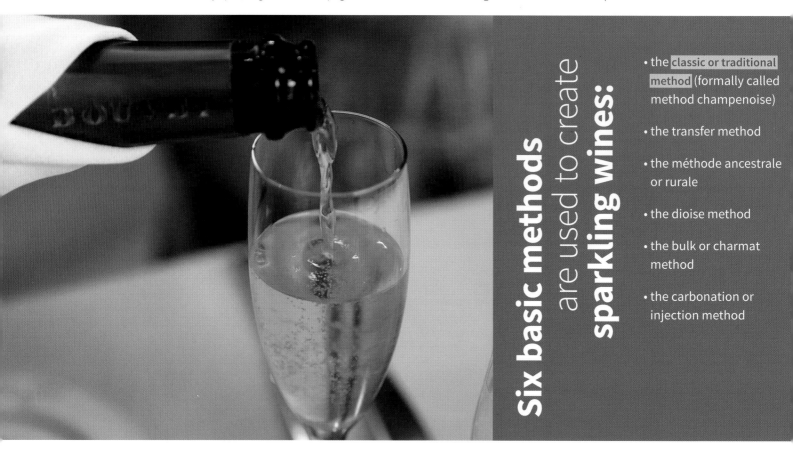

Six basic methods are used to create sparkling wines:

- the classic or traditional method (formally called method champenoise)

- the transfer method

- the méthode ancestrale or rurale

- the dioise method

- the bulk or charmat method

- the carbonation or injection method

CLASSIC OR TRADITIONAL METHOD

True champagne is produced only in the Champagne region of France, though other wine-makers may adapt the **classic or traditional method.** The European Union does not allow using the term *méthode champenoise* on labeling for non-champagne wines.

Champagnes are made from one, or a blend of up to three, grape varieties: Chardonnay, Pinot Noir, and Pinot Meunier. Other classic method wines may use other varieties. The grapes are hand harvested and carefully pressed to avoid contact with skin and pips. The free run of juice is called the *tête de cuvée* and is reserved for prestige wines such as Dom Pérignon. The juice from the first pressing is called the *cuvée,* and the second pressing is called the *premières tailles,* which may be used by some producers. The total yield of juice is strictly enforced by the *Comité Interprofessionnel du Vin de Champagne* (CIVC) to 2550 liters for each marc or 4000 kg/8800 lbs. of grapes. The must settles and ferments in steel tanks or old oak vats, and then most of the wines undergo malolactic fermentation.

The wine is then blended according to the style desired by the winemaker, and 20% is held in reserve for future years. Next, a solution composed of sugar and yeast, known as *liqueur de tirage,* is added to the wine, which is then bottled and capped. The carbon dioxide produced in the bottle during the second fermentation, or prise de mousse, causes champagne's characteristic effervescence. The pressure caused by trapped carbon dioxide is between five and six bars or 90 pounds per square inch, which translates to 200 – 250 million bubbles per bottle. After the wine finishes the second fermentation in 3–4 weeks, the bottle is aged on its side for a minimum of one year en *tirage* or on the lees (from January 1 following the vintage) to qualify for non-vintage champagne. (The minimum requirement is nine months in the United States.) The lees or yeast cells are partially absorbed in a process called autolysis, which lends added flavor and complexity to the wine.

The next stage in the classic method is to move the lees stuck to the side of the wine bottle down to the neck. The bottle is angled neck down at 45°, shaken, and turned by hand or by machines (gyropalettes) in a process called **riddling,** or *rémuage,* that may last several weeks. *See 10.25a and 10.25b.* After the lees are in the bottle's neck, the bottle may further age upside down (sur pointe) or have its lees expelled through a process known as **disgorgement,** or *dégorgement* in

which the neck of the bottle is placed upside down in a solution to freeze the top inch or two of wine and trapped lees. When the cap is removed, the gas expels the frozen plug. Then the bottle is topped off with identical wine called a **dosage** or *liqueur d'exposition,* which may have a dose of varying degrees of cane sugar solution dictating the level of sweetness. **The levels of sweetness are as follow:**

- **Brut Sauvage or Natural** bone dry: 6 g/l of sugar (extra brut)
- **Brut** very dry; <15 g/l of sugar; no noticeable sweetness
- **Extra Dry; Extra Sec** slightly sweet; 12-20 g/l sugar
- **Sec or Dry** noticeable sweetness; 17-35 g/l sugar
- **Demi-Sec** quite sweet; 33-50 g/l sugar
- **Doux** extremely sweet; more than 50 g/l sugar

TRANSFER METHOD

Similar to the classic champagne method, the **transfer method** produces a pleasantly carbonated sparkling wine. In this method, the wine is aged on the lees but is neither riddled nor disgorged. It is filtered and dosed in bulk before being rebottled. The wine will tend to have a coarser texture than champagne because of the resulting loss of carbonation.

10.25a Hand riddling on a pupître

10.25b Mechanical riddling through the use of a gyropalette

MÉTHODE ANCESTRALE OR RURALE

This method is the most ancient way of producing sparkling wine. The wine is fermented at cold temperatures and bottled prior to its completion. The resulting wine is less bubbly, sweeter, and may have deposits. This style of wine is found in the Blanquette de Limoux.

DIOISE METHOD

The *dioise method* is a variation of the *Méthode Ancestrale* whereby the wine's first slow fermentation in sealed vats is filtered, bottled, and the wine continues to ferment in the bottle until it reaches 7.5% alcohol. The wine is then disgorged and filtered so that it is low in alcohol and has residual sugar. This method is used for Asti and Clairette de Die Tradition.

BULK/CHARMAT/ CUVE CLOSE METHOD

In the **bulk, Charmat, or cuve close method**, wine is fermented a second time in bulk and then bottled. Cheaper and faster than either the transfer or classic champagne method, the bulk method can produce a good wine, but one that lacks the complexity of a classic or traditional method sparkling wine.

CARBONATION/ INJECTION METHOD

The least expensive and lowest-quality sparkling wines are made by the carbonation/injection method, in which carbon dioxide is injected into the wine vat, and the wine is then bottled under pressure, much in the way that a soft drink is produced. Because the resulting wine is coarser and the effervescence dissipates rapidly, only the least expensive sparkling wines are prepared in this way.

Fortified Wines

Fortified wines are those that have had neutral spirits or brandy added to fermenting or fermented wine to generally raise the level of alcohol from 16% to 22%. When fermentation stops and the wine retains sweetness, the process is called **mutage.** Winemakers also fortify wines to ensure their stability. The most common fortified wines are Port, Sherry, Madeira, Marsala, and Vin Doux Naturel.

PORT

Port, which originated in the Douro Valley of northern Portugal, begins its transformation to a fortified wine with grapes that are fermented to the 6%–9% alcohol stage. Then the winemaker mixes in *aguardiente* brandy (77% alcohol) so the wine is about 20% brandy and 80% grape wine. The Port is then aged in old wooden barrels called pipes for varying lengths of time, depending on the type of Port desired.

Two basic types of Port are wood and vintage. **Wood Port** is aged in wood and is ready to be consumed shortly after it is bottled. Of the wood Ports, ruby and tawny are the most significant styles. **Ruby Port** is aged for 2–3 years, and **Tawny Port** is aged for at least six years and up to 40 years. The more Ports age in wood, the more they lose their hard tannins and color. Ruby Ports, named for their deep red color, have a very sweet fruit flavor and are one of very few wines that can stand up to dark chocolate without being overwhelmed. **Colheita ports** are wood aged ports from a single vintage but are quite distinct from vintage ports. They must be aged in pipes for a minimum of 7 years.

Vintage Port, made from the best available grapes from a single vintage year, are aged 2–3 years in wood and then require at least 10–15 years in the bottle. Some vintage Ports may be aged for 50 or more years. With so much bottle aging, vintage Ports require decanting to separate the wine from its thick sediment. Extensive sediment is so common and prevalent that Port aficionados say that the wine is "throwing a crust."

Recently, a hybrid style of Port has been developed in response to the high cost of vintage Port. Called Late Bottled Vintage (LBV) Port, it is made from a specific vintage, traditionally aged 4–6 years in wood, and then bottle aged. It can continue to improve in the bottle before being consumed. It may also need to be decanted based on the length of the bottle aging.

SHERRY

Sherry is produced in the southern region of Spain known as Andalusia. It is made from grapes grown in the chalky soils, called albariza, around the town of Jerez de la Frontera. (Sherry is based on the Arabic name Sheris). Although similar fortified wines have been called sherry, the European Union has now restricted the use of the title sherry to sherries produced in this region, when they are sold in Europe. The Palomino makes up 95% of the grapes grown in that region. Pedro Ximénez, or PX, and Moscatel grapes make a very sweet wine for blending and are an added component for making sweet cream sherry.

Unlike Port wines, sherry is fortified after fermentation. The Palomino grapes are mostly hand harvested, gently pressed to form must, fermented, and then fortified. Two fundamental processes make sherry unique: biological aging through yeast *flor* development, and fractional blending through the *solera* system. *See 10.26.* Many sherries also go through an oxidative process of aging to allow the wine to become not only intentionally oxidized, but also more intense because the water content has evaporated, and the dry extract is more concentrated.

10.26 The Sherry Solera System in a cathedral-like bodega

There are two basic types of sherries: fino and oloroso. **Fino** sherry is light with a very distinctive nose that stems from biological aging and the development of acetaldehyde (a compound the human body produces as it breaks down alcohol). To produce a fino or its lightest style manzanilla, winemakers use the best free run juice. All wines develop a secondary yeast called **flor.** For the flor yeast to develop, the wine is fortified to 15.5% alcohol and placed in American oak casks until they are five-sixths full. The flor yeast feed on oxygen, alcohol, and glycerin in the wine. These components need to be replenished by blending new wine into the older wine. This process of fractional blending or "tipping the scales," is called the solera system and continues during its three to six years of aging for fino sherry. True **amontillados** are finos whose flor yeast have died naturally or are wines that have been fortified to 16% ABV or more. Most commercial amontillados are blends that are sweetened. Finos and manzanillas look like white wines and are light bodied, dry, and consumed upon release. Once opened, they deteriorate as quickly as a white still wine.

Oloroso sherry is fortified to 18% alcohol so the flor cannot develop. The wines undergo aging by oxidation, resulting in mahogany colored, fuller bodied wines that have a different nutty pungency. The wines still go through fractional blending to maintain a consistent style and added complexity. Olorosos are some of the most difficult wines for consumers to appreciate, and they need to be paired with intensely flavored or seasoned foods. When blended with PX, Oloroso becomes a sweet cream sherry. A recent development has been the creation of VOS (Vinum Optimum Signatorum but also known as Very Old Sherry) and VORS (Vinum Optimum Rarum Signatorum) made of sherry blends that are a minimum of 20 years and 30 years respectively.

MADEIRA

Madeira wines, named after the Portuguese island of Madeira, once functioned as ballast in ships that came to this island's revictualing station on voyage from England to the American colonies. It was soon discovered that hot aging in the hold of the ships improved these fortified wines. In fact, Madeira was used by the colonists to toast the signing of the Declaration of Independence.

Madeiras are fortified after fermenting to produce dry styles but fortified during fermentation for sweeter styles. They undergo a unique baking process called the estufagem system. The best wines are those that are baked naturally in lofts or attics by the heat of the sun called Vinhos de Canteiro aged for 20 years minimum in 600L pipes.

Those of a lesser quality are stored for a minimum of three months at 40°C–50°C in a steampipe heated room (estufa) or are heated directly by heating coils running in the wine vats. This process causes the sugars to caramelize and promote oxidation to make the wines virtually indestructible. A few wines may also go through a sherry-like solera process. The best Madeiras are special reserve, extra reserve, and vintage. Special reserves are blends that are at least ten years old. Extra reserves are at least 15 years old, and vintage Madeiras must be from a single vintage and aged a minimum of 20 years in the barrel and two years in the bottle. Since the formation of the European Union, producers cannot label their wines varietally unless they contain 85% of that variety. Previously, much of the wine sold as Madeira had little of the varieties that originally made Madeiras famous. **There are, however, four varietally and one non-varietally labeled Madeiras:**

• **Sercial** Very dry and acidic
• **Verdelho** Dry and smoky
• **Rainwater** Dry but slightly fruity and softer
• **Bual** Medium sweet, aromatic, and reminiscent of nuts and dates
• **Malmsey** An English corruption of Malvasia, the sweetest Madeira, but balanced by high acidity with great, dark, and rich dried-fruit aromas.

MARSALA

Originally named for the city of Marsala on the isle of Sicily, Marsala was first produced in 1770 by an English merchant named John Woodhouse. **Marsala** is fortified by alcohol and sweetened by concentrated grape must and has an alcohol content of 17%–19%. These wines may be golden, amber, or ruby-colored, and the sugar level in each color can vary from secco (dry), to semi-secco (semi-dry), to dolce (sweet). Most Marsalas labeled fine (pronounced fee-nay) are aged one year, although a number of quality Marsalas that are labeled *Superiore Riserva* (aged four years), *Vergina* (aged five years) and *Stravecchio* (aged ten years) make for delightful sipping.

VIN DOUX NATUREL

French for "naturally sweet wine," *Vin Doux Naturel* is actually the product of mutage. A majority of these wines are made from Muscat grapes. Especially satisfying as dessert wines, these French sweet wines are best if balanced by acidity. The most famous come from the village of Beaumes de-Venise in the Rhône Valley. The other famous appellations that use the red Grenache grapes are Rasteau and Banyuls. These Port-like wines are sometimes deliberately exposed to air and topped off with new wine every six months to help develop the quality of rancio, a blue cheese bouquet, also found in old Cognacs.

Aromatized Wines

Aromatized, or apéritif wines are best served before a meal because their bitter and aromatic ingredients are appetite stimulants. Any number of aromatic ingredients may be infused into an apéritif, including herbs, spices, flowers, and barks. Aromatized wines such as Vermouth, Dubonnet, and Lillet, are fortified and have an alcohol content of at least 15%. There are wine cocktails that are considered aperitifs when they are blended with a liqueur such as Kir.

Vermouth Vermouth stems from the German term *vermut,* meaning "wormwood," an herb that was once frequently used in beverages. Both dry white and sweet red Vermouth are made in France and in Italy. Dry Vermouth is the result of a white wine fermented to dryness, infused with aromatics, and fortified with brandy to an alcohol content of 19%. After it is bottled, it is aged for 3 1/2–4 years. Dry Vermouth is served chilled and is sometimes substituted for dry white wine in cooking.

Sweet Vermouth uses sweeter white grape varietals fortified to 17% alcohol and infused with aromatics and quinine. After sugar and caramel coloring are added, sweet Vermouth is aged for two years. Sweet Vermouth is usually served on the rocks with soda. Both dry and sweet vermouths are often used in cocktails such as Martinis and Manhattans.

Dolin Vermouth de Chambery Appellation d'Origine Dolin Vermouth de Chambery Appellation d'Origine, the only vermouth with an A.O.C in France. It comes in 3 styles: red, white, and dry.

Carpano Antica Carpano Antica formula is one of the best vermouth in Italy.

Dubonnet French Dubonnet is available in dry white and sweet red varieties. It is best served chilled or on the rocks with a twist of lemon.

Lillet Infused with citrus flavors, Lillet may be red or white, dry or off-dry. It is best served chilled or on the rocks with a twist of lemon or orange.

Kir Kir is not an aromatized wine per se but is an example of a classic apéritif made by blending the acidic Aligoté white grape wine with Crème de Cassis, a black currant liqueur.

11. Decoding *the* Label

In addition to having a knowledge of the various types of wines and how they are made, servers need an overall understanding of the information provided on wine labels. Unfortunately, there is no standardized universal labeling system for all of the wine producing regions of the world. Some wines are labeled by variety, others by appellation, quality standards, brand names, or a combination thereof. Furthermore, wine labels may be in various languages with terms unfamiliar or foreign to both guests and servers. Good servers need an overall understanding and recognition of these terms to help customers decode the wine list.

Wine Purchasing *and* Tasting

Most restaurants and other beverage establishments, whether on or off-premise, purchase wine from distributors, who in turn, buy from suppliers or importers. This system is known in the U.S. as the **three tier system.** In most states, it is illegal for an establishment to purchase wine directly from a wine producer unless it is from a small local producer. When food service establishments purchase wines for their wine lists, a number of factors are considered including: the brand name, the place of origin, and the variety; the reputation of the distributor, négoçiant, and/or importer if applicable; the cost of the wine; and finally the wine list's compatibility with the food menu.

WINE PURCHASING

Several factors influence the purchasing decisions for wines:

Brand name Wines may be purchased solely on the basis of the brand name and the reputation of the producer. Names such as Château Lafite Rothschild®, Robert Mondavi®, or Opus One® are often the only guarantee of quality a purchaser needs. *See 11.1 and 11.2.*

Place of origin In the European Union, the appellation or place of origin reflects the most significant differences in the aroma and taste of wines. Generally speaking, the more delimited an area, the better the wine quality is thought to be. *See 11.3 and 11.4.* Appellations are becoming increasingly important as the awareness of consumers evolves. Quality wine producers in the United States and the New World are marketing their wines by stressing increasingly recognized appellations such as Napa Valley or Sonoma County. There are now approximately 220 American Viticultural Areas (AVA) in the United States. *See 11.5.*

Varietal labeling The marketing of wines by varietal labeling, such as Chardonnay, is a fairly recent phenomenon. In response to the less distinctive wines sold under semi-generic labels such as California Burgundy, producers in the 1940s and 50s, began differentiating their better wines by labeling them varietally. Many consumers make the varietal the primary factor in their purchasing decision. *See 11.6 and 11.7.*

11.1 Famous wines of Bordeaux are known by their brand names.

11.2 Some American wines are primarily marketed using their brand names.

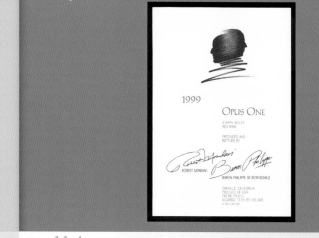

11.3 Beaujolais-Villages is a district of 39 designated villages within the Beaujolais region of Burgundy.

11.4 Moulin-à-Vent is one of ten Beaujolais Cru Villages.

11.5 Russian River Valley AVA is a more narrowly defined appellation within the Sonoma County AVA.

11.6 Most New World fine wines are varietally labeled.

11.7 Unlike other AOC French regions, Alsatian wines are most often varietally labeled.

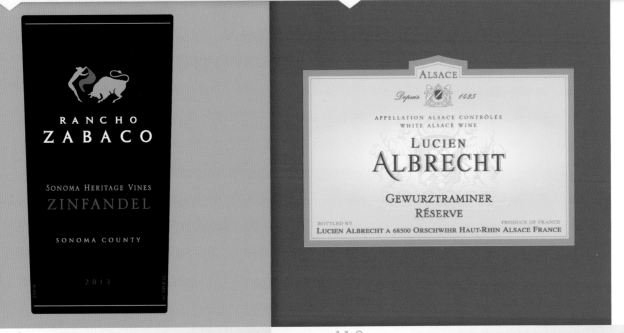

11.8 Very often the négociant or importer is listed on the back label as with Kobrand's name on this label.

11.9 Sassicaia—This world renown wine with a proprietary name is also one of the most expensive.

Reputation of the négociant, importer, and distributor Many négociants, who in France are wine merchants, importers, and distributors, have built reputations for their expertise by either producing or selecting, storing, and transporting wines, and then delivering them in optimum condition. Their customer service support is important and it is imperative that they keep their restaurant accounts apprised of any wine shortages and changes or special pricing that may help the establishment's profitability. They may also support additional staff training with seminars and wine tastings, as well as providing point of sale materials such as table tents to augment sales. *See 11.8.*

Cost Cost is a factor in any purchasing decision. For a food and beverage establishment, the cost of the wine purchased must fall within the budget parameters of the menu. A casual-dining restaurant, for example, would not offer a wine list featuring rare and expensive vintages. *See 11.9.* It is worth noting that price does not dictate quality, but rather often reflects the marketing, and the wine critic ratings and perceptions. In general, an establishment in the United States looks for a return of 100% or more on the cost of wine. Volume purchases usually result in significant savings.

Compatibility with the food menu Wine lists should not only reflect the restaurant's price compatibility but should also reflect the food menu's theme and tastes. If the restaurant is Tuscan themed, the wines should reflect the style and profile of Tuscan foods even if they are not from that region. If the menu reflects a preponderance of seafood and light sauces, the wines should be lighter in style and have moderately high acidity to pair best with the food.

DECODING THE WINE LABEL

Knowing how to read a wine label can provide a wealth of information. Unfortunately, no standard, universal method, or legal requirements exist for labeling. Today, however, all European Union wines conform to one set of standards. The information of greatest concern to the purchaser or server is the place of origin, the quality level, the vintage year, and the varietal or proprietary labeling.

Place of Origin

The place of origin is determined and guaranteed by the official state or regulatory agency of each country. The entire appellation system is based on the primacy concept of the place of origin. The wine may be labeled primarily for the location in which the grapes are grown, especially in the case of some quality French, Italian, Spanish, Portuguese, German, Austrian, and Hungarian wines. In Europe, if a label identifies a geographic area, 100% of the grapes must be grown in that area. In Australia, New Zealand, and the U.S., however, the requirement is 85%.

When determining the place of origin, one must examine the geographic level given on the label. In general, the more defined the area, the higher the quality of the wine. **The five levels ranging from the broadest to the narrowest geographically defined areas are:**

Country
- France
- U.S.A.

Region
- Bordeaux
- California

District
- Médoc
- Napa/Sonoma

Commune/village
- Pauillac
- St. Helena/Dry Creek

Vineyard
- Château Latour
- Mario's Vineyard/ Stefani Ranch

See 11.10.

11.10 Mario's Vineyard is located in the AVA of St. Helena which is one of the 16 AVAs of the Napa Valley AVA.

Quality Level

Although much of the world shares similar standards, these are by no means uniform. Members of the European Union must meet hierarchic criteria that vary considerably. Each country has a governmental or regulatory agency to oversee viticultural and winemaking practices. These agencies qualify the level of each wine on the basis of place of origin, which determines viticultural practices and winemaking processes. In the European Union, there are two overall quality levels, with Protected Designation of Origin (POD) and Protected Geographical Indication (PGI) in the first, and "Wine" in the second. In countries with less clearly defined appellation-based or hierarchical systems than those of the European Union, there is greater freedom to experiment. The United States also has a federal regulatory agency, the Alcohol and Tobacco Tax and Trade Bureau (TTB), as well as state regulatory agencies to oversee the wine industry.

The brand name or name of a producer may be as significant as the quality rating given by a regulatory agency. For example, Angelo Gaja in Italy produces unconventional wines of the highest quality. His Chardonnay is nontraditional in Piedmont and has not been designated by the Italian regulatory agency as a highest quality wine with a rating of DOCG. In addition, the purchaser should be aware of the reputation of the négociant, wine merchant, or importer (Frederick Wildman and Sons, Neal Rosenthal, or Kobrand Corporations are reputable examples.)

Vintage

Vintages reflect the weather for a particular year. Thanks to scientific developments, vintages matter less today than in the past. Although winemakers are able to manipulate wines to extract the greatest amount of flavors possible, there are limits as to what they can achieve. Winemakers can make a good wine, but not a great one, in an "off year." A great vintage increases the potential of a quality wine to develop greater complexity and aging potential than a wine created from a mediocre or poor vintage. In disastrous vintages, the producer may decide not to sell the wine under his primary label in order to protect the label's integrity.

Varietal, Generic, or Proprietary

Wines can be labeled with varietal, generic, or proprietary names. Australian and European varietal wines must contain a minimum of 85% of the grape variety stated on the label. In the United States, varietal wines must contain a minimum of 75% of the stated variety, except in Oregon, where a 90% minimum is required for certain varieties such as Pinot Noir, Chardonnay, and Pinot Gris.

Lower-quality American wines are often **semi-generically labeled**—for example, as California Chablis, Claret, or Madeira. These wines may be composed of any blend of any variety of grapes and typically bear little resemblance to their European namesakes. **The United States has 17 acceptable semi-generic labels, which include the following:**

- Burgundy
- Claret
- Moselle
- Sherry
- Chablis
- Hock
- Port
- Tokay
- Champagne
- Madeira
- Rhine wine
- Chianti
- Malaga
- Sauterne or Haut Sauterne
- Marsala
- Angelica

Many wines are also marketed under an exclusive **proprietary or brand name** such as Opus One® from the United States. Those wines do not reflect any single quality. Some proprietary labels, such as Blue Nun® from Germany, represent European table wines, and others, such as Sassicaia® from Italy, represent the best quality.

United States Wine Regions

The United States is currently the world's fourth largest wine producer and is the world's number one wine consuming nation since 2014. Wine production reached over 750 million gallons in 2013 with over 7,700 wineries located in 50 states. California represents 90% of U.S. production and contributes more than 60 billion dollars to the state's economy. While California has 152 American Viticultural Areas (as of 2014), there are six regional AVAs that encompass most of the others. **They are:**

- The North Coast AVA, which includes Napa Valley, Sonoma, Mendocino, and the Lake counties. This is the most famous region because it includes Napa Valley and Sonoma County, which produce some of California's finest wines. *See 11.11.*
- The Central Coast and Santa Cruz Mountain AVAs, which are frequently, divided into the North Central and South Central Coast divisions by wine writers, although neither of those exists as AVAs. The Central Coast includes: San Louis Obispo, Paso Robles, and Santa Barbara counties.
- The South Coast area, which primarily includes Temecula County.
- The Sierra Foothills area, which includes six AVAs.
- Klamath Mountains in northern California, which have three AVAs including Trinity Lakes.
- The Central Valley, which is the largest production zone and includes Lodi AVA and Clarksburg AVA.

California and Oregon's wine growing regions are protected by coastal mountain ranges that keep the inland regions dry. The cold Pacific Ocean and San Pablo Bay effect, drawn inland by the desert heat, forms cooling mists that allow for the successful growth of cool climate grape varietals such as Chardonnay and Pinot Noir in areas closer to the coast. Sunny interior hot weather is equally conducive to warm climate varietals. There are enormous differences in temperatures based on the location of the vineyard as demonstrated by the example of the Carneros AVA at the southern end of Napa where it can be 15 degrees cooler than at the Calistoga AVA in the northern end of Napa just 30 miles away. The same is true of Sonoma County, which is considerably larger in size than Napa and has the cool climate of the Russian River Valley as opposed to the warm climates of Dry Creek Valley or the Alexander Valley. The top varieties produced in descending order of production are: Chardonnay (W), Cabernet Sauvignon (R), Merlot (R), Zinfandel (R) Pinot Noir (R), Syrah (R), Sauvignon Blanc (W), and Pinot Gris/Pinot Grigio (W).

California

11.11 The North Coast area includes some of the most significant wine growing AVAs due to the cooling influence of the Pacific Ocean and waters of San Pablo Bay.

Oregon & Washington

Oregon

Oregon is less well protected by the Coast Range in the northern half of the state, resulting in a cooler and wetter climate. Oregon produces a small quantity of the United States total production (less than 1% of California's coastal region). It is home to 540 small producers who have developed a world renowned reputation particularly for Pinot Noir and Pinot Gris wines. There are currently 17 AVAs, six of which are sub-appellations of the most significant region of the Willamette Valley AVA. This area is sandwiched between the Coast Range in the west and the Cascade Mountains to the east.

Washington State

Washington State is the second largest producer of vinifera wines in the U.S. Unlike Oregon, most of Washington State's vineyards are located west of the Cascades in the arid Sonoran Desert and are irrigated with water from the Columbia and Yakima Rivers. The desert soils allow growers to plant ungrafted vines to save considerable costs. The climate is continental with short hot summers and cold winters with the ever present danger of frost in the fall. Due to significant diurnal temperature fluctuations and long summer days, many varieties are able to ripen while maintaining high acidity. There are 13 AVAs, the largest of which is the Columbia Valley. This area covers almost 1,000 square miles and includes 9 sub-appellations including Horse Heaven Hills and Wahluke Slopes AVAs. There are now 800 wineries, some of which have developed a deservedly high reputation for producing Chardonnay (W), Cabernet Sauvignon (R), Merlot (R), Riesling (W), Syrah (R), and Sauvignon Blanc (W).

New York & other states

New York is the third largest producer of wines with over 400 wineries although over 80% represents vitis labrusca varieties such as Concord (R), Delaware (R), and Catawba (B) and production made from hybrids such as Vidal Blanc (W), Seyval Blanc (W), and Chambourcin (R). There are 5 AVAs including Long Island, the Finger Lakes, the Hudson Valley, Niagara Escarpment and Lake Erie. Riesling (W) and Gewürztraminer (W) from the Finger Lakes AVA, and Merlot (R), Cabernet Franc from North Fork AVA in Long Island have developed reputations for quality wines. Humidity and climatic variations in the growing and harvesting seasons create the biggest challenges to growers on the eastern seaboard.

Virginia has become a significant producing state with 7 AVAs and over 250 wineries with Viognier and Cabernet Franc displaying world-class pedigree. States such as Rhode Island, which is part of the Southeastern New England AVA, has 7 wineries. North Carolina (especially in the northwest corner of the state) has 4 AVAs including the Yadkin Valley AVA and over 140 wineries with Cabernet Sauvignon, Cabernet Franc, Merlot, and Sauvignon Blanc. Colorado with its high altitude river valleys (Grand Valley AVA and West Elks AVA), are all producing quality vinifera wines in an industry that has grown from 5 wineries in 1990 to over 120 wineries. While all 50 states produce wine, the combined vinifera production total of all states other than that of California, Washington State, Oregon, and New York equals less than 2.5%. Florida ranks 6th in total production, which is derived almost totally from Muscadine native grapes, hybrids, and other fruit wines.

11.12

Brand Name ┈┈
Type of Wine ┈┈
Place of Origin ┈┈
Alcohol Content ┈┈

11.13

Name and Address of Bottler ┈┈
Net Contents ┈┈
Health Warning ┈┈
Sulfite Statement ┈┈

United States Labeling Laws

United States law requires that the following information is listed on wine labels:

1. Brand Name: Either the name of the producer or the proprietary name
2. Type of Wine: Semi-generic, table (red, white or rosé), or sparkling
3. Country or Place of Origin: The country or state or appellation must be included
4. Name and Address of the Bottler
5. Alcohol Content: For table or still wines, a variance of 1.5% is allowed; for sparkling wines < 1%
6. Net Contents of the Bottle
7. Sulfite Statement: States whether or not the wine contains sulfites (most do)
8. Health Warning: To advise pregnant women and heavy machinery operators against consuming alcoholic beverages. *See 11.12 and 11.13.*

U.S. Labeling Terms

Accepted labeling terms in the United States include:

- Vintage–95% of grapes must be from that vintage year
- Estate Bottled–100% grown, made, and bottled at the winery
- Produced by–75% or more crushed, made, and bottled at the winery
- Cellared and Bottled by–10% or less crushed, made at the winery
- Vineyard Name–95% or more grown at the particular vineyard

Australia

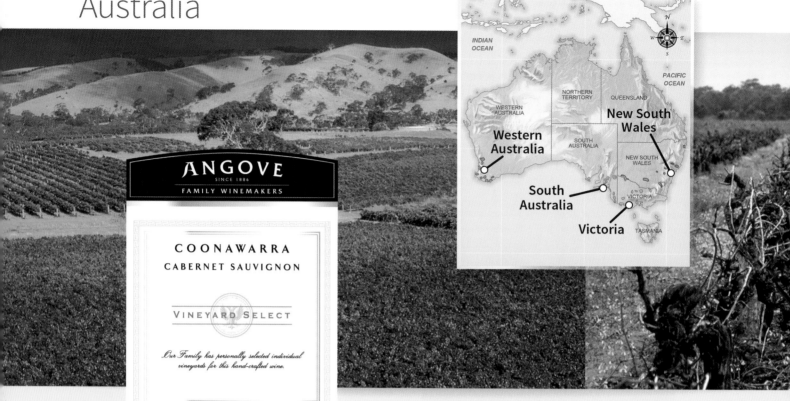

The huge island continent of Australia ranks sixth in the world's wine production and is the second largest producer of imported wine into the U.S. While wine is produced in all of the Australian states, the most important regions lie in the southern third of the country in the 30° latitude (South) where almost all Australian wine is produced. This region includes the states of New South Wales, South Australia, Victoria, the island state of Tasmania, and parts of Queensland; all of which form the super appellation of Southeastern Australia. Bulk wine regions are located in the arid Outback region of New South Wales and Victoria. This area is irrigated by the Murray, Darling, and Murumbidgee Rivers and is similar to California's lush Central Valley. The best growing region for quality wines is along the southern coast along the Tasman Sea where there are cold ocean breezes and moderate temperatures. The famous Barossa Valley, Coonawarra, Eden and Clare Valleys, and the Yarra Valley appellations are found here.

While Australia's export oriented wine industry may be best known for its inexpensive, easily quaffable, fruity "critter" wines, it does produce high quality white wines primarily from Chardonnay, Sémillon, and Riesling, and reds from Shiraz (a synonym for Syrah), Merlot, and Cabernet Sauvignon. While these wines may be sold varietally, they are frequently blended so that one may find the designations GSM (short for Grenache, Shiraz, and Mourvèdre) on the label.

Australian Labeling Laws

Australia's Wine and Brandy Corporation is the regulatory agency that enforces labeling laws through an annual audit of the Label Integrity Program. **The LIP enforces the following regulations:**

1. A minimum 85% of the wine must be made from the stated varietal.

2. A minimum of 85% of the wine comes from the stated region.

3. If a wine is composed of more than one variety, the varieties must be named in descending order. For example, a wine labeled Cabernet Shiraz would contain more Cabernet Sauvignon than Shiraz.

4. Semi-generic labels that are named for European appellations are not allowed.

5. If the term "reserve bin" or "bin number" is listed, the wine must indicate distinctiveness and higher quality.

6. If the term "show reserve" is used, the wine must have won a medal at a wine tasting competition, an event that is taken very seriously by wine makers.

7. Geographic indications are an official description of Australian wine zones, regions, and subregions. They are increasingly important, just as American Viticultural Areas are in the United States. There are now 114 Geographic Indications that have been classified as of 2014. *See 11.14.*

11.14

CLARENDON HILLS

Minimum 85%
(actual 100%) ········· **GRENACHE**

South Australia 85% ·· CLARENDON

Vintage ················· **2006**

Vineyard Name *Kangarilla*

750ML

New Zealand

New Zealand is a newcomer to the international wine scene since having developed a reputation primarily for two varietals: Sauvignon Blanc and Pinot Noir. Its two islands (North and South Islands) span the wine growing latitudes of 35° to 45° south. The vineyards are almost all located on the eastern side of the islands as they are protected by mountainous ranges that act as a rain shadow. New Zealand's primary appellations include: Marlborough and Central Otago in South Island, and Hawke's Bay and Martinborough in the North Island.

New Zealand Wine Laws

New Zealand has adopted the Food Standards Code where the wine's minimum content for the stated variety, appellation, or vintage must be at least 85%. *See 11.15 and 11.16.*

11.15 Sauvignon Blanc is the most popular variety for which New Zealand has become known. Marlborough is a major appellation in South Island.

WHITEHAVEN

Marlborough

SAUVIGNON BLANC

2013

NEW ZEALAND

ALC 13.6% BY VOL

11.16 Though a recent phenomenon, Pinot Noir has cemented New Zealand's reputation as an up and coming fine wine producer. Some of the best of New Zealand's Pinot Noir comes from the world's most southerly vineyards in Central Otago.

AMISFIELD

PINOT NOIR
2005

CENTRAL OTAGO
WINE OF NEW ZEALAND

South Africa

Although South Africa is considered a New World wine producer, its production first started in 1659 with the settlement of European colonists who established a revictualing station for European traders travelling to India and the Far East. South Africa's wine growing region is located mostly along the coast especially in the Capetown area where the Atlantic Ocean meets the Indian Ocean, and the cold Benguela current from Antarctica creates winds that cool the hot inland temperatures to produce an ideal Mediterranean wine growing climate. The geographic breakdown of wine areas makes them super regions, which incorporate regions formed by districts composed of wards. The most significant region is the Western Cape, which encompasses the Coastal Region including the Stellenbosch and Paarl districts.

South Africa had a well-deserved, reputable reputation until phylloxera struck in the mid 19th century, and its industry became dominated by a single co-op early in the 20th century. Due to the international boycotts created in response to apartheid policies, only 30% of the grapes grown were used for wine production. South Africa's wine industry has since seen a resurgence of quality, which has led it to seek a worldwide export market.

Chenin Blanc, also locally known as Steen, is the most significant variety, although noble international varieties such as Chardonnay (W), Sauvignon Blanc (W), Cabernet Sauvignon (R), Shiraz, and Merlot are also now produced and are earning South Africa a highly regarded reputation. It is also the home of Pinotage, which is a cross between Pinot Noir and Cinsaut that was developed in South Africa almost a century ago.

South African Wine Laws

The wine laws are overseen by the South African Wine and Spirits Board, which supervises the Wine of Origin system certifying that any wine with a stated appellation must be 100% from the region, district, or ward, and that if there is a stated vintage or variety, it must consist of a minimum of 85%. The Board samples all wines for certification and affixes a white paper seal over the cork but under the capsule to verify its acceptance. *See 11.17.*

11.17 South African Labels with "Cape Blend" refer to red wines blended with a minimum 20% Pinotage.

Chile & Argentina

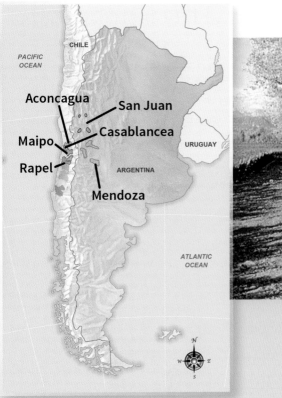

CHILE

Chile is another international player, which has been producing wines since the Spanish settled the Central Valley in the 16th century. Its wine quality was not well considered despite its use of Bordeaux varieties that were planted in the mid 19th century. The dominant varieties were Pais and Muscatel, and the wines were mostly insipid. It was only once tariffs and legislative barriers were removed in the 1980s that investments were made so that the number of wineries soared with a focus on the export market.

Due to Chile's long (3000 miles) thin land mass, which is positioned between the Pacific Ocean and the Andes Mountains, Chile enjoys a Mediterranean climate similar to that of California with a wide diurnal temperature range and a lack of rain during the growing season. The traditional location of its vineyards was near the capital, Santiago, in the Central Valley. In the last 15 years, there has been an expansion of vineyards to hillsides and bench sites that are more conducive to high quality wine production. Large foreign investments, 'flying winemakers' and improved viticultural knowledge have led Chile to become an important exporter of wines to the U.S. The dominant red varieties are Cabernet Sauvignon, Merlot, and Carmenère (a Bordeaux variety that was misidentified as Merlot until the 1990s), and Sauvignon Blanc and Chardonnay for whites.

Chilean Wine Laws

1. If a wine label has the name of a place, such as a region, sub-region or appellation, 75% of the grapes must come from that place. Chile created a Denominación de Origen system that recognizes larger regions, which incorporate more distinct terroirs forming sub-regions.

2. If a wine label carries the name of a grape variety, the wine must be made from at least 75% of that grape variety, although most are composed of 85% for the export market in the EU.

3. If a wine label carries a vintage, 75% of the wine must come from that vintage. *See 11.18.*

ARGENTINA

While Argentina is a much larger land mass and produces far more wine than Chile, its wines are made for its domestic rather than export market. Ninety percent of its production is consumed domestically. It is only recently that Argentina has begun exporting quality wines to Europe and the U.S. Argentina's major wine producing region of Mendoza, which is situated east of the Andes and distinguished by its high elevation, has developed a reputation primarily for Malbec, a red wine, and Torrontés, a white wine. The diurnal range helps to keep the wines lively with acidity, and the vines benefit from long hang time. One of the greatest challenges is hail storms, which can devastate a crop in minutes.

Argentina's Wine Laws

Argentina has modeled an appellation system on its European counterparts with a DOC at the highest quality ranking. Only two sub-appellations of Mendoza have achieved this designation: Luján de Cuyo and San Rafael. The next level is Indicación Geográfica (IG), which is used for more regional designations, and the third ranking is for Argentina's table wine. For a wine to be varietally labeled, it must be 80% of the particular variety. *See 11.19.*

11.18 The label is representative of the partnerships and the impact of foreign investments in the Chilean wine industry and the dominance of Bordeaux varietals.

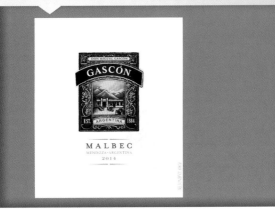

11.19 Malbec grown in high elevations in Mendoza is the varietal that Argentina has become known for.

The European Union

The European Union is now comprised of 27 countries with a combined population of nearly 500 million people, and almost 8 million acres of vineyards that produce 1.5 billion (12liter) cases of wine.

European Union Labeling Requirements and System of Quality

As the new rules for individual members are currently insufficiently clear, this text will reflect only those now used. All European wines must meet the standards established by the European Union Office International du Vin (OIV) and must be labeled accordingly. The label should reflect the primacy of typicity of style from a specific region or terroir.

The European Union currently identifies five different categories for still wines. As of January 1, 2011, the system includes five similar general quality levels, which are mandatory for all members. There are two broad quality types of wines, those with geographic indications, and those without. For those with geographic indications, there will be two definitions: **Protected Designation of Origin** (PDO's) and **Protected Geographical Indications** (PGI's). The third category simply referred to as "Wine" with the name of the country added allows for both the vintage and the variety to be mentioned on the label.

Protected Designation of Origin These regions must be registered with the European Union, and each defined region is governed by regulations established by EU criteria and legislated within the respective member countries.

The categories include:

1. Grape varieties recommended or authorized
2. Viticultural practices
3. Maximum yields
4. Winemaking practices
5. Minimum alcoholic content
6. Analysis of the finished wine.

Appellation d'Origine Contrôlée (AOC) for France, and Denominazione di Origine Controlata e Garantita (DOCG) and Denominazione di Origine Controlata (DOC) for Italy are all examples of designations of origin.

Protected Geographical Indication This second level refers to wines produced from a specific European country that has less stringent rules. Whereas 100% of the wine from a PDO must come from that appellation, only 85% need come from the PGI. The wine may also have a vintage and include up to two varieties on the label. This level will include the current French classification of Vin de Pays (VdP) for France, which will change to Indication Géographique Protégée that is similarly used for other agricultural products such as cheese. *See 11.20.* It is currently unclear as to how the member states will respond to the new regulations when reconfiguring their own label terminology.

Wine The third level is called "Wine" and can refer only to European-produced wines. The label may include either the variety or vintage.

Non-EU Wine with Geographical Description The fourth level, Wine with Geographical Description, refers to wines produced from specific recognized wine regions outside the European Union such as a wine from Napa.

Non-EU Wine The fifth level is for non-EU wines of lower quality that cannot include either a vintage or a variety on the label. While the U.S. health-warning requirement had been forbidden in the European Union, some EU countries, such as France, now mandate a health warning as it relates to wine and pregnancy.

11.20 Vin de Pays will be changing to Indication Géographique Protégé.

France

France is viewed by many in the world as a leader in quality wine production and a barometer by which to measure one's own wines. Its historical influence is undeniable as most of the recognized "international" varieties, such as Chardonnay, Sauvignon Blanc, Pinot Gris, Pinot Noir, Cabernet Sauvignon, Merlot, and Syrah, originated from France. With a vineyard area that is only surpassed by Spain, France is one of the leading wine producers with almost half a billion cases. France's wines are currently the third most imported into the U.S. and also represent about a third of all wines exported in the world. France's climate is ideal for its many varieties because it enjoys the characteristics of all three major climates: Continental, Maritime, and Mediterranean.

The primary regions of quality wine production (AOC) are:

- **Champagne** recognized as the birthplace of the classic or traditional method for sparkling wine. *See 11.21.*
- **Loire** famous for Chenin Blanc and Sauvignon Blanc for whites, and Cabernet Franc for reds.
- **Alsace** home to varietals such as Riesling, Gewürztraminer, Pinot Gris, and Muscat. *See 11.22.*
- **Rhône** the white Viognier is the world's model while Syrah and Grenache play a similar role for red wines.
- **Bordeaux** produces high quality Sauvignon Blancs generally blended with Sémillon, which is the primary variety used for botrytized Sauternes. Bordeaux also produces the apogee of blended red wines based on Cabernet Sauvignon, Merlot, and Cabernet France. *See 11.23.*
- **Burgundy** home to some of the world's greatest Chardonnays and Pinot Noirs. It has become the role model for the rest of the world. Burgundy is also the most important producer of Gamay and a user of the carbonic maceration technique for bright fruity reds. *See 11.24.*

The Languedoc-Rousillon is equivalent to California Central Valley where the bulk of wine production still takes place. While most of its wine falls under the lowest wine classification, it is the most important region for IGP wines, and many AOC sub-appellations have developed within its boundaries to produce wines based on Grenache, Carignan, Syrah, and Mourvèdre.

11.22 Specific sites that face southeast and are at higher elevations provide an ideal climate and soil conditions for ripened grapes in Alsace.

11.21 Hand harvesting in some quality wine producing areas such as Champagne is required by law.

French Wine Laws

The renamed *Institut National de l'Origine et de la Qualité (INAO)* is France's regulatory agency, which governs wine production and labeling. The enforcement arm of this group is called the *Service de Répression des Fraudes,* which enforces the law and punishes fraud. **French wines are categorized into three broad classifications:**

PDO Appellation d'Origine Contrôlée (AOC or AC or AOP), or Appellation d'Origine Protégée (AP) is the highest classification, representing 57% of all wines produced in France. **Different classifications are unique to each AC region, but most have a tiered system that is defined by the geographic boundaries. In sequence of quality, from highest to lowest, they are as follows:**

- **Grand cru classé** generally a single vineyard site. *See 11.25.*
- **Premier cru classé** single vineyard in some regions such as Bordeaux is the highest designation but may not consist of one contiguous vineyard
- **Village** named after a village or commune but may incorporate the surrounding region
- **District** a larger geographic designation, but one that still shares the same viticultural characteristics
- **Region** a broader geographic designation where there is less of a defined personality to the wine, but one that is still recognizable as coming from a single region

Indication Géographique Protégée (IGP) represent about a third of France's production. As opposed to AOP/AOC wines, which must be made from 100% of grapes grown in the designated appellation, wines with this designation need only have a minimum of 85% grapes grown in the designated region.

Vin de France is table wine with geographic indication and may mention a vintage and varietal. However, there are some iconoclasts who rebel against some of the proscriptive elements of the AOC system and choose to market their wines as Vin de France.

11.23 The clay, limestone, and gravelly soils, and the maritime climate provide perfect growing conditions for Merlot and Cabernet Sauvignon based wines.

11.24 This neatly rowed and tidy Pinot Noir site of the AOC Domaine Romanée Conti represents some of the most expensive agricultural land in the world.

French Labels

- Vendange/Récolte–Vintage/harvest
- Mis en bouteille au château–Estate bottled
- Cru–"Growth," indicating a specific vineyard of high quality, which is often used as a classification level as well
- Cuvée–Blend
- Clos–Walled vineyard
- Brut–Very dry
- Sec–Dry
- Moelleux–Sweet

European Wine Categories

PDO | Protected Designation of Origin
PGI | Protected Geographical Indication
Table wine | without geographic description but with varietal and vintage

French Wine Categories

AOP/AOC | Appellation d'Origine Protégée/ Contrôllée
IGP | Indication Géographique Protégée
Vin de France

11.25 Bâtard-Montrachet is one of 33 Grand Cru appellations of Burgundy.

Italy

Although Italy has produced wines for millennia, its modern wine history has been for the most part undistinguished up until the last 40 years. Its mostly Mediterranean climate, mountainous or hilly landscapes, and perfectly suited volcanic based soils blended with limestone and other soil types provide a perfect backdrop for the production of fine quality wines. Italy has the third most planted vineyards in the world and frequently ranks as a top wine producer by volume. Italy is divided into twenty different regions, and it is often said, "they are in search of a country." This saying reflects how different each region is from the other culturally, and how varied the wines are as well. There are over 1,000 varieties grown, including Sangiovese, which is the most predominant black grape variety. Other very important red grape varieties include Montepulciano, Merlot, Barbera, Negroamaro, Nero d'Avola, Cabernet Sauvignon, Aglianico, and Nebbiolo. For white wines, the most significant are: Trebbiano (which is predominant but not known for making distinctive wines), Catarratto, Malvasia, Pinot Grigio, Chardonnay, Garganega, and Moscato.

The last four decades have seen a wine revolution in Italy, making it one of the most dynamic wine regions of the world with innovative viticultural and vinification techniques. Until Italy developed a sufficiently large urban middle class, wine, for the most part, had been perceived as an essential condiment to a meal, akin to olive oil, which should be well made but not something about which to necessarily contemplate. Most Americans are less well acquainted with these Italian varieties. Italy's most famous wines are sold under the names of a varietal or an appellation such as Chianti or a combination of grape variety and appellation as in the case of Moscato d'Asti. **The most significant regions of Italy include:**

Piedmont Piedmont in the northwest, a name that translates as "at the foot of the mountain," is home to many of the highest quality zones including Barolo, Barbaresco, Asti, and Gavi to name but a few. Due to its cooler climate, wines from here have greater acidity and are very food friendly.

The Veneto The Veneto in the Northeast produces the highest volume of DOC/DOCG wine in Italy. It is best known for Soave and Pinot Grigio for whites, and Valpolicella, Amarone della Valpolicella, Bardolino, and Merlot for reds.

Tuscany Tuscany has developed a worldwide reputation for its food and wine. The most famous regions of Tuscany are Chianti Classico, Brunello di Montalcino, and Vino Nobile di Montelpulciano. Tuscany is representative of the Italian wine Renaissance with new DOC's and DOCG's being created and exciting developments taking place on its western coast in the areas of Bolghieri and the former swamplands of Maremma.

Southern Italy and the Islands Southern Italy and the Islands are where the ancient Greeks settled and planted vineyards naming it Oenotria, or land of the vine. With a sunny Mediterranean climate on volcanic soils, this region is undergoing a more recent transformation than its northern counterparts. Sicily is proving to be a particularly exciting and emerging quality region, especially around the active volcano of Mt Etna. Vineyards in Sicily and Southern Italy were at one time known mostly for bulk wine production, but now appellations such as Taurasi or Greco di Tufo in Campania and Salice Salentino have helped to transform that impression.

European Wine Categories

PDO | Protected Designation of Origin

PGI | Protected Geographical Indication

Table wine | without geographic description but with varietal and vintage

Italian Wine Categories

DOC/DOCG | Denominazione di Origine Controllata/ Denominazione di Origine Controllata e Garantita

IGT | Indicazione Geogafica Tipica

Vino d'Italia

Italy's Wine Laws

The wine laws of 1963 created the Denominazione di Origine Controllata (DOC), which was patterned after France's AOC. These laws spurred the Italian wine industry toward modernization and quality. Approximately 15% of Italy's total wine production is classified DOC or DOCG, and within that category, more than 900 types of wines are produced in more than 450 appellations.

Because of the very stringent DOC and DOCG regulations, many producers refused to abide by them and were therefore excluded, even though they were producing some of Italy's finest quality and most expensive wines. This anomaly precipitated changes with the Goria laws of 1992, creating the IGT category. It is no wonder that Italian wine labeling is difficult to understand. **Generally, the wines are labeled in four ways:**

- **The name of the village, district, or region** Barolo. *See 11.26.*

- **The name of the variety** Pinot Grigio. *See 11.27.*

- **The name of a variety and the region** Brunello di Montalcino. *See 11.28.*

- **The proprietary names** such as Summus® or Ornellaia®

Italy has three wine classifications fitting the three EU wine classifications:

PDO Denominazione di Origine Controllata e Garantita (DOCG) This most stringent category requires that the producer follows the requirements of the DOC and guarantees what is stated on the label. How this category falls into the new system is anyone's guess. There are 73 DOCG wines as of 2013.

PDO Denominazione di Origine Controllata (DOC) Equivalent to the French AOC designation and governed by the same kinds of regulations, this classification includes more than 332 wines.

PGI Indicazione Geographica Tipica (IGT) This classification is meant to upgrade 40% of Italy's table wines. Producers must apply for this status, and currently more than 118 have done so.

Vino d'Italia encompasses 26% of Italy's total wine production.

Italian Labeling Terms:

- *Vendemmia*–Vintage
- *Azienda agricola, fattoria, tenuta*–Estate (each)
- *Imbottigliato all' castelo*–Estate bottled
- *Imbottigliato all' Origine*–Estate bottled
- **Classico**–From the original part of a DOC wine region
- **Riserva**–A DOC(G) wine with additional aging
- **Superiore**–A DOC(G) wine with 0.5% or more alcohol than is required
- *Bianco*–White
- *Rosso*–Red
- *Nero*–Dark red
- *Rosato*–Pink
- **Secco**–Dry
- **Abboccato**–Semi-dry
- **Dolce**–Sweet
- **Spumante**–Sparkling
- *Frizzante*–Sparkling
- *Cantina Sociale*–Vine-growers cooperative
- *Marchio Nazionale*–Appears on a red seal on the neck of a wine bottle, indicating compliance with government controls for wines exported to the United States

11.27 Pinot Grigio, synonymous with Pinot Gris, has become a world favorite in just the last two decades.

11.26 Barolo is a small town for which one of Italy's great wines is named.

11.28 Brunello is a Sangiovese clone most famous around the medieval Tuscan town of Montalcino.

Germany

Because Germany lies in the most northern latitude where the ripening season is shorter, almost all the wine regions are in the southwestern corner of the country. Germany's vineyards cover approximately 250,000 acres, which is about the size of Bordeaux' vineyards alone. Germans consume most of their own wines and provide a significant import market for others. The U.S. is an important import market for Germany's high end wines.

The Romans were the first to plant vineyards in the thirteen wine growing regions of Germany and used the Rhine as a natural defensive border against its opponents. The best wine growing sites are located on the steep slopes of rivers such as the Mosel and the Rhine where warmer waters moderate ambient temperatures and reflect sunlight back onto the vineyards. Eighty percent of Germany's wines are white and Riesling is the most important in terms of quality. *Spätburgunder,*

which is German for Pinot Noir, has undergone a transformation because of global warming and has allowed producers to make wines that are comparable to those produced in Burgundy. Müller-Thurgau, which is the second most planted grape variety and is a cross between Riesling and Silvaner, is still important commercially. It is hardier than Riesling, but it does not have the same attributes.

The most important wine growing regions are:
- **Rheingau** renowned for its Rieslings from south facing slopes and grown in blue and red slate
- **Rheinhessen** the largest of the 13 wine growing regions with quality Riesling and red wines
- **Pfalz** produces one quarter of all Riesling grown in Germany
- **Mosel** incredibly steep slopes on the banks of the twisting and winding Mosel River, and its tributaries producing some of Germany's most distinctive wines

11.29 Traditional labels are difficult for English speaking people to understand, though they have a great deal of useful information.

11.30 The latest marketing efforts are represented by labels such as this one, which is easy to read and will attract less traditional wine drinkers in their 20s and 30s.

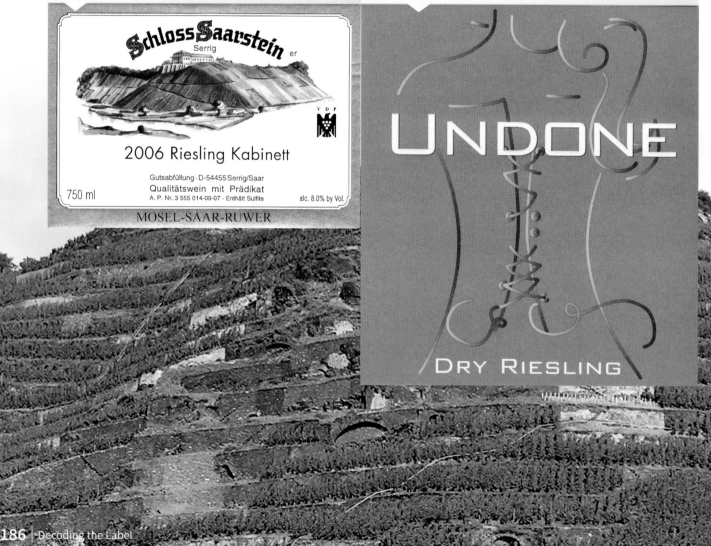

German Wine Labeling

German wine labels are the most detailed and also, at times, among the most unintelligible. *See 11.29.* Fortunately for the U.S. consumer, many have become very modern looking and easier to understand. *See 11.30.* **In accordance with the EU standards, German wines are divided into three categories:**

European Wine Categories

PDO | Protected Designation of Origin
PGI | Protected Geographical Indication
Table wine | without geographic description but with varietal and vintage

German Wine Categories

Qualitätswein and Prädikatswein or gU (Geschützte Ursprungsbezeichnung)
includes QBA/QMP | Qualitätswein bestimmter Anbaugebiete, Qualitatswein mit Prädikat
Deutscher Landwein or ggA | Geschützte Geographische Angabe
Deutscher Wein

Consumers in the United States are particularly concerned with Qualitätswein, the quality wines now also known as gU(Geschützte Ursprungsbezeichnung), which are divided into two sub-classifications:

PDO or gU Qualitätswein bestimmter Anbaugebiete (QbA) This category is the largest and includes quality wines from one of the 13 specified wine regions. These wines tend to be light, fresh, and fruity and are allowed to be enriched with süssreserve, or sweet reserve made of sterile unfermented must.

ggA Deutscher Landwein is produced from the German landwein regions from permitted grapes and must be trocken (dry) or halbtrocken (semi-dry) in style except in Franken region.

Deutscher Wein is produced exclusively from legally recognized grapes and can mention the vintage as well.

PDO or gU Qualitätswein mit Prädikat (QmP) This quality wine with special distinction is the best of Germany's wines. These wines are further classified into six categories with special attributes in ascending order of ripeness at harvest. They include: *Kabinett, Spätlese, Auslese, Beerenauslese, Eiswein,* and *Trockenbeerenauslese. See 11.31.*

- **Kabinett**–Normal harvest time; lightest of Prädikat wines
- **Spätlese**–Late harvest with more intensity and richness; not necessarily sweet
- **Auslese**–Hand-selected grapes; intensely flavored, but may have been affected by botrytis and are not usually sweet
- *Beerenauslese (BA)*—Overripe berries that are individually selected; a rare sweet wine that is rich and flavorful
- *Eiswein*—Literally means "ice wine;" has the ripeness of BA and is harvested and pressed while frozen; remarkable acidity balancing sweetness
- *Trockenbeerenauslese (TBA)*—Grapes that are affected by botrytis and individually picked, making a very rich, sweet, honeylike wine.

Consumers also see the term *trocken* and *halbtrocken* on labels, indicating dry or semi-dry styles of wine.

Because the Prädikat system is not based on a sense of place or *terroir,* this has posed a bit of a challenge to the EU system, which is based on the concept of place. There is another concurrent system, which is a wine producer based classification movement based on *terroir.* This system has more stringent viticultural and vinification requirements than the official system and now extends from Rheingau, where it originated to include all 13 growing regions. The association is called the **VDP,** which stands for *Verband Deutscher Prädikat und Qualitätsweingüter* and is symbolized by an eagle holding a cluster of grapes, which is found on the capsule of the wine bottle. The VDP wines, if dry, can be designated as Erste Lage (First Class) or as Grosses Gewächs (Great Growth). VDP Grosse Lage that are naturally fruity and sweet are classified by the Prädikat system.

In addition to this classification, vintage 2000 marked the beginning of the use of "Classic" and "Selection" terms. "Classic" wines are the equivalent of above-average quality QbA wines, made with traditional varieties. "Selection" wines must be hand harvested from a single vineyard, and thus present German wine producers the opportunity to develop a French "cru" system.

Although confusing, the elements for a classification system based on terroir are already in place—13 regions *(anbaugebiete),* 39 districts *(bereiche),* 165 collective vineyard sites *(grosslagen),* and 2,643 individual vineyard sites *(einzellagen).*

Finally, German wine bottles may have seals and awards placed on them, indicating that the wine has qualified as exceeding the standards for a particular classification. A gold seal on the neck indicates a dry wine, a green seal indicates an off-dry wine, and a red seal indicates that the wine is sweet.

German Labeling Terms:
- *Rotwein*–Red wine
- *Weissherbst*–Rosé QbA or QmP wine made from a single variety of black grapes
- *Rotling*–Rosé made from a blend
- *Schillerwein*–QbA or QmP rosé wine from Württenberg
- *Perlwein*–A red or white wine with a light sparkle, usually by carbon dioxide injection
- *Deutscher Sekt*–A quality sparkling wine with less alcohol than champagne
- **Trocken**–Dry
- *Halbtrocken*–Semi-dry
- *Erzeugerabfüllung*–Estate bottled
- *Gutsabfüllung*–Estate bottled
- *Winzergenossenschaft*–Wine growers' cooperative

11.31

Producer ·····
Variety ·····

Category of special attributes (late harvest)

The Vineyard Spiced Garden from the town of Urzig

Contents ·····

The alcohol level

Quality level ·····

Region from which the product hails

The wine was tasted by a board from the region in March 2006

(Label text:) GRAFF — RIESLING SPÄTLESE — 2005 ÜRZIGER WÜRZGARTEN — MOSEL · SAAR · RUWER — 750 ml — Qualitätswein mit Prädikat · A. P. Nr. 2602034/03/06 — ALC. 8% BY VOL. — BOTTLED FOR AND SHIPPED BY CARL GRAFF GMBH & CO. KG, WORMS, GERMANY, IN D-67547 WORMS

Spain

Spain has a long wine history, yet most of its wines were unknown until recently, with the exception of Rioja and Sherry. Once Spain joined the EU, it was jolted out of its languor by a massive infusion of capital and the creative forces unleashed after decades of fascist rule. Wines of Spain coming from regions unknown even to "wine experts" of a decade ago are now found in every major market of the U.S.

Spain is very mountainous and has distinct regions and climates: the wet fjord region of Ríaz Baixas of Galicia in the northwest; the mountainous northern regions of Rioja and Navarra at the foot of the Pyrenees Mountains; the hot and arid plateau of La Mancha and the Mediterranean coastline of Penedés and Tarragona; to the southern tip of Sherry where the Atlantic meets the Mediterranean. *See 11.32.*

Spain's most widely planted grape, Airén, is also the world's most planted and is used to produce indistinct bulk wine. The most famous, distinctive, and the most widely spread is the Tempranillo variety, which has many names depending on its location. Garnacha, known as Grenache in France, plays an important role both as a stand alone and a component of blends. Minstrel, also known as MA taro and Mourvèdre in France, is the third most significant black grape. Maccabee, known as Vera in parts of Spain, is the most significant white variety along with Palomino for Sherry, and Pedro Ximénez for sweet solera wines.

Rioja is still one of the most famous regions and is only one of two regions holding the highest labeling designation of Denominación Geográfica de Origen Calificáda (DOCa); the other region is **Priorat** in Catalonia. There are about one thousand growers in Rioja who sell their grapes to three hundred producers, though some may be using their own grapes. The wines are medium bodied with floral and cherry aromas with distinct leathery bouquets and are bottle aged. They have medium high acidity with light to medium tannins and are very food friendly. Roija also produces very good quality whites and rosés.

Other regions include:

- **Ribera del Duero,** which is the home of one of the world's most expensive wines, Vega de Sicilia's Unico. This hot region in the Duero River Valley has a wide diurnal range due to its altitude, which allows its Tempranillo based wines (frequently blended with Cabernet Sauvignon, Garnacha and Merlot) to maintain their acidity despite their richness.
- **Toro** and **Cigales** are other appellations in the Duero that make similar wines.
- **Rueda** is strictly a white wine appellation in the Duero, which produces quality acidic food friendly Verdejo based wines.
- **Cava** refers to a classic or traditional method-made sparkling wine produced mainly in Penedés.
- **Rías Baixas** is located in the northwest and produces a fine quality white wine that is sold varietally as Albariño.

There are now as many as 78 DOs in Spain and their island possessions, which represent an exciting new era for wine aficionados.

DENOMINACIÓN DE ORIGEN CALIFICADA

2012 / PRODUCTO DE ESPAÑA

> 11.32 Spain's climate, topography and soils are varied from the mountainous regions of Navarre to the chalky plains of Sherry, all resulting in very different wines.

Spanish Labeling Laws

Although Spain has long been producing wine, it is only as recently as 1972 that it adopted a modern regulatory system with the establishment of the *Instituto de Denominaciónes de Origen (INDO)*. The INDO works in tandem with the local or regional *Consejo Regulador* to maintain and certify that the regulations and standards are applied. **Spanish wines are grouped under six classifications:**

PDO Vino de Pago This classification is relatively new for "estate wines" that are particularly distinguished. If in an official DO, it becomes Vino de Pago Calificado. The estates must reach the most stringent standards set for that particular appellation and produce wines that have been evaluated as being distinguished. There are currently 15 Vino de Pago and Vino de Pago Calificado.

PDO Denominación de Origen Calificáda (DOCa) This classification guarantees high standards and is comparable to an Italian DOCG wine. Only Rioja and Priorat are designated DOCa, although several appellations may soon join this rank. *See 11.33.*

PDO Denominación de Origen (DO) Equivalent to the AC designation of French wines; there are over 70 DO appellations. *See 11.34.*

PDO Vino de Calidad con Indicación (VCIG)- a minor category with only 6 appellations designed for up and coming regions eligible for promotion after 5 years to DO.

PGI Vino de la Tierra (VdlT) These wines must come from a single geographic indication and meet specific alcohol and sensory standards.

Vino This table wine classification is the lowest classification.

In addition to following the EU regulations, Spain's DOCa and DO also follow aging criteria.

Spanish Labeling Terms

- *Vino Joven*–Intended for immediate drinking upon release in the spring following the vintage
- *Crianza*–Aged a minimum of 6 months in oak and 2 years in the bottle; Rioja and Ribera del Duero wines are aged 1 year in oak
- *Reserva (white)*–Aged 6 months in oak and released after 3 years
- *Reserva (red)*–Aged 1 year in oak and released in the fourth year
- *Gran Reserva*–Only from exceptional vintages; whites are aged 6 months in oak and released in the fourth year; reds are aged 2 years in oak and 3 more in the bottle

Other Spanish Terms

- Fino–A light, dry type of sherry
- *Manzanilla*–The lightest sherry, similar to fino
- Amontillado–A type of aged fino sherry
- Oloroso–A type of oxidized sherry
- Cava–Sparkling wine, classic method from designated regions
- *Cosecha*–Vintage
- *Mistela*–A blend of grape juice and alcohol

European Wine Categories

PDO | Protected Designation of Origin

PGI | Protected Geographical Indication

Table wine | without geographic description but with varietal and vintage

Spanish Wine Categories

DOCa | Denominación de Origen Calificada, Vino de Pago/Vino de Pago Calificado

DO | Denominación de Origen

V.C.I.G | Vinos de Calidad con Indicación Geográfica

Vinos de la Tierra | Country wine

Vino | Wine

11.33 Rioja is one of two DOCa's where wines are Tempranillo based.

11.34 Catalayud is one of the 70 plus Do's and Garnacha is one of the most prominent grape varieties in Spain.

Portugal

Portugal has an ancient wine history and has one of the earliest protected appellations, *Oporto*, which dates back to 1756. Until recently, most consumers in the world thought of Port and Madeira wines and perhaps rosé wines such as Mateus and Lancers as Portugal's only offerings. Portugal's wine industry is one of the most recent to undergo an innovative wine revolution, and the results are not only promising but have also provided consumers with excellent value wines. Continental Portugal and its islands have 18 regions. The mainland has two very distinct climates with the weather in the northern tier above the Tajo (Tagus) River cooler and wetter (with the exception of its interior), and the southern tier with weather that is hotter and drier. The primary white varieties that are making a name for themselves are Arinto, Loureira, Alvarinho (synonym for Albariño in Spain), and Touriga Nacional, and Tinta Roriz or Aragonez (Spanish Tempranillo) for reds. **The primary regions include:**

- **Minho,** which produces both white and red Vinho Verde though only the whites are note worthy as they are among the most tart wines of the world. They are a wonderful accompaniment to seafood dishes. *See 11.35.*
- **Douro** is located along the Douro River and is famous for its Port wines but is gaining respect for its blended still reds, which are intense but elegant.
- **Dão** is located inland in the northern tier and is known for good quality value driven red wines.
- **Alentejo,** in southeastern Portugal produces excellent red wines with the Trincadeira and Aragonez indigenous varieties. It also produces international varietals such as Syrah.

Portuguese Labeling laws

It is only since joining the European Union that Portugal's regulatory system, through the *Instituto da Vinha e Vinho (IVV)*, has established a comparable tiered system. **Portuguese wines are classified as:**

DOP Denominaçâo de Origem Controlada (DOC) This classification is similar to a French AC or Italian DOC wine; there are currently about 29 DOC regions. DOC wines are required to have a paper seal, the *Selo de Origem,* which is placed over the cork but under the capsule.

PGI Indicação de Geográfica Protegida A geographic indication designation applies to wines produced in a specific region with a minimum of 85% of grapes from that region.

PGI Vinho Regional Specifies traditional term used for the labeling of wines with a geographical indication. The reference to this statement precludes the use of Protected Geographical Indication.

Vinho The variety and the vintage may be mentioned on the label.

Portuguese Labeling Terms

- *Reserva*–Must be from a single vintage and have .5% higher alcohol than the minimum for DOC wines
- **Garrafeira**–Aged 2 years in cask and 1 year in bottle for red wine, 6 months in wood and 6 months bottle aging for white wine
- **Colheita**–Vintage
- *Colheita selecionada*–For high quality vintage wines with 1% higher alcohol
- *Engarrafado na origem*–Estate bottled
- **Quinta**–Estate

11.35 Touriga Nacional is an indigenous Portuguese variety that has developed into a hallmark of Portuguese red wine (note the English description on the label).

European Wine Categories

PDO | Protected Designation of Origin

PGI | Protected Geographical Indication

Table wine | without geographic description but with varietal and vintage

Portugal Wine Categories

Vinho

DOC | Denominação de Origem Controlada

IGP | Indicação Geográfica Protegida Vinho Regional

IG | Indicação Geográfica

Storing Wine, Wine Tasting, Food *and* Wine Pairing

While it is important to have an understanding of wine service, which includes decoding the label, it is also necessary to master how wine is stored. Proper storage preserves wine so it tastes the way the winemaker intended. It can also allow the best wines to slowly evolve into complex drinkable works of art.

Poor storage will quickly cause wines to degrade and lead to off-flavors and imbalances. A knowledge of the effects of improper wine storage allows servers to better identify and evaluate wines that have deteriorated. An understanding of how wine interacts with food provides servers with an additional tool to enhance the guest's dining experience.

STORING WINE

Because wine is a living entity, it can either suffer or thrive, depending on how it is treated. *See 11.36.* When storing wine, five important factors must be controlled: temperature, humidity, light, position, and stability. The organization of a wine cellar is also important to food service establishments that purchase wine in volume. Because most wines are made to be consumed within two to three years, it is important to keep track of when the wine was purchased. An efficient inventory system also records the name, vintage, price, amount purchased, distributor, shipper, and the bin numbers.

Temperature Wine should be stored at a constant temperature of 50°F–55°F (10°C–13°C), although temperature stability is more important than the actual temperature level because some bacteria become active as temperature fluctuates. However, the lower the temperature (down to 50°F/10°C), the slower the maturation of the wine. Wines should not be refrigerated for any length of time because refrigeration can cause the cork to dry out and allow oxygen to enter the bottle.

Humidity Wine should be stored in a well-ventilated space with a relative humidity of 70%–85% to prevent the cork from drying out.

Light Avoid storing wine in direct light, whether natural or artificial. Too much light causes heat, and therefore, deterioration.

Position Wine bottles should be stored on their sides to keep the corks moist and to inhibit oxidation.

Vibrations Wine should be stored in a location that is free of agitation or vibration as these conditions can cause rapid deterioration.

11.36 Maintaining an organized temperature and humidity controlled storage environment is key to successfully managing an extensive wine list.

WINE TASTING

Wine tasting can be both simple and complex. *See 11.37.* It is simple to quaff wine and enjoy its attributes without contemplating its subtleties. A fuller appreciation comes with learning to distinguish the subtle characteristics of color, aroma, bouquet, flavor, texture, intensity, balance, and the length of the finish. For a professional wine taster, all of these characteristics must be recognized, identified, and recorded. For the novice and the appreciative amateur, part of the enjoyment of tasting wine comes from exploring and learning about a world of subtle sensations.

Types of Tastings

There are four basic types of wine tastings:

General tastings General tastings are often conducted by retailers or distributors, special event organizers of food and wine expositions, or fund-raisers. Tasters try a variety of wines in an arranged sequence, typically beginning with dry white wines and ending with sweet fortified wines.

Horizontal tastings Horizontal tastings are for evaluating wines of a particular region or vintage. Horizontal tastings allow the taster to evaluate the differences among wines produced by several winemakers from the same region, or within the same parameters of varieties and vintage.

Vertical tastings Vertical tastings evaluate wines of different vintages, usually from a limited number of producers. The taster focuses on the wine's maturation and the factors that differentiate the vintages.

Blind tastings Blind tastings are the most complex in that the tasters have no prior information about the wines. The wines are generally chosen from the same varietals or vintage. A blind tasting allows tasters to sharpen their skills at differentiating subtleties among wines. *See 11.38.*

Set-Up and Requirements

An appropriate atmosphere is key to a professional wine-tasting event:

- The room should be well lighted, ideally with natural daylight or nonfluorescent lighting to allow for accurate color evaluation.
- Glassware should be clean and free of any lingering odor of detergent.
- The room should be void of any extraneous scents such as flowers or air freshener.
- Tasters should not wear cologne or other heavy scents that might interfere with accurate sensory evaluation.
- Glasses should be the appropriate size and shape for the wines being tasted. They should be placed on a white background so that tasters can accurately discern a wine's color and intensity.
- Water should be served to cleanse the palate and no foods other than flavorless bread or water biscuits should be served. Spittoons should be provided.
- Each taster should have an evaluation sheet and a pen or pencil for making observations and for evaluating each wine.
- The room should be silent throughout the tasting exercise so tasters are not distracted.

During wine tastings, wine is served in 1.5- to 2-ounce portions and grouped in flights, or groupings of similar vintages, varietals, or other comparable factors. Groupings allow the taster to evaluate the wines against one another and to prevent dissimilar wines from interfering with the subtle tastes of other wines.

When different styles of wine are being evaluated, the sequence in which they are tasted is significant to the taster's ability to discern the subtleties—light-bodied wines before full-bodied wines; dry wines before off-dry or sweet wines; and generally, whites before reds.

11.37 An organized and systematic approach to tasting is a key ingredient to wine knowledge.

11.38 Blind tastings are generally chosen from the same varietal or region.

VINOS DE JEREZ SHERRY WINES

CONSEJO REGULADOR

7

The Six S's of Wine Tasting

The six S's of wine tasting are see, swirl, sniff, sip, swallow or spit, and savor.

See Although sight is the least accurate of the senses with which to evaluate wine, it provides clues to, and anticipation of what is to come. First, examine the upper surface of the wine, known as the **disc.** The edge or **rim** of the disc may appear colorless. The variation of color or hue between the rim and the core of the wine will indicate possible aging, origin, and vinification to an experienced taster. Note that the disc is not flat, but rather forms a concave curve, called the **meniscus,** as the wine extends a short way up the sides of the wine glass.

The color or **hue** of the wine is sometimes referred to as the **robe.** The robe gives important clues about the wine. A white wine with little or no color indicates the fruit was immature, and the wine will probably lack aroma and flavor. Pale and light-colored wine often comes from cooler climates. Most white wines tend to range from straw green-yellow to light yellow. As white wine barrel or bottle wine ages, it develops more color. Medium yellow and light gold wines tend to be sweet dessert wines. If the wine is brown, it has either been fortified or has oxidized.

A red wine with a blue or purple rim indicates immaturity. Light reds indicate thin-skinned varietals such as a Pinot Noir. The majority of red wines are medium cherry red, but they may develop a red tile or brick hued rim with age. Red wines lose color with age, so examining the color gives clues about the wine's age.

Swirl Swirling the wine lightly coats the upper level of the glass, aerating the wine and allowing it to "breathe" and open. As the wine evaporates off the side of the glass, flavor components are released. The residual wine that clings to the glass is called **legs,** tears, or arches. Legs are caused by alcohol and glycerol levels in the wine. The greater the alcohol content, the denser and more pronounced the legs.

Sniff Smell is the most important sense for wine tasting. The olfactory sense allows tasters to discern hundreds of smells. The taster differentiates between aromas and bouquets. **Aroma** descriptors include such terms as fruity, spicy, floral, or vegetative. **Bouquet** descriptors include nutty, caramelized, woody, earthy, and petroleum. Some wines may have off odors as a result of faulty winemaking or storage. When sniffing wine, the taster should sniff once, then swirl the wine and tilt the glass toward himself or herself so the nose is directly in the glass, and then sniff again.

Taking short sniffs without inhaling deeply, the taster notes an initial impression, often called the attack, or first nose. After 30 seconds or so, the wine is sniffed again for second impressions, called the second nose. After a short interval, the sniffing process is repeated to verify or add to the earlier impressions. Sniffing too frequently will result in palate adaption, in which the taster is unable to discern any differences whatsoever.

Sip Using the mouth alone, humans are able to distinguish only five tastes: sweet, sour, salty, bitter, and umami (the best example to convey its sense is the taste of monosodium glutamate MSG). Research has shown that although most taste buds are concentrated on the tip and sides of the tongue, they are also located on the roof and back of the mouth. This is why it is important to roll the wine on and around the tongue to coat these taste buds. Saltiness is not a typical component of a wine's taste, and bitterness is only slightly less so.

Tasters describe the degree of sweetness in a wine as dry, off-dry or mildly sweet, sweet, and very sweet. Although most wines lack bitterness, wines that are bitter are described as slightly bitter, moderately bitter, and very bitter. Sourness or acidity can be described as "flatness" if the wine is not sufficiently acidic. "Fruitiness" is used when it is normally acidic and "acidulous" when excessively acidic.

Wine tasting also involves tactility (the texture or **"mouthfeel"** of the wine), which is a function of tannins, glycerol, and alcohol. **Astringency** is the "drying out" effect or rough feeling a taster perceives from tannins. Tannic wines may be described as slightly astringent or chalky, moderately tannic, or astringent.

Alcohol gives the taster a perception of sweetness and a tactile sensation of heat. Glycerol, like alcohol, exhibits a perception of richness and weight on the palate.

Swallow or Spit A taster cannot remain alert and assess a wine accurately if he or she is consuming it. Spitting between tastes is necessary for proper assessment.

Savor Savoring wine involves the taster's appreciation and evaluation of a wine by focusing on the way it lingers in the mouth. The key to tasting wine is to determine the balance between the acidity and the tannins on the one hand and the sweetness and alcohol on the other. The combined sensations of taste, smell, texture, balance, and length, or how quickly or slowly those perceptions remain on the palate, determine the evaluation of the wine's finish.

The best wines have a balanced finish that is integrated into a satisfying whole. If one element dominates, the wine is unbalanced. Wines are described as having a short, medium, or long finish, depending on how long the sensations linger. Wines with short finishes leave lingering flavors for less than 15 seconds. Great wines, on the other hand, have finishes that linger from one to several minutes.

Wine-Tasting Terms

In the past, wine tasters tended toward the poetic when they described the taste of wine because it is difficult to communicate abstract and subjective sensations such as taste. To help improve communication among wine tasters, Professor Anne Noble at the University of California-Davis developed the aroma wheel in an attempt to make the adjectives that describe wines more uniform and scientific.

The following terms have become accepted within the wine trade:

- Austere–Unyielding, possibly too young
- Baked–Lacks freshness and acidity
- **Big/Full**–Full-bodied and full-flavored
- Buttery–Soft, round whites with bouquet of malolactic fermentation
- Coarse–Lacking complexity or finesse
- Complex–Multilayered and multifaceted
- Creamy–Denoting richness
- **Crisp**–Good acidity
- Dense–Intensely flavorful and colorful
- Dried-out–Fruit flavors have dissipated
- **Earthy**–Aromas reminiscent of soil or minerals
- Elegant–Great finesse and balance
- Fat–Full-bodied but lacking acidity
- **Firm**–Structure backed by tannins, acid
- Flabby–Lacks acidity or is "flat"
- Fragrant–Flowery
- Green–A young wine or wine made from unripe grapes
- Hard–Tannic; too young
- Heavy–Overly alcoholic
- Herbaceous–Aromas of grass; herbs
- **Jammy**–Overly ripe fruit
- Lean–Limited flavor; high acidity
- **Long**–A lingering finish
- Mouthfilling–Richly textured
- Pétillant–Spritzy, slight carbonation
- Robust–Full-bodied
- Rough–Coarse; unpolished
- Sharp–High acid
- Short–Lacking finish
- Silky–Smooth; mature tannins
- Simple–Lacking distinction
- Smooth–Mature tannins
- Soft–Mellow flavors
- Sour–Overly acidic; vinegary
- Spritz–Prickly from carbon dioxide
- Stalky/stemmy–Bitter vegetal taste
- Steely–Good acidity
- Supple–Sensuously smooth
- **Thin**–Lacks body
- Vegetal–Vegetable aroma (e.g., bell pepper)
- Velvety–Rich silkiness
- Watery–Weak and thin
- Woody–Odors of old casks
- Zesty–Crisp and fresh

The following terms are used for wines that are spoiled:

- Acetic–Vinegary
- **Corked**–Affected by cork mold TCA
- Maderized–Baked, flat, partly oxidized
- Moldy–Smells of mold
- Oxidized–Cardboardy and papery from air exposure
- Sulfurous–Smells of burnt matches or bad eggs; too much sulfur dioxide

The Six *S*'s
of Wine Tasting

Professional wine tasters have trained their senses to make subtle comparisons and judgments.

Use the following steps to fully appreciate wine:

1. SEE–Examine the color of the wine against a white background.

2. SWIRL–Swirl the wine to release its aroma.

3. SNIFF–Sniff the wine to form a first impression; then sniff again to enjoy the wine's subtle aroma and bouquet.

4. SIP–Sip the wine, and roll it around in the mouth so it touches all the taste buds.

5. SWALLOW (or spit)–Spit the wine into a cup or sink, and cleanse the palate with water or plain crackers or wafers.

6. SAVOR–Savor the finish, or aftertaste, of the wine, and take notes of your impressions before tasting the next sample.

Food *and* Wine Pairing

Pairing wine with food used to be a straightforward, if not rigid, and a matter of following the French tradition of specific wines with specific dishes. The classic dictum held that red wine was always served with red meats and white wine was served with fish and poultry. Over the past several decades, however, Western cuisine has expanded and has come to incorporate many cultural ingredients and techniques. As a result, Western society has become much more adventurous with wine pairings. There do remain, however, some common sense guidelines for matching wine with food. *See 11.39.*

GUIDELINES

It is important to remember to match the intensity of flavors in both the food and the wine. **Use these guidelines to best pair food and wine:**

Match or contrast the components of both the food and the wine Having similarities in components (sweet, sour, salty, bitter) may be safe, but not necessarily interesting. For example, sweet food with sweet wines match perfectly as long as the wine is always sweeter than the food; but sweet Sauternes are perhaps more interesting with a salty and creamy rich Roquefort cheese.

Think about the acidity Acidic foods need to be accompanied by acidic wines such as Sauvignon Blanc and cool-climate Chardonnays. Highly acid foods will wash out low-acid wines. Acidic wines also pair well with salty and oily foods. The effect is similar to pairing citrus with fish.

Modify bitterness Bitter food and bitter wine reinforce bitterness, while a, sweetness or acidity can modify it. A mixed green salad with grilled chicken, for example, might be paired with a white wine such as white Zinfandel or Chenin Blanc.

Match or contrast dominant flavors of both the food and the wine Herbs, spices, seasonings, and cooking techniques can enhance flavors in wine. For example, thyme or basil in a dish will bring out the herbaceous character of a Sauvignon Blanc. Grilled foods such as salmon will match the spiciness and toastiness of Pinot Noir. Contrasting smoky and floral flavors can also be interesting, when serving smoked salmon with a floral Riesling.

Match the intensity of textures To make sure that one does not overpower the other, match the intensity of textures. Lightly textured foods pair well with light-bodied wines, and rich foods with full-bodied wines—a California Cabernet goes well with grilled sirloin steak, for example.

Remember that tannins are less perceptible with fat A hard tannic Cabernet Sauvignon will not taste astringent if accompanied by salty fatty beef, duck, cheese, or rich sauces. Accompany a fine older wine with simpler food that acts as a foil. Use good, drinkable quality wine for cooking. Use the same style wine in cooking as will be served with the meal for better harmony. Be aware of interactions between food and wine: artichokes compete with acidity in wine. Foods high in umami, such as anchovies, soy sauce, bonito, or smoked salmon, react badly to tannins and leave a metallic flavor on the palate. Corn is difficult to pair with very dry wine because of its high starch and sugar content.

Remember that mixed green salads, especially those with vinaigrette, will ruin the taste of wine. If possible, avoid using vinegar, and substitute citrus juice; then serve with a slightly off-dry wine with good acidity, such as a Chenin Blanc. Be alert to the difficulty of pairing egg dishes with a wine, especially those without other taste components. Poached eggs, for example, will coat the tongue and palate and limit the perception of the wine. A Western-style omelet, however, has taste and flavor components such as onions, tomatoes, peppers, and cheese—all of which enhance compatibility with wine. Consider the intensity of chocolate; it is difficult to pair if it is very sweet or bitter. It is less of a problem if it is merely a component of a dessert.

If possible, avoid serving wine with very spicy foods, which will not only overwhelm a wine's flavors, but will also enhance the perception of tannins if present. Remember that the best wine is the wine the taster most enjoys and that many psychological factors are involved in a consumer's wine choice that have little to do with the gustatory senses.

- **Seasonality** Most people enjoy light and white wines in warm seasons and full-bodied red ones in cold weather.
- **Prestige** Consumers often want to pair fine quality food with expensive wines, regardless of the wine's suitability.
- **Ethnicity** Consumers enjoy pairing regional wines with cuisines of the same region.
- **Occasionality** Some wines, like champagne, are associated with celebrations.
- **The company** Sharing a bottle of wine may make an experience most memorable.

When serving more than one wine with dinner, here are a few general guidelines:
- Serve dry wine before sweet wine.
- Serve light-bodied wines before full-bodied ones.
- Serve whites before reds.
- Serve young wines before older ones.

11.39 Food and wine pairings are based on demonstrable tasting principles of balancing one against the other.

As the ancient Greek philosopher Socrates noted, "Wine moistens and tempers the spirit, lulls the cares of the mind to rest; it revives our joys and is oil to the dying flame of life. If we drink temperately and smell drafts at a time, the wine distills into our lungs like the sweetest morning dew. It is then the wine commits no rape upon our reason, but pleasantly invites us to agreeable mirth."

Appendix A

COMMON MEASUREMENT CONVERSIONS

WEIGHT

U.S. Standard	Metric
0.035 ounce	1 gram
1 ounce	28.35 grams
16 ounces (or 1 pound)	454 grams
2.2 pounds	1 kilogram

VOLUME *(liquid)*

U.S. Standard	Metric
0.034 ounce	1 milliliter
1 ounce	29.57 milliliters
8 ounces (or 1 cup)	237 ml
16 ounces (or 1 pint)	474 milliliters (or .47 liter)
2 pints (or 1 quart)	946 milliliters (or .95 liter)
33.8 ounces (or 1.06 quarts)	1,000 milliliters or 1 liter
4 quarts (or 1 gallon)	3.79 liters

COMMON CONVERSION FACTORS

WEIGHT

To convert:	Multiply by:
ounces to grams	28.35
grams to ounces	.03527
kilograms to pounds	2.2046

VOLUME

To convert:	Multiply by:
quarts to liters	.946
pints to liters	.473
quarts to milliliters	946
milliliters to ounces	.0338
liters to quarts	1.05625
liters to pints	2.1125
liters to ounces	33.8

COMMON TEMPERATURE CONVERSIONS

Degrees Fahrenheit	Degrees Celsius	Degrees Fahrenheit	Degrees Celsius
32°F	0°C	325°F	163°C
41°F	5°C	350°F	177°C
140°F	60°C	375°F	191°C
150°F	66°C	400°F	204°C
160°F	71°C	425°F	218°C
166°F	74°C	450°F	232°C
180°F	82°C	475°F	246°C
212°F	100°C	500°F	260°C
300°F	149°C		

VOLUME *(dry)*

U.S. Standard	Metric
1 pint	.55 liter
0.91 quart	1 liter
2 pints (or 1 quart)	1.1 liters
8 quarts (or 1 peck)	8.81 liters
4 pecks (or 1 bushel)	35.24 liters

LENGTH

U.S. Standard	Metric
0.39 inches	1 centimeter
1 inch	2.54 centimeters
39.4 inches	1 meter

LENGTH

To convert:	Multiply by:
inches to millimeters	25.4
inches to centimeters	2.54
millimeters to inches	.03937
centimeters to inches	.3937
meters to inches	39.3701

PRONUNCIATION GUIDE

Abboccato	*ahb-bok-KAH-to*	Calvados	*kahl vah dohs*
Aglianico	*ah-lyAH-nee-ko*	Carmenère	*kahr muh nehr*
Alentejo	*ah-len-TEH--zhoo*	Catawba	*kuh TAW bah*
Alsace	*ahl sahss*	Chablis	*shah blee*
Amontillado	*ah mohn te YAH doh*	Champagne	*shahm PAH nyah*
Amuse bouche	*ah mews boo-sh*	Château	*shah toh*
Añejo	*ah neeyeh ho*	Châteauneuf-du -Pape	*shah toh nuf doo pahp*
Arabica	*ah RAH bee kah*	Chef de rang	*shef duh rahng*
Armagnac	*ar mah nyahk*	Chenin Blanc	*sheh nahn blahn*
Auslese	*aows lah zeh*	Chianti	*kee AHN tee*
Asti	*ahs tee*	Cloche	*klush*
Banyul	*ban yul*	Clos	*cloh*
Barbera	*bar BEH rah*	Colheita	*ko leeAY tah*
Bardolino	*bar doh LEEN oh*	Cosecha	*Koh seh kah*
Beaujolais	*boh zhoh lay*	Crianza	*kree AHN zah*
Beaune	*bone*	Cru	*kroo*
Beaumes-de-Venise	*bohme duh vuh nees*	Cuvée	*kew vay*
Beerenauslese	*bay rehn aows lay zeh*	Cynar	*CHEE nar*
Bernkastel	*BEHRN kahs tel*	Débarrassage	*day BAH rahs sahje*
Bianco	*bee AHN ko*	Denominazione di Origine Controllata	*deh no mee nah tsyo neh dee o reejee neh con trohl LAH tah*
Blanc de Blancs	*blahnk duh blahnk*	Dolcetto	*dohl CHET toh*
Bordeaux	*bohr doh*	Dão	*DA oo*
Brut	*brewt*	Digestif	*dee djehs teev*
Bual	*boo ahl*	Dolce	*DOL cheh*
Cabernet Sauvignon	*kah behr nay soh vee nyohn*	Doux	*doo*
Cahaça	*kah SHAH sah*	Dubonnet	*doo boh nay*

Entremets	*ehn treh may*
Eiswein	*IYS vihn*
Erzeugerabfüllung	*ehr tsoy geh AHB fool oong*
Fino	*FEE noh*
Frizzante	*freets SAHN teh*
Garganega	*gahr gah NEH gah*
Garrafeira	*gah rah FAY rah*
Gewürztraminer	*geh VURTZ tra meen er*
Graves	*grahv*
Gutsabfüllung	*goots AHP fool loong*
Gyokuro	*gee oh koo roh*
Haut-Médoc	*oh may dohk*
Indicazione Feographica Tipica	*in dee kah tsiO neh jeh o grAH fee ha tEE pee kah*
Imbottigliato all'Origine	*im bot tee lyAH to al lo rEE jee neh*
Islay	*eye lay*
Kabinett	*KAH bee neht*
Kräusen	*kroy zen*
Liebfraumilch	*LEEB frow milkh*
Lillet	*lee lay*
Loire	*lwahr*
Madeira	*mah DEER ah*
Malaga	*MAH lah gah*
Malmsey	*MALM zee*
Malvasia	*mal vAH zyah*
Manzanilla	*mahn thah nEE yah*
Marchio Nazionale	*mAHr keeo nAH tsyiohn nAH leh*
Malvasia	*mahl vAH zyah*
Marsala	*mahr SAH lah*
Médoc	*may dohk*
Minho	*meen ho*
Moelleux	*mweh luh*
Moscato	*mohs KAH toh*
Mosel	*MOH zel*
Montepulciano	*mont teh pool chAH no*
Moulin-à-Vent	*MOO lan AH vahn*
Muscadet	*moos kah day*
Nebbiolo	*neb bee OH loh*
Negroamaro	*neh gro ah MAHR ro*
Nero	*nEH ro*
Oidium	*OH id dee yum*
Oloroso	*oh loh ROH soh*
Pauillac	*po yahk*
Pétillant	*peh TEE yahnt*
Pfalz	*fahltz*
Phylloxera	*fill LOHK suhr rah*
Piña	*pee nyah*
Pinot Blanc	*pee noh blahnk*
Pinot Noir	*pee noh nwahr*
Pouchong	*POO shuhng*
Prädikat	*preh dee KAHT*
Qualitätswein	*kval ih TAYTS vine*
Quinta	*Keen tah*

PRONUNCIATION GUIDE

Réchaud	*Reh Show*		Verdelho	*vehr DEL yo*
Recioto	*reh chee OH toe*		Vin de Pays	*vehn duh payee*
Rémuage	*reh mew Ahj*		Vino Comarcal	*vee no ko mahr kahl*
Rheingau	*RINE gow*		Vino da Tavola	*vee nO dah tAH vohla*
Rheinhessen	*RIYN EHs sen*		Vouvray	*voo vreh*
Rhum Agricole	*room AHg gree cole*		Weissherbst	*viys hEH r bst*
Riesling	*REES ling*		Wit	*vit*
Rotwein	*ROHT viyn*		Zinfandel	*TZIN fahn dehl*
Saint-Émilion	*sahn tay meel yohn*			
Sake	*SAH keh*			
Sancerre	*sahn sehr*			
Sauternes	*soh tehrn*			
Sec	*sehk*			
Secco	*sEHk ko*			
Sekt	*zehkt*			
Sémillon	*seh mee yohn*			
Shiraz	*shEE raas*			
Spätlese	*shpAYt lay zeh*			
Superiore	*soo peh ryOh reh*			
Tavel	*tah vel*			
Torrontés	*toh rohn TEHS*			
Trebbiano	*trehb byAH no*			
Trocken	*trOH*			
Ullage	*uhl ledje*			
Valpolicella	*vahl poh lee CHEH lah*			
Vendemmia	*veh dEHm myah*			

Notes

Bibliography

Books

Anderson, Burton. Best *Italian Wines.* London: Websters International Publishers Ltd., 2001.

Anderson, Burton, and Stuart Pigott. *The Wine Atlas of Italy.* UK: Antique Collector's Club, 1997.

Axler, Bruce, and Carol Litrides. *Food And Beverage Service.* New York: John Wiley & Sons, Inc., 1990.

Bastianich, Joseph, and David Lynch. Vino Italiano: *The Regional Wines of Italy.* New York: Clarkson Potter/Publishers, 2002.

Bird, David. Understanding Wine Technology: *The Science of Wine Explained.* UK: DBQA Publishing, 2005.

Bird, Owen. Rheingold: *The German Wine Renaissance.* UK: Arima Publishing, 2005.

Blom, Philipp. *The Wines of Austria.* New York: Faber and Faber Inc., 2000.

Brook, Stephen. *The Complete Bordeaux: The Wines / The Châteaux / The People.* UK: Octopus Publishing Group, 2007.

Broom, David, and Jordan Spencer. *The Complete Bartender's Guide.* Buffalo, NY: Firefly Books, 2003.

Brostrom, Geralyn, and Jack Brostrom. T*he Buisness of Wine: An Encyclopedia.* Westport, CT: Greenwood Press, 2009.

Brown, Jared, and Anastatia Miller. *Spiritous Journey: A History of Drink.* New York: Jared Brown Publishers, 2008.

Calagione, Sam. *Brewing Up a Business: Adventures in Entrepreneurship from the Founder of Dogfish Head Craft Brewery.* Hoboken, NJ: John Wiley & Sons, Inc., 2005.

Cass, Bruce, and Jancis Robinson, eds. *Oxford Companion to Wines of North America.* New York: Oxford University Press, 2007.

Cecil, Sam A. *The Evolution of the Bourbon Whiskey Industry in Kentucky.* Nashville, TN: Turner Publishing Company, 2001.

Cernilli, Daniele, and Marco Sabellico. *The New Italy: A Complete Guide to Contemporary Italian Wine.* San Francisco, CA: The Wine Appreciation Guild, 2001.

Clarke, Oz. *New Wine Atlas.* London: Websters International Publishers Ltd., 2002.

Clarke, Oz. Bordeaux: *The Wines, The Vineyards, The Winemakers.* London: Websters International Publishers Ltd., 2006.

Cocks, Charles. *Bordeaux and its Wines.* 17th ed. Bordeaux, FR: Éditions Féret, 2004.

Combe, B. G., and P.R. Dry. *Viticulture: Volume 1 Resources. 2nd ed.* South Australia: Winetitles Publishing, 2004.

Combe, B. G., and P. R. Dry. *Viticulture: Volume 2 Practices.* South Australia: Winetitles Publishing, 2006.

Consejo Regulador of Denominations of Origin Jerez- Xérès- Sherry, Manzanilla-Sanlucar de Barameda, and Vinagre de Jerez,ed. *The Big Book of Sherry Wines.* Spain: Regional Ministry of Agriculture and Fisheries, Sub- Ministry: Department of Publications and Dissemination, n.d., 2007.

Cooper, Michael. *Wine Atlas of New Zealand.* 2nd ed. Auckland, New Zealand: Moa Beckett Publishers Ltd., 2002.

Coulombe, Charles A. *Rum: The Epic Story of the Drink that Conquered the World.* New York: Citadel Press, 2004.

Crestin-Billet, Fédérique. *Veuve Clicquot: La Grande Dame de la Champagne.* Translated by Carole Fahy. Grenoble, FR: Editions Glenat, 1992.

Damrosch, Phoebe. *"Service Included: Four-Star Secrets of an Eavesdropping Waiter."* New York: HarperCollins Publishers, 2007.

Daniels, Ray. *Designing Great Beers: The Ultimate Guide to Brewing Classic Beer Styles.* Boulder, CO: Brewers Publications, 2000.

DeGroff, Dale. *The Craft of the Cocktail: Everything You Need to Know to Be a Master Bartender, with 500 Recipes.* New York: Clarkson Potter/Publishers, 2002.

DeGroff, Dale. *The Essential Cocktail: The Art of Mixing Perfect Drinks.* New York: Clarkson Potter/Publishers, 2008.

Erickson, William. *Noble Rot: A Bordeaux Wine Revolution.* New York: W.W. Norton & Company, Inc., 2004.

Fielden, Christopher. *Exploring the World of Wine & Spirits.* UK: Wine & Spirits Education Trust, 2009.

Fix, George. *Principles of Brewing Science: A Study of Serious Brewing Issues.* 2nd ed. Boulder, CO: Brewers Publications, 1999.

Friedrich, Jacqueline. *A Wine and Food Guide to the Loire.* New York: Owl Books, 2001.

Giglio, Anthony, ed. *Mr. Boston Platinum Edition: 1,500 Recipes, Tools and Techniques for the Master.* Hoboken, NJ: John Wiley & Sons, Inc., 2006.

Goldstein, Evan. *Perfect Pairings: A Master Sommelier's Practical Advice for Partnering Wine with Food.* Berkeley, CA: University of California Press, 2006.

Goode, Jamie. *The Science of Wine: From Vine to Glass.* Berkeley, CA: University of California Press, 2006.

Gregory, Conal R. *The Cognac Companion: A Connoisseur's Guide.* New York: Running Press, 1997.

Grimes, William. *Straight Up or On the Rocks: The Story of the American Cocktail.* New York: North Point Press, 2001.

Hall, Lisa Shara. *Wines of the Pacific Northwest: A Contemporary Guide to the Wines of Washington and Oregon.* UK: Octopus Publishing Group, 2001.

Halliday, James. *Australia and New Zealand Wine Companion.* Australia: HaperCollins Publishers, 2001.

Hanson, Anthony. *Burgundy.* UK: Mitchell Beazley, 2003.

Herbst, Sharon Tyler. *The New Food Lover's Companion: Comprehensive Definitions of Nearly 6,000 Food, Drink, and Culinary Terms. 3rd ed.* Hauppauge, NY: Barron's Educational Series, 2001.

Hindy, Steve, and Tom Potter. *Beer School: Bottling Success at the Brooklyn Brewery.* Hoboken, NJ: John Wiley & Sons, Inc., 2005.

Illy, Andrea, and Rinantonio Viani. *Espresso Coffee: The Chemistry of Quality.* Amherst, NY: Elsier Academic Press, 1995.

Jackson, Michael. *Great Beer Guide: 500 Classic Brews.* New York: Dorling Kindersley, 2000.

Jackson, Michael. *Michael Jackson's Complete Guide to Single Malt Scotch: A Connoisseur's Guide to the Single Malt Whiskies of Scotland. 5th ed.* Philadelphia, PA: Penguin Group, 2004.

Jamieson, Ian. *German Wine.* UK: Faber & Faber, 1991.

Jefford, Andrew. *The New France: A Complete Guide to Contemporary French Wine. Revised.* UK: Mitchell Beazley, 2006.

Jeffs, Julian. *Sherry. Fully revised and updated.* UK: Mitchell Beazley, 2004.

Johnson, Hugh. *The Story of Wine.* UK: Octopus Publishing Group, 1989.

Johnson, Hugh, and Jancis Robinson. *World Atlas of Wine. 6th ed.* UK: Mitchell Beazley, 2007.

Katsigris, Costas, and Chris Thomas. *The Bar & Beverage Book. 4th ed.* Hoboken, NJ: John Wiley & Sons, Inc., 2007.

King, Carol A. *Professional Dining Room Management.* New York: Van Nostrand Reinhold Co., 1988.

Lipinski, Robert, and Kathleen A. Lipinski. *The Complete Beverage Dictionary.* New York: Van Nostrand Reinhold Co., 1992.

Litrides, Carol A., and Bruce H. Axler. *Restaurant Service: Beyond the Basics.* New York: John Wiley & Sons, Inc., 1994.

MacDonogh, Giles. *Portuguese Table Wines: The New Generation of Wines and Wine Makers.* UK: Grub Street Publishing, 2001

MacNeil, Karen. *The Wine Bible.* New York: Workman Publishing, 2001.

Markowski, Phil, with Tomme Arthur, and Yvan De Baets. *Farmhouse Ales: Culture and Craftsmanship in the Belgian Tradition.* Boulder, CO: Brewers Publications, 2004.

Mayson, Richard. *Portugal's Wines & Wine Makers: Port, Madeira & Regional Wines. New Revised Edition.* San Francisco, CA: Wine Appreciation Guild, 1997.

McGovern, Patrick. *Ancient Wine: The Search for the Origins of Viniculture.* Princeton, NJ: Princeton University Press, 2003.

McInerney, Jay. *Bacchus & Me: Adventures in the Wine Cellar.* Guilford, CT: The Lyons Press, 2000.

Myer, Danny. *Setting the Table.* New York: HarperCollins Publishers, 2006.

Norman, Remington. *Rhône Renaissance: The Finest Rhône and Rhône-Style Wines from France and the New World.* San Francisco, CA: Wine Appreciation Guild, 1996.

Paston-Williams, Sara. *The Art of Dining: A History of Cooking & Eating.* London: The National Trust, 1993.

Bibliography

Pendergrast, Mark. *Uncommon Grounds: The History of Coffee and How It Transformed Our World.* New York: Basic Books, 1999.

Plotkin, Robert. *The Original Pocket Guide To American Cocktails and Drinks.* Tucson, AZ: BarMedia, 2004.

Price, Freddie. *Riesling Renaissance.* UK: Mitchell Beazley, 2004.

Radford, John. *The New Spain: A Complete Guide to Contemporary Spanish Wine.* UK: Mitchell Beazley, 2007.

Regan, Gary. *The Joy of Mixology: The Consumer Guide to the Bartender's Craft.* New York: Clarkson Potter/Publishers, 2003.

Robinson, Jancis. *How to Taste: A Guide to Enjoying Wine. Revised Updated Edition.* New York: Simon & Schuster, 2008.

Robinson, Jancis. *The Oxford Companion to Wine. 3rd.ed.* New York: Oxford University Press, 2007.

Saunders, Lucy. *Cooking With Beer: Taste Tempting Recipes and Creative Ideas for Matching Beer & Food.* Canada: Time Life Books, 1996.

Schuster, Michael. *Essential Winetasting: The Complete Practical Winetasting Course.* Revised Edition.UK: Mitchell Beazley, 2009.

Simon, Joanna. *Wine with Food.* New York: Simon & Schuster, 1996.

Smith, Barry C. *Questions of Taste: The Philosophy of Wine.* New York: Oxford University Press, 2007.

Smithsonian Cooper-Hewitt, National Design Museum. *Feeding Desire: Design and the Tools of the Table 1500-2005.* New York: Assouline Publishing Inc., 2006.

Spang, Rebecca. *The Invention of the Restaurant: Paris and Modern Gastronomic Culture.* Cambridge, MA: Harvard University Press, 2001.

Standage, Thomas. *A History of the World in 6 Glasses.* New York: Walker & Company, 2006.

Stevenson, Tom. *The New Sotheby's Wine Encyclopedia: The Classic Reference to the Wines of the World.* 4th ed. New York: Dorling Kindersley, 2007.

Stevenson, Tom. *World Encyclopedia of Champagne and Sparkling Wine. Revised and Updated Edition.* San Francisco, CA: Wine Appreciation Guild, 2003.

Strianese, Anthony J. *Dining Room and Banquet Management.* Delmar, NY: Delmar Publishing, 1990.

Taber, George M. *Judgment in Paris: California vs. France and the Historic 1976 Paris Tasting that Revolutionized Wine.* New York: Scribner, 2005.

Taber, George M. *To Cork or Not to Cork: Tradition, Romance, Science, and the Battle for the Wine Bottle.* New York: Scribner, 2007.

Wagner, Paul, Liz Thach, and Janeen Olsen. *Wine Marketing & Sales: Success Strategies for a Saturated Market.* San Francisco, CA: Wine Appreciation Guild, 2007.

Warner, Jessica. *Craze: Gin and Debauchery in an Age of Reason.* New York: Random House, 2003.

Wilson, James E. *Terroir: The Role of Geology, Climate, and Culture in the Making of French Wines.* Berkeley, CA: University of California Press, 1999.

Wondrich, David. *Imbibe! From Absinthe Cocktail to Whiskey Smash, a Salute in Stories and Drinks to "Professor" Jerry Thomas, Pioneer of the American Bar Featuring the Origina.* New York: Penguin Group, 2007.

Zraly, Kevin. *Windows on the World Complete Wine Course. 25th Anniversary Edition.* New York: Sterling Publishing, 2009.

Bibliography

Web Sources

BeerAdvocate. 1996-2009.
<http://beeradvocate.com>.

Brewers Association/American Homebrewer's Assocation. N.d.
<http://www.beertown.org>.

"Coffee Chemistry—Aroma." Coffee Research Institute. March 2002
<http://www.coffeeresearch.org/science/aromamain.htm>.

Master Brewers Association of the Americas. 2009.
<http://www.mbaa.com/>

Selected Web Resources

American Culinary Federation <http://www.acfchefs.org >

American Dietetic Association <http://www.eatright.org>

American Disabilities Act Information
<http://www.usdoj.gov/crt/ada>

American Institute of Wine and Food <www.aiwf.org>

Cook's Thesaurus <http://www.foodsubs.com>

Epicurious <http://www.epicurious.com>

Food Network <http://www.foodtv.com>

Green Restaurant Association <http://www.dinegreen.com>

Hunger Information <http://www.secondharvest.org> and
<http://www.strength.org>

International Council on Hotel, Restaurant, and Institutional
Education <www.chrie.org>

Internet Wine Guide <http://www.internetwineguide.com>

The James Beard Foundation <www.jamesbeard.org>

Johnson & Wales University <http://www.jwu.edu >

Les Dames d'Escoffier <www.ldei.org>

National Restaurant Association <http://www.restaurant.org>

Recipe Archives <http://recipes.alastra.com >

U.S. Bureau of Labor Statistics <http://www.bls.gov >

U.S. Department of Agriculture <http://www.ers.usda.gov> and
<http://www.mypyramid.gov>

U.S. Department of Health and Human Services
<http://www.hhs.gov>

U.S. Department of Labor <http://www.oalj.dol.gov>

U.S. Environmental Protection Agency <http://www.epa.gov>

U.S. Equal Employment Opportunity Commission
<http://www.eeoc.gov>

U.S. Food Safety and Inspection Service <http://www.fsis.usda.gov>

U.S. Small Business Administration <http://www.sba.gov>

Glossary

A

à la carte menus with items priced either individually or as combination meals; customers place their orders and pay at the counter or the drive-thru window

à l'assiette service American service, the most popular service around the world; simple and quick because all the food is plated in the kitchen

abboccato Italian labeling term meaning "semi-dry"

acetaldehyde a compound the human body produces as it breaks down alcohol

acetic wine-tasting term meaning "vinegary"

acetic acid produced by acetic bacteria which consume alcohol and convert it to vinegar

acetobacter the organism that turns wine to vinegar

adjuncts additional ingredients, such as fruits, herbs, spices, coffee, chili peppers, and other grain or sugar sources like rice or corn, added to beer to create lightness, to economize, and to add more flavor

aging process that takes place in charred oak barrels, which give color to the spirit, absorb impurities, and mellow the flavor

air pot brewer coffee maker that dispenses brewed coffee into an insulated serving decanter and holds the product at 185°F (85°C) for one hour

alcohol a volatile, colorless liquid obtained through the fermentation of a liquid containing sugar

Alcohol and Tobacco Tax and Trade Bureau (TTB) the agency that collects taxes owed and ensures that alcohol beverages are produced, labeled, advertised, and marketed in accordance to federal law

alcoholic beverage any potable liquid containing from 0.5% to 75.5% ethyl alcohol by volume

alcoholic distillation the process by which the alcohol from a fermented liquid is evaporated, captured, and cooled to liquid form

ale yeasts the yeasts that collect at the top of the fermentation vessel to create a floating bubbling mass that protects the fermenting wort from oxygen and bacteria

ales (*Saccharomyces cerevisiae,* or, as it is now known, *S. uvarum*); a classification of beer yeast

alewives women who are ale house keepers; term first used in 15th century England

alpha acids contribute to the bitterness of beer

alt bier ales produced before the evolution of lagers; a lighter, smoother style of ale that lacks many of ale's fruity esters due to cooler fermentation temperatures

American service also known as plated à l'assiette service; the most popular service around the world; simple and quick because all the food is plated in the kitchen

American style a dining style defined by typically cutting a bite-sized piece of food and then pausing to switch the fork from the left hand to the right hand before placing the knife onto the rim of the plate and then eating the food from the fork, with the left hand on the lap or on the edge of the table

American Viticultural Areas (AVA) certain geographic areas resulting from the concept and centrality of place or terroir; does not designate quality

americano a single shot of espresso with 6 to 8 ounces (177 to 237 ml) of hot water added

amontillado fino whose flor yeast have died naturally or a blend of fino and oloroso

amuse-bouche a small bite-sized sampler

amylase class of enzymes needed for brewing

analyser two tall linked columns that make up the Coffey Still

añejo tequila tequila aged for a minimum of one year in small barrels less than 600 liters

antimicrobial an agent that kills microorganisms or inhibits their growth

apéritifs drinks served before dinner

Appellation d'Origine Contrôlée (AOC or AC) system that delimited the name of a wine to a region and determined the varieties best suited to the particular environment of that region; also represents the highest classification, representing 57% of all wines produced in France

Appellation d'Origine Protégée a French language appellation regimen in Europe to designate food and wine with a particular origin

aquavit a liquor from Scandinavia distilled from a fermented potato or grain mash and flavored with caraway, cumin seeds, citrus peel, cardamom, aniseed, or fennel

Arabica the highest-quality coffee; grows best in a narrow band on either side of the equator at altitudes ranging from 2,000 to 6,000 feet (610 to 1,829 m)

Armagnac brandy the oldest French brandy mostly produced in the unique alembic armagnaçais, a type of column still, which dates back to the earliest days of brandy production

aroma how a wine smells; descriptors include terms like *fruity, spicy, floral,* or *vegetative*

aromatized wines wines that are best served before a meal because their bitter and aromatic ingredients are appetite stimulants

Assam a rich, black tea from the Assam province of northern India, valued as a breakfast tea by connoisseurs

assumptive selling a sales technique that uses open-ended questions to guide guests in making their choices

astringency the "drying out" effect or rough feeling a taster perceives from tannins

attenuation degree to which how much sugar will be converted to alcohol, versus how much will be left as the body of the beer

auslese hand-selected grapes; intensely flavored but may have been affected by botrytis and are not usually sweet

austere wine-tasting term meaning "unyielding, possibly too young"

autolysis the breakdown of yeast cells

automatic urn coffee maker that yields 60 5-ounce (148-ml) servings of coffee, brewed with 2 1/2 gallons (9.46 l) of water to one pound (.45 kg) of coarse-ground coffee

azienda agricola Italian labeling term meaning "estate"

B

back a chaser on the side

back bar displays bottles in an attractive way to promote sales and market premium, super-premium, and ultra-premium brands

back waiter this position serves as a bridge between the brigade and the kitchen; has the primary responsibility of placing and picking up orders from the kitchen

bag-in-a-box system soda system that uses a single line flowing from a container of syrup to a pump that enables the syrup to travel to the soda dispenser known as a soda gun

baked wine-tasting term meaning "lacks freshness and acidity"

banquet a meal or event in which food and beverage has been ordered for a predetermined number of people

banquette refers to the continuous seating positioned against a wall

banquette service in a banquette, guests are seated facing the server, with their backs to the wall; the server should number the guests clockwise from the focal point when taking food and beverage orders

bar sundries non-edible supplies, such as sip sticks, beverage straws, sword picks, and cocktail napkins, needed for bartending

barback this position assists and supports the bartender by performing various tasks during the set up, service, and break down of the bar area

barrel a 31.5 US gallon unit used to measure beer production

bartender also known as a mixologist; must be knowledgeable about an expansive range of alcoholic and non-alcoholic products and be skillful in marketing and selling to the guest

bâtonnage a process of lees stirring

beer clean the highest standard of cleanliness for serving glasses

beer engine a siphon pump that gently pumps the ale leaving a thick, creamy head

Beerenauslese (BA) overripe berries that are individually selected; a rare sweet wine that is rich and flavorful

beverage manager also known as the beverage director; a senior-management position within high-volume establishments that have large wine lists and liquor inventories; knowledgeable in all aspects of beverages including beer, wine, spirits, and non-alcoholic offerings

beverage tray a round, 12" to 14" in diameter, hand-held skid-free tray on which to carry beverages

bianco Italian labeling term meaning "white"

bière de garde rather strong, intensely flavored beers that improve with bottle age

big/full wine-tasting term meaning "full-bodied and full-flavored"

bitters very bitter or bittersweet liquids distilled from various herbs and roots

black dragon a type of oolong tea from Taiwan

black grapes refers to grapes whose colors range from red to purple, to deep blue violet

black tea tea that, when steeped, is strongly flavored and amber or coppery brown

blazer pans oval, rectangular, or round pans made of copper or stainless steel

blend procedure using a blender to mix a drink's ingredients thoroughly to develop a creamier, frothier texture

blended scotch a mixture of grain whisky and malt whisky; may contain as many as 40 different malt whiskies

blended whiskeys are light bodied with at least a 20% straight whiskey content blended with unaged neutral spirits

blind tastings the most challenging type of wine tasting in that the tasters have no prior information about the wines

Bock stronger styles of beer that usually carry the symbol of the goat on their label

Bohemia today's Czech Republic

bomber the 22 oz. bottles becoming popular for specialty beers and bottle-conditioned beers

bone china a specific type of china that was primarily manufactured in England; contains a high proportion of bone ash that produces a greater translucency, whiteness, and strength

booth service in establishments with booths, guests are numbered clockwise around the booth for the purpose of organizing the kitchen order and food service; service begins with the guest seated farthest away from the server

bottle-conditioned a slight secondary fermentation that leaves a small yeast sediment visible in the bottle

bouquet refers to secondary wine smells that evolve due to winemaking techniques and bottle aging

Bourbon whiskey whiskey that contains a minimum of 51% corn; must be produced in the United States

braggot mead made with the addition of malt sugars

brandy distilled wine

bread-and-butter service sequence service that varies from restaurant to restaurant but typically serves bread as a welcoming gesture after the water has been poured or after the food order has been taken

brettanomyces various strains of beer yeasts such as wild

brew pub a restaurant-brewery that sells 25% or more of its beer on site

brewsters widows who made ends meet by selling their beers

brigade a team of service personnel who can work together as one

brigade system a full-service team made up of as many as seven positions

brut French labeling term meaning "very dry"

bual a grape variety for which the Madeira wine is made into a medium sweet aromatic wine reminiscent of nuts and dates

buffet service this service can be conducted in an à la carte or banquet environment; can be simple and unstaffed, modified deluxe with staff members serving beverages and assisting at the buffet, or deluxe with the most extensive service

buffetier this position supervises the correct positioning of the buffet tables and the organization of the display

bulk or charmat method the process by which wine is twice fermented in bulk and then bottled

busser also known as a server assistant, usually an entry-level position; primarily responsible for clearing and grooming the table

butler service similar to Russian service, but this style allows for the guest to select the food portion from the platter or tureen

butter service may be served in the form of wrapped patties, chips, curls, balls, florets, or whipped or compounded forms in a ramekin, dish, or specialty butter cup

buttery wine-tasting term meaning "soft, round whites with a bouquet of malolactic fermentation"

Glossary

C

cachaça the spirit of Brazil; it is produced from sugar cane juice and shows distinctive vegetal notes

caffè breve a single shot of espresso and 4 ounces (118 ml) of steamed half-and-half, served in a 6-ounce (177-ml) cup with sugar on the side

caffè latte a single shot of espresso topped with steamed skim milk and a layer of frothed skim milk

caffeine a nitrogen compound found in plants; a mild stimulant that may increase the heart rate and cause sleeplessness in some people

Camellia sinensis a tree or shrub that grows best at higher altitudes under damp, tropical conditions; produces tea leaves

Campbeltown single malts have a distinctive, briny taste

Canadian whisky whisky that is six years old or older

canopy management a manipulation technique whereby the canopy is made up of the grape leaves that absorb sunlight for photosynthesis

cantina sociale Italian labeling term meaning "vine-growers cooperative"

cap the remaining grape stems and skin forced to the surface by carbon dioxide and heat during fermentation

cappuccino a single shot of espresso, topped with 4 1/2 ounces (133 ml) of thick foam of steamed emulsified milk served in a 6- to 8-ounce (177- to 237-ml) cup or glass with sugar on the side

captain the position that supervises and organizes every service detail for his or her station or room, including the taking of orders and synchronizing the service for the station

carbonation/injection method the process by which carbon dioxide is injected into the wine vat, and the wine is then bottled under pressure, much in the way that a soft drink is produced

carbonic maceration a red winemaking method common in, but not limited to, the Beaujolais region of Burgundy, France

caramelization when carbohydrates like sugar are heated to temperatures of 300 degrees or higher, causing them to turn brown

cask-conditioned a secondary (final) fermentation that occurs in a 9-gallon metal cask (known as a Firkin), served without the use of additional CO2 pressure by a siphon system called a beer engine that gently pumps the ale into the traditional 20-ounce "pint"

casserole service service where the dinner plate and any accompaniments are preset on the table from the guest's right side

casual, family restaurants establishments that offer customers a relaxed atmosphere; feature moderate prices, home-style cooking, and child-friendly menus

cava Spanish labeling term meaning "sparkling wine, classic method"

cellared and bottled U.S. label meaning "10% or less of grapes crushed, made at the winery"

centerpieces decorative attention-getters used to enhance table presentations; five types—floral and foliage, edible, sculpted, ceramic, and lighting

certified organic coffees coffees that have been endorsed by an accredited, independent, third-party inspection

Ceylon the former name for Sri Lanka known for a full-flavored black tea with a delicate fragrance; ideal for iced tea because it does not turn cloudy when cold

chambré brought to room temperature

chaptalization a process where winemakers can correct an imbalanced condition with sugar prior to fermentation

chauffe-plats heat-retaining panels that may be stacked in a small battery at a convenient service point inside the dining room and then brought to the guéridon when required; used for keeping foods warm when tableside plating is performed

chef de rang the station captain

chef de service/chef de salle dining room manager or maître d'

cider traditionally, a fermented apple beverage; in the United States, the term usually refers to unfiltered non-fermented apple juice

cinnamon roast the lightest commercially available roast; these coffee beans have no visible oils on their surface, and the flavor and body are light

clarification/hot break occurs when dissolved proteins coagulate and form floating chunks; also known as hot break

classic or traditional method the same method used to make sparkling wine as champagne in the Champagne region of France

classico Italian labeling term meaning "from the center of a DOC wine region"

clip-on printed menu piece that attaches to the menu to highlight special selections

cloche service the French word for "bell;" refers to the bell-shaped domes that are used as sophisticated and impressive plate covers at fine dining restaurants to keep plated food warm

clos French labeling term meaning "walled vineyard"

coarse wine-tasting term meaning "lacking complexity or finesse"

cocktail a fairly short drink, made by mixing liquor or wine with fruit juices, eggs, and/or bitters

cocktail servers responsible for the sales and service of cocktails and beverages to guests

Cognac home to the world's elite brandies, stemming from the kinds of grapes from which they are distilled, the soil and climate of the Cognac region, and the skill of the distillers

cold compounding a simple method of flavoring liqueurs by blending in essences and concentrates to the base spirit

colheita Portuguese labeling term meaning "vintage"

colheita ports wood aged ports from a single vintage but are quite distinct from vintage ports

colheita selecionada Portuguese labeling term meaning "high quality vintage wines with 1% higher alcohol"

Colombian milds grown primarily in Colombia, Kenya, and Tanzania, these coffees constitute 16% of the world's production and are graded principally on bean size

Column still fashioned after the Coffey Still invented in 1827

commis de débarrassage the waiter's assistant or busser

commis de rang the front waiter

commis de suite the back waiter

complex wine-tasting term meaning "multilayered and multifaceted"

compounded beverages drinks made by combining either a fermented beverage or spirit with a flavoring agent

compounding the process of blending spirits with other flavorings, including sweeteners. Conditioning process at the end of fermentation where the beer is chilled, causing the yeast to collect or flocculate at the bottom of the tank where it is then racked to a clean beer tank; allows the beer to further clarify and permits its flavors to subtly combine

congeners flavor and aroma compound that gives a distinctive characteristic to wine and liquor

consumer protection providing that alcoholic beverages conform to the Standards of Identity and are produced, labeled, advertised, and marketed according to federal law

Continental style dining style defined by holding a fork and knife in the left and right hands respectively, cutting a bite-sized piece of food and then placing the food onto the tines of the fork and into the mouth, while still holding onto the knife in the right hand

continuous distillation method that utilizes a variety of column stills fashioned after the Coffey Still invented in 1827

contract brewery when one brewery hires another brewery to produce a recipe

conventional water method in this process, green coffee beans are treated with steam and water to open their cellular structure then flushed with a decaffeinating agent, such as methylene chloride or ethyl acetate

conversion also known as saccharification; at a critical temperature range, enzymes begin to break down the starches into fermentable and non-fermentable sugars; end product is a sweet, sticky liquid known as wort

cookingware broad term applied to earthenware, stoneware, porcelain, and china designed for cooking, baking, or serving; has a smooth, glazed surface and is strong and resistant to thermal shock

cooperages producers who make barrels using carefully controlled processes

cordials also known as liqueurs; highly refined, sweet spirits to which flavorings, such as fruits, nuts, herbs, or spices, have been added

corked wine-tasting term meaning "affected by cork mold TCA"

corretto a single shot of espresso with a 1-ounce (30 ml) shot of liqueur, served in a demitasse

cosecha Spanish labeling term meaning "vintage"

cover setting; may be as simple as a napkin and a bread-and-butter plate or as elaborate as a show plate, appetizer fork and knife, soup spoon, salad fork and knife, dinner fork and knife, a dessert fork and teaspoon, a bread and butter plate, a water glass and three wine glasses

craft beer beer produced in small, independent, and traditional breweries

creamy wine-tasting term meaning "denoting richness"

crema the amber foam that floats on top of a well-made espresso; a complex suspension of emulsified coffee oils, carbon dioxide bubbles, and suspended particles that float on the surface of freshly brewed espresso

crème called crème liqueurs for their creamy texture and sweet taste; crèmes take their name from the dominant flavoring ingredient, such as a fruit (crème de banana)

crianza Spanish labeling term meaning "aged a minimum of six months in oak and two years in the bottle"; Rioja and Ribera del Duero wines are aged one year in oak

crisp wine-tasting term meaning "good acidity"

cru French labeling term meaning "growth," indicating a specific vineyard of high quality; often used as a classification level as well

crumbing procedure used for clearing the table of crumbs and other food particles

crushing splitting the skins of grapes to release free-run juice

cultivar any variety originating through cloning or hybridization

cutlery originates from the old French word for "knife," coutel; the term silver is also frequently used because flatware was made from silver until the mid 19th century

cuvée juice from the first pressing of grapes; French labeling term meaning "blend"

cyser mead made with the addition of apple

D

Darjeeling located in the foothills of the Himalayas, lends its name to a full-bodied, black tea with a Muscat flavor

dark rum traditional, full-bodied, rich rum, dominated by overtones of caramel

decanting allowing some wines to "breathe" so the full aromatic bouquet may be revealed

demitasse a half cup

Denominaçâo de Origem Controlada (DOC) classification similar to a French AC or Italian DOC wine; there are currently about 27 DOC regions. DOC wines are required to have a paper seal, the Selo de Origem, which is placed over the cork but under the capsule

Denominación de Origen (DO) equivalent to the AC designation of French wines; there are 78 DO appellations

Denominación de Origen Calificáda (DOCa) a classification that guarantees high standards and is comparable to an Italian DOCG wine

Denominazione di Origine Controllata (DOC) equivalent to the French AOC designation and governed by the same kinds of regulations; approximately 15% of Italy's total wine production is classified DOC or DOCG

Denominazione di Origine Controllata e Garantita (DOCG) this most stringent category requires that the producer follows the requirements of the DOC and guarantees what is stated on the label

dense wine-tasting term meaning "intensely flavorful and colorful"

destemming a process where the stalks and stems are generally removed in the winery after the grapes are harvested

deutscher sekt German labeling term meaning quality sparkling wine

dextrins fermentable and non-fermentable sugars

diacetyl buttery aromas and flavors acceptable in certain beer styles in small amounts

digestifs drinks served after dinner

dining room manager/maître d' position with close contact with every department of the restaurant; knows all aspects of the business

dinner-house restaurants establishments that provide moderately priced, easily prepared meals

dioise method a variation of the Méthode Ancestrale whereby the wine's first slow fermentation in sealed vats is filtered and bottled; the wine continues to ferment in the bottle until it reaches 7.5% alcohol

disc the upper surface of the wine

disgorgement also known as dégorgement; after the lees are in the bottle's neck, the bottle may further age upside down (sur pointe) or have its lees expelled when the neck of the bottle is placed upside down in a solution to freeze the top inch or two of wine and trapped lees

distilled spirits spirits born from the distillation of fermented beverages

district a larger geographic designation, but one that still shares the same viticultural characteristics

DMS (Dimethyl Sulfide) the flavor and aroma of creamed corn usually resulting from stale or low quality grains or improper kettling techniques

doily an intricately patterned lace mat that was traditionally made of cotton or linen thread and is named after Doily, a 17th century London draper

dolce Italian labeling term meaning "sweet"

dollies carts of different shapes and sizes with casters, which are used for storing and transporting glassware

doppelbocks double-strength bock beers; carry two goats on the label

doppio a double shot of espresso served with sugar on the side

dosage also known as liqueur d'exposition; when the cap is removed, the gas expels the frozen plug and then the bottle is topped off with identical wine

doser to measure out the precise portion

dough in a process in which grist and warm liquor are gradually combined in a large heated and/or insulated container called a mash tun

dram shop laws also known as third-party liability laws; these regulations hold restaurants, bars, and their employees liable for illegal acts committed by patrons under the influence of alcohol served to them in the establishment

dried-out wine-tasting term meaning "the fruit flavors have dissipated"

dry hopping adding hops to beer after fermentation, when it is dry, and allowing the alcohol present to extract the aromatics without as much bitterness

dry method produces a sweet, smooth, complex coffee taste; this method is used primarily in areas such as Yemen or Ethiopia where robusta is the dominant coffee crop

DUI driving under the influence

dump box a receptacle with a screen over a drain that allows ice or water to drain without allowing garnishes and sundries to clog the plumbing

DWI driving while intoxicated

E

Earl Grey a popular choice for afternoon tea; Earl Grey is flavored with oil of bergamot

earthenware a porous ceramic product that is fired at comparatively low temperatures to produce an opaque body that is not as strong as stoneware or china; may be glazed or unglazed

earthy wine-tasting term meaning "aromas reminiscent of soil or minerals"

eiswein literally means "ice wine;" has the ripeness of BA and is harvested and pressed while frozen; remarkable acidity balancing sweetness

elegant wine-tasting term meaning "great finesse and balance"

engarrafado na origem Portuguese labeling term meaning "estate bottled"

English breakfast a full-bodied black tea; a robust blend of Indian and Sri Lankan teas

English service service in which the server spoons or plates portions directly onto a dish that is in front of the guest; in the United States, it is often called Russian service or silver service

entremets a small course, such as a sorbet or small dessert, served between courses

erzeugerabfüllung German labeling term meaning "estate bottled"

espresso a hot coffee beverage; a very complex beverage that requires the use of excellent quality beans produced and roasted to exacting specifications

espresso macchiato a single or double shot of espresso topped with a heaping teaspoon of steamed milk

estate bottled U.S. label meaning "100% grown, made, and bottled at the winery"

esters fruity notes

evaporate to change from a liquid or solid state into vapor

extra añejo a new category that signifies a 100% agave tequila has been aged for three years or more

F

Fair Trade Certified marketing label that states that the coffee was purchased in a fair trade agreement, supporting a livable income of $1.61 per pound for the coffee of small growers' and supporting organic farming in shade grown areas by offering further premium pricing

family-style service service where the chef prepares the dishes in the kitchen, and then servers place platters, casseroles, or tureens in the center of the guests' table with the appropriate serving utensils

faro an unusual style beer, to which rock candy is added for priming and to add sweetness.

fat wine-tasting term meaning "full-bodied but lacking acidity"

fattoria Italian labeling term meaning "estate"

fermented beverages beverages made from products like grains and fruits with alcoholic strengths ranging from 3.2%–14%

fine china a thin, translucent, vitrified product that is generally fired twice at relatively high temperatures; the highest quality tableware made for the domestic or retail trade

fine-dining restaurant an establishment that offers excellent food, fine wines, and highly skilled and attentive service

fining a clarification process used to give wines their brilliance

fino a sherry that is light with a very distinctive nose that stems from biological aging and the development of acetaldehyde (a compound the human body produces as it breaks down alcohol)

firkin a gallon cask used for cask conditioned ales

firm wine-tasting term meaning "structure backed by tannins, acid"

fixed, or focal, point the entrance of the restaurant; used to number tables, each seat, and thus each guest

flabby wine-tasting term meaning "lacks acidity or flat"

flatware all dining utensils, such as forks, spoons, and knives

flavored teas these teas gain their distinct character by the addition of the essence of citrus fruits, berries, vanilla, or other flavoring components to tea leaves

float the final liquid ingredient added to a drink after the usual procedure is performed; a float finds its own space and should not be incorporated into the drink

flocculation how well yeast settles out of the beer after fermentation

flor secondary yeast developed by all wines

food auctioning serving guests by asking what was ordered

fork a utensil produced in different sizes and shapes for specific functions; standard sizes include: dinner fork, appetizer fork, fish fork, and cocktail fork

formosa oolong a delicate, large-leafed oolong tea, with a taste reminiscent of ripe peaches

fortified wines wines that have had neutral spirits or brandy added to fermenting or a fermented wine to generally raise the level of alcohol from 16% to 22%

fragrant wine-tasting term meaning "flowery"

free-pour pouring spirits or liqueurs without using a measuring device, such as a jigger. Less accurate than a measured pour and therefore less professional

French press coffee maker that comes in 10- to 20-ounce (296- to 591-ml) sizes and uses medium grind coffee at a rate of 1–1 1/2 ounces (30–44 ml) per 20 ounces (591 ml) of boiling water

French roast heavily roasted coffee beans, bringing out a strong, characteristically bitter flavor and aroma

French service a key element of this service is tableside preparation and plating; servers prepare and plate special dishes tableside in full view of the guest

frizzante Italian labeling term meaning "sparkling" with less CO2 than spumante

front waiter assistant to the captain; performs all duties in the absence of the captain

fruit brandies brandies flavored with apples and pears; stone fruits, such as plums, peaches, or apricots; or berries, such as blackberries or elderberries

fruit-flavored liqueurs bearing a label that identifies the fruit that flavors the liqueur, such as Midori®, made with melon

Full City roast a medium coffee bean roast

G

garrafeira Portuguese labeling term meaning "aged two years in cask and one year in bottle for red wine, six months in wood and six months bottle aging for white wine"

generic or value brand a category, such as coffee brandy, that is a general category that any number of companies can produce

geuze a style of Lambic where new beer is added to older beer to increase the acidity and alcohol

gin an unaged liquor, made from grains, such as barley, corn, or rye, and flavored with juniper berries, coriander, and other herbs and spices

glassware used for serving beverages, includes common glass, fully tempered, and crystal

gluten reduced achieved by the use of a clarifying agent that removed suspended proteins, including gluten proteins, from a finished beer

gold tequila the same as blanco tequila but with caramel added for color

golden rum also called amber rum, a medium-bodied liquor usually aged for at least three years in oak casks

gran reserva Spanish labeling term meaning "only from exceptional vintages;" whites are aged six months in oak and released in the fourth year; reds are aged two years in oak and three more in the bottle

grand cru classé a single vineyard site

grappa "firewater style" of pomace brandy produced primarily in Italy

green wine-tasting term meaning "a young wine or wine made from unripe grapes"

green beer the result when wort is oxygenated to allow the yeast to quickly begin fermentation

green tea tea that is unoxidized and yellowish green with a slightly bitter flavor; steaming or heating the leaves immediately after picking prevents enzymatic oxidation that turns tea leaves into black tea

grind describes how coffee beans are ground, from coarse to fine

grist grain that has been separated from its chaff in preparationfor grinding; coarse meal

groom the table clean the table before serving a course if needed, particularly after the entrée

growler the half gallon glass jug traditionally sold at brew pubs and craft breweries due to their space saving features and ease of transport

gruit old fashioned herb mixture used for bittering and flavoring beer

guéridon a service cart or trolley; a portable work station used for all tableside preparations, including portioning, cooking, finishing, and plating

gunpowder the highest Chinese grade green tea; it is rolled into tiny balls

gutsabfüllung German labeling term meaning "estate bottled"

gyokuro the finest grade of exported Japanese green tea

H

halbtrocken German labeling term meaning "semi-dry"

hand tray a small tray used to carry a single small item, such as a drink, a napkin, or the check

hang time time spent on the vine

hard wine-tasting term meaning "tannic, too young"

head foam of the beer

heads compounds first released at the lowest boiling point during distillation; volatile and harmful

heart middle compounds released during distillation

heavy wine-tasting term meaning "overly alcoholic"

herbaceous wine-tasting term meaning "aromas of grass or herbs"

herbal teas also called tisanes; infusions made from herbs like chamomile, spearmint, ginseng, and lemon balm

high tea service also called afternoon tea; a light, midday meal that bridges the gap between early-morning breakfast and late-evening dinner

highballs beverages that consist of carbonated mixers, water or juices, and the appropriate liquor, served tall in highball glasses on ice

Highland malts whiskies that are generally sweeter and have more body and character than Lowland malts

highlighting drawing a guest's attention to particular menu items by using vivid and enthusiastic descriptions

hold/no garnish served without garnishes

holloware service pieces; examples include: chafing dishes, coffee urns, samovars, coffee pitchers, tea pots, creamers, and water pitchers

honeymoon derived from the Viking tradition of encouraging newlywed couples to consume mead for the first month, or lunar cycle, after marriage ensuring conception

hop back a separate vessel packed full of fresh hops used in adding hoppy flavor and aroma to any beer

hops grain that helps preserve beer and impart aromas and bitterness

horizontal tastings type of tasting used to evaluate wines of a particular region or vintage

host/hostess a charming and inviting personality focused on greeting and seating guests using proper etiquette and protocol

hue the color of a wine

hybrids a cross between two species of grape, such as a vitis vinifera and an American species

I

IBUs International Bittering Units

ice frozen water; a key component of drinks

ice down-pour procedure to place ice in a service glass and then add liquor and the mixer; serve as is

ice machine machine that produces ice in a quantity that the establishment needs over the course of a day; should be able to fully recover the maximum quantity for the next business day

ice wine or eiswein as it is known in Germany (from where it originated); wine produced from grapes that have been allowed to freeze naturally on the vine before being harvested and pressed

imbottigliato all' origine Italian labeling term meaning "estate bottled"

imperial a green tea grade from Sri Lanka, China, or India

Indicação de Proveniência Regulamentada (IPR) classification comparable to the French VDQS, phased out as of 2009

Indication Geographique Protégé (IGP) identifies a wine or spirit if the wine or spirit originates in the territory indicated by the indication

Indicazione Geographica Tipica (IGT) classification meant to upgrade 40% of Italy's table wines

infusion steeping flavoring agents through the use of heat

intermezzo a pause or intermission between two courses; usually a sorbet, sherbet, or granita is served to cleanse the palate between two courses of very different flavors

Irish whiskey a whiskey that must be produced in Ireland; usually triple distilled, usually in pot stills, from Irish grain; aged in wooden casks for three years

iron stoneware historic term for durable English stoneware; composition and properties are similar to those of porcelain but lacks translucency and is off-white in color

Islay malt the most pungent and heavily peaty of all the malts; takes characteristics from the peat that is used to dry the barley and from the closeness to the sea

isomerization occurs when hop compounds change shape and become soluble

Italian roast the darkest stage of roasting; the coffee beans become carbonized and coated with a film of oil; usually reserved for espressos

J

jammy wine-tasting term meaning "overly ripe fruit"

jigger a legal measure of 1.5 ounces (45 ml)

job knowledge a thorough understanding of the workplace, including the layout; flow; equipment; communication between departments; and familiarity with the food, wine, and beverage menus

junmai sakes that are 100% rice and are graded according to the level of milling of the rice

K

kabinett normal harvest time; lightest of Prädikat wines

keg a half-barrel, or 55.5 gallons

kettling process in which the wort is brought to a boil and then simmered for about one hour to sterilize it

knife utensil mainly used for cutting food; comes in different shapes and may have a serrated or a flat edge; standard industry knives include: dinner knives, with or without serrated edges; steak knives; fish knives; appetizer knives; and bread-and-butter knives

koji a type of mold that converts starches to fermentable sugars

koumis fermented mare's milk; one of the earliest alcoholic beverages

kräusen a process in which sweet unfermented wort is added to the aging beer to cause a secondary fermentation

L

lager German for "storage;" a style of beers that tolerate cooler temperatures

lager yeasts yeasts that ferment at cooler temperatures and rest at the bottom of the tanks and ferment slowly

lagering a process by which the beer is stored at cold temperatures, and stubborn sugars continue to slowly ferment

lagers *Saccharomyces carlsbergensis*; a classification of beer yeast

lambic beers fermented with wild yeasts in oak casks and then bottled for a second fermentation with the addition of fruit purées, which add alcohol, color, and flavor to the finished beers after aging

lapsang souchong a black tea with a tarry, smoky flavor and aroma

lautering the process of removing the sticky, sweet wort from the spent grains

lees the sediment containing dead yeast and other solids that collect in the bottom of the wine tank or barrel following fermentation

legs the residual wine that clings to the glass when swirled

light a drink containing a reduced amount of liquor but the normal amount of mixer

light struck occurs when beer has been exposed to ultraviolet and visible light; skunky beer

linen tablecloths; may be 100% natural fiber, a 50-50 blend of cotton and polyester, or 100% polyester

liqueurs also known as cordials; highly refined sweet spirits to which flavorings, such as fruits, nuts, herbs, or spices, have been added

liquor term used to describe Brewers' brewing quality water; water comprises 90% to 96% of beer's volume

log straight 5 gallon keg used by home brewers

long wine-tasting term meaning "a lingering finish"

lowland malts whiskies that are drier than Highland malts; usually lighter

lungo a single shot of espresso served in a demitasse with sugar on the side

luxury brands one of four sales categories of alcohol beverage products in the greater than $30.00 per liter bottle price range

M

maceration soaking a material in liquid to separate softened parts of the material from the harder ones; occurs when an aromatic or flavoring agent is immersed in the base spirit until the spirit absorbs the flavoring or aroma

Madeira wine from the island of Madeira that is fortified to produce dry or sweet style wines

maderized wine-tasting term meaning "baked, flat, partly oxidized"

malmsey an English corruption of Malvasia; the sweetest Madeira wine made from 85% minimum Malmsey grapes but balanced by high acidity with great, dark, and rich dried-fruit aromas

malolactic fermentation process caused by lactobacteria that converts harsher malic acid in the wine to softer lactic acid

maltase one of the most important enzymes needed for brewing; maltase amylase

malting an essential process in beer making with three steps: steeping, germinating, and kilning

marc pomace brandy that is produced in all wine-producing regions of France

marchio nazionale Italian labeling term meaning "indicating compliance with government controls for wines exported to the United States;" appears on a red seal on the neck of a wine bottle

marking a table restaurant jargon for adjusting flatware

Marsala wine that is fortified by alcohol and sweetened by concentrated grape must; has an alcohol content of 17%–19%

Märzen beers named after the month of March in which they were often brewed

mead fermented beverage made from honey; many use 100% honey, although some are combined with fermented grain, fruit, or cider

meadery produces mead by diluting honey with clean water to the appropriate consistency or sugar content

mechanical method coffee bean harvesting method used when the trees are planted on relatively flat terrain in even rows; the harvester straddles the row and agitates the trees to cause the beans to fall onto a conveyor belt

melomels meads made with additional fruits added

meniscus the concave curve that the disc forms

menu board used to highlight daily specials, usually handwritten

mescal an agave-based distillate

metheglin mead made with the addition of spices

méthode ancestrale or rurale the most ancient way of producing sparkling wine; the wine is fermented at cold temperatures and bottled prior to its completion

milling grinding the barley into a coarse meal; performed before brewing to preserve freshness and flavor

mineral waters waters with flavors and tastes that provide consumers with a different experience

mis en bouteille au château French labeling term meaning "estate bottled"

mistela Spanish labeling term meaning "blend of grape juice and alcohol"

mixed drinks tall drinks, combined with liquor, and served over ice

mixologists also known as bartenders; those who study mixology; highly skilled professionals who must master hundreds of beverage recipes and techniques

mixology the study of cocktails, mixed drinks, and their ingredients

mocha a blend of coffee and chocolate; not to be confused with Moka brewing

mocktails nonalcoholic cocktails and alcohol-free beverage alternatives

modular brewer coffee maker that combines a fixed-location brewing module (the heating and volume control) with mobile brewed coffee containers of various capacities (5, 10, and 20 liters)

moelleux French labeling term meaning "sweet"

moka a common European form of home coffee frequently used in the United States

moldy wine-tasting term meaning "smells of mold"

mouthfeel the texture of a wine

mouthfilling wine-tasting term meaning "richly textured"

must the extracted juice, with minimal fragments of stems, seeds, or skins

mutage the point when fermentation stops and the wine retains sweetness

N

napperon a linen overlay placed over a tablecloth for both protective and decorative purposes

near beer any of several malt beverages similar to beer but usually considered nonalcoholic because they have an alcohol content under 2% ABV

négociants merchants who not only distribute but also "raise" the wines purchased from the owners of small vineyards

nero Italian labeling term meaning "dark red"

Ninkasi Goddess of beer

noble hops classic European variety of hops

Non-EU wine the fifth level; for non-EU wines of lower quality that cannot include either a vintage or a variety on the label

Non-EU wine with Geographical Description the fourth level; refers to wines produced from specific recognized wine regions outside the European Union, such as a wine from Napa

non-verbal body language communication of attitudes and feelings, knowingly and sometimes unknowingly

O

oidium a powdery mildew fungus originating from the United States that devastated many of France's vineyards, particularly in Bordeaux

Oktoberfest most famous festival in Munich marking the beginning of the brewing season

oloroso sherry that is fortified to 18% alcohol so that the flor cannot develop

on the rocks when a beverage is served on ice, usually in a rocks glass

oolong tea a type of tea that combines the characteristics of black and green teas; the leaves are partially oxidized, the process is interrupted, and the leaves are rolled and dried

oxidation usually caused by age or faulty packaging; the beer may smell like cardboard or wet paper and may appear darker in color than it should be

oxidized when dissolved oxygen reacts with beer or when and aromas and flavors are dissipated and taste stale

Glossary

P

percolation process that allows the spirit to trickle through a flavoring agent much in the way that water trickles through ground coffee, except that the process is repeated

perlwein German labeling term meaning "a red or white wine with a light sparkle," usually by carbon dioxide injection

Perry cider made from pears

pétillant wine-tasting term meaning "spritzy, slight carbonation"

phenols flavors produced by yeast

photosynthesis the process that allows the formation of sugars from carbon dioxide and a source of hydrogen–such as water–in the chlorophyll-containing tissues of plants exposed to light

phylloxera a microscopic pest accidentally introduced to vineyards in France through the importation of American vines by the French merchant Borty to the Rhône Valley

pilsner German style of beer with a light straw to golden color and a more bitter, earthy taste

piña a large bulbous core which weighs up to 170 pounds (77 kg)

pince technique used by a server to transfer appropriately sized and shaped food from a platter, breadbasket, or other serving dish to the guest's plate; requires a large serving spoon and fork, called a serving set

pips grape seeds

Pisco a specialty brandy of Peru and Chile

platter service when a chef prepares and places food on a platter in the kitchen

pomace brandies made from the pressed skin, pulp, seeds, and stems of grapes that remain after wine pressing. They are seldom aged and are usually harsh and raw

pool when all tips are placed together and shared equally by waitstaff of the same ranking or level

porcelain a term frequently used for china in Europe

portafilter filter holder where the espresso grind is held once dispensed

POS point-of-sale system

potable spirit ethyl alcohol

potage spoons soup spoons

pottery clay products made of unrefined clays; includes all fired clayware, but more specifically, it describes low-fired porous clayware

Pouchong a light styled oolong tea grown both in China and Taiwan

premier cru classé a single vineyard; in some regions, such as Bordeaux, it is the highest designation but may not consist of one contiguous vineyard

premières tailles second pressing of grapes

premium brand a proprietary brand, both domestic and imported, that falls into a higher price range based on its perceived quality and brand recognition

pre-set menu a menu that has been established ahead of time

priming adding additional sugars to a beer to induce a secondary fermentation

prix fixe French for "fixed price;" the prix fixe menu consists of multiple courses offered at one fixed price regardless of the entrée selected

produced by U.S. label meaning "75% or more crushed, made, and bottled at the winery"

prohibition time in 20th century U.S. history when the sale and alcoholic beverages was prohibited and the production of sacramental or medicinal wines was limited

proof percentage of alcohol by volume; (American method) the strength of a liquor, which was at one time called "gunpowder proof"

proprietaries trademarked liqueurs that are made according to specific, usually highly secret recipes

proprietary brand a trademarked brand, such as Kahlúa, that no one else can replicate

Protected Designation of Origin (PDOs) regions registered with the European Union; each defined region is governed by regulations established by EU criteria and legislated within the respective member countries

Protected Geographical Indications (PGIs) second-level wines produced from a specific European country with less stringent rules

protein rest a portion of the mashing process during which enzymes, such as peptidas and proteinase break down proteins into soluble amino acids for the yeast to use during fermentation, and glucanase breaks down tough cell walls

pulped natural method cherries are pulped and the beans are dried without going through a fermentation stage to remove the mucilage

pyment mead made with the addition of wine grapes

pyrolosis as coffee beans reach a temperature of about 400°F (204°C), they begin to turn brown, and the oils, called coffee essence, start to emerge; this process produces the distinctive flavor and aroma of a coffee

Q

Qualitätswein bestimmter Anbaugebiete (QbA) largest German category, includes quality wines from one of the 13 specified wine regions; these wines tend to be light, fresh, and fruity and are allowed to be enriched with sweet reserve made of sterile unfermented must

Qualitätswein mit Prädikat (QmP) quality German wine with special distinction; further classified into six categories with special attributes in ascending order of ripeness at harvest: Kabinett, Spätlese, Auslese, Beerenauslese, Eiswein, and Trockenbeerenauslese

quick-service restaurants establishments that provide a limited, fairly consistent selection of food at very reasonable prices

quinta Portuguese labeling term meaning "estate"

R

racking process that gives controlled exposure to air; the limited contact with oxygen can help wines mature

rainwater dry but slightly fruity and softer madeiras

real ales cask-conditioned ales produced by craft brewers

réchaud a portable stove designed to cook, flambée, or keep food warm; usually made of stainless steel, copper, brass, or silver plate

rectifier one of two columns that comprise the Coffey Still; it contains a number of perforated plates located at different heights

redistillation distilling a spirit with a flavoring agent; used mostly for flavoring agents like seeds, citrus peel, or mint; employs an extraction method

region a broader geographic designation where there is less of a defined personality to the wine but one that is still recognizable as coming from a single region

Reinheitsgebot German laws, passed in the 1500s and still in effect today, to ensure the purity of beer; allows for the use of four main ingredients in beer: malted grains, water, hops, and (with its discovery by Pasteur) yeast

rémuage also known as riddling; process where the wine bottle is angled neck down at 45°, shaken, and turned by hand or by machines (gyropalettes)

reposado tequila tequila that is aged 2 to 11 months; made from 100% blue agave

reserva Portuguese labeling term meaning "must be from a single vintage and have .5% higher alcohol than the minimum for DOC wines"

reserva (red) Spanish labeling term meaning "aged one year in oak and released in the fourth year"

reserva (white) Spanish labeling term meaning "aged six months in oak and released after three years"

restaurant a place where anyone can go to enjoy a complete meal prepared and served by someone else; the first restaurant was opened in Paris by A. Boulanger, a soup vendor, offering sheep's feet simmered in white wine

restaurant china a uniquely American blend of china and porcelain designed and engineered specifically for commercial operations

revenue collection the bureau that collects revenues from all producers of beverage alcohol on the basis of proof gallons

Rhum Agricole a style of rum produced from sugar cane juice rather than molasses

riddling also known as rémuage; process where the wine bottle is angled neck down at 45°, shaken, and turned by hand or by machines (gyropalettes); may last several weeks

rim the edge of the disc

riserva Italian labeling term meaning "DOC(G) wine with additional aging"

ristretto a shot of espresso, served in a demitasse with sugar to the side and a "water-back"

robe the color of a wine

robust wine-tasting term meaning "full-bodied"

robusta also called coffea canephora; hardier than Arabica with a significantly higher percentage of caffeine; grows well at lower altitudes in wet valleys and tropical forest climates

rosato Italian labeling term meaning "pink"

rosso Italian labeling term meaning "red"

rotling German labeling term meaning "rosé made from a blend"

rotwein German labeling term meaning "red wine"

rough wine-tasting term meaning "coarse, unpolished"

Ruby port port that is aged for two to three years

rum spirit made from fermented sugar juice, sugarcane syrup, sugarcane molasses, and other sugarcane by-products

Russian service when the food is carried from the kitchen, presented, and then finished and served to the guest

rye whiskey spirit produced from a grain mash containing at least 51% rye grain; it may not be distilled at higher than 160 proof and must be aged in new, charred oak barrels

S

saccharification also known as conversion; at a critical temperature range, enzymes begin to break down the starches into fermentable and non-fermentable sugars; the end product is a sweet, sticky liquid known as wort

sake a fermented rice beverage most associated with Japan; a form of beer because it is made from grain

sapidity reflects the minerality present in water

scented tea a beverage made by blending aromatic petals from flowers, such as jasmine, lavender, gardenias, or magnolias with tea leaves

schillerwein German labeling term meaning "QbA or QmP rosé wine from Württenberg"

Scotch whiskies blended Scotch whisky, vatted malt scotch, and single malt whisky

sec French labeling term meaning "dry"

secco Italian labeling term meaning "dry"

section also called a station; group of tables (usually three or four) for which a server is responsible

seed-based liqueur which, although one seed predominates, is usually made from several kinds of seeds

selective method picking only ripe berries from the tree by hand

semi-à la carte menu items are served together and priced as a combination on a menu; entrées may be priced with the inclusion of a salad or a side dish, while the appetizer, soup, dessert, and beverage are priced separately

semi-generic labels 14 different labels that are still used today from when U.S. producers first began to market their wines and were unable to label them by variety as they were for the most part made from inferior blends

semi-generically labeled lower-quality U.S. wines

sencha the most common Japanese green tea; popular in restaurants and sushi bars

sercial very dry and acidic madeiras

servers waiters, waitresses, wait-staff, sales associates, or cast members

service actions that enhance a guest's dining experience; goes beyond the mechanics or procedures for delivering food; a critical ingredient in a restaurant's recipe for success; conveys the feeling to guests that the server is there for them

service à la russe French service that incorporates elements of Russian service

service plate used as an underliner for all courses other than the entrée

service set a service spoon and fork that are used to pince or pincer

service tray a large, oval food tray that allows servers to carry several dishes to the table at one time; usually lined with cork or rubber to prevent slippage

serviceware all utensils, glassware, china, and service pieces used in the coverage of a meal

serviette a napkin-lined dinner plate used for to carry clean flatware to the table

session beers low alcohol beers like Mild or Ordinary Bitter

shake procedure agitating energetically with ice to disperse or incorporate heavy ingredients

sharp wine-tasting term meaning "high acid"

short wine-tasting term meaning "lacking finish"

shot a measure of liquid (quantity determined by the house) served straight up

shou mei a Chinese green tea known as "old man's eyebrows"

show plate decorative plate preset at each place setting during formal meals, which is removed before service begins

shushibori method where cheesecloth bags of wet rice are stacked on top of each other, allowed to drain, and then restacked; utilized when fermentation is completed

side work varies by establishment, but typically includes: setting tables for service; cleaning and refilling salt and pepper shakers; refilling sugar bowls; folding napkins for service; polishing flatware and glassware; vacuuming, sweeping, and washing floors; and cleaning doors, mirrors, and designated surfaces

silencer a custom-made pad or a linen or felt cloth that is placed on a table underneath the tablecloth; gives the linen a richer texture and reduces the noise level when plates are placed on the table

silky wine-tasting term meaning "smooth, mature tannins"

simple wine-tasting term meaning "lacking distinction"

simple syrup a solution created by dissolving superfine sugar with equal parts water

single batch distillation process that is not sufficient to concentrate the wash into a desirable and potable spirit

single malt a whisky brewed from a single batch of wort, also known as a green or mash beer, from one particular Scottish distillery

single-pot brewer coffee maker that yields 60 ounces (1.77 l), or 12 5-ounce (148-ml) servings and may be pour-through or plumbed systems

skirting specialized linen used for draping tables; available in three types of pleating: sheer, accordion, and box

skunky beer that has been exposed to light and oxidized by exposure to excessive UV or florescent light, which reacts with the hop compounds in the beer

smallwares all beverage products, standard condiments, sauces or syrups, and paper goods. They also include garnish tongs, measuring cups, shakers, pumps, and pieces of coffee or tea service equipment that can be easily lost or damaged

smooth wine-tasting term meaning "mature tannins"

soft wine-tasting term meaning "mellow flavors"

soju a Korean beverage made with all rice but sometimes includes tapioca or sweet potato

sommelier formerly just a wine steward and today a beverage manager who must have extensive knowledge of wines, spirits, and beverages.

sour wine-tasting term meaning "overly acidic, vinegary"

sour mash the result of the fermentation process, in which the mash is soured with a lactic culture such as that used for sourdough bread

sour mix the combination of simple syrup, lemon or lime juice, or egg whites used in preparing beverages

sours drinks that use a sour base, such as lemon or lime juice

sous cloche large, domed plate covers placed over the food and then removed by servers simultaneously in front of the guests to add to the drama of dining

sparging the process of rinsing all of the sugar from the grain hulls and using those same hulls as a natural filter to clarify the wort

spätlese late harvest wine with more intensity and richness; not necessarily sweet

specialty coffees beverages made with coffee; includes lattes, espressos, and cappuccinos

speed racks equipment designed for bartenders to easily access the most commonly used spirits and mixers; located in the well which is mounted to the sinks and the ice bin

speed-shake procedure agitating with ice in a service glass to disperse or incorporate heavier ingredients

spent grains the left over grain husks at the end of the mashing process

Speyside single malts whiskies with a distinctive, briny taste

spiced rum rum infused with spices

spiced teas a blending of flavorings, such as cinnamon, nutmeg, coriander, and cloves with tea leaves

spirit a highly alcoholic beverage produced by both fermentation and distillation

spoons type of utensil, includes: teaspoons; demitasse spoons; soup spoons; bouillon spoons; a sauce spoons; and other specialty spoons, such as long handled ice tea spoons.

spritz wine-tasting term meaning "prickly from carbon dioxide"

spumante Italian labeling term meaning "sparkling"

SRM Standard Reference Method

stackable plate covers covers specifically sized to plates so they remain firmly in place, allowing the server to carry as many as 12 to 16 entrées on an oval service tray

stalky/stemmy wine-tasting term meaning "bitter vegetal taste"

station also called a section; group of tables (usually three or four) for which a server is responsible

statler a square table that opens into a round

steam beer an American invention, made famous by Anchor Brewing Company in San Francisco; an ale brewed with a lager yeast that gives it good body, lower maltiness and esters, and emphasizes the fine hop aroma

sterilized to destroy microorganisms in or on, usually by bringing to a high temperature with steam, dry heat, or boiling liquid

still an apparatus in which alcohol is vaporized and then recondensed

stir procedure gently agitating with ice to chill and blend cocktail ingredients

stoneware a nonporous ceramic product made of unprocessed clays, or clay and flux additives, which are fired at elevated temperatures; quite durable and resistant to chipping but lacks the translucence and whiteness of china

STP standard transport plate used to carry flatware

straight up or neat served without ice; the drink never comes into contact with ice

straight whiskey whiskey produced by one distiller, aged at least four years, bottled at 100 proof, and stored in bonded warehouses under government supervision

strip method harvesting method used for coffee varieties that ripen their berries at the same time; one swift movement sweeps the branches clean of berries

suggestive selling sales technique that incorporates highlighting, assumptive selling, and upselling

sulfurous wine-tasting term meaning "smells of burnt matches or bad eggs, too much sulfur dioxide"

supercritical carbon dioxide decaffeination method that uses carbon dioxide as the solvent agent extracting 96%–98% of the caffeine

superiore Italian labeling term "DOC(G) wine with 0.5% or more alcohol than is required"

supple wine-tasting term meaning "sensuously smooth"

Swiss water processing method similar to the conventional water method but uses charcoal filtration rather than chemicals to remove caffeine

T

table accessories a variety of items that make serving convenient and dining more enjoyable for guests: ashtrays and matches, salt and pepper shakers, and condiments, such as vinegar, ketchup, sugar, and creamers

table d'hôte a menu in which the price of a multiple-course meal changes according to the entrée selected

table etiquette rules founded on respect and consideration for other diners, and the property of others

table manners behaviors considered acceptable or unacceptable by most in today's society

table tent printed menu piece that sits on the table; highlights special selections

table wine a third level, referring only to European-produced wines

tableside service type of service that includes assembling, saucing and garnishing, sautéing and flambéing, and carving and deboning

tableware all utensils, glassware, china, and service pieces used in the coverage of a meal

tails compounds released last during distillation

tall/long a drink served in an 8- to 16-ounce (240- to 500-ml) highball or zombie glass; the amount of the mixer is increased, not the amount of liquor

tannin a chemical compound found in grape skins

Tawny port port that has aged for at least 6 but up to 40 years or more

tea a beverage made from an infusion of the leaves of Camellia sinensis prepared in boiling water

tencha powdered green tea used in Japanese tea ceremonies

Tennessee whiskey whiskey that is leached or filtered through sugar maple charcoal in mellowing vats before it is diluted with demineralized water and aged in charred oak barrels

tenuta Italian labeling term meaning "estate"

tequila a distillate made from the fermented and distilled juice of the blue agave plant

terroir French term loosely translated as "territory"; in viticulture, terroir encompasses all the elements that comprise growing conditions–soil, climate, topography, geology, and hydrology

tête de cuvée free run of juice, reserved for prestige wines, such as Dom Pérignon

thin wine-tasting term meaning "lacks body"

third-party liability laws also known as dram shop laws; regulations that hold restaurants, bars, and their employees liable for illegal acts committed by patrons under the influence of alcohol served to them in the establishment

three-tier system system where most restaurants and other beverage establishments, whether on or off-premises, purchase wine from distributors, who in turn, buy from suppliers or importers

tiger stripes a visible pattern of thin lines on good crema

tip credit monies that make up the difference between the hourly wage paid to servers and the federal minimum wage

tips said to be an acronym for "To Insure Proper Service" or "To Insure Prompt Service"

tisanes also called herbal teas; infusions made from herbs, such as chamomile, spearmint, ginseng, and lemon balm

trade practices practices that promote voluntary compliance

transfer method when wine is aged on the lees but is neither riddled nor disgorged but filtered and dosed in bulk before being rebottled

trappist beers brewed by monks to support the monastery; only six monasteries (five in Belgium and one in Holland) can use the term Trappist

tray stands also known as jacks; collapsible frames on which to rest trays; frames may be plastic, wood, or metal

trocken German labeling term meaning "dry"

Trockenbeerenauslese (TBA) grapes that are affected by botrytis and individually picked, making a very rich, sweet, honeylike wine

trub a deposit that forms on the bottom of the kettle

truth-in-menu guidelines twelve guidelines used to help servers avoid misrepresenting the products they are selling

tureen a large, deep covered dish for serving soup, stew, or other foods; part of Russian service

tureen service a part of Russian service used when soup is ordered; with the tureen in the left hand, approach and serve guests from the left, drawing the handle of the soup ladle toward yourself. Service proceeds counterclockwise around the table

U

ullage airspace in a barrel or a bottle

ultra-premium or luxury brands alcohol brand categories in the $25.00 to $40.00 per liter bottle price range; typically considered the highest quality brands

up when a beverage is prepared with ice to chill, but served strained from the ice in a stemmed glass

upselling a technique that promotes the sale of items of a better quality or of a larger size than what was originally contemplated by the consumer

V

varietal coffee a coffee that comes from a single varietal region

vatted malt also called blended malt; malted scotches or pure malt scotches are blends from more than one distillery

VDP Verband Deutscher Prädikat und Qualitätsweingüter; association symbolized by an eagle holding a cluster of grapes

vegetal wine-tasting term meaning "vegetable aroma" (e.g., bell pepper)

vegetal a broccoli or cabbage aroma usually indicating the use of stale hops or poor sanitation in the packaging

velvety wine-tasting term meaning "rich silkiness"

vendange/récolte French labeling term meaning "vintage/harvest"

vendange vert also known as green harvest; technique used to reduce yields through pruning and crop thinning

vendemmia Italian labeling term meaning "vintage"

veraison the onset of ripening when the berries develop color and begin to soften

verdelho dry madeira wine made from 85% verdelho grapes

vertical tastings wine tastings used to evaluate wines of different vintages, usually from a limited number of producers

Vienna roast describes both a medium coffee roast that is chocolate brown with dark speckles and a particular blend of different roasts

village named after a village or commune but may incorporate the surrounding region

Vin de Pays refers to "country wine;" created to upgrade winegrowing regions from table wine production but now becoming obsolete and replaced by Indication Geographique Protégé

vin doux naturel naturally sweet wine; the product of mutage

vineyard name U.S. label meaning "95% or more grown at the particular vineyard"

vinho the variety and vintage mentioned on a label

Vinho Regional classification comparable to France's Indication Geographique Protégé

Vino Comarcal (VC) indicates one of 23 regional appellations for wines that are outside the bounds of a DO

Vino da Tavola (VDT) table wine; now referred to as a Vino

Vino de la Tierra (VdlT) equivalent to the French Vin de Pays; these wines have a regional character and are striving for DO status

Vino de Mesa (VdM) table wine classification; the lowest classification

vino de pago classification for "estate wines" that are particularly distinguished whether in official DOs or technically not so

vino joven Spanish labeling term meaning "intended for immediate drinking upon release," in the spring following the vintage

vintage from the French word *vendange* meaning "harvest;" U.S. label meaning "95% of grapes must be from that vintage year;" a vintage reflects the weather for a particular year

Vintage Port port made from the best available grapes from a single vintage year; aged 2–3 years in wood and then require at least 10–15 years in the bottle

viticulture the science of growing grapevines

Vitis vinifera species of grapes that produces most wines

vodka spirit produced primarily from grain, potatoes, molasses, or beets; a neutral spirit that mixes well with other beverages

Volstead Act U.S. law that made the production and sale of alcoholic beverages illegal

W

waiter's friend a corkscrew that has a knife blade to cut the capsule of the wine bottle and sharpened edge; it should have five turns to the screw, and the server should ensure that the worm is not bent, in order to maximize its effectiveness

waitron a term coined in the 1980s; reflects a common view that servers take orders robotically and serve without any social skills

wash fermented liquid

watery wine-tasting term meaning "weak and thin"

weissherbst German labeling term meaning "rosé QbA or QmP wine made from a single variety of black grape"

well a shelf mounted to the sinks and the ice bin; houses the speed rack

wet kilning a process where the germinating grains of crystal or caramel malts are brought to kilning temperature without drying

wet method the process by which coffee processors first depulp the berries mechanically then soak them in tanks of water until fermentation softens the mucilage layer for easy removal

whiskey spirit made from a grain mash, distilled at 90% alcohol by volume (ABV) or less

white grapes any light-skinned grape that ranges from pale green to gold

white rum this rum is generally the highest in alcohol content and is light-bodied and clear, with a subtle flavor

white tea a tea that is unoxidized and silvery in color with the highest concentration of caffeine; made from the youngest shoots or buds of specific tea varietal plants

white tequila tequila labeled blanco or plata (silver); it is unaged or slightly aged and filtered to remove color

wild yeasts yeasts that give the finished beer an acidic tang

wine steward position with extensive knowledge of wines and spirits and who may be in charge of the purchasing and service of wine

winzergenossenschaft German labeling term meaning "wine growers' cooperative"

wit a style of wheat beer that uses adjunct flavorings of coriander, orange peel, and other such spices and herbs; sometimes known as "Belgian Wheat"

Wood Port port aged in wood and that is ready to be consumed shortly after it is bottled

woody wine-tasting term meaning "odors of old casks"

wort the end product produced through conversion; a sweet, sticky liquid

Y

yeast a single-celled fungus that is essential to fermentation

Z

zesty wine-tasting term meaning "crisp and fresh"

Index

S

Adam Woolfitt/CORBIS, **87**

Aveleda, **190**

Cardinal International, **23**

Castello Banfi, **163, 168, 185, 179, 184, 185**

Charles O'Rear/CORBIS, **160**

Chateau Ste. Michelle, **168, 174**

Cintas Corporation, **33**

Classic Wine Imports, **168**

Constellation Brands, **168, 170**

Contino. CVNE, **189**

Culinary Arts Museum at Johnson & Wales University, **82, 144**

Depositphotos, Inc. USA, **1, 11, 19, 31, 63, 71, 81, 103, 113, 169**

Dogfish Ale Craft Brewing Company, **83**

Dudson USA, **25, 26, 78**

Edward Korry, **83, 104, 105, 107, 111, 144, 140, 147, 153, 154, 157, 159, 160, 161, 165, 182, 188**

E. & J. Gallo Winery, **146, 168, 170, 171, 172, 176, 177, 179, 180, 185, 188, 189**

George Howell Coffee Company, **74, 75**

George Lavioe Photography, **Front Cover**

Illy USA, **45, 72, 73, 75, 77**

Kobrand Corporation, **108, 168, 170, 171, 175, 177, 181, 183, 185**

Marc DeMarchena, **13, 14, 22, 74, 76, 115, 119, 144, 145, 147, 148, 149, 151, 152, 153, 153, 154, 155, 156, 157, 158, 161, 163, 173, 181, 186**

Moët Hennessy USA, **108, 163**

Mulderbosch Vineyards, **168**

Owen Franken/CORBIS, **160**

P. J. Valckenberg, **161, 168, 186, 187**

Pasternak Wine Imports, **168, 170, 171, 179, 183, 189**

Quady Winery, **168**

Rodney Strong Vineyards, **160, 168, 178**

Russian River Brewing Company, **88**

TransFareUSA, **73**

Trinchero Family Estates, **168, 170, 172, 176, 178, 184, 186**

United States Department of Agriculture–Agricultural Marketing Services, **73**

Warwick Estate, **178**

Notes